HENRY HUDSON

HENRY HUDSON
Dreams and Obsession

COREY SANDLER

CITADEL PRESS
Kensington Publishing Corp.
www.kensingtonbooks.com

CITADEL PRESS BOOKS are published by

Kensington Publishing Corp.
850 Third Avenue
New York, NY 10022

Copyright © 2007 Word Association, Inc.

All Kensington titles, imprints, and distributed lines are available at special quantity discounts for bulk purchases for sales promotions, premiums, fund-raising, educational, or institutional use. Special book excerpts or customized printings can also be created to fit specific needs. For details, write or phone the office of the Kensington special sales manager: Kensington Publishing Corp., 850 Third Avenue, New York, NY 10022, attn: Special Sales Department; phone 1-800-221-2647.

CITADEL PRESS and the Citadel logo are Reg. U.S. Pat. & TM Off.

First printing: April 2007

10 9 8 7 6 5 4 3 2 1

Printed in the United States of America

Library of Congress Control Number: 2006935123

ISBN-13: 978-0-8065-2739-0
ISBN-10: 0-8065-2739-0

To the people I met who shared their lives and stories with me,

and to my father who taught me how to ask.

Contents

Acknowledgments

The hardest part of writing this book was selecting from the immense riches I collected during my journeys and my research. I worked with some of the most interesting people I have ever met, living in some of the most unusual places on Earth. Many of them are worth a book of their own.

I was greatly helped in my travels by Brad Ball of Silversea Cruises, Dugald Wells of Cruise North Expeditions and the Makivik Corporation of Quebec, Maria Prezioso of American Canadian Caribbean Lines, Michelle McPherson of the Ontario Northland Transportation Commission, and Monica Campbell-Hoppé of the Canadian Tourism Commission.

In London, Angela West helped me to commune with Henry Hudson at the altar rail of St. Ethelburga's Church.

On a fascinating cruise to the polar ice barrier, the incomparable Magdalenefjord, and the war-of-the-worlds movie set town of Longyearbyen, I am indebted to Captain Marco Sangiacomo of the *Silver Cloud* for his knowledge and enthusiasm. I was greatly helped in Svalbard by Tove Eliassen of the tourism bureau and the Longyearbyen administrative leader Sigmund Endahl.

My guides on the ground in northern Canada, each contributing a unique piece of the puzzle, included James Wilson Brown of Waskaganish, the archaeologist James V. Chism in Waskaganish, Albert Diamond, Nellie Faries of Moose Factory Island, Eric Hamel of Hydro Quebec, the Reverend Tom Martin of Whapmagustui-Kuujjuarapik, Clarence Trapper of the Moose Cree First Nation on Moose Factory Island, and Chief Robert Weistche of Waskaganish.

Aboard ship in Hudson Strait, I learned much from the expedition leader Brad Rhees, Jessie Annanack, and Bruce Qinnuajuak.

In the Hudson River Valley of New York, I benefited immensely from the knowledge and experience of Walt Lipka of Cohoes, the environmentalist Andy Mele, Captain Chip Reynolds of the replica *Half Moon* and the New Netherland Museum in Albany, and Captain Mike Valenti of the *Grande Caribe.* A special note of thanks to the folksinger Pete Seeger, a personal philosophical and spiritual touchstone and one of the keepers of the modern river.

Thanks, too, to Kaitlin Funaro, a research associate at the New York City Arts Commission.

I am lucky enough to live on an island that has played its own very special role in the history of exploration and maritime commerce; Henry Hudson sailed just off Surfside Beach on August 6, 1609. The Nantucket Atheneum possesses a superb collection of research material including a near-complete collection of the original *Hakluyt Society* publications; thanks to Lincoln Thurber for his assistance. I also sought information, theories, and lessons in geography at the Nantucket Historical Association research library.

Thanks to the National Aeronautics and Space Administration for use of satellite images of portions of the Northeast and Northwest passages. You can see many more at visibleearth.nasa.gov.

There were hundreds of other people I interviewed and met in my travels. Many of them are quoted by name in the book; to all of them I give thanks.

On the publishing side, Gene Brissie was the godfather and Gary Goldstein delivered the goods. As always, my wife, Janice Keefe, was the essential first reader, first editor, and first critic of the book.

The reason I began this book was my great interest in the almost-forgotten story of Henry Hudson and the even-less-known account of the places he visited then, and as they are now. I found a huge amount of information to sift through, not all of it accurate. There were a great many oral histories, many of them embellished over time.

As best I could, I have presented what I learned with a journalist's objectivity. Any mistakes are mine, not my sources.

Preface

No one knows where Henry Hudson's bones lie.

They may have been beneath the keel of my ship as I sailed in James Bay. They may have been under my feet as I hiked on one of the hundreds of little islands in Canada's cold northern territory of Nunavut. Or they may have been buried in the tundra below the stubby wings of a small plane as I flew over the mostly untouched vast wilderness of Nunavik and northern Quebec.

This book is about Henry Hudson and his voyages, about the remote places he visited in the early 1600s, and about the still astounding sights and people I found when I retraced his steps four centuries later.

My journey took me to Hudson's home base in bustling London, to the end-of-the-world settlement of Longyearbyen in Svalbard near the North Pole, to New York City and up the Hudson River to its navigable top, and through the roiling Hudson Strait into Canada's Hudson Bay and down into the dead end of James Bay.

Hudson made four trips in three different small wooden ships that were dependent on the winds and the currents, and all but defenseless against the unforgiving ice that blocked the Northeast and Northwest passages. He had only the most primitive of navigational instruments and charts and almost no knowledge of the scattered groups of people he met in North America.

I made my trips by jumbo jet, luxury cruise ship, spartan icebreaker, cold and wet inflatable raft, freighter canoe, shallow-draft riverboat, twin-engine bush plane, car, ferry, train, bus, subway, taxi, and in the backseat of a police paddy wagon. I hitched a ride in the cargo basket of an all-terrain beach buggy driven by an elderly Inuit woman, and I explored an unpopulated island in Hudson Bay with an Inuit rifleman by my side as we kept the proper distance from a hungry polar bear.

This book is a form of time travel. I am not a historian and this is not a history. The bones of Henry Hudson's story are based on a relatively thin written record: some logbooks, mostly by members of his crew; some contracts and correspondence; and snippets of court documents.

Four hundred years later, I went where Hudson went, touching an altar rail where he sought communion, walking on frozen Arctic and subarctic tundra where he explored, and sailing through waters where he ventured.

Lector, circumspice

Beneath St. Paul's Cathedral in London lies the tomb of Christopher Wren, the architect who helped rebuild the city after the great fire of 1666. Near his grave marker a tablet advises: "*Lector, si monumentum requiris, circumspice.*" (Reader, if you seek his monument, look around you.)

Henry Hudson walked the streets of London before the great fire. We don't know exactly where he lived, but the offices of his financial backers and the church where he took communion before his first voyage were not that far from St. Paul's.

Hudson was one of history's great explorers, though every one of his voyages failed to meet their common goal: finding a northern route from England and Europe to China and Asia. He had four voyages as master and at least three mutinies, the last of which resulted in his abandonment and probable death in a small boat in the icy waters of James Bay.

There is no gravestone raised to Hudson because his bones have never been found. If there was one, though, here's what it might say:

If you seek his monument, look at New York City. The Big Apple, the financial and cultural capital of the world and home to 8 million people, was beach and forest in 1609 when Hudson was the first European to sail through the Narrows at the mouth of the river that to-day bears his name.

If you seek his monument, look at the Hudson River. One of the most beautiful rivers in the world, the broad and deep harbor at its southern end gave birth to New York City. Hudson explored 150 miles up the river to its navigable top near modern-day Albany. Two centuries later that region flourished when the Erie Canal was dug by hand to continue navigation to the breadbasket of Chicago and the Midwest.

If you seek his monument, see and hear the art. The Hudson Valley's palisades, mountains, and vistas inspired artists such as Thomas Cole and Frederic Edwin Church, authors such as Washington Irving, and musicians from Aaron Copland to Pete Seeger.

If you seek his monument, look at Svalbard, Novaya Zemlya, and Bear Island. There are not many more remote places on this planet; Hudson's voyages above the Arctic Circle were in many ways as daring and dangerous as voyages to the Moon.

If you seek his monument, look at Canada. Within a few years of Hudson's failed voyage, the British owners of what became known as the Hudson's Bay Company became de facto landlords and governors of the vast natural riches of Canada. And the reclusive hunter-gatherer peoples of the far north, the Inuit and the Cree, began a spiral that eventually marginalized and weakened them. More recently, the demand for different natural resources has brought them back to the table as a political and economic force.

This book is about the remarkable connections between disparate people and places across a span of 400 years.

HENRY HUDSON

Why Did Henry Hudson Go to Sea?

We don't know where he died; we have only the suggestion of where he disappeared.

We don't know what he looked like; we have only the imagined images of artists who drew his face after he was gone. Some of the most famous of the paintings of Henry Hudson are incorrect fabrications that show icebergs and mountains where none existed; some of the most interesting paintings and artifacts have gone missing.

His ships, which went on to sail under different masters, have never been found. There is only one known substantial direct connection between Hudson and today: the altar rail at St. Ethelburga's Church in London, at which he knelt to receive communion before setting out on his first voyage in 1607: a piece of wood in a place where almost everything else has been changed or destroyed.

What we do have are famous places and monuments: one of the great rivers in the world, one of the largest and most significant bays, several towns with his name, and a few obscure statues and plaques.

Hudson's Thin Resume

We know of only four voyages he made as master of a ship. There may have been others; captains do not often spring forth full-born, especially considering the expense and responsibility given these men by their sponsors. But his resume is remarkably short: the only verified details exist in the period between 1607 and 1610.

He probably served as a lower-ranked sailor on earlier voyages, and he had an education beyond the ordinary: he knew how to read and write and he conducted some of his own research among existing charts and logs of contemporary explorers.

Here are the four star-crossed expeditions of Henry Hudson:

- **1607.** From London to Greenland and then north and east to the frozen arctic archipelago of Svalbard, in a torturous attempt to go from Europe to Asia over the North Pole.

- **1608.** From London to bleak Novaya Zemlya, looking for a route across the top of northern Russia past Siberia and on to China.

- **1609.** From Amsterdam, under orders from his new Dutch backers to go back to Novaya Zemlya. After a brief reacquaintance with the ice above Russia, he made a U-turn across the Atlantic for a tour of the North American coast. He worked his way down from Newfoundland and Nova Scotia, past the eventual sites of Boston and Plymouth, and all the way to a close approach to the British settlement of Jamestown in Virginia. Turning around again, he eventually made a hopeful but unsuccessful voyage 150 miles up the Hudson River in today's New York in search of a shortcut to Asia.

- **1610.** Back in the service of British investors, he sailed from London directly to northern Canada, through the icy Hudson Strait above Labrador and into the massive Hudson Bay. Then he turned away from a northwest bearing and headed south into James Bay—a geographic dead end and the place where he met his own cruel end at the hands of some of his crew.

For Exploration's Sake

Hudson was a ship's captain and an explorer, not a conqueror. He made no claims of ownership.

He did not sail to Svalbard or Novaya Zemlya to claim these cold, rough places for England or for Holland. When he entered the North River (now the Hudson), he did not plant the Dutch flag at its deep mouth near Manhattan or its shallow navigable end near Albany. And when he traveled to the north of Labrador and through the Furious Overfall and the floating ice and the treacherous tides of the strait that now bears his name, he did so as a private citizen.

The driving force behind Hudson—and many of the others who followed in his wake—was trade and commerce. Hudson's financial backers were looking for a route from Europe to China and Japan. They wanted to sell finished goods from Great Britain and return with valuable spices, tea, and minerals.

Was he one of the greatest explorers of all time?

Was he merely an accidental tourist who stumbled into history?

Or was he the world's worst ship's captain, master of four failed expeditions, enabler of at least three mutinies, and creator of an atmosphere that led to his own ignominious death?

Bloviators and Fablemongers

In my travels, I ran into all sorts of people who had something to say about Hudson.

There were bloviators who knew exactly how Hudson had died, but not where. I met self-proclaimed experts who told of red-headed Cree who were direct descendants of the missing captain. I heard stories of the captain's son held prisoner by natives. I was told of markings on rocks that indicated Hudson had survived and headed inland into the wilds of Ontario. There were well-meaning natives who repeated stories they said had been passed down to them by elders but could have just as readily been thirdhand retellings of imagined histories from school books. And there were many people—in Svalbard, in London, in New York, and in Canada—who had no idea whatsoever of any true details of the explorer's voyages and his fate.

Along the way, I developed my own rule: anyone who claimed any certainty about Hudson's fate had no facts to back up their story.

The full story of Henry Hudson—beginning, middle, and end—is probably lost to time. But I did find a rich fabric of stories, events, and people in the 400 years since Hudson sailed to some of the most interesting places on the planet.

Retracing Hudson's Path

Everywhere Hudson traveled has undergone extraordinary change, much more than just the ordinary passage of four centuries has brought to other places. I came to think of Captain Hudson as the original Forrest Gump, an accidental tourist who left a vacuum that has since been filled by remarkable occurrences.

I went to Spitsbergen, which is part of the Svalbard archipelago 500 miles from the North Pole, a place that lives in total darkness for three months of the year, total daylight for three more, and somewhere in between for most of the rest of the time.

There were most likely no humans living there when Hudson arrived in 1607 on his first voyage of discovery, although the Vikings wrote about the islands in ancient Icelandic texts. Hudson got stuck in the ice and turned back to England, but his failure was followed almost immediately by a frenetic whaling boom that all but wiped out the whales and walruses that had populated the surrounding waters.

In boiling down the whale and walrus blubber, the lonely men who worked there discovered outcroppings of coal they could use to fire their tryworks. Three centuries later, an entrepreneur from Boston passed through the barren fjords on a ship—one of the first vacation cruises—and saw the coal. He returned to launch a mining enterprise that extracted and shipped coal from one of the most remote places in the world.

Literally a no-man's-land until 1920 when an international treaty gave sovereignty of Svalbard (but not ownership) to Norway, the place also became the launching point for the first polar expeditions by airplane, airship, and sled, the location of one of the most bizarre small-scale battles of World War II, and the site of the final surrender of German troops some four months after the end of that war.

4

I sailed near Nova Zembla (now called Novaya Zemlya), the scarcely known set of islands that are an extension of the Ural Mountains in Russia's western Siberia, separating the Barents Sea from the Kara Sea. Hudson came here in 1608 and again in 1609, ordered by his financial backers to pass through or beneath the islands and continue on to Asia. He was blocked by ice both times.

He never saw a native on the cold and mostly barren land, which is not surprising. Today, the entire population consists of about 100 Nentsy people on 35,000 square miles, an outpost of a small tribe of about 40,000 indigenous people who live on the mainland in the far north. They were mostly ignored by the Soviet Union until the mid-1950s, when the government decided to use the island as one of its primary nuclear test sites. In 1961, at a place called Sukhoy Nos—at almost the exact place where Hudson tacked back and forth looking for a strait through the island to the Northeast Passage—the Soviets dropped the fifty-megaton Tsar Bomba, the largest known airborne nuclear weapon ever detonated.

I sailed into the glorious harbor of Manhattan, past the point where Hudson first made landfall—ten years before the Pilgrims landed at Plymouth Rock—and then up the magnificent Hudson River. I saw how the water was salty and the tides were strong; as we passed through the area called Tappan Zee—where the river widens to more than three miles—I could imagine Hudson's hope. Somehow it seemed possible that this waterway was a strait that led through the inconvenient North American continent that lay between Europe and Asia.

But then our little boat moved onward to near West Point, where the river dramatically narrows and twists in an S-turn; from a mile out, it seemed as if the waterway was coming to a dead end at the base of the mountains ahead. I could picture the crew's concerns that this was nothing more than an unfrozen fjord like the ones they had tried to pass through in Svalbard and Novaya Zemlya.

Past West Point, I could imagine cautious hope as the river straightened. But the final leg of the navigable Hudson River runs narrower and shallower until it shoals out in gravel, sand, and rapids near Waterford above Albany.

I traveled by car and on foot to near the tiny source of the grand river, a little splash of a pond called Lake Tear-of-the-Clouds that is fed by snowmelt from New York's highest peak, Mount Marcy. An explorer of poetic bent named the outflow the Opalescent River; the bubbling stream gives no hint of what it will become when it meets the Atlantic Ocean at New York City and makes no allowance for Hudson's dream of a passage to China.

And then I went up to the Ungava Peninsula at the top of Canada's immense province of Quebec and through the roiling waters of Hudson Strait in the company of icebergs, whales, and polar bears. I passed through the strait between the top of Ungava and the bottom of Baffin Island (still called Meta Incognita—the unknown shore—on twenty-first-century maps) and approached the open but threatening waters that led to the northwest. But like Captain Hudson, my ship made a left turn south into the immense Hudson Bay and then farther south into the dead end of James Bay.

I left the water and ventured into Inuit and Cree settlements that are still in their early years as an experiment in nation-building by the Canadians. Hudson and his men met only a few natives—some cautiously friendly and some aggressively warlike—when they entered in 1610 and when the survivors straggled out in 1611.

Then, the people were entirely hunter-gatherers. They lived in the bush and followed the crops: caribou, geese, fish, and plants. Their settlements were temporary gathering places for social and spiritual events a few times each year.

Although the white man brought about some changes in these patterns through the establishment of the trading empires of the Hudson's Bay Company and the North West Company, the Cree and Inuit mostly ignored (and were certainly ignored by) the Canadian government until the second half of the twentieth century. The biggest changes have come in the past few decades as Quebec has discovered and begun to harness a vast source of energy in the Ungava and James Bay region: not oil, but huge flows of water.

I met with some of the Cree who are engaged in a difficult fight with the government and the massive Hydro Quebec power dams and reservoirs that have flooded their traplines and drained some of their fishing rivers. In return, Canada has offered money and prefab houses and community centers with hockey rinks to people with a culture that had no use or want of any of these material possessions then, and in many cases, now.

New York's Almost-Invisible Man

In New York's ornate Federal-style layercake of a City Hall is a small, formal reception area called the Governor's Room. The space is directly across the hallway from the office of the mayor, a job some call the second most difficult elected position in the nation.

City Hall is just off Chambers Street, less than half a mile from the original eastern shoreline of the Hudson River.

Completed in 1816, the three connected rooms have been visited by dignitaries from the Marquis de Lafayette to Albert Einstein. President-elect Abraham Lincoln was a guest in 1861, and his coffin was laid in state there four years later.

On one wall is President George Washington's writing table of 1789; we know that because some long-ago government functionary inlaid that information on a plaque in its top. Nearby is another piece of furniture, the desk of the flamboyant Mayor Fiorello H. La Guardia; did the "Little Flower" rest his elbows here when he read the comic strips over the radio during the newspaper strike in 1945?

The walls of the Governor's Room are covered with fine formal portraits of notables and some ordinary works of very obscure mayors and governors of New York. As I stood there, it was obvious that the organizing principle for the room was finding works of art that fit the nooks and crannies.

Each of the rooms has a grand fireplace, and space for a major painting above. In the first room, there is a large painting of Dewitt Clinton, very deserving of the place of honor for a room decorated at that time. Clinton had served in the state assembly, state senate, and U. S. Senate before being elected mayor of New York and serving from 1803 to 1815; during that time, in 1812, he narrowly lost the race for president to James Madison. He went on to be governor of New York from 1817 to 1823, and again from 1825 to 1828.

And, of course, he championed "Clinton's Ditch": the Erie Canal that runs west from the top of the navigable Hudson River to the Great Lakes and that established New York City as one of the world's most important harbors and cities.

To Clinton's right is a small painting of Christopher Columbus by the eminent artist and telegraph inventor Samuel F. B. Morse. Columbus, of course, never visited New York; Morse, though, lived at an estate called Locust Grove near Poughkeepsie, seventy-five miles up the Hudson River.

And to Clinton's left, squeezed into a perfectly sized space twelve feet off the floor, between the lintel above the door and the white plaster trim below the ceiling, is a dark and murky painting. It is the only portrait of Henry Hudson in New York City Hall.

Actually, we're not even sure it is a portrait of Hudson. To begin with, no one has ever uncovered a picture of Hudson made before his death; every one of the hundreds of commemorative and tragic-heroic portraits of Hudson come from the imagination of some seventeenth-century artist or a painter who embellished on the theme in the 400 years that followed.

Here's what we do know about the painting tucked away above the door in City Hall: it is about twenty-four inches wide and thirty inches tall, oil paint on canvas. It shows a middle-aged man with short hair and a beard, his neck surrounded by a formal ruff of pleated fabric, in the style of a western European gentleman.

We're not even sure it is *supposed* to be Henry Hudson, and the archivists of the Art Commission of the City of New York can't explain how it came to hang on the wall. I found a letter in the city archives that served to confuse the matter nicely; according to the note, researchers had seen vague records, possibly compiled during the Great Depression by U.S. Works Projects Administration workers, reporting that the painting could be seen, unframed, in an 1830 engraving of the Governor's Room.

Another document from the archives says that the prolific self-taught historian Benjamin J. Lossing made a "shrewd guess" in 1866 that the painting was by the Flemish artist Paul van Somer, who was quite active around the time of Hudson's death. After Hudson's dis-

A portrait of Henry Hudson in the Governor's Room
of New York City Hall.
*Photo by the author. Painting from the
Collection of the City of New York*

appearance, there came a small boomlet in mawkish paintings of the captain.

But then the story of the portrait in New York gets weird again. In 1909, the city's art commission declared that it had found the name "Count Pulaskie" in the lower right corner of the painting; Casimir Pulaski was a Polish military man of some wealth who offered his services and some of his cash to General George Washington during the American Revolution. As a general of the American cavalry, he organized and led an independent light infantry corps

The portrait that may be Henry Hudson,
in the Governor's Room of New York City Hall.
*Photo by the author. Painting from the
Collection of the City of New York*

known as the Pulaski Legion. He was mortally wounded in the battle of Savannah and died in 1779. All the portraits of Pulaski I have
seen—many of which seem to have been made while he was alive—
show him as a young man with a mustache. He had no beard and
did not affect a ruffled collar.

So back to the archives. In 1929, the 1926–1927 annual report of
the art commission adds a question mark: Count Pulaski? And then
in 1929, when the portrait was undergoing cleaning and restoration,
the name Count Pulaski was found to have been penciled in white
crayon and easily rubbed off.

This time conservators reported they found a monogram in the
lower left corner similar to the one used by Somer on other portraits
hanging in the National Portrait Gallery and in Hampton Court
Palace, both in London. There was also a date: 1620, nine years after Hudson's disappearance.

Paul van Somer was born about 1577; he was a successful painter of historic scenes and portraits in Amsterdam and came to London about 1616, settling in St. Martin's Lane—the city's art district. He was a favorite of King James I, and most of his later works included royal portraits and women of the court. He died in 1621 or 1622. There is no documentation that said he ever painted a portrait of Henry Hudson, and nothing that says he didn't.

With that information in hand, the Art Commission of the City of New York contacted Lionel Cast, the retired "Surveyor of the King's Pictures" at Hampton Court Palace near London, who muddied up the answer once and for all: in 1929 Cast wrote a letter to the art commission saying that the picture hanging on the wall was not of Henry Hudson, but of "a Spaniard of high position."

I can testify to the high position, twelve feet off the floor. Like almost everything else about Henry Hudson, the rest of the story seems lost in the fog.

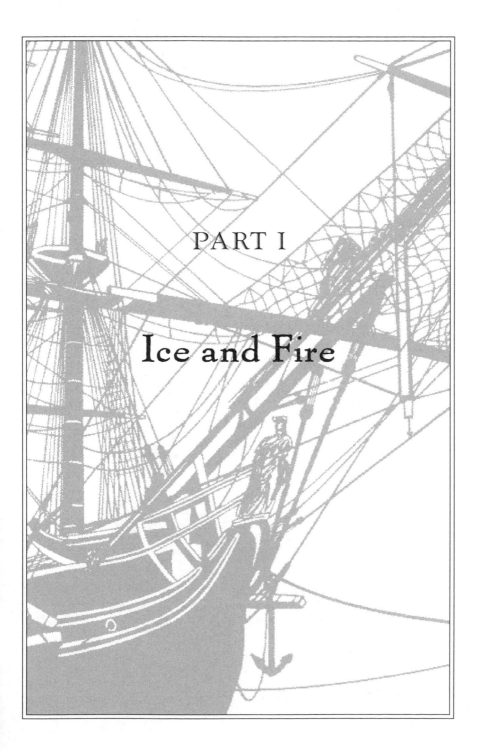

PART I

Ice and Fire

In the seventeenth century, one common theory held that the path from Europe to Asia lay due north of Europe and England. It was believed that the North Pole was free of ice in the summer and that a carefully timed voyage could pass over the pole to reach the Pacific Ocean.

CHAPTER 1

The Northeast-Northwest Obsession

Anno 1607, April the nineteenth, at Saint Ethelburge, in Bishops Gate street, did communicate with the rest of the parishioners these persons, seamen, purposing to go to sea four days after, for to discover a passage by the North Pole to Japan and China.

First, *Henry Hudson,* master. Secondly, *William Coltnes* his mate. Thirdly, *James Young.* Fourthly, *John Colman.* Fifthly, *John Cooke.* Sixthly, *James Beubery.* Seventhly, *James Skrutton.* Eighthly, *John Playse.* Ninthly, *Thomas Baxter.* Tenthly, *Richard Day.* Eleventhly, *James Knight.* Twelfthly, *John Hudson,* a boy.

Three hundred and ninety-eight years later, I stood at the same spot where Henry Hudson knelt to take communion. I touched the arches that framed the northern wall of the church and felt for signs of the presence of the captain and his crew.

Ghosts, legends, and names on a map are all that truly remain of Hudson. It is a reasonable guess that our captain was related to one of several other Hudsons and one Henry Heardson (accuracy in spelling not being an essential skill of the time), who had been involved in the founding of the small but ambitious Muscovy Company, the investors who would sponsor Hudson on his first two voyages as master.

Hudson may have had a small house near the site of the Tower of London along the Thames, where he lived with his wife, Katherine, and their children, John, Richard, and Oliver. Thomas Hudson, who may have been his brother, had a house a mile or two farther west in the area of London called Limehouse.

Between the Tower and St. Paul's Cathedral is a small stub of a road called St. Dunstan's Lane; a bit farther west is another little road named Budge Row that may have been the location of the offices of the Muscovy Company. Less than half a mile north is St. Ethelburga's Church on Bishopsgate. It is reasonable to believe that those three places can be threaded together.

So we can envision a path that could have been taken by Hudson and some of his crew that April day in 1607. Hudson may have walked or ridden in a carriage westward along the Thames to the offices of his sponsors on Budge Row.

Small as it is, Budge Row was once part of one of the main highways of the city of London, connecting to Watling Street; records show its existence at least as far back as 1294. *Budge* is a word for lambskin made with the wool dressed outward; it was used as a decorative ornament on capes and other articles of clothing, including the formal wear of the Budge Bachelors, who used to accompany the lord mayor of London to his inaugural ceremonies. As with many of the guilds of London, the budge makers congregated in one area: Budge Row.

It was almost certainly not a coincidence that Hudson's backers were located near Budge Row. In the mid-1500s when the Muscovy Company was founded, England was not Great Britain; it was a second-class economic and military power at a time when Spain and Portugal were ascendant in Europe. England's biggest export was wool—Budge Row was one of its important wholesale marketplaces—but its ability to reach international markets was hampered by complex global politics.

As Hudson made his way from the Tower, to his left was Old London Bridge, begun about 1176. The crude stone crossing was lined with shops and taverns; for many centuries this was the only permanent crossing over the Thames near the city.

On the opposite bank was Southwark, which grew as a staging point. In its early days, the wait to cross the bridge could be as much as several hours, and the gates to the city would close at night. And so Southwark (pronounced *sutherk*) became a somewhat lawless rest stop, outside of the jurisdiction of the city of London, an entertainment district with few rules. It was a place of pubs, houses of prostitution, prisons, and churches intertwined in a crazy quilt of little streets and alleys.

In nearby Bankside, alongside the brothels, bear-baiting pits, and other forms of low entertainment, was the Globe Theatre, built about 1598 by the actor Richard Burbage and his partner William Shakespeare. There is no indication that Hudson ever met Shakespeare or attended one of his plays, but they did share an acquaintance in common: Richard Hakluyt, a collector of maps, charts, and stories of exploration.

Back on the north side of the Thames, the city of London was the center of commerce, although it was hardly a shining city on the hill. It was actually a bit of a dump.

On St. Dunstan's Lane was a large church called St. Dunstan in the East. We don't know for a fact that Hudson stopped there on his trip to St. Ethelburga's, but it is likely that he was aware of one of the gravesites there.

Today, all that remains of St. Dunstan in the East is the tower and walls, the interior an empty shell. The church was destroyed in the Great Fire of 1666, rebuilt using a grander design by the great architect Christopher Wren, and then destroyed once again by German bombs during World War II.

But still buried on the church grounds is the tomb of Henry Heardson, who died on December 22, 1555. The inscription reads:

Here lyeth Henry Heardson's corps,
Within this Tombe of Stone:
His soul, through faith in Christ's death,
To God in Heaven is gone.
Whiles that he lived an Alderman
And skinner was his state:

To Verture bare hee all his love,
To Vice bare he his hate.
He had to wife one Barbara
Which made this tombe you see
By whom he had of issue store,
Eight sonnes and daughters three.

What can be learned from this inscription, other than an affirmation of George Bernard Shaw's observation that "England and America are two countries divided by a common language"? Heardson had been an alderman of the city of London and a skinner (fur trader), and with his wife, Barbara, had eight sons and three daughters.

A reasonable supposition is that the alderman was at least moderately wealthy, and there are indications that he had been one of the founders of the Muscovy Company. From that fact, and his age, he is believed by many to have been Henry Hudson's grandfather. And though long dead by 1607, he may have been the reason Henry received special consideration in obtaining the post of captain for the company.

The Northeast-Northwest Obsession

In 1776, the economist Adam Smith famously branded England as a nation of shopkeepers who founded a great empire for the sole purpose of creating a market of customers. At that time, this had been accurate for several centuries and would continue to be true for at least another century. Think of India, Africa, Asia, the Caribbean, and North America; all were primarily economic colonies, places for a nation of shopkeepers to buy low and sell high.

The Muscovy Company was founded in 1553 by a group of London businessmen and gentry to finance and benefit from expeditions to discover a Northeast Passage to Cathay (China). Why go to the trouble of sending ships thousands of miles into unknown seas and to unknown lands? The short answer, of course, was money.

There were fortunes to be made in trade: fish, furs, spices, tobacco and other crops, whale oil, and gold. And there was huge profit in the outright theft of gold and treasure from the natives and in secondhand robbery by pirates and privateers who raided the ships heading back to Europe with their plunder.

A cargo of silk or spices from Asia or the Spice Islands could yield huge profits for shipowners and financiers. Silk—because it was exotic and because fashion drove an influence-setting segment of the economy—was a valuable import. A later fashion craze for beaver skin hats and apparel would fuel much of the early exploration and commercial claims in Canada. Spices were also valued because they were exotic, but on a more practical basis they were much wanted because they could mask the flavor of poorly preserved meat.

The longer answer is a matter of politics, religion, and geography: a trio of considerations in exploration for as long as humans have trod the earth. Europeans already knew of the existence of Cathay and Cipangu (Japan) and other places in Asia. Marco Polo had traveled mostly overland from Venice to Mongolia and on to China as early as the 1260s.

The Portuguese had a profitable and expanding market in India, China, and elsewhere in Asia. King Manuel I dispatched Vasco da Gama in 1497 to bring back spices and other goods from India and "porcellanas," impressive Chinese ceramics that were first described by Marco Polo.

The Portuguese established trading posts at Goa in southwestern India in 1510 and at Malacca in Malaysia the following year. By 1513, they had their first settlement in China itself; another important foothold was in Macau, which was underway by about 1550.

Meanwhile, the Dutch were looking for their own source of marketable spices including clove, nutmeg, and mace. They sought and found a sea route to the Moluccas that avoided the land routes controlled by Venice since the time of Marco Polo.

And in any case, the exploration of the New World—the Americas—did not start with Christopher Columbus in 1492. It is generally believed that Leif Eriksson and other Vikings ventured from their original base in Norway to Iceland and Greenland many centuries earlier, and in about 1000 landed somewhere in northern Canada.

The first landfall in Canada may have been a place they called Helluland, the "Land of Flat Stones," which was probably on the coast of Baffin Island due west of Greenland. From there they sailed south and landed at Markland, the "Land of Woods," believed to be what is today called Cape Porcupine on Labrador. And finally the Viking explorers found a place they considered hospitable enough to stay a while: they called it Vinland, after the wild grapes that grew in the area; the settlement they built—which is still being studied by archaeologists—is L'Anse aux Meadows (Meadow Cove) in Newfoundland.

But even before the Vikings there were ancient legends of voyages by Europeans westward. Oral histories said that when the Moors (Muslim armies backed by Arab caliphates originating in Damascus) invaded Portugal in the eighth century, seven Catholic bishops and their flocks of followers fled from the motherland and went to sea. Leaving in 714, they were said to have found safe haven at a place called the Seven Islands or the Seven Cities.

Attention numerologists: the 700s, seven bishops, and seven cities. Add to that the fact in the pre-Columbian era the widely accepted view of the world was that there were "seven" seas . . . not including the Atlantic, which was right on the shores of Europe but very little understood. Seven was given to mean "many," and the seas that were mapped were the Mediterranean Sea, the Adriatic Sea, the Black Sea, the Caspian Sea, the Indian Ocean, the Persian Gulf, and the Red Sea.

Over time, the story became embellished to become the Seven Cities of Gold because of a completely unsupported but widely accepted belief that they held great repositories of gold and silver.

The concept was well known to Christopher Columbus. Most of us were taught as schoolchildren that Columbus had this singular idea—as if it had occurred to him in a dream—that the world was not flat and that there was land to be explored to the West. In fact, speculative maps of the time showed England and the continent of Europe on the right side of the page and Cathay and Cipangu to the left, with a large island called Antilia in between.

And Columbus had—according to his own account given near the end of his life—already made a number of voyages as a trader-merchant as far as Iceland and had heard of more land to the West. In other words, he had already established to himself that there was no edge of the world.

When Columbus sailed west, he was expecting to find Asia, but when he encountered the Bahamas, he decided one of these hundreds of sand spits and cays must be Antilia and therefore he named that section of the "West Indies" as the Antilles. Columbus was a driven man, searching all through the Bahamas, Hispaniola (today's Haiti and Dominican Republic), and all the way over to the east coast of Mexico for the Seven Cities.

Columbus never found much in the way of gold, but that did not prevent later Spanish expeditions to northern New Spain—colonial Mexico, which extended into today's California, Texas, and New Mexico—from searching for the Seven Cities, which now had a name: Cíbola. Though the myth originated with the Spanish, the natives may have been eager to please (or distract) the conquistadors with directions and details of such a wondrous city.

Just five years after Columbus made his first voyage, the Italian explorer Giovanni Caboto—called John Cabot by his English employers—sailed from Bristol across the Atlantic. In 1497, he came across on the shorter, more northern route that leads from England to Newfoundland. (The Great Circle Route is much like the one followed by most modern jetliners and ships of today as they cross in an arc from New York or Boston toward Greenland and then on to London or Paris. It looks bowed on a map projected onto a flat map but because it follows the curvature of the earth, it is closer to a straight line than other courses.)

Cabot coasted along Newfoundland and found the entrance to Hudson Strait and Hudson Bay, before continuing south down past today's New England and heading back to England. It was a very tentative thrust, but a probe nevertheless in the direction of the much-sought Northwest Passage.

Cabot died not long after his return to England. The family business was continued by his son, Sebastian Cabot, who had sailed with his father on the trip to Newfoundland and perhaps on other voyages. Like many of the explorers of his time, his personal story is a bit sketchy. He may have entered Hudson Bay sailing for a British syndicate in 1509; he sold his services to the Spanish in 1512 and was made that nation's official mapmaker in 1518.

In 1526, the younger Cabot set sail from Sanlúcar de Barrameda in the Andalucia district of southern Spain on a voyage that was supposed to pick up spices from the Moluccas. In a turnabout that would be echoed by Hudson eight decades later, Cabot instead crossed from Spain to the South Atlantic Ocean and spent several years exploring the South American coast below the equator.

He returned from Argentina and Uruguay with little to show for his efforts and the investment in his expedition other than reports of hostile natives; his Spanish backers were less than pleased and sent him off to Africa in near exile for four years.

There was, along the way, a bit of politics. England's prestige, fortunes, and military strength were nowhere near their height at this time. The ruling monarch was Henry VIII, who had many fish to fry (and wives to divorce, disown, and execute). The king had enough troubles with the Roman Catholic Church, and he did not want to antagonize Spain and Portugal. Henry VIII's tumultuous reign ended with his death in 1547, and he was succeeded by his ten-year-old son, Edward VI.

By 1548, Cabot was back in England, too old to command his own vessel but with enough influence to maneuver for royal backing by the young king for new voyages. The boy king—the only male heir of his father—lived just five years before succumbing to disease; most of the decisions were made by his adult protectors in the court.

In 1553, Cabot became one of the founders and the governor of a joint-stock company with the intended goal of sailing to China by way of the Northeast Passage; that group would eventually become the Muscovy Company. And as we have seen, one of the other early members of the consortium was Henry Heardson, an influential alderman of the city of London.

The economic challenge was this: the island nation of England needed new markets for its products (mostly textiles) as well as sources of raw materials and precious metals. The primary goal of the early explorers was commerce, not dominion; profits not glory. The adventurers were not seeking to convert the savages, but to change their shopping and trading practices.

The geographic challenges were even more daunting. Thus far, fifty years into the organized exploration of the New World, England had barely profited from the exploration. And the most promising areas of Florida, Mexico, Central America, and South America were already being exploited by the powerful fleets of Spain and Portugal.

It seemed that the markets with the most potential for England were in Asia, specifically in China and Japan. However, the land route across Europe and deep into Asia was long and difficult and the sea route that went south and down under the Cape of Good Hope at the bottom of Africa was a perilous voyage by itself. Add to the mix the fact that the ships were also subject to Islamic pirates, privateers, and other brigands.

Portuguese interests had struck protective trade deals for ships flying their flag, but ships from Britain and most other countries were tempting targets.

The solution arrived at by Cabot and his group was twofold: one was to seek passage by northern routes that were shorter in length and stayed away from Portuguese, Spanish, and pirates. The other was to seek markets in colder climes. Selling heavy English clothing and textiles made more sense in places like Russia than in Mexico.

The trick was how to get from England to Asia by sea. There were a number of theories put forth by geographers, mariners, and supposed scientists:

1. North America was but an island and all that was necessary was to find the passage that went through it to Asia.

An assumption that unexplored major land masses had such passages was what drew Henry Hudson into the ice-filled fjords of Spitsbergen on his first voyage and caused him to search for a river through Novaya Zemlya on his second. In 1609, Hudson would poke at several openings in the midsection of the U.S. East Coast before eventually sailing up the great river that opens to the sea at Manhattan in hopes it led to China. And in 1610 he tried to make it through the ice at the top of Canada.

2. There was a belief in mathematical or artistic symmetry; if the world was truly a globe, then the waters and the land masses of the Northern and Southern hemispheres had to balance and be equal.

Portuguese explorers had reported that Africa's east coast (on the other side of the Horn from Europe) veered eastward at the top. Spanish explorers in the Pacific who were sailing off Panama to the North said that the American continent trended to the West.

Therefore, the theory held, Africa and Asia were joined at the top, and the New World was actually a huge peninsula sticking out of Asia. From this there was a relatively easy jump to believing that rivers crossing the Americas led to Cathay.

3. The North Pole could not possibly sustain ice through the entire summer because of the constant daylight.

Mariners could see how icebergs broke off the shelf and how the ice barrier advanced in winter and retreated in summer. Therefore, it was thought, a well-timed voyage up Norway and across the top of the planet at just the right spot would find the North Pole to be open water . . . with Asia on the other side.

The Merchants Adventurers

The "Merchants Adventurers of England for the Discovery of Lands, Territories, Isles, Dominions, and Seignories Unknown, and Not before That Late Adventure or Enterprise by Sea or Navigation, Commonly Frequented" gathered more than 200 investors and about £6,000 in capitalization. With the sponsorship of the Duke of Northumberland, the protector of the boy king Edward VI, the company was given a royal charter and a monopoly over lands to the Northeast, North, and Northwest.

In its short form, the investors became known as the Muscovy Company, or the Company of Merchants Trading with Russia, or simply as the Russia Company. At the heart of its charter was the right to trade with Russia without paying customs duties.

Besides its other firsts, the Muscovy Company was the first English joint-stock company, operating much like a modern corporation. The capital investment of its members was held by the company rather than being returned with or without a profit after each voyage.

From Russia, the Muscovy Company imported furs, timber, flax, hemp, tallow, and wax. From the nation of shopkeepers, the main export was finished cloth.

On May 10, 1553, the syndicate sent out its first expedition. The three ships were the *Bona Esperanza*, commanded by Sir Hugh Willoughby; the *Edward Bonaventure*, under charge of Richard Chancellor with Stephen Borough as navigator; and the *Bona Confidentia*. Proceeding out of London on the Thames, the ships fired a salute to the members of the court at the palace at Greenwich; young Edward VI was too ill to come out to see them off.

The ships exited the Thames and headed north and then east to follow the coast of Norway toward the top of Russia. Off the Lofoten Islands inside the Arctic Circle a major storm blew up and the ships were separated. Chancellor and the *Edward Bonaventure* continued on, hoping to meet up with the other ships at an agreed on location; after a week there, Chancellor struck out alone.

Meanwhile, Willoughby and the *Bona Esperanza* crossed the Barents Sea and reached the Russian island of Novaya Zemlya. As many other later explorers including Hudson would find, there was not much to the place other than ice. At the end of the summer, the ship turned back toward Norway and home, but along the coast of Russia near present-day Murmansk the ship became locked in ice. The next summer the ship, filled with frozen corpses, was found by nomadic Sami tribesmen. They had provisions, but not proper clothing for the difficult winter.

At least Willoughby and his men were accounted for; the *Bona Confidentia* and its entire crew were never found.

Chancellor did not get as far as Novaya Zemlya, but instead rounded the top of Norway and entered the White Sea. He came ashore near present-day Arkhangel'sk at the mouth of the Severnajya Dvina (North Dvina) River.

Chancellor's greatest accomplishment was securing a meeting 600 miles inland at Moscow and successfully negotiating a trading agreement with Ivan IV, the tsar of Russia, better known (outside of his presence) as Ivan the Terrible. The company's first factory for its agents (or factors) was in Moscow; in 1717, it was moved north to Arkhangel'sk and in 1723 to St. Petersburg.

Most of the early records of the company were destroyed in the great London fire of 1666; included may have been mention of Hudson's history with the institution. The Muscovy Company continued through the Russian Revolution; since 1917, its operations have been mostly as a charity supporting English chaplains working in Russia.

Hudson's Incomplete Biography

Without any documents or certainty, many historians believe Hudson was born about 1570, which would have made him (for the times) solidly middle aged when he took command of the *Hopewell* in 1607 at age thirty-seven. He may have been raised in Hoddesdon in Hertfordshire, northwest of London and nearly twenty miles solidly inland from the Thames or the ocean.

When I was a reporter for the Associated Press, I had an all-purpose maxim for unproven statements: "Interesting, if true." The following snippets fit into this category:

- Henry Heardson, the alderman and one of the founders of the Muscovy Company, *may* have been our captain's grandfather, and if so that may have been Captain Henry Hudson's admission ticket.

- Christopher Hudson, most likely an older brother to Henry, was an agent for the Muscovy Company in Russia about 1560.

- Thomas Hudson, believed to be another older brother, was a captain for the company, and among his expeditions was one to Persia in 1580. In 1583 or 1585, he met at his home in Limehouse in London's east end with Captain John Davis before that man's trip to upper Canada.

26

There is no proof, but some historians have speculated that our Captain Henry Hudson may have been a junior member of the crew on Davis's expedition in 1587 in search of the Northwest Passage; Davis approached but did not pass through the roiling waters at the eastern end of what we now call the Hudson Strait. Davis called the strong currents the "Furious Overfall."

Another line of speculation places Henry Hudson as a sailor on an English vessel in battles against the Spanish Armada in 1588, or as a merchant sailor trading in the Mediterranean and Africa.

Even less is known about Hudson's wife, Katherine. We don't know her family name. However, we do know she did bear three sons for her husband: Richard, John, and Oliver.

CHAPTER 2

Ashes, Ashes, All Fall Down

In 1607, London was hardly what most of us would have imagined the eventual capital of the British Empire to be; it was a rough, dirty collection of hovels and shops interspersed with some impressive but still crude cathedrals, churches, guildhalls, and palaces. It was the perfect place for two dreadful calamities that were on the horizon.

First came the Black Death of 1665, a plague spread by the rats that lived in the open sewers of London. By some estimates, 100,000 people died that summer and in a smaller outbreak the next year.

Think of that the next time you hear a child sing, "Ring around the rosies, a pocketful of posies, ashes ashes, we all fall down." That's an Americanized version, devoid of its original meaning, of a macabre old British nursery rhyme. The old version of the rhyme was:

> *Ring a ring o' roses*
> *A pocketful of posies.*
> *Atishoo! Atishoo!*
> *We all fall down.*

To many historians, the rhyme can be decoded to describe the events of 1665. The ring of roses was the blotchy rash that spread across the body of plague victims. Doctors and scientists had not made the link from bad sanitation, rats, and the bacterium that caused the disease; there was a belief that the disease was caused by "bad air," also known as a miasma. The pocketful of posies, a sweet-smelling flower, could have been meant to clear the air or at least mask the stench. Atishoo! means "achoo," a reference to severe sneezing fits that were another mark of the disease. And then the victims fell down, dead.

The second awful calamity awaiting London was the Great Fire of 1666, which stopped the plague by killing rats and forcing new construction and sanitation methods. It also burned down much of the city that Henry Hudson may have known when he made his way to St. Ethelburga's to pray in 1607.

The Little Church

Like almost everything else about Hudson, the little church of St. Ethelburga's combines a fabulous and tragic history. The place was already a few centuries old when Hudson and eleven others of his crew came to seek a blessing before sailing alone to the North.

The first mention of the parish was in 1250, and the church was probably built sometime in the late fourteenth or early fifteenth century; there is a mention of Ethelburga's in documents dated 1366 and another indication that it was rebuilt in 1430 using stonework from earlier structures.

Ethelburga was the sister of the fourth bishop of London, St. Erconwald; the Bishop's Gate in central London was named for him in 685. He appointed his sister as the original abbess of Barking, the first religious house for women in England. Ethelburga's good work came through her tending to many nuns and priests who were stricken by a plague in 664; when she died in 676, officials of the church recorded the requisite visions and miracles necessary to award her sainthood.

St. Ethelburga's was not a grand edifice like St. Paul's Cathedral, which is located a little more than half a mile to the west. By 1607, there had been at least four major cathedrals in the city. The first church on the spot had been erected in 604; after it was destroyed by fire, it was rebuilt in 685 by Bishop Erconwald. The Vikings destroyed the second St. Paul's church in 962 during one of their many raids. Another church was destroyed by fire in 1087.

But in 1240, at the end of a 150-year construction project, a grand Norman cathedral was opened. With the addition of a spire in 1314, St. Paul's Cathedral was the tallest in all of Europe and one of the longest on the continent.

Through the years, little St. Ethelburga's stood nearly untouched. It was the smallest church in the City, just fifty-six feet long and about thirty feet wide, an intimate space with a peaceful little garden at the rear. This was a neighborhood church that mostly offered daily services and sanctuary for workers at the local guilds; at one time, there were forty-two churches within the square mile officially known as the City.

When the Great Fire swept through London for four days beginning on September 4, 1666, flames stopped short of St. Ethelburga's. The great cathedral of St. Paul's, though, burned to the ground.

The architect Christopher Wren, who had been engaged before the fire to make renovations, instead oversaw its complete reconstruction. His master achievement is the cathedral that dominates the financial heart of London today, with its 360-foot-high dome, second only to St. Peter's in Rome.

St. Paul's went on to be the site of the funerals of Lord Nelson, the Duke of Wellington, and Sir Winston Churchill. It was at St. Paul's that peace services marked the end of World War I and II, and it was there that Prince Charles married Lady Diana Spencer.

St. Ethelburga's was one of only five medieval churches in the central City to survive both the conflagration and then the German blitz bombing raids of World War II, receiving a direct hit from a flying bomb but sustaining only minor damage to its roof.

The little church mostly served workers in the area, including employees of the Hudson's Bay Company (HBC). That enterprise was first incorporated in 1670 at offices in the shadow of the great cathedral. For nearly three centuries the company ruled over its vast empire as an absentee landlord; for the first 264 years of its existence, not one of its governors had visited a single one of its distant posts in Canada.

Although St. Ethelburga's witnessed the growth of the City all around, in the more than 600 years it has been in existence, there seem to have been just two events of great historical significance that occurred there.

The first great event was the visit of Henry Hudson on April 19, 1607. A painting commissioned by the HBC purports to show the scene: Hudson, his son, and two others kneel before a priest who is holding a chalice. Hudson wears a white ruffled collar and has reddish hair and a short goatee; the early twentieth-century artist most likely borrowed the visage of Hudson from one of the various imagined portraits done in the years after his death.

At the time that Hudson and his men arrived at St. Ethelburga's, the little church had already been diminished in its importance. In about 1570, the wardens of the underfunded church had decided to raise some money by building a small shop on one side of the front door and renting it out. A matching shop was added in 1613. The rough wooden structures were joined at the top with a gallery and sleeping rooms.

The shops almost obscured the fact that there was a little church behind them; old engravings show a painted sign reading "Church of Saint Ethelburga" awkwardly emblazoned across its front.

The odd camouflage continued into the twentieth century. In the 1920s, one of the shops was used by an optician who hung an oversized pair of eyeglasses from a hook above the door.

Meanwhile, St. Ethelburga's received a protector in the form of W. E. Geikie-Cobb, the rector of the church from 1900 to 1941. He devoted his life to polishing the little gem on Bishopsgate. He was responsible for converting the tiny burial ground in the backyard into a contemplative garden with a goldfish pond and a small fountain; the interior of the church was restored, undoing some of the modernization that had taken place since the sixteenth century.

And then Geikie-Cobb set to work on commemorating Henry Hudson with a memorial window. In 1919, Geikie-Cobb approached the English-Speaking Union, a group that aimed to bridge the British Empire and the United States, asking for a contribution to cover an estimated cost of £500, "more or less" to install a Hudson window.

Among the respondents was the HBC, which gave £25 to the campaign. Eight years later, in a great historical coincidence, the HBC moved into a new headquarters, Hudson's Bay House, right next door to St. Ethelburga's on Bishopsgate.

By that time, Geikie-Cobb's plan for a single window had grown to a set of three, and the HBC upped its donation to £500 just a month before the dedication. The original minutes of the HBC board meeting noted that the contribution was for a window to commemorate Hudson's visit to the church "prior to setting out on his voyage of discovery to Hudson's Bay." The minutes were corrected by hand to say "Hudson River" and the dedication went forth on April 19, 1928, the 321st anniversary of the communion.

A second window was paid for by contributions from individuals and groups in England, and a third commemoration from U.S. sources gathered by the HBC's New York agent. All three Hudson windows, in the Arts and Crafts style, were created by the English artist Leonard Walker; a fourth window by Walker memorialized Geikie-Cobb in 1947.

The principal window showed a formally dressed Captain Hudson standing in front of an imposing three-masted ship, almost certainly much grander than either Hudson's uniform and the secondhand *Hopewell* in which he actually sailed.

The unattractive shops that obscured the front were finally taken down in 1932, and the little church looked much as it had 500 years before.

But in 1940, while war raged in Europe and trade of fur pelts and consumer products with Canada was suspended, the head office of the HBC moved from Bishopsgate to the appropriately named Beaver House in Great Trinity Lane. By 1950, the HBC no longer had any offices neighboring St. Ethelburga's.

By the early 1990s, the little church had lost most of its congregants; only a few thousand people maintained homes in the city and there were many other, more opulent places of worship. St. Ethelburga's was in the process of being declared, as the British say, "redundant," and would be used as a "chapel of ease," secondary to other church buildings in the area.

St. Ethelburga's Church in London.
Photo by the author

The second major event in the history of St. Ethelburga's took place at 10:20 in the morning on Saturday, April 24, 1993.

The City of London, also called the Square Mile, was the original heart of medieval London. In more modern times, it had become the financial center of one of the greatest cities of the world, home to banks, insurance companies, and historical and cultural icons including Christopher Wren's glorious St. Paul's Cathedral, the Tower of London, and the Royal Courts of Justice.

On that quiet Saturday, while most of the 300,000 or so workers who pack the City during the week were at home, a truck packed with one ton of ammonium nitrate fertilizer, fuel, and a detonator pulled up directly in front of the door to St. Ethelburga's. A photog-

Interior arches of St. Ethelburga's Church.
Photo by the author

rapher for the *News of the World*, dispatched by his newspaper because it had been alerted by the Irish Republican Army (IRA), was
standing a few yards away when the truck exploded.

The cameraman was killed, forty-four others were injured, and St.
Ethelburga's church—a survivor of the Great Fire, the blitz, and urban renewal—was almost leveled. The entire west wall facing Bishopsgate was destroyed, along with most of the northern wall; all the
stained glass windows, including the three Hudson memorials, were
obliterated. The belfry and the roof collapsed and nearly all the
wooden interior pews and fixtures were gone.

Damage to buildings in the City was estimated at £350 million. St.
Ethelburga's had been appraised at £2 million, but its insurance pol-

The interior of St. Ethelburga's Church
in about 1900.
Photo from "Henry Hudson"
by Thomas Janvier, 1909

icy against terrorist attack had been reduced to just £100,000 after another IRA bombing at the Baltic Exchange a year before.

The first reaction of Anglican Church officials was that St. Ethelburga's was too badly damaged to be rebuilt; they considered a plan to incorporate the remains of the church in a monument to the victims of terrorism. The winner of a design competition proposed encasing the ruins within a glass "coffin" with income-generating offices built in the tiny garden at the back of the plot. That plan was fiercely opposed by the Friends of St. Ethelburga's as well as by the Royal Fine Art Commission. Members of the church and the general public, helped along by political maneuvering, launched a fundraising campaign for a reconstruction.

The rubble was carefully moved to a site in North London and archaeologists and engineers sifted through the fragments of stone, brick, glass, and wood for salvageable pieces. Experts from the Museum of London made preliminary identification of pieces including stonework from the twelfth century, fifteenth-century masonry, and timbers from the roof and bell tower that had once decorated the front of the church. The goldfish from the pond in the little garden at the back of the church survived the blast and were evacuated to a watery sanctuary at the Vicar of St. Mary's in Paddington Green.

It took more than eight years—June 2001—before rebuilding began, with a total price tag of about £3.6 million. The plan called for reconstruction of the medieval facade and the north wall (minus the Hudson stained glass windows) using recovered stones and masonry.

Under the sponsorship of London's bishop and cardinal, and with John McCarthy and Terry Waite, plans came together for converting the former church into a center for peace and reconciliation. McCarthy and the American Terry Anderson (both journalists) had been held for five and six years, respectively, by the militant group Islamic Jihad in Beirut. Waite, a representative of the Anglican Church, was taken captive when he went to Lebanon to seek their release and was himself held for more than four years. "It is a wonderful idea for a building which has itself been a victim of conflict," McCarthy said.

On November 12, 2002, the rebuilt church was reconsecrated by the bishop of London. He held the same silver chalice believed to have been used at Hudson's communion; it had been retrieved from its storage place in a London vault. The next day, the St. Ethelburga's Centre for Reconciliation and Peace was officially opened by Prince Charles.

The west front of the church, facing Bishopsgate, looks much like it did before the bombing. The main tower, which was somehow left mostly intact after the explosion, was completely restored. A new cupola sits above, containing within it the original eighteenth-century bell; the weather vane, dating from 1671, was restored and put back in place.

Within, the columns along the south side were left standing after the blast; pieces of original stone were used to patch and extend them. The north wall, which once held the Hudson windows, is new brickwork.

The ammonium-nitrate fertilizer bomb used by the IRA in 1993 was a favorite weapon of the IRA, the Tamil Tigers of Sri Lanka, and some Middle Eastern terrorist groups. The same recipe was used to construct the 5,000-pound truck bomb that destroyed the Oklahoma City Federal Building in 1995, killing 168 people; the explosion in Oklahoma took place on April 19, coincidentally the same day and month Hudson took communion 388 years before.

When I visited St. Ethelburga's, London was still very jittery as the result of four bombings by Islamic militants that had taken place just two weeks before in the Underground and on a double-decker bus. The Peace and Reconciliation Centre had responded with several interfaith services and gatherings. The centre manager Angela West, who showed me around, told me that area police had been warning local institutions, including St. Ethelburga's, that the City was once again a prime target for terrorists.

CHAPTER 3

Voyage One: From London to Svalbard and the Ice

Henry Hudson and his crew had good reason to seek a blessing at St. Ethelburga's in 1607. They were about to set sail in a small ship to a place scarcely known, in pursuit of an unproved, sketchy theory. The goal was to find a Northeast Passage from Europe to Asia by sailing over the top of the North Pole; Hudson had been employed by the Muscovy Company at least in part because one of its directors had recommended him as someone who had in his possession "secret information" related to the passage.

It is generally believed that Hudson's plan was neither secret nor information, but instead a sketchy, published eighty-year-old theory put forth by Robert Thorne, an agent for a Bristol trading company living in Seville. It began as a letter from Thorne to King Henry VIII in which he revealed that all logic supported the idea that it was possible to sail from England to the Spice Islands directly over the North Pole.

Thorne's route was based on an unproven assertion that the three months of constant daylight in the Arctic summer would melt the polar ice cap.

In 1527, Thorne began his letter to the king with a statement of the geopolitically obvious: "The Spaniards hold the westward route, by the Straits of Magellan; the Portuguese the eastward, by the Cape of Good Hope. The English have left to them but one way to discover and that is by the North."

Herewith the secret, which Thorne claimed had been hidden by parties not specified. "I know it is my bounden duty to manifest this secret unto your Grace," Thorne wrote. "By sailing northward and passing the Pole, descending to the Equinoctial line, we shall hit these islands, and it should be a much shorter way than either the Spaniards or Portingals have."

When the court declined to bankroll an expedition, the concept was published as a pamphlet called "Thorne's Plan." Thorne, a global booster for exploration, declared: "There is no land uninhabitable nor sea innavigable."

Thorne was not the first to postulate a northern route; the Roman scholar Pliny the Elder had put forth a similar idea in an encyclopedia of natural science written in the first century A.D. According to Pliny, there was a circular sea at the top of the world with a connection to the Indian Ocean through a land called Tabis.

Hudson may have studied Thorne's sketchy plan in the library of Richard Hakluyt, who was one of the directors of the Muscovy Company and one of the era's greatest collectors of charts, logs, and maritime theories. Another follower was the Dutch mapmaker Peter Plancius, who would become one of Hudson's supporters on his third voyage, from Amsterdam.

Another visitor to Hakluyt was William Shakespeare; some literary scholars say the plot outline for *The Tempest* came from an account Hakluyt had of the wreck of the *Sea Venture* in 1609 in Bermuda, on its way to the Virginia colonies.

There is no known record of an encounter between Hudson and Shakespeare; *The Tempest* is considered to be Shakespeare's final play, first performed in 1611 or 1612. The great playwright died in 1616, and we can only imagine the tragedy he could have written about the fate of Hudson.

A Secondhand Boat

Captain Hudson was given command of a relatively sturdy, shoebox-like ship, the *Hopewell*. The vessel was about three years old. The previous year, 1606, Captain John Knight had sailed the ship to Labrador in search of the Northwest Passage.

Knight's exploration had ended badly. Hakluyt wrote about Knight in his book *Voyages in Search of the North-West Passage*:

> Nor ought we to pass on without calling to mind the melancholy fate, in 1606, of Master John Knight, driven, in the *Hopewell*, among huge masses of ice with a tremendous surf, his rudder knocked away, his ship half full of water, at the entrance to these straits. Hoping to find a harbour, he set forth to explore a large island, and landed, leaving two men to watch the boat, while he, with three men and the mate, set forth and disappeared over a hill. For thirteen hours the watchers kept their post; one had his trumpet with him, for he was a trumpeter, the other had a gun. They trumpeted often and loudly; they fired, but no answer came. They watched ashore all night for the return of their captain and his party, "but they came not at all."

Knight's remains were never found; Canada's Natural Resources Agency posted a photo of the lonely, barren Labrador beach on its Web site.

The *Hopewell* was of about forty tons capacity; a ship's tonnage has traditionally been calculated based on the amount of revenue space it holds—tax collectors used to figure their fees based on an estimate of the number of tuns or barrels a vessel could hold. A gross ton is roughly 100 cubic feet; the refrigerator in your kitchen is about 40 to 50 cubic feet in overall size, so the *Hopewell* could have carried something like 80 boxes of that size as cargo. (Today, a midsized modern freighter may be 100,000 tons in size, and a megacruise ship or container ship twice as large.)

The ship was outfitted as a bark, with square rigging on the fore- and mainmast, and fore and aft rigging on the mizzenmast. The crew had a compass, some crude charts from a handful of western European explorers who had been in the general area, and a set of rudimentary navigational tools that were capable of giving a rough estimate of latitude. They were heading north into an area where in summer the Sun never sets, the stars are not visible, and the magnetic compass is almost unusable because of the proximity to the pole.

It was not until May 1 that the *Hopewell* was able to leave its mooring at Gravesend and head out to sea; we can assume the delay was caused by bad weather and unfavorable winds.

The first of May 1607, we weighed Anchor at Gravesend, and on Tuesday the six and twentieth day in the morning we made the Iles of Shotland . . . and at noon we were 60°12' and six leagues [twenty-one miles] to the Eastward of them.

The *Hopewell* had set out from Gravesend, about twenty-six miles east and downriver from London on the south bank of the Thames; on the other side of the river is Tilbury, which today is the main container ship and cruise terminal for the Port of London. Only a relatively few major ships sail further west through the Thames Flood Barrier and through the Tower Bridge.

Gravesend dates back to at least 1086, when it was listed in the Domesday Book as Gravesham, probably derived from *graaf-ham*, meaning the home of the bailiff of the lord of the manor. Another possible source of the name is *Grove's End* or *grafs-ham*, meaning a place at the end of the grove. The grimmest theory ties the town name to the bubonic plague of the 1600s, as a place where bodies—no longer being buried on land—were dumped into the river.

It was shipboard protocol to take a reading of the ship's position every day at noon. According to the log, on May 26 the *Hopewell* was about twenty-one miles east of the Shetland Islands at the north end of Great Britain.

The log of Hudson's first voyage as captain for the Muscovy Company, from May 1 through September 15, 1607, was collected and transcribed by the historian Samuel Purchas and published in book three of *Purchas His Pilgrimes* in 1625 in London. Purchas says that the document was written by the crewman John Playse and by the master Henry Hudson. Midway through the log the voice changes from second person to first person; Hudson may have taken over the log at that point, or it may have been that Playse had recopied the first half of Hudson's log, changing the voice.

I have corrected or made consistent spellings of the names of the crew, sometimes presented in multiple versions. And I have updated some of the archaic or incorrect spelling.

The log and other documents were also collected in *Hudson the Navigator*, an 1860 publication of the Hakluyt Society in London.

The Pocahontas Connection

In 1607—the same year Hudson was setting out on his voyage in search of the Northeast Passage—Pocahontas met Captain John Smith at the English settlement in Jamestown, Virginia.

Let's not confuse Disney's fairy tale (Romeo and Juliet meet cute forest animals and a wise, talking tree in the wilderness of Virginia) with the true facts as they are known. Born in about 1595, Pocahontas's real name was Mantoax or Matoaka, which means "Little Snow Feather"; she was a daughter of Powhatan, the leader of the Powhatan Indian confederacy in Virginia. Her second, most famous name, Pocahontas, means "Little Wanton." The chief's daughter was apparently a bit of a wild child.

The Powhatans spoke an Algonquian language; they were linguistic cousins to the Mohicans and the Leni-Lenape tribes of the Hudson River Valley and the Cree of James Bay.

Henry Hudson and John Smith were well acquainted as ambitious explorers; they may have shared plans and schemes under Hakluyt's stewardship. In 1609, Smith sent a letter back to England to Hudson; on Hudson's third journey that year, he sailed near the settlement at Jamestown but did not come ashore, perhaps in fear that his ship—which on that one voyage flew the Dutch flag—would not be welcomed.

Smith, unlike Hudson, was embarked on a plan to colonize a portion of North America. The Virginia Company operated under a charter from King James I. His three-ship expedition landed in Virginia in April 1607, just as Hudson was taking communion at St. Ethelburga's and preparing to head north into the ice.

The outlines of the legend of Pocahontas are based on two somewhat different accounts, both by Smith, in a pair of books he wrote about his adventures in Virginia. Smith was quite a self-promoter; he almost certainly would be quite pleased to learn of his installation in the Disney pantheon of legends.

Smith relates that he led a group of Jamestown colonists beyond the walls of their fort on an expedition in search of food in late December 1607. He writes that they crossed paths with a hunting party led by Powhatan's brother, Openchancanough; all the settlers were killed except for Smith, who was brought to Powhatan's village as a prisoner. It was there that the twenty-eight-year-old Smith met Pocahontas, whom he described in a book he wrote a year later; *A True Relation*, as "a child of ten years old which in feature, countenance and proportion much exceeded any of the rest of her people." (If Disney had stuck to the record, the resulting movie might have been classified as kiddie porn.)

It wasn't until Smith's later book, *The General History of Virginia, New England, and the Summer Isles*, first published in 1616 after he had returned to England, and in later writings, that he either gave more details or greatly embellished the story of his capture by the natives and his supposed rescue by Pocahontas.

The summary of Smith's story, pieced together from the first and second relating, is this: he was held by the Powhatans and made to go through a sort of ritual trial. In *A General History*, he writes of his own story in the third person:

A long consultation was held, but the conclusion was two great stones were brought before Powhatan: then as many as could laid hands on him, dragged him to them, and thereon laid his head. And being ready with their clubs to beat out his brains, Pocahontas, the King's dearest daughter, when no entreaty could prevail, got his head in her arm, and laid her own upon his to save him from death. Whereat the Emperor was contented he should live to make him hatchets, and her bells, beads, and copper; for they thought him as well of all occupations as themselves.

One reason some historians are very careful in their appraisal of his tale is that this lucky young man also claimed an earlier rescue by a beautiful princess. In his writings, he tells of how he served as a soldier of fortune for the Austrians in battles against the Ottoman Turks in 1601. Smith says that after he personally killed three of the most important of the Turkish enemy he was captured and brought to Istanbul and made the slave of Princess Charatz Tragabigzanda. But he says that the princess found the twenty-one-year-old Smith so handsome and attractive that she fell in love with him and sent him away to safety.

(The residents of seaside northern Massachusetts had another close escape. In 1614, Captain Smith anchored in what is now Sandy Bay in Rockport. He wrote that he saw attractive cliffs, "fronted by three isles." He named the place Tragabigzanda in honor of his princess heroine; he called the three islands the Turk's Heads to commemorate the glory of his action on the battlefield. Luckily for modern real estate agents, Prince Charles—later King Charles I from 1625 to 1649—renamed the cape in honor of his mother, Anne of Denmark. And the three Turk's Heads of Cape Anne became Straitsmouth, Thacher's, and Milk islands.)

Back to the story of Pocahontas: some historians say it may have been partly true, perhaps a ritual demonstration of power by Powhatan. In any case, Captain Smith was quickly released and returned to Jamestown in January 1608.

The biggest impact of Pocahontas came later. Smith returned to England in 1609, after suffering an injury in a gunpowder explosion; we are told that the princess was told the captain was dead.

After Smith left, relations between the settlers and the Powhatans deteriorated. In 1610, Pocahontas married a native named Kocoum and went with him to live with the Patawomeked (Potomac) Indians, a related tribe. But in 1613, Captain Samuel Argall—a somewhat harsh leader who went on to be deputy governor of Virginia—sailed up the Potomac River and kidnapped Pocahontas and brought her back to Jamestown as a hostage. (No mention is made of her husband and any children they might have had.)

Argall demanded of Powhatan that he release English prisoners he held and supply the colony with some food; the English were released, but Pocahontas remained with the settlers at Henrico, inland up the James River. It is not clear whether she was held against her will or chose to stay. She was placed in the care of the Reverend Alexander Whitaker, who had set up an outpost of the Anglican Church there.

Pocahontas converted to Christianity in 1614; Whitaker baptized her as Rebecca in 1614. A painting that imagines the ceremony hangs in the rotunda of the U.S. Capitol in Washington, D.C. The work was completed in 1840; the artist John Gadsby Chapman shows Pocahontas in a white dress, kneeling before a priest and a baptismal font. She is surrounded by colonists and a few members of her family, including Chief Powhatan; her brother, Nantequaus, turns his back on the ceremony. Her eventual husband, John Rolfe, stands behind her.

It was during her captivity at Henrico that she met the English colonist Rolfe; he had brought tobacco plants from the Caribbean to the colony and the crop went on to become Virginia's leading export. Eventually, the tobacco plantations would also become intertwined with the introduction of slavery.

When Rolfe and Rebecca were married in an April 1, 1614, wedding at Jamestown, it served a great political purpose. The marriage—said to be the first formal union between a European settler and a native—established a temporary truce between the English settlers and the area tribes that lasted until Powhatan's death in 1618.

Now known as Rebecca Rolfe, she gave birth to a son in 1615 and named him Thomas after the colony's governor, Sir Thomas Dale. In that same year, the Virginia Company formally recognized Pocahontas/Rebecca's contributions to the colony, awarding her an annual stipend.

In 1616, Sir Dale brought the Rolfe family and about a dozen other Native American men and women to England on one of the company's ships; it was basically a public relations tour to boost royal and private interest in developing the colony. Pocahontas was introduced at court to King James I and Queen Anne; she was also reunited with Captain Smith. It was in the midst of this seven-month grand tour of England that Smith published his second, larger account of his exploits in Jamestown; this version included the story of Pocahontas's role as his protector from execution.

In March 1617, the Rolfe family boarded a ship to make their return from England to the Virginia colony. Almost immediately, Pocahontas became gravely ill (pneumonia or tuberculosis or other pulmonary diseases were quite common) and she was taken ashore. She died on March 21, 1617, at the age of about twenty-two; she is buried at St. George's Parish Church at Gravesend.

Fog, Wind, Ice, and Ill Will

For the first few weeks after it left London in 1607, the *Hopewell* made very little progress because of contrary winds; on June 4, the ship was no more than ninety miles from the northern part of the Shetland Islands. A week later, it was within the Arctic Circle and sailing northwest toward Greenland.

On June 11, the *Hopewell* was at 67°30′, about the latitude of the top of Iceland to the west. The crew spotted six or seven whales near the ship. That was the good news, but the ship's journal—maintained by a member of the crew, John Playse—also gives the first adverse weather report: "All the night proved a great fog with much wind."

> *June 13, 1607.* Between one and two o'clock in the morning we saw some land on head of us, and some ice; and it being a thick fog, we steered away northerly . . . Our sails and shrouds did freeze. At eight

in the morning it cleared up, the wind being at North-east and by East, with much wind we were hardly able to maintain a sail. This is a very high land, most part covered with snow. At the top it looked reddish, and underneath a blackish clay with much ice lying about it . . . We saw much fowl. Also we saw a whale close by the shore. We called the headland which we saw Young's Cape; and near it standeth a very high mount like a round castle, which we called the Mount of God's Mercy.

The ship was off the east coast of Greenland, a place that is still barely touched by humans; the log does not give latitude and the precise locations of the landmarks are not known.

The headland was named after one of his sailors, James Young. Mount of God's Mercy would seem to be a nod toward the British explorer John Davis, who explored northern Canada in 1584 in search of the Northwest Passage and was an acquaintance of Thomas Hudson and possibly the master of a ship that Henry Hudson had sailed on. Among the places Davis named was the Cape of God's Mercy at the bottom of the Cumberland Peninsula on Baffin Island.

June 20, 1607. All the morning was a thick fog with the wind at south; we steered north-east till noon. Then we changed our course and steered away north north-east hoping for a sea free of ice in our course to fall with the body of Newland.

Newland was one of the names given the area today called Svalbard (Norwegian for Cold Coast), an archipelago that reaches to just above 80° of latitude. The principal island in the group is Spitsbergen (Jagged Peaks). For the next few days, Hudson struggled against strong winds, ice in the water, and fog. Unable to move to the east, the *Hopewell* hugged the coast of Greenland and carefully moved north.

June 21, 1607. In the morning while we steered our course north north-east, we thought we had embayed ourselves, finding land on

NASA image of the Svalbard Peninsula; the western side
is approachable, but ice chokes the top and eastern sides.
Jacques Descloitres, MODIS Rapid Response Team,
NASA/GSFC

our larboard, and ice upon it, and many great pieces of drift ice. We
steered away north-east, with diligent looking out . . . for land, having
a desire to know whether it would leave us to the east, both to know
the breadth of the sea, and also to shape a more northerly course.
And considering we knew no name given to this land, we thought
good to name it Hold with Hope, lying in 73 degrees of latitude.

Here is to be noted that when we made the Mount of God's Mercy
and Young's Cape, the land was covered with snow for the most part,
and extreme cold when we approached, but this land was very temperate to our feeling.

Old maps and atlases show a dot of land on Greenland marked as Cape Hold with Hope at about 73.3° North, 22.5 West, roughly 950 miles due west across the Greenland and Norwegian seas from Tromso in Norway and 700 miles southwest of Svalbard. Modern maps often don't bother with names for the almost untouched eastern side of Greenland; nearly all the settlements are to the west.

Hudson and all other explorers of the time dreaded becoming "embayed," which meant becoming trapped in a bay. At best, it meant that what they thought to be a strait between land masses had come to a dead end; at worst—and this was a significant threat in the Far North—it might mean that a ship could become trapped by ice closing in around the mouth of a harbor after the explorers had entered.

June 22, 1607. This morning when it cleared up, we saw the land, its nearest part trending east northeast and west southwest. . . . It was a main high-land, nothing at all covered with snow and the north part . . . was very high mountainous. The many fogs and calms with contrary winds, and much ice near the shore held us from further discovery of it.

It may be objected against us as a fault for hailing so Westerly a course. The chief cause that moved us thereunto was our desire to that part of Greenland which (for ought that we know) was to any Christian unknown. And we thought it might as well have been open sea as land, and by that means our passage should have been . . . to the Pole.

And considering we found land contrary to that which our cards make mention of, we accounted our labor so much the more worth.

At this point in the log, we find a bit of after-the-fact backfilling ("It may be objected against us . . ."). and perhaps a bit of geographic pipe dreaming ("this land was very temperate to our feeling"). Remember that Hudson was managing a commercial enterprise on behalf of his financial backers and had to account for his expenditures of time and money, and he also did not want to quarrel with their underlying plan for the voyage, which was based on a belief that there was an ice-free passage over the North Pole in the summer.

June 27, 1607. About one or two o'clock in the morning we made Newland, being clear weather on the sea but the land was covered with fog, the ice lying very thick all along the shore for 15 or 16 leagues [fifty-two to fifty-five miles] which we saw. . . . This day at noon, we accounted we were in 78° and we stood along the shore. This day was so foggy that we were hardly able to see the land many times, but by our account we were near Vogel Hooke.

Vogel Hooke or Voegl-hoeck (Bird Cape)—named by William Barents on his 1596 voyage—is near the northwest end of Prince Charles Foreland, a barrier island that stands off the west shore of Spitsbergen. Today, the same area bears the Norwegian equivalent names of Prins Karls Forland and Fuglehuken. The south end of the island is near the entrance to Isfjorden, which leads to today's settlement of Longyearbyen; north of Prince Charles Foreland on Spitsbergen is Magdalenefjord.

July 1, 1607. About noon we were embayed with ice, lying between the land and us. By our observation we were at 78°42', whereby we accounted we were thwart of the Great Indraught.

And to free ourselves of the ice we steered between southeast and south, and to the westward. . . . About six this evening it pleased God to give us clear weather, and we found we had shot far into the Inlet, being almost a bay, and environed with very high mountains. . . . Then, being sure where we were, we steered away west . . . and found all our ice on the northern shore and a clear sea to the south.

Hudson was constantly on the lookout for fast-moving water going into or out of significant bays; the conventional wisdom was that one of these was certain to be a strait that led through to China.

Based on the latitude reported in the log, the Great Indraught is probably the Kongsfjorden, which is near today's settlement of Ny Ålesund. Some historians suppose that Hudson may have been not quite as far north as he thought and may have instead entered the Isfjorden, which leads to what is now Longyearbyen; that larger fjord is six miles wide at its entrance and broadens to as much as thirteen miles in width as it runs fifty miles inland, almost splitting Spitsber-

The logbooks and journals of the time used British nautical measurements. In seventeenth-century England, a *league* was three nautical miles in length; a nautical mile was a bit longer than a terrestrial mile. (A nautical mile is 6,080 feet, whereas a mile on land is 5,280 feet.) So, a league is equal to about 3.45 miles.

And just to make things more confusing, other seafaring nations had different definitions: for French sailors, a league was equal to about 2.42 miles on land; in Spain, a league was equal to about 2.63 land miles; and for Portuguese navigators the league was about 3.84 miles. I've used the British measure in this book.

The depth of the sea, something especially important in bays, rivers, and near land, was measured in *fathoms*; one fathom is equal to six feet.

gen in half. Forced to take shelter against high winds and ice, Hudson stayed in the inlet for several days. On July 4, the weather turned cold and the *Hopewell*'s shrouds and sails were frozen.

On July 11, as the *Hopewell* pushed north, the voice in the log changes from second person to first person; a margin note in Purchas's transcript says, "From hence it seemeth is taken out of Henry Hudson's own notes." One explanation: John Playse had copied over the first part of the log from Hudson's notes.

July 11, 1607. We were come out of the blue sea into our green sea again, where we saw whales . . . Here we saw plenty of seals, and we supposed bears had been here, by their footing and dung on the ice. This day, many of my company was sick with eating of bear's flesh the day before.

July 12, 1607. This morning we had our shrouds frozen. . . . This afternoon we steered away north. . . . Then we saw ice ahead of us . . . we were very near ice, being calm, and the sea setting onto the ice, which was very dangerous. It pleased God at the very instant to give us a small gale, which was the means of our deliverance.

In these two matter-of-fact journal entries are the stuff of legends and easy death on the seas. The crew, always subject to disease and injury, falls ill because they ate spoiled meat. There was also the constant threat of scurvy from vitamin C deficiency; it was not until the mid-eighteenth century that a British doctor realized the preventative and suggested that sailors eat limes, hence the nickname "limeys" for Britons at sea.

The next day's journal entry tells how the insubstantial *Hopewell* drifted toward the ice without wind to help them sail away until a last-minute gale gave them steerage.

July 14, 1607. At noon being a thick fog, we found ourselves near land . . . and running farther we found a bay open to the west. . . . The northern side of this bay's mouth . . . is a small island which we called Collin's Cape by the name of our boatswain who first saw it.

In this bay we saw many whales, and one of our company having a hook and line overboard to try for fish, a whale came under the keel of our ship and made her held. Yet by God's mercy we had no harm, but the loss of the hook and three parts of the line.

In the bottom of this bay, John Colman, my mate, and William Collin, my boatswain, with two others of our company went on shore and there they found and brought aboard a pair of morse's teeth in the jaw; they likewise found whale's bones, and some dozen or more of deer's horns, they saw the footings of beasts of other sorts, they also saw rote-geese, they saw much driftwood on the shore, and found a stream or two of fresh water. Here they found it hot on the shore, and drank water to cool their thirst.

This night proved clear, and we had the sun on the Meridian, on the North and by East part of the compass, from the upper edge of the horizon with the cross-staff we found [its] height 10°40' . . . from a north sun to an east sun, we sailed between north and north north-east for eight leagues [twenty-eight miles].

On this day's journal entry, Hudson mentions almost in passing the midnight sun; July 14 is very close to the peak of the summer in Svalbard with the sun never descending below the horizon.

According to later marine historians, Hudson makes an error here in calculating his latitude. He thinks he has reached above 80°23', and some writers place the location of Collin's Cape on Nordaustlandet (Northeast Land), which is another large island around the top of Spitsbergen and to the east.

Sir Martin Conway, in his 1906 book *No Man's Land: A History of Spitsbergen from Its Discovery in 1596 to the Beginning of the Scientific Exploration of the Country,* refigured the latitude based on Hudson's report of the height of the sun. Conway says Collins Cape and Whale's Bay where Colman and Collin went ashore was approximately 79°5'.

That would place Collin's Cape at what is now called Cape Mitre or Kapp Mitra, about fifty miles short of the top end of the main island of Spitsbergen. Whale's Bay would be what is now called King's Bay or Kongsfjorden, a fjord just below Cape Mitre that splits north toward virtually untouched land and south toward the tiny community of Ny Ålesund.

Based on these more-modern calculations, the *Hopewell* proceeded to the next logical safe harbor, a bit farther north at Magdalenefjord at about 79°50'. The area at the top of the northwest corner of Spitsbergen offers several protected harbors.

Hudson's claim of exploration to 80°23' would stand as a record for the farthest north exploration by any captain, a mark that would not be broken for 166 years.

July 16, 1607. This morning we saw that we were compassed in with ice in abundance. . . . We saw more land . . . trending north in our sight . . . stretching far into 82°, and by the bowing or showing of the sky. I hoped to have had a free sea between the land and the ice and meant to have compassed this land by the north. But now finding by proof it was unpossible by means of the abundance of ice compassing us about by the north and joining to the land.

And this I can assure . . . that between 78°50' and 82° by this way there is no passage. But I think this land may be profitable to those that will adventure it. In this bay . . . and about this coast, we saw more abundance of seals than we had seen any time before.

Once again, Hudson's entry for this day is an attempt at balancing the books. Though the stated purpose of the voyage—to find the Northeast Passage to China—was not accomplished, "this land may be profitable."

Within a few years after Hudson's visit, Magdalenefjord and the island of Smeerenburg (Blubbertown) about fifteen miles north, would become two of the most active whaling outposts in the Arctic. A decade later, the massive invasion all but killed off the area's whales and many other marine mammals to the great profit of their backers.

The log does observe that the land seems to extend farther than Hudson had expected; the "bowing" of the sky could have been an Arctic mirage caused by temperature differentials between the water, land, and the air.

There is a particular type of mirage seen on the ocean and especially in Arctic and Antarctic latitudes: scientists and explorers with a literary bent call this mirage fata morgana. The name comes from Morgan le Fay, the shape-shifting goddess-witch half-sister of King Arthur. A fata morgana is an optical mirage caused by a temperature inversion, warm air over cold, dense air near the water acting like a refracting lens that produces a distorted, upside-down image. An iceberg, cliff, or ship may appear elongated and twisted in shape, floating above the surface like a castle.

> *July 27, 1607.* We heard a great . . . noise with the ice and sea, which was the first ice we heard or saw since we were at Collin's Cape. The sea heaving us westward toward the ice, we heaved out our boat and rowed to tow out our ship farther from the danger which would have been to small purpose [because] the sea went so high. But in this extremity it pleased God give us a small gale at Northwest . . . we steered away southeast.
>
> Then we had a good gale . . . and found by the icy sky, and our nearness to Greenland that there is no passage that way; which, if there had been I meant to have made my return by the north of Greenland to Davis his Straits, and so for England.
>
> *July 31, 1607.* Finding the fog more thick and troublesome than before . . . and our time well nigh spent to do further good this year,

I commanded to bear up for our return for England, and steered away south southwest.

We were thwart of Cherie's Island the next morning . . . Knowing we were near it, we looked out farefully for the same, and it proving clear, we saw it . . . a very ragged land on the western side rising like haystacks.

After several more days sailing along the coast, the return home began on July 23, 1607, with *Hopewell* headed due west from Spitsbergen toward Greenland.

Cherie's Island, at 74°30' North latitude, had been named Bear Island in 1596 by Willem Barents. Seven years later another explorer, Stephen Bennet, passed by the island and thought he was the first to see it; he named it after Sir Francis Cherie, one of his financiers in the Muscovy Company. Today, the island goes by the Norwegian translation of Bear Island: Bjørnoya.

Bear Island is a very recognizable landmark in the cold emptiness of the Barents Sea. Its northern end is mostly flat, like the landing platform of an aircraft carrier; at the southern end, cliffs rise into peaks. The largest is the evocatively named Mount Misery at 1,830 feet above the cold waters. At the extreme southern tip is the 260-foot tall Sylen, a rock needle that punctuates the landscape.

August 15, 1607. We put into the Iles of Farre [Faeroe Islands] . . . and the fifteenth of September I arrived in Tilberie Hope in the Thames.

Hudson's log does not make note of it, but according to two captains also employed by the Muscovy Company the *Hopewell* sighted a previously uncharted island on his way back from Spitsbergen to England, apparently after passing Cherie (Bear Island) and before putting into the Faeroes.

Captain Thomas Edge produced a paper called "Brief Discoverie of the Muscovia Merchants" and included in it some further detail that may have come directly from Hudson or a member of his crew. Edge said that "in ranging homewards he discovered an island lying in 71°, which he named Hudson's Tutches."

The curiously named island was probably today's Jan Mayen Island, which lies about 400 miles west of the direct path that leads from the bottom of Spitsbergen, past Bear Island, to the Faeroe Islands. Was Hudson blown that far off course on his trip home? (He makes no mention of a significant storm that would have caused such a deviation.) Or was Hudson heading for Greenland and the "temperate" touchstones of Hold-with-Hope and Young's Cape with plans to spend the winter there and then continue on to the west coast of Greenland and into the Davis Strait in northern Canada?

We can only guess; there is no known expansion of the log or a personal journal by a member of the crew. Did Hudson decide to return to England on his own, or were there rumblings (or open revolt) at the prospect of spending a cold winter away from home? All we know is that there is a great gap of detail between leaving Bear Island and docking at Tilbury on the Thames.

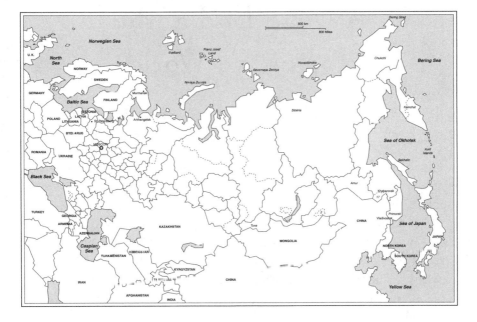

Another proposed Northeast Passage from Europe to Asia followed a route to the top of Norway and then along the coast of Russia through or below Novaya Zemlya and on to the Bering Strait.

CHAPTER 4

A Dead End at the Top of the World

Silversea Cruises's *Silver Cloud* is the polar opposite of Henry Hudson's *Hopewell*. His humble wooden ship could have been drydocked on the pool deck of the luxurious Italian cruise ship.

We boarded *Silver Cloud* in Copenhagen along with about 150 other guests who were paying from $500 to $2,000 per night for a sixteen-night cruise. The intinerary called for a trip up the coast of Norway to near its top and then a left turn due north to approach as close as possible to the polar ice barrier. From there we would proceed to Svalbard, the Cold Coast.

We traveled in the lap of luxury. Champagne and wine flowed like bottled water. Our suites were heated or cooled to our exact preference. The chef would stop by our table each evening to discuss the dishes he had prepared and to inquire about our special preferences. The 514-foot-long ship could travel at twenty knots; wing-like gyroscopically controlled stabilizers extended from each side to dampen the roll of rough seas. The ship's doctor supervised a fully equipped hospital in case one of the passengers felt below the weather.

Up on the bridge, Captain Marco Sangiacomo had detailed charts of the Norwegian Sea, the Bering Sea, and the islands of Svalbard. A global positioning satellite receiver pinpointed the *Silver Cloud*'s location to within 300 feet. Another satellite delivered detailed weather forecasts. Several radar systems scanned the seas in all directions in search of other ships (we saw none for more than a week), land, and ice.

And as we crossed the Arctic Circle and moved toward the North Pole, the ship's Italian officers and Filipino sailors were on extra vigilance, scanning the horizon for large icebergs and floes.

It was the captain and crew's first visit to Svalbard, and they had prepared in every way they could to cautiously maneuver the $200 million ship and its paying customers up to the ice that surrounds the pole and into the fjords of Spitsbergen. The young captain—at thirty-eight the junior master in the fleet and one of the younger captains of a major cruise ship anywhere—was confident but very tense.

On July 31, we moved due north up the prime meridian of 0° of longitude to the outer fringe of the North Pole ice pack: the polar ice barrier. The prime meridian is the line of longitude that divides the earth into the Eastern and Western Hemispheres; the equator is the line of latitude that separates the globe into the Northern and Southern Hemispheres.

Hudson was able to come up with a fairly accurate reading of his latitude by measuring the height of the Sun at various points on his voyages, but it was not until the 1740s that the English clock designer John Harrison perfected a timepiece and a system that could accurately measure longitude.

The prime meridian mostly traverses ocean, but its official measuring point is at the Royal Observatory at Greenwich, England, near London; if we had turned around and sailed south from the ice barrier, there would have been no land between us and the east coast of England near Hull. South of Greenwich, the line passes near Rouen in France and the east coast of Spain, through the African countries of Algeria, Mali, Togo, Burkina Faso, and Ghana, and then entirely over water to Antarctica.

It's an odd feature of the navigational system in use for thousands of years that when you approach the North Pole every direction is north; when you turn your back on the geographic location of 0°0' every direction is south. (Similarly, standing at the south geographic pole, all paths are northward.)

At about 2:00 P.M., the ship reached 79°42' North latitude and 0°0' of longitude. Sangiacomo slowed the ship to near its minimum maneuvering speed of five knots and scanned the horizon with binoculars; the first officer stood alongside him with another set of glasses, and a sailor was posted out on the port side flying bridge. On the large radar screens a faint white line was visible directly ahead of us and to our west; small compact car-sized chunks of ice bobbed alongside us in the water.

The ship's wing-like stabilizers had been pulled in so that they wouldn't strike any low-hanging ice floes; in any case, they would not have been of much use while the ship was barely moving forward. The bow thrusters—a set of powerful side-facing propellers that can quickly push the ship's nose or stern to one side or the other—were on standby.

Coming to the Ice Barrier

In Ålesund, before the *Silver Cloud* sailed away from the mainland toward the polar ice barrier—a three-day journey from the Norwegian Sea to the Barents Sea—we had picked up a local pilot. Cato Lorentsen was familiar with the waters in and around Svalbard and available to give advice on things like ice, currents, and anchorages.

As insubstantial as the barrier looked, according to Lorentsen the ice was about eleven to thirteen feet thick at its edge. Though most of the ice was below the surface of the water, our ship's hull extended eighteen feet into the sea. A head-on meeting would be like hitting a wall.

The pilot drew his finger down the nautical chart to reinforce the markings already in place: there were three notable currents to be aware of, rivers within the ocean that could move icebergs broken off of glaciers or ice floes from the polar cap into our path.

The East Spitsbergen Current flows south from the ice barrier on the remote eastern side of Spitsbergen; one branch continued due south toward Bear Island behind us and the other hooked around to the west below the bottom of Spitsbergen. The third current in the area is the Norwegian Atlantic Current, which is the far northern extent of the warm Gulf Stream; that current is the one that keeps the western side of Spitsbergen mostly clear of ice for much of the year while the eastern and northern sides are usually blocked.

Captain Sangiacomo was younger, more communicative, and notably more excited about his current assignment than most masters of cruise ships I have met. No one aboard the *Silver Cloud* was more eager to be making a first visit to the Arctic than he was.

Earlier in the week, the *Silver Cloud* had tied up alongside its slightly larger sister ship *Silver Whisper* in Ålesund and Sangiacomo had met with that ship's more-experienced captain. (The other ship was staying closer to the European mainland on a different itinerary.)

"I have in this yellow envelope all of my notes about the ice," Sangiacomo told me. "He gave me some advice for when we arrive close to the ice. He told me to pay attention to how the ice was drifting and also to always pay attention on my back because the ice is closing behind you."

Up at the top of the world the ice moves generally from north to southeast because of currents and the effects of the rotation of the earth. Sangiacomo said the advice he received was to always keep an opening on the port side so that if ice closes in the ship can turn to the left and away from danger.

The ice in the water around us were floes—pieces broken off of the polar ice pack or calved off of glaciers to our east in Spitsbergen. We were too far north to be in the path of the huge icebergs that travel south from Greenland; those bergs circulate around Labrador (as the *Titanic* discovered in 1912) and often enter into the St. Lawrence River or Hudson Strait on the Canadian side of the Arctic.

Sangiacomo had a full suite of high-tech instruments to help him navigate. He was surprised to find that his global positioning satellite (GPS) receiver was still functioning, even at this high latitude. He also had a gyroscopic compass that kept track of his position from the last certain reading in port, and there were several radar systems that showed the ice pack. But the primary navigation method at the top of the world involved lookouts, binoculars, and charts.

Every Tuesday, Norwegian authorities broadcast a bulletin with information about the position of the ice barrier and floating ice. On the other side of the pole, Canadian and U.S. agencies plot icebergs and there are Web sites where mariners can see satellite photos of the waterways.

We were no longer able to connect to the Internet from the ship because the satellite—somewhere down around the equator—was below the horizon. A radio crackled with weather reports transmitted from Svalbard and the Norwegian mainland.

I asked him if he ever gave thought to the really old-fashioned sailing methods. When Henry Hudson came through these waters in 1607, he had no GPS, no radar, no Internet, and no radio. All he had were a few incomplete maps, a magnetic compass that became increasingly inaccurate the farther north he proceeded, and some primitive instruments to measure latitude.

"What they did was unbelievable," Sangiacomo said. "There is poor visibility. We are too far north to fix the position with a sextant; there are not so many stars and the horizon is not so visible. And it is daylight all day."

And then with a nod he took in the luxurious appointments of the *Silver Cloud*. "We have heating in case it is too cold. They had nothing."

On my previous visits to the bridge, the captain had maintained an easygoing happy chatter with the crew, switching back and forth from Italian to English as needed and leaving the manipulation of the controls—the wheel, which controlled the rudder, and the levers that adjusted the speed of the propellers—to one of the mates. Now, he moved to the wheel himself; he directed one of the officers to block any incoming phone calls to the bridge. If the social hostess had a special request for the captain to make an appearance at a cocktail party, this was not the time to ask.

Our first spotting of the ice barrier was an Arctic mirage; it looked like land but was actually a reflection off the ice to the clouds and back. When I put my binoculars to the image, I could see it moving up, down, back, forth, left, and right as the wind played with the clouds and temperature layers.

We moved within a mile of the ice barrier and slowed to a crawl. Now we could see the thin line of ice with the naked eye. The winds were calm, and the ship was able to hold relatively stationary.

The outer band was like a broken Cheerio. We could see a bit of open water beyond, but in the distance and to the west all was white.

There was a moment of silence as we all took in the scene, and then the captain motioned the Filipino sailor on duty to take the wheel. Suddenly, he bolted away from the bridge and trotted up the hallway. The officers watched him leave, and then quickly turned back to their binoculars and the radar screens. Was something wrong?

A few moments later Sangiacomo returned to the bridge; he had run to his cabin to get his personal camera and he asked one of the mates to take a picture of him with the shelf of ice over his shoulder. He smiled for the first time that day.

"I come once in my life," he explained.

The Northernmost Cruise Director

Ray Solaire, the puckish cruise director of *Silver Cloud*, came up to the bridge and posted a magazine photo of a polar bear with her cubs onto a wall. He pointed the video camera for the ship's onboard television channel at it and moments later he took the microphone to announce the first wildlife spotting. Solaire, born in northern England, is a former vaudevillian who has been at sea for more than twenty-five years; it was his first visit to the ice barrier.

Ten minutes later, the wind suddenly shifted to come off of the ice and toward us. With it came a lowering fog; half a mile away, we all knew, was that solid wall, moving in the current. And we also knew that large bergs and growlers were in the water around us.

At that moment, we were less than 700 cold, windy, and empty miles due south of the geographic North Pole, as close as we could get by sea from this approach. Sangiacomo directed a slow turn to the west and we swung in a U-turn all the way around to the south and the *Silver Cloud* moved away from the ice barrier.

On the pool deck, Solaire was organizing a volleyball game in the heated pool. "Bring your swimming costumes," he announced. "This is a once-in-a-lifetime chance."

A Barkeep As Pilot

Some pilots, like the ones who guide ships through the Panama Canal or into a busy harbor like New York, bring the sort of intensity you find in a person who knows everything there is to know about one small but important place. I met a pilot in the Cape Cod Canal who had spent his entire career guiding ships back and forth through that one 500-foot-wide 17-mile stretch of water.

The man who came aboard *Silver Cloud* in Ny Ålesund seemed cut from different cloth. To begin with, he didn't have much to say to the captain, or to me. "He is not talking too much," said Sangiacomo. "He is a Scandinavian man. He is yes, no, maybe."

Cato Lorentsen had the look of a man who had been to sea and back, windblown and ruddy-faced. He told me that in the eighteen years he had been in Svalbard—a long time to be a temporary resident there—he had seen the ice conditions change. This year, he said, it was possible to go past the end of the island at about 81° of latitude and go around to the east side; that was not usually the case—Hudson had been blocked 400 years ago—although conditions changed from year to year. A dozen years back, Lorentsen said, the ice pack had been especially heavy and navigation to the east was impossible.

He did seem to know the waters, giving me a great number of informative yes, no, and maybe answers to my questions as we studied the charts in the ship's library. Lorentsen told me that in years past he had run a small cruise ship that went out to the ice pack and has been on fishing vessels that have been around Svalbard and as far away as twelve miles offshore the Russian island of Novaya Zemlya to hunt minke whales.

So, what do you do when you're not sailing on a cruise ship coming into your home waters, I asked. "I have a big pub in Longyearbyen, the Carlsberger," he said. I made a note to check it out on our visit to Longyearbyen later in the week.

Magdalenefjord: Beauty, Death, and Cocktails

The next day *Silver Cloud* sailed slowly into Magdalenefjorden, a six-mile-long east-west indentation into Albert I Land at the top end of Spitsbergen. The skies were a perfect cerulean with high fluttering streaks of insubstantial clouds; the Arctic Sun moved in its odd overhead loop, giving no clue about the time of day.

The outer flanks of the fjord included several sharp valleys filled with active glaciers. As we came toward the shore, the passage curved gently to the right, just enough to obscure our view of what lay ahead.

Up on the bridge the effusive Captain Sangiacomo, aided by the occasional hand signal or yes or no contributions of the pilot Cato, steered the ship into the fjord.

Finally, we reached the end of the waterway and the ship fell silent. Around us was the view most of the passengers (and the captain) had traveled a lifetime plus ten days to see, one of those places that is meant to be absorbed in contemplation.

Off the bow of the ship was a major glacier, in retreat up the valley toward an ice field on a crownlike mountain called Hommentoppen. To our left, a bright blue glacier was advancing toward the sea. At right, a scattering of ice fields hung up in the hills. And at our stern was a small beach with what looked like piles of rock up from the shore. Chunks of blue ice, broken off from the glaciers, bobbed in the water.

We set anchor, and two boatloads of deckhands and crew headed for the beach. As they approached, four men came down from a bright orange tent that was pitched on the flank of one of the hills; they were carrying serious rifles and binoculars and after scanning the beach and nearby hills they moved out to form an armed perimeter.

My wife, daughter, and I were on the first boat of passengers to

The *Silver Cloud* bobs like a toy boat in the historic harbor of Magdalenefjord.
Photo by the author

go ashore. As befits a luxury cruise, even in the most remote of places, preparations had been made to ease our way; the crew had constructed a temporary landing ramp for the tenders, and we arrived with dry feet on the beach. A few yards up from the landing spot the ship's sommelier stood overseeing the operation of a refreshment stand offering champagne, wine, and mixed drinks served in crystal glasses from a silver platter; a sign, created for the moment, read: THE NORTHERNMOST BAR IN THE WORLD.

We chose to ignore the bar for the moment and make the most of this unique place. The *Silver Cloud* is not a monster like the *Queen Mary 2* or one of the Carnival or Royal Caribbean shopping mall/disco/skating rink/food courts at sea; but it nevertheless is a significant vessel. Stood on end it would be equal to a fifty-story building. In the pool at the end of the fjord, though, it seemed almost like a toy; it was dwarfed by the craggy mountains, the huge glaciers, and the very high sky.

On the other side of the temporary bar were several areas marked off by low metal poles in the ground; a sign demanded no trespassing on this natural cultural monument. A bit farther, a rock bore a small plaque: "Whaling Station and Burial Ground 1612–1800. The whaling station was used by Dutch, English and Basque expeditions 1612–1650. British, Dutch and German whalers are buried here."

This was Gravneset, the Grave Point.

A Beach with a View

The beach was literally a dead end—a place where thousands of whales were butchered and processed in tryworks set up on the sand. And it also served as a graveyard for more than a hundred whalers who had made their way all the way up north from their homes in England, Germany, Holland, and the Basque region but succumbed to accidents and disease.

The British called the place Trinity Harbour; the first to arrive may have followed Hudson by just a few years. Trinity reached its peak around 1620 and was abandoned about three years later.

Very few of the sites have been fully explored. Scientists believe that the whalers were predisposed to scurvy; many came from the lower classes including northern England. Their diets at home had little in the way of fresh meat, fruit, and vegetables; the menu got worse at the isolated whaling stations. A modern examination of twelve corpses at Smeerenburg (Blubbertown), about fifteen miles farther north in Amsterdamøya, showed nine out of twelve bodies had signs of scurvy.

Smeerenburg was the Dutch whaling headquarters in the first half of the seventeenth century. There were at least eight stone and brick tryworks with copper boilers installed there for the processing of whale blubber, with a population of about 200 men working ashore.

Whaling began in earnest almost immediately after Hudson returned from his voyage in 1607, and continued through the end of the eighteenth century. Prices were high enough for whale oil and walrus tusks. The third product derived from the fishery was baleen, the comblike filters in the mouths of the baleen species of whale;

this material was used in the manufacture of such essentials as buggy whips, umbrella ribs, and corset stays.

At its peak, there were as many as 300 vessels in the waters around Svalbard, and the annual harvest ranged from about 750 to 1,250 whales. The Dutch had the largest fleet, but there were also British and German companies in the area. One species, the great bowhead whale, was completely killed off in the region.

The best of the early whalers were the Basques—seamen from the western end of the Pyrenees, along the coast of the Bay of Biscay, where Spain meets France. They had hunted whales for centuries in their home waters and as far away as Labrador in northern Canada.

Archaeologists have located at least fifty former whaling stations in Svalbard, with remnants ranging from foundations of houses and other buildings to blubber pots. Many of the sites are carpeted with bones from whales and walruses, and there are additional grave-yards for some of the whalers who did not return home.

Russian hunting and trapping settlements, established from about 1700 to 1850, harvested walrus tusks, oil and hide, polar bear and fox hide, and down.

As each whaling station, hunting area, or coal mine was abandoned, much of the equipment was left in place. The cost of disassembling and transporting items was usually more than its value.

Whaling companies established by Dutch and English interests squabbled in the waters in and around Svalbard, with minor fights also erupting among fleets from Norway, Denmark, France, Spain, and Germany. Many of the English ships were funded by the Muscovy Company—the same group that had financed Hudson's first two voyages in search of the Northeast Passage. This company based its claim on its deal with Ivan IV that gave it a monopoly on trade with the northern parts of Russia. (Svalbard was not Russia, but apparently it was close enough in the eyes of the Muscovy Company.)

In the 1620s, there were several seasons in which a British fleet—accompanied by naval vessels—would board and seize boats belonging to the Dutch and take the year's catch and equipment. In other years, Dutch boats would do the same to British whaling and freight vessels.

By the mid-seventeenth century, though, an agreement between the two whaling groups divided the hunting areas: the English worked south of Magdalenefjord and the Dutch to the north of that location. It was after that deal was reached that the Dutch built their celebrated whaling station of Smeerenburg.

On the beach at Magdalenefjord are the remains of four tryworks, held together by four-century-old "blubber cement": congealed whale oil, sand, and gravel. Behind the ovens, Graveneset has about 130 graves. The dead were buried as deep as the permafrost would allow. There once had been small crosses carved by knife with the name and hometown of the whalers; almost all the markers are gone, taken by nature or collectors.

The French woman Léonie Thévenot d'Aunet visited the area in 1838 onboard *La Recherche*. The vessel was engaged in yet another search for a Northeast Passage to Asia, this one sponsored by the Commission scientifique du Nord. A collection of her letters to her brother, published under the matter-of-fact title *Voyage of a Woman to Spitsbergen*, became a best seller in France and Europe. She was just nineteen at the time and was traveling with her fiancé, the painter François Biard.

D'Aunet described the graveyard as a somber place surrounded by the bones of whales and walrus, remnants of an extinct giant race. She found several of the graves pushed out of the ground, forced up by the permafrost below. Many were open and empty, ravaged by polar bears. She gathered up some of the loose human bones, placed them in an open coffin, and closed it.

She wrote of "coffins without memorial stone, without monument, without a wreath or a flower, without anyone to shed a tear or say a prayer, without a friend to mourn the departed and visit their barren, frozen resting places where the wild howls of polar bears and storms are all that break the eternal silence."

In 1845, the now-married Mme. Biard became one of Victor Hugo's numerous mistresses. She was eighteen years younger than the celebrated writer; he wrote a series of explicit poems about their liaison. In that year, the pair was found "in criminal conversation" and she was arrested and jailed. Hugo was freed; a few months before Louis-Philippe—the last king of France—had named him a "peer."

Hugo was said to have consoled himself about the arrest of his latest lover by beginning work on what would become one of his best-known books, *Les Miserables*.

Frisbee at the Top of the World: Magdalenefjord

Near the end of the day, most of the passengers returned on the tenders to the *Silver Cloud* for hors d'oeuvres, cocktails, team trivia, a golf putting competition, a predinner show, and a seven-course Italian dinner featuring gnocchetti alla Genovese (small potato gnocchi with pesto sauce) and pesce spada alla ligure (pan-fried swordfish with olives, tomatoes, and pine nuts).

We lingered as the northernmost bar was packed up and loaded on the tender and watched as the armed guards began to move in from their posts on the perimeter of the beach. I caught up with one of them, Audun Gjerland, who carried a radio, a modern hunting rifle, and a belt of three-inch-long 9.3mm bullets (fatter around than a .357 Magnum).

These are bullets intended to bring down big game; the threat at Magdalenefjord, of course, is *ursus maritimus*, the polar bear. The largest polar bear ever recorded weighed 2,209 pounds and was 12 feet long; a merely ordinary male bear is in the range of about 775 to 1,430 pounds and 8 to 10 feet long.

Gjerland was nearing the end of a forty-day assignment living in an orange tent surrounded by two circles of trip wire. An animal touching the outer ring would set off flares and small explosions; if the inner wire was tripped, an alarm would sound. That is, of course, if the intruder had not already been convinced to move elsewhere by one of Gjerland's three partners who took turn on sentry duty outside the tent all through the bright-as-day night.

The guards are employed by a private company that contracts with cruise ships, outfitters, and guides who bring innocent visitors to this extraordinary place in the Nordvest-spitsbergen Nasjonalpark. Their tent is pitched on the side of the hill near a small hut that belongs to the governor of Svalbard. He visits—by helicopter and with his own guards—from time to time.

When tourists are not in the area, the guards mostly share the beach with gulls; even here at the top of the world, seagulls have the same nickname they do on my beach in Massachusetts and most everywhere else. They call them *fliegen rotter* (flying rats).

Gjerland said his summer on the beach had been pretty uneventful; there were bears on the hills, but like the ones I would soon see on Mansel Island in Hudson Strait in the Canadian Arctic, they mostly sit around fat and lazy in August. In about three weeks, the area would see its first short dusk of the season, and by mid-November the bay would be in total darkness for three months. Neither he (nor I) would want to stand guard over Gravneset in winter, we agreed, when the bears are on the hunt for seals and most anything else.

Taking care not to disturb the dead, nor rile the living polar bears, my daughter and I spent our last moments in this extraordinary place seeking to set or at least tie a world record. We played Frisbee on the beach, at 79°57" North, 11°11" East. Then we covered our footsteps with sand and caught the last tender back to our floating five-star hotel.

CHAPTER 5

Longyearbyen: No-Man's-Land

Not to be unkind, for everyone I met there was gracious, welcoming, and alive, but Longyearbyen felt a bit like a scene from the *Night of the Living Dead*. There was a sense of making hay—or coal or tourist dollars—while the Sun was shining. And every conversation of any depth would sooner or later turn toward the subject of the impending night.

All around us were skeletons above ground. Great rusting towers, like the alien machines of *War of the Worlds*, marched across the landscape, up the valleys, and into town. Some still held aloft cables and barrel-sized buckets. Silent now, it didn't take much imagination to think of the clanking, squealing, and rumbling noise of the funiculars carrying their loads of coal from one of the mines to processing plants and the docks.

The last of the overhead conveyors ran until 1987, and it wasn't until a few years ago that local stores stopped insisting that visitors remove their shoes so that they would not track coal dust everywhere they went. It is still considered proper etiquette to have indoor and outdoor shoes when you arrive at a public building or someone's house.

Years before stylish women in Manhattan began commuting to work in Nikes with their Manolo Blahniks in a shoulder bag, everyone in Longyearbyen would leave their muddy and blackened boots in the entrance hall and change to slippers or fleece socks.

There are other skeletons above ground, too: whale and walrus bones scattered around like giant white tree limbs near the harbor. At Gravneset in Magdalenefjord and at the cemetery in Smeerenburg, human bones had been pushed up from the permafrost. At the small museum in Longyearbyen, which was housed in a former pig sty (with plans for removal to a more modern building soon), I came face to face with the intact skeleton of a long-dead miner.

Today's mostly young population of Longyearbyen could not support much of a graveyard. A few graves had been chiseled into the ground just above town at the base of the original coal mine; a few others had been mounted in above-ground crypts. But as a town official told me, you really aren't allowed to grow old or even very sick in Svalbard; the privileges of advanced medical care and a proper burial are reserved for the mainland of Norway or Russia or wherever your true tax base is.

And then there was the matter of the Midnight Sun, which made me feel like a semipermanent zombie. I am a morning person by nature, obnoxiously full of energy and creativity at the crack of dawn back in my own part of the world; as dusk and darkness arrive, I fade rapidly. I dread the prospect of a late dinner or a later show; I fear falling asleep in my soup or snoring through "Moonlight Sonata."

When I first began speaking with locals about life in a place with three months stuck at about 3:00 P.M. and three months frozen at 3:00 A.M., I assumed they would complain about the dark. That seemed like the natural response. Humans gravitate to the light like moths; we plan our summers around visits to the beach and go to sleep after the Sun goes down.

Instead, they told me that they enjoyed, or at least tolerated better the three months of sunless winter. They could always turn on a light to do their work or meet with friends; it was peaceful and tranquil, they said. And when the occasional beautiful day or night or whatever it was would arrive—especially when it coincided with a

A polar bear warning in Longyearbyen "applies for all of Svalbard."
Photo by the author

full moon—troops of them would head out into the country on their Skidoos or on cross-country skis with miner's lamps on their heads. Of course, they also would carry a rifle and flares out of respect for polar bears—it's the law.

An Institutionalized Rootlessness

Spitsbergen—the principal island of Svalbard—was already a no-man's-land when Willem Barents first visited in 1596 and Henry Hudson sailed there in 1607. There were no indigenous people; there may have been visits by Vikings and by nomadic tribes venturing (on purpose or by accident) 600 miles north from Tromsø on the mainland of Norway or 1,000 miles northeast from Iceland.

And even though it was formally claimed by England in 1614 and Denmark in 1615, it was still without formal ownership for almost

400 years more. Norway, the closest country to the archipelago, also threw in a claim, and later so did Russia and Germany.

Spitsbergen and the surrounding lesser islands including Bear Island and Jan Mayen became home to a series of transients: first came the whale and walrus hunters, then the coal miners, a short period of military presence, and now a mix of miners, tourist enterprises, and researchers.

The rootlessness of Svalbard continues. An agreement among European powers in 1872 declared the archipelago as *terra nullius*, which allowed any nation to claim land or resources. Finally, the Treaty of Paris in 1920, part of the cleaning up after World War I, gave sovereignty—but not complete ownership—to Norway.

The coal companies effectively owned and operated the economy through the 1980s, and it wasn't until about 1990 that the concept of promoting Spitsbergen as a tourist destination was accepted. Today, there's a small four-star hotel and a more modest guesthouse in town, and cruise ships make occasional visits.

In 2006, there were just five semipermanent settlements in the 24,300 square miles of the islands. Longyearbyen, the Norwegian administrative center, was home to about 1,700; Ny Ålesund, a former Norwegian mine now used as a research center, had about 40 residents; Svea or Sveagruva has about 200 miners; and Barentsburg, the Russian mining settlement, has about 900 residents who come and go from a base in the Ukraine. And for those who want to get away from the crowds, there is the Polish Polar Station at Polar Bear Bay in Hornsundfjord; about eight workers and occasional visitors occupy the site, which is run by the Polish Academy of Science.

Longyearbyen is ever-so-slightly warmer than the eastern and northern sides of the archipelago. About 60 percent of the land is covered with snow and ice year-round, and permafrost can go down 1,500 feet or more, with only the top six to ten feet thawing in the summer.

The average annual temperature for Longyearbyen is 28 degrees. In the coldest months of winter, the thermometer plunges to as low as -22 degrees Fahrenheit; the monthly average temperature in January is just 5 degrees. Add in regular gales, and the wind chill equivalent can feel as cold as 100 degrees below zero. (In balmy July, the monthly average is about 43 degrees.)

The Gulf Stream passes by to the west, melting and moving the sea ice and allowing ports and harbors including Longyearbyen, Ny Ålesund, and Magdalenefjord to be open to shipping for a few months each summer. The east side (facing the Taymyr Peninsula of Western Siberia 1,000 miles away or Novaya Zemlya 600 miles to the east southeast) usually remains locked in ice year round, although in recent years more and more of the coast is clear in August.

Sunny Days on the Cold Coast

The day I arrived in Longyearbyen, August 1—the middle of summer—was hardly a day to go to the beach, but the weather was comfortable and the Sun had six weeks or so until it would set. Why, then, was it apparent that half the town had gone on vacation to the mainland or elsewhere in Europe?

I met with Tove Eliassen, the manager of Svalbard Tourism, in her office in Longyearbyen; as I walked through the lobby, I was slightly behind schedule and I ignored the stacks of shoes stored in cubbyholes by the front door.

"We don't find the summer better," she said. "It is milder during the summer, but today is a foggy day, which is normal, and there is a lot of difference between an average temperature of six degrees Celsius [43 degrees Fahrenheit] here and an average of twenty degrees Celsius [68 degrees Fahrenheit] on the mainland. It's also a school holiday and because of industrial holidays things slow down in the mining production."

But there's an even more unusual reason about why residents go away in August and stick around home in the dead of winter.

"I don't think locals find the summers the most spectacular time of the year. That would be February and March. After four months of darkness, when the light comes back in March that is when we start living," she said. "And then you live like crazy until the end of May and then come the holidays."

The holidays: we're not talking about your basic American

worker's vacation schedule. In Norway, the government guarantees workers an annual four-week holiday with full pay. Even the manager of tourism was quick to admit that—for a local—spending four weeks of vacation in Longyearbyen would be a bit of a bore.

After four months of darkness, there is a bit of light in the sky for a few minutes beginning in mid-February, but because the town of Longyearbyen sits in the bowl of a valley, the big event comes on March 8 a bit after noon, give or take a day and a few minutes. That is *Soldagen* (Sun Day), the heart of a week-long Sun festival.

On that day, most of the town shuffles through the darkness to find the stairs of the old Skjæringa hospital; the building itself was torn down a number of years ago but the stairs were rebuilt to honor the tradition. When the first rays of the Sun strike the huddled moles on the steps, the place goes crazy. Adults celebrate as adults tend to do, the children dance in little Sun costumes, and then the Sun goes down until the next day.

When the Sun sets for the winter in late October, there's a dark season blues festival. The polar night, when the midday is just as dark as midnight, arrives in mid-November.

An Island of Transients

When I'm not out on the road following the wake of Henry Hudson or working on other books, I live on an American resort island with a wintertime population of about 9,500; by the time the wind stops blowing, the snow stops falling, and the fog lifts in May, we pretty well know each other. Not so in Longyearbyen, Eliassen told me.

"We don't really know each other because the annual turnover is so very high, something like twenty-eight percent," she said. "Within a four-year period, almost everyone has changed." Eliassen is one of the old-timers; she has been in Longyearbyen for eight years. She told me that she regularly reads notices in the local newspaper that say something like, "I want to thank all my friends for a wonderful couple of years, and I am now moving to the mainland," and then she realizes that she has never met the person who is making a formal adieu.

The principal industries of Longyearbyen include a small research institute and college, tourism and outfitting, and a few small mining operations. About 250 people work directly in the mines, and then there are jobs in transporting the coal and preparing it for use in the power plant or for shipment by sea to Norway or Russia.

A few days before my arrival, a small fire had broken out in one of the mines, and it appeared that the industry might have to shut down for a few months to deal with the fire and to pump water out of the shafts; as many as 600 people might be without work for a period of time. The wide and deep social safety net of Norway requires the mining companies—with assistance from taxpayers—to continue the wages of the workers.

The wording of the Treaty of Svalbard still leaves the citizens in a bit of a no-man's-land. The governor of Svalbard, the chief administrator of the archipelago, is appointed by Norway's Ministry of Justice for a limited term of office. And, like almost everyone else in Svalbard, he doesn't technically reside there. He is a transient from the mainland.

"Even though I live here," Eliassen said, "I am registered as living just outside of Oslo, which was my last address on the mainland. I have no connections there whatsoever, but my social security number is linked to that address.

"There really are no inhabitants here. You may be a resident, but you have to register in and you have to register out.

"It can be very frustrating for people living here. For example, I just had some news about my life insurance policy the other day and it was sent to the address in Oslo, the one that I don't live at anymore. Even though I've told them god knows how many times that this is where I have been living for the last eight years, they still send letters there. I have no relatives or friends living at that address, so mail kind of circles in the system or it is lost."

Eliassen said that it is only just recently that a small number of people have started building and owning their own houses, buying or leasing land from one of the coal companies. "The majority of people here are in rented apartments they obtain through their place of employment," she said. "If they are not working there anymore, they are out."

Headlamps and Moonshine

What kind of person chooses to come to live in a place with months of constant darkness, months of midnight Sun, and months of severe weather?

I asked Eliassen about studies in places where people are generally less adventurous and more desirous of comfort and conformity—the United States, let's say—where researchers are convinced there is a form of depression that is linked to the short and gray days of winter. They call it Seasonal Affective Disorder, which makes for the cute acronym of SAD. The experts blame it on a shift in our internal clocks, the circadian rhythm, caused by changes in the amount and quality of sunlight.

Not so in Svalbard, Eliassen told me. "They have done some research on that here because certain doctors and scientists are surprised that there is not a problem. There are fewer people here with depression than in Oslo, for example. It could be because it is totally dark and then totally light. You live by your watch. There is no gray weather, no twilight."

Actually, she said, it is the period of constant sunlight that can be more depressing than the darkness. The changeover from total darkness to total daylight seems to happen very quickly, and many people—herself included—find it hard to adjust their internal clocks to the light. When the Sun first comes above the horizon in mid-February until the first day of complete light in mid-April, daylight increases by forty minutes a day; sunrise comes twenty minutes earlier and sunset twenty minutes later. The process reverses every fall.

"When it changes, I have problems sleeping," Eliassen said. "I feel terribly tired with no energy. It really stresses me."

By the time I met Eliassen, I had been in the land of the Midnight Sun for about a week and I could understand the problem already. There were no external cues for my body clock other than the lavish changing menus for breakfast, lunch, and dinner aboard ship. After a long day of eating, drinking, stage shows, eating, and drinking again, it was very disconcerting to head for bed at 11:30 P.M. and find bright Sun peeking through the curtains. If we made the mistake of opening the curtains, it was like turning on the lights in the middle of a night's sleep: instant jitters.

"December and January are the darkest months," Eliassen told me, but her face brightened. "That is our lowest tourist season, but people—mostly Norwegians—do come to experience the darkness.

"A full moon in the dark day I wouldn't swap with anything. Give me Hawaii, give me whatever, I won't swap it.

"Normally, you get around with your headlamp when you are outside in the dark, and then suddenly you have got this day where you can actually see shadows of yourself on the snow because of the moonlight. It is fantastic."

Headlamps. In the land of the blind, the one-lamped man is king.

Graves and Gruves

All through the valley near Isfjord and elsewhere on the west coast of Spitsbergen are hulking wooden remnants of the great funicular system that once transported coal from the *gruves* (mines) to the town and the docks; steel buckets still dangle from some of the towers like a crude ski lift. The earliest date back to the 1920s, but most of the remnants were built after World War II.

The tramway system moved as many as 120 buckets (called *kibbs*) per hour, each carrying nearly a ton of coal, bridging gullies and streams and crossing roads. At Ny Ålesund, the flatter landscape permitted installation of a narrow-gauge steam railway in 1917. The toy-like locomotive still stands on a short stretch of track near the quay, rusted in place.

The overhead system has been replaced by trucks that rumble back and forth to the docks. There are hardly any people in Longyearbyen who have been there long enough to have seen the funiculars in action, but Eliassen recounted descriptions of a hellish scene: a constant clanking and banging as the cars moved from

Abandoned coal tramway in Longyearbyen.
Photo by the author

tower to tower and a mist of black coal dust in the air. Loads sometimes spilled from the kibbs or the buckets crashed into each other
at unloading stations right in the heart of the settlement of Longyearbyen.

"When I first arrived, you took your shoes off when you went to
the supermarket. Here in my office, we still have the sign out front
and most of us have really nice indoor shoes," she said, glancing at
my boots. "I should have told you about taking off your shoes when
we set up the appointment," she said. "Your shoes are not too dirty,
but ten years ago it would have been very bad."

The extreme isolation of island life plus the dark, cold winter
sounded to me like a perfect recipe for alcohol binges; I was not surprised to find in my research that in the coal mine company towns
of the 1920s there was a selective ban on alcohol. What does the all-
protective mother country do now to deal with this threat?

"Oh, we still have ration cards," Eliassen said; she pointed to her *alkoholkort* (alcohol card), which was pinned to the bulletin board at the back of her desk. Beer, wine, and hard liquor for drinking at home are sold only by ration card; area pubs and bars can sell by the drink but they are required to monitor the habits of their customers. And even tourists can only purchase a certain amount of alcohol, based on the length of time between their scheduled arrival and departure date.

"The miners used to be served water or cranberry juice at the canteen," Eliassen said. "Until quite recently, before we had bars and restaurants, the miners could buy beer at the community hall once or twice a week.

"The senior staff lived in better housing quarters. They had tablecloths and candlelight dinners and they had wine with their meals. The idea was that the senior staffers were educated people and they knew how to control their consumption."

The Long Arm of the Law

Shoeless, I entered the thoroughly modern office of Sigmund Engdahl, the administrative leader of the Community Council—roughly equivalent to the city manager for Longyearbyen. The council is in charge of Longyearbyen, including the settlement, the local mines, and the airport.

"Most of the people here see Spitsbergen as a temporary stay for one year, two years, or five years. But some also enjoy the place so much that they stay for thirty years," Engdahl told me.

"But you can't stay here if you are old, at least that's what the authorities say. If you need special care you do not have the possibility to get it here."

Norwegians are expected to return to the mainland and their permanent address to get care and assistance in their old age; foreigners are expected to go back to their native countries.

The Community Council is not allowed to levy any taxes; it owns the power station and the water supply and is able to charge for those services but not make a profit.

"Some things are more expensive here; a liter of milk costs seven kroner in Norway and twenty-two here [about $3.33 for a bit more than a quart], because all fresh food has to get here by plane. But there are no taxes on alcohol or on cigarettes. So some things that are highly taxed in Norway are cheap here."

Norway's social services come at a high price; on the mainland, most purchases are subject to a value-added tax (VAT) of about 20 percent. Residents of Svalbard, though, can apply for a rebate of VAT on purchases, just as if they were a foreigner visiting Norway. Engdahl is of the opinion that it evens out: the higher cost of items purchased in Longyearbyen is balanced by the lower cost of items purchased on the mainland or shipped from there. Like most of us—and that includes people like me who live in remote parts of the United States—the Internet has become the way to shop.

The Treaty of Svalbard

The primary reason why all Norwegians are equal but some are more equal than others is the status of the islands set by the Treaty of Svalbard. The international agreement was signed in 1920 at the peace conference in Paris, but not fully implemented until 1925. Among the nine original signers were Norway, Great Britain, the United States, Australia, Denmark, France, India, Netherlands, and Sweden. It is still open for newcomers; the Soviet Union signed in 1935; there are now about forty signatories.

In changing from a no-man's-land to something akin to an open territory, the treaty also required that the archipelago remain demilitarized. Drafted in the short period of forced goodwill that followed World War I and the establishment of the League of Nations, the treaty states: "Subject to the rights and duties resulting from the admission of Norway to the League of Nations, Norway undertakes not to create nor to allow the establishment of any naval base in the territories specified in Article 1 and not to construct any fortification in the said territories, which may never be used for warlike purposes."

Although the islands are considered part of the Kingdom of Norway, the treaty allows citizens of any country that is a signatory the right to come to work and stay and benefit from those elements of Norwegian social services that are extended to the islands. "We now have sixty or seventy people from Thailand working here," Engdahl said. "In Norway, that would be impossible because they could not get work visas."

In essence, Norway is permitted to set the rules for Svalbard but cannot discriminate in any way against foreign nationals. Norwegian companies must pay taxes to cover the cost of health insurance, but foreign companies have no such requirement and their workers do not have this automatic protection.

The general atmosphere of Spitsbergen also still owes much to the vestiges of a hundred years of near-dictatorial rule by the coal companies; they owned the land, they controlled the jobs, and when people were no longer on the payroll they were expected to move out of their company-owned apartment and leave the islands.

And then there is the Russian settlement of Barentsburg, near the entrance to the Isfjorden about twenty-five miles west of Longyearbyen; there are no roads that connect the two settlements. Barentsburg is still very much of a company town, like Longyearbyen was a few decades ago. It is also one of the most remote places in the world to have a Russian consulate. Many of the miners are from the Ukraine, and they shuttle back and forth.

"What are we going to do with the Russian settlement if we give the Norwegians the right to stay and get old up here?" Engdahl asked.

Technology Shrinks the Isolation

The paved airport runway at Longyearbyen was built in the 1970s. "Before that, you had to come up here in the autumn and there was no communication with the mainland before May or June because of the ice. So we were isolated more than six months of the year. Today, it is quite different because there is a plane almost every day, and in summer there are two planes every day."

Another way in which Longyearbyen has lost a great deal of its isolation is the arrival of high technology. Just past the airport is a farm of gigantic white mushroom caps, a ground station for downlinks from low-polar orbit satellites. Among the operators and owners of the domes are the National Aeronautics and Space Administration (NASA) and National Oceanic and Atmospheric Administration (NOAA) agencies, the Eumesat European consortium that operates low-altitude polar orbiting satellites, and the Norwegian Space Center.

One of my guides in Longyearbyen also gave me a wink-and-a-nudge, saying that the United States had some secret spy satellite receivers there as well. The presence of what's left of the Russian Northern Fleet in and around the port of Murmansk on the mainland and the nuclear test site of Novaya Zemlya might lend some credence to a Svalbardian Area 51 at Longyearbyen. I could get no closer than a distant chain-link fence with monitoring devices.

A low-polar orbit satellite has a number of advantages, starting with the fact that it is much closer to the earth. Typically, low-earth orbit satellites are somewhere between about 200 and 1,000 miles above the ground; to keep from being pulled to the earth by gravity, they must travel at a high rate of speed, about 17,000 miles per hour.

That means these satellites can make a complete orbit in as little as ninety minutes, completing as many as sixteen trips per day. It also means that military and civilian owners of this type of satellite need to launch a whole series of them, spread out over a range of longitudes, to cover the entire planet.

Polar orbit satellites are in constant movement northward and then southward, while the earth rotates west to east beneath them. Because of that pattern, it makes sense to install earth stations at very high latitudes because this allows more regular communication with them as they pass overhead the North and South Poles on every orbit.

This makes Svalbard a perfect place for observation stations because it reaches to about 80° North latitude; there is no equivalent permanent settlement that far south in Antarctica.

(By contrast, geostationary satellites sit at a fixed place in the sky but some 22,300 miles up, above the equator; at that distance, their orbits are synchronous with the earth. Put another way, their latitude remains at 0° while their longitude is constant at whatever location they are placed.)

A benefit of the satellite station at Longyearbyen was the installation in 2003 of a pair of 20 gigabit-per-second fiber-optic submarine cables from Spitsbergen 550 miles to mainland Norway. That is about as fast and wide a communications pipeline as any civilian can find anywhere, four or five times quicker than the speediest broadband link most of us are used to in our homes and offices.

The very expensive project included two cables, just in case one of them is somehow cut or damaged by a fishing boat or a natural event on the ocean floor. "When I came up here in 1998, we had only the two Norwegian television channels," Engdahl said. "When you spoke on the phone, it was over the satellite and it was very difficult . . . and you had to wait two or three seconds to get the response. Today, we have twenty-five or thirty television channels and this very high-speed Internet."

I borrowed his keyboard for a twenty-second excursion from Longyearbyen to Boston to check on the Red Sox score from the night before.

The Playboy Prince and His Great-Great-Grandfather's Footsteps

While I was in town, I checked out the Carlsberger, the bar of Cato Lorentsen, the pilot of the *Silver Cloud*. This is a serious drinking establishment in the heart of Longyearbyen, a small room decorated almost entirely by bottles of liquor that lined its walls.

I learned that Prince Albert of Monaco, still officially in mourning for his father, Prince Rainier III, had stopped by for a pint a month or so before, just weeks before his investiture as His Serene Highness in Monaco.

If you Google the words *Playboy Prince* and *Albert*, you'll find a few days' worth of reading that tell the story of the son of Rainier and the glamorous movie star Grace Kelly. In the middle of the year-long mourning period, headlines had erupted again to tell of the claim—acknowledged by Albert—of a former flight attendant that she and the prince had conceived a son. Alexandre, who was now two years old, may well have a claim on a piece of the prince's fortune of perhaps $2 billion, but probably not on the throne.

It turned out that Albert II—his driver's license might read Albert Polignac Grimaldi—had come to Longyearbyen as part of his effort to retrace the expeditions of his great-great-grandfather Albert I, who had organized and participated in four voyages to Svalbard at the end of the nineteenth century and early in the twentieth century. (The spectacular Magdalenefjord is officially in the Albert I land subdivision of Svalbard.)

His Serene Highness Prince Albert was making plans to travel by dog sled from the ice barrier off Svalbard to the North Pole, 100 years after his namesake made the same trip. Playboy image aside, Albert has shown a serious commitment to environmental issues in his tiny principality and has used his celebrity in some global efforts.

When I asked about other celebrities who had set foot in Spitsbergen recently, a local who appraised me as an American had a different name to offer: "You know that Hillary Clinton was here, don't you?" I didn't, but a bit of research turned up the fact that Senator Clinton, accompanied by her occasional gadfly supporter or opponent Senator John McCain, had made a two-day fact-finding trip to the archipelago in the summer of 2004 to learn about the Arctic's changing climate and be briefed on the Arctic Climate Impact Assessment prepared by an international consortium of scientists. A statement by the World Wildlife Fund said the "historic" visit of the two senators put the spotlight on global warming's "ground zero."

The Final Battle

Although Svalbard was officially a nonmilitarized zone under terms of the 1920 treaty, once World War II broke out, it became a focus of interest to both sides. The Allies were concerned that German forces would make use of the coal for their naval operations, and they also feared that weather stations on the islands could be used to give forecasts to army and air force operations in Europe.

That is, of course, exactly what happened. During the war, Svalbard became perhaps the most remote location for the projection of two of Germany's largest and most powerful naval ships, the military equivalent of using a sledgehammer to swat a mosquito.

Germany invaded Norway in April 1940; in response, plans were made in the summer of 1940 to land Canadian troops on Spitsbergen as an occupation force to deny the Germans use of the islands. But the short summer passed and no action was taken.

A year later, in August 1941, a new plan was put into action using British, Canadian, and free Norwegian troops. At first, the idea called for installation of a large number of troops, but after training in Scotland and some reconsideration of the isolation and other difficulties of life in Svalbard, the plan was scaled back.

Instead, a squadron of small destroyers, naval trawlers, a cruiser, and the converted ocean liner *Empress of Canada* headed from Scotland to the North. At 4:30 A.M. on August 25, troops landed at the outside of the Isfjord and secured the small Norwegian wireless station there; a few hours later, the larger ships arrived at the Russian settlement of Barentsburg. There was no opposition; the jetty was lined with unarmed civilians with their luggage. Hundreds of miners and family members were evacuated to the *Empress*.

The next step involved the demolition of mining equipment at Grumantby; in the process, a fire broke out that destroyed the entire town of wooden buildings. At Barentsburg, heavy equipment including a crane and tracks for the narrow-gauge railway were disabled. According to military reports, the Russians were quite willing to get off the island and go back home; apparently, the Norwegian miners and the remaining residents in Longyearbyen had expected troops to land and defend them.

Instead, the aerial funicular for transportation of coal and the power plant in Longyearbyen were disabled. And finally, hundreds of thousands of gallons of fuel and oil, as well as approximately half a million tons of coal were set ablaze.

During the entire ten-day operation, there was no sign of German opposition. The *Empress of Canada* returned to Glasgow on September 7, 1941.

Congratulating themselves on their success back home in Scotland, they had left no one behind to tell them that a grand invasion force of about ten German scientists and construction workers came back to Longyearbyen a month later; a few other weather stations were set up elsewhere in the islands.

But a year later, the Allies decided to reoccupy strategic positions in Svalbard and set up their own weather stations. What followed was a Marx(ist) Brothers tragic version of *Duck Soup*. Two small ships, the *Selis* (an old Norwegian seal catcher) and *Isbjorn* (a mini-icebreaker built in 1894), attempted to make their way into the ice in Barentsburg harbor in May 1942 with a force of about eighty-two men.

It was much too early in the season to ensure an easy entrance into Isfjord. Less than a mile from shore, both became stuck in the ice—they were literally sitting ducks.

German observers called in an air strike, and while some of the troops and sailors scrambled across the ice to safety, the *Isbjorn* was struck by two bombs and sank immediately, while *Selis* caught fire. Varying reports said somewhere between twelve and seventeen men died, and the survivors had to hide in some of the buildings at Barentsburg until they were rescued in July; several German air sorties attacked the settlement while they waited.

There were no further direct contacts between the scattered German and Allied observers for the remainder of the war.

The biggest military event in the history of Svalbard, though, came when the massive battleship *Tirpitz*—the sister ship to the famed *Bismarck*—sailed into Isfjord and shelled Longyearbyen in September 1943. Also participating was the *Scharnhorst*, which lobbed a shell at Mine 2, opened in 1922; the resulting fire continued to burn in isolated pockets until 1962.

Operation Cicilien turned out to be the final German naval bombardment of the war. The *Scharnhorst* was sunk in a naval engagement near Murmansk three months later. Members of the Norwegian resistance had made radio contact with British forces, reporting that the ship had left safe haven in a fjord and had gone out to sea; this was confirmed in Bletchley Park near London, where German radio transmissions were being read by mathematicians, who had cracked the Kriegsmarine's "Enigma" code. The 770-foot-long ship was attacked by ships and aircraft and sank on December 26, 1943, due south of Spitsbergen, about 115 miles off the northern end of the mainland of Norway, between Tromsø and Murmansk. Only 36 of the *Scharnhorst's* crew of 1,968 men survived.

Tirpitz was to survive almost another year. After several attempts at destroying it, including the use of midget submarines and an attack by aircraft from a carrier, the ship was finally sunk in a fjord on the mainland of Norway, at Håkøybotn, west of Tromsø on November 12, 1944. An estimated 1,000 German sailors were killed in the assault.

And then in a footnote to the War of Svalbard, and indeed to the entire World War II, the eleven lonely German troops and scientists at the weather station at Station Haudegen on Nordaustlandet (Northeast Land) became the last German combatants to surrender; they turned themselves in to the Norwegians in September 1945, nearly four months after the war ended.

Northeast Land is above the top and to the northeast of the main island of Spitsbergen, not far from where Henry Hudson ended his first voyage in pursuit of the Northeast Passage.

CHAPTER 6

The Vikings,
the Coal Company Town,
and Mary Baker Eddy

The Vikings and probably the Russians were there first; there is mention of the islands of Svalbard in ancient Icelandic texts from about the twelfth century. But it was the Dutch explorer Willem Barents who was given credit for "discovering" or at least rediscovering the islands in 1596 on the third of his voyages in search of the Northeast Passage.

On his first expedition, in 1594, he commanded two ships from Amsterdam that followed the coast of Norway and Russia, reaching as far as the west side of Novaya Zemlya; he was forced to turn back because of ice and weather conditions at the northern end of that island.

In 1595, he led a well-financed expedition of seven ships to the same area, this time trying to drop below Novaya Zemlya and pass between Vaygats Island and the coast of Russia, but once again he was blocked by ice.

On his final voyage in 1596, back down to just two ships, he passed by and made some crude charts of Bear Island and Spitsbergen. The two vessels separated to conduct independent expeditions and Barents continued on, retracing his first voyage up the west side of Novaya Zemlya. At the northern end of that island his ship became caught in the ice and the crew was forced to winter over there; they took apart some of the timbers and structure of their ship to build a cabin, where they huddled for the winter.

Barents and crew finally left Novaya Zemlya on June 13, 1597, in two open boats; the men were rescued by the second vessel in the expedition after they reached Samiland at the top of Scandinavia on the mainland. Barents, though, had died aboard his boat on June 20.

A great deal of the story and some charts was made known when the diary of Gerrit de Veer, the ship's carpenter, was published. In 1871, the cabin in which Barents and his crew spent the winter was found on Novaya Zemlya, with relics from the ship and the crew inside; the structure was moved to a museum in The Hague.

De Veer was also the first person to write about a particular form of polar mirage known as the Novaya Zemlya effect. This rarely seen atmospheric oddity, caused by the refraction of sunlight between differing temperature layers, makes it appear that the Sun is rising even when it is still as much as 5 degrees below the horizon in the polar winter. In certain weather conditions, the Sun appears to be a flat line, a square, or a distorted hourglass shape.

Black Coal in a White Landscape

Many of the tourists who come all the way to Svalbard expect a pristine polar environment—snow-capped mountains, blue glaciers, and unspoiled valleys of wildflowers. Most are probably surprised to find that they have landed in the middle of a coal mining town littered with abandoned equipment and wooden and iron industrial tramways. In other parts of the archipelago are the remnants of another once-great industry: the huts and tryworks of the whale hunters.

After Henry Hudson's visit, the whale and walrus harvest became a major industry. Whalers and sealers found readily available coal on the mountainsides, which they used to fire their blubber pots and eventually to refuel early steamships that came to Spitsbergen. And it was coal that brought the first semipermanent residents to the archipelago at the end of the nineteenth and the beginning of the twentieth centuries. Without the whales or the coal, Svalbard might well be an uninhabited, inhospitable dot in the sea, much as it was when Hudson and the *Hopewell* became stuck in the summer ice.

Another reason why Svalbard holds—tenuously—to a population is that it was a minor chess piece in World War II and the cold war that followed. I've already mentioned how British and Allied forces wanted to block the German military from using outposts for weather forecasting. After the war, the existence of a Soviet-run coal mine at Barentsburg helped convince the Norwegians to keep Longyearbyen alive.

It was a way for the Norwegians (and by proxy, the Americans and their friends) to keep an eye on Soviet activities in the area. It is fair to speculate that the passage of ships and submarines in the Soviet Union's Northern Fleet and its nuclear testing activities on Novaya Zemlya were monitored from the area.

When the BBC reporter Alex Kirby visited Barentsburg in 2000, he concluded that while both sides in the cold war went through a pretense of mining, the primary reason the Russians and the Norwegians stayed in Svalbard was so that they could keep an eye on each other.

He reported that when he asked one Norwegian why anyone would want to stay there, he was told, "Well, if we left, the Russians would simply take over, or the French, or even you."

Mary Baker Eddy and the Great Norwegian Coal Company

Although Spitsbergen is not on most lists of places to see before you die, I was not the first person to visit Spitsbergen by luxury cruise ship.

For most of the twentieth century, only a small number of tourists made their way to Longyearbyen; this was the sort of place that made its way into the pages of *National Geographic*. Today, though, a double handful of ships sail in the waters around Svalbard each summer, mostly on world cruises or adventure tours of Scandinavia.

But more than a century ago there was another boom in construction of passenger liners (for transport) and cruise ships (for tourism). In the summer of 1901, the *Kaiserin Auguste Viktoria,* one of the most deluxe cruise ships of its time—it included a Ritz-Carlton Restaurant onboard—visited the fjords of Spitsbergen. Among the guests were John Munro Longyear and his wife, Mary Beecher Longyear.

Longyear, born in Lansing, Michigan, in 1850, had worked his way into becoming one of the wealthiest men in the United States. His father had been a Republican congressman from Michigan during the Civil War and was later a federal judge.

He obtained a job surveying state lands in the Upper Peninsula in 1873, and after the Panic of 1873—a serious economic depression that brought down 89 of the country's 364 railroads and thousands of other companies that had boomed on speculation after the Civil War—he used the information he had gained to make investments in large tracts of land in Michigan. The family biography, and many other histories of the area that must have been based on it, say that in 1873 he was too poor to buy a new pair of boots, but he still managed to buy up every interesting piece of land he could. He was said to have a "nose" for minerals.

He married Mary Beecher in 1879, and as the country came out of the depression, he began to cash in. The land he controlled was rich in iron ore and other minerals, and came to include the Menominee and Mesabi iron ranges. Like many modern fortunes, Longyear's was mostly built with the exchange of paper and information. He owned the land but kept away from risk by leasing mining and exploration rights to other companies. He collected royalties on projects that used other people's money.

About the same time, Longyear explored the vast timberland holdings of the Pillsbury (as in flour) family in the Mesabi Iron Range of Minnesota near Nashwauk. The deal with the Pillsburys gave Longyear and his partner 50 percent of the mineral rights for anything they found on the land, and this paid out a huge amount of dough.

Nashwauk is just west of Hibbing, Minnesota, which has two distinctions: home of the world's largest open-pit mine and the birthplace of Robert Zimmerman, best known under his assumed name of Bob Dylan.

Longyear parlayed his investments into becoming a bank director and logging and lumber baron, and in 1890 he was elected to a term as the mayor of Marquette. One estimate of Longyear's wealth was $15 million, and he used some of that to build a sixty-five-room stone home on Lake Superior. The mansion, with landscaping by Frederick Law Olmsted, was completed in 1892.

But in 1900, Howard, their eighteen-year-old son drowned in the lake and Mary Longyear did not want to live in a home that looked out at the place where one of her children had died. In 1901, John and Mary Longyear traveled to Europe and took the cruise that explored the fjords of Spitsbergen.

While the other passengers were playing shuffleboard or drinking hot toddies, Longyear was considering the fact that his nose told him there seemed to be abundant coal in Spitsbergen.

When the Longyears returned to the United States in 1902, they decided to move their huge mansion away from the shores of Lake Superior. It was taken apart, stone by stone, and loaded—according to a *Ripley's Believe It or Not* cartoon of the day—on 172 box cars and flat cars and transported to Brookline, Massachusetts, where it was reassembled. While they were at it, twenty more rooms were added.

Mary Longyear had become a friend and follower of Mary Baker Eddy, one of the founders of the Christian Science religion, headquartered in Boston. She devoted much of her remaining life, and much of Longyear's fortune, to the church.

With his wife and home safely relocated to Massachusetts, Longyear made another visit to Spitsbergen. This time he came as a buyer; together with a financial partner, Frederick Ayer of Boston, in 1905 he bought up Norwegian land claims and established the Arctic Coal Company on the south side of Adventfjord.

The first, small-scale, commercial mining had been begun by a Norwegian on the north shore of Isfjorden in 1899; before then, workers had just picked at any coal visible on the surface.

The Arctic Coal Company was an audacious idea: extracting coal in one of the most remote places on Earth, in extreme cold weather and near-total darkness for months at a time, in a port that is only free of ice for a few months of the year. Nevertheless, Longyear again prospered from his nose for minerals and money.

The first three shiploads of coal reached mainland Norway in the summer of 1907. The town that grew up around the mine was modestly named Longyearbyen, meaning Longyear City.

On January 3, 1920—during the dark season—a coal dust explosion in Mine 1 killed twenty-six people; that mine was abandoned, although the wooden roof at its entrance still stands above the town. Four of the dead were buried at the cemetery in the valley; nearby are several of the victims of the 1918 Spanish Flu, which reached all the way to Longyearbyen.

Existing in no-man's-land, the American-owned mine was technically outside the jurisdiction of any nation. A British competitor proved unable to sustain its operations. But a Russian operation established in 1912 at Grumant was more successful, despite Longyear's objections.

In 1916, he sold his interest to a syndicate of Norwegian banks, industrial companies, ship owners, and a few insider politicians, including the prime minister of Norway. The new company was called Store Norske Spitsbergen Kulkompani (Great Norwegian Coal Company).

Longyear died in Massachusetts in 1922; his wife died in 1931. She bequeathed the mansion to the Christian Science Church for use as a museum and foundation offices; it continued in that function until 1998, when the church sold it off to become the centerpiece of a luxury condominium project. The Longyear Museum, devoted to Eddy and the church, is now in another leafy Boston suburb, Chestnut Hill.

The Company Island

Longyearbyen's coal mines went well beyond the concept of a company town; it was more of a company nation. Store Norske had near-complete control over the operation of the mines and the regulation of the miners. Its powers began with the fact that the company owned nearly all the land and had all the jobs. The syndicate even went so far as to issue its own money; from 1916 until 1979, workers were paid in Spitsbergen cash, which was readily accepted at Spitsbergen stores (owned by the syndicate) but not so easily used anywhere else.

The only regular way in and out was by boat; freighters and passenger ships were able to visit Longyearbyen and the western side of Svalbard from May to October of each year. Store Norske owned and operated its own fleet of boats until 1928.

If the ports were iced over, the ships would set anchor at the edge of the ice and passengers would walk in to shore and freight would be brought in by sled. During the cold and dark months of the remainder of each year, the community was completely cut off from the outside world.

The company ruled its workers and the local economy with a stern hand. There were numerous labor disputes over wages and living conditions, including a near-war in 1917. That summer the Norwegian government sent a naval force to Longyearbyen to break a strike; according to accounts of the time, the navy split the village in two with workers segregated to the south and management and their families to the north. The strikers were removed from Spitsbergen and new workers, who were affiliated with a new union, were brought in to replace them.

Conditions were quite rough, with ordinary workers housed six to eight in a room. Steam baths, for occasional use only, were added in 1920. And there were no women on the miners' side of the community; the few women in Longyearbyen were among the families of the managers.

In 1929, the worker's union successfully lobbied for the hiring of women for housekeeping and cooking jobs. According to the company's official history, "These women had a stabilizing effect on local society. Cohabitation was quietly accepted."

Each fall, before the scheduled departure of the last boat back to the mainland for the season, all the women workers were tested. "Pregnant women were dismissed or given an abortion," according to the records.

At the Paris peace conference that cleaned up some of the issues in the aftermath of World War I, the Norwegian government pushed for sovereignty over Svalbard; four of the seven members of the government committee that prepared for the conference were connected to Store Norske, and the private draft the group prepared formed the basis of the official Norwegian proposal to the international community.

It wasn't until the 1960s that the company began to allow, if not encourage, workers to bring their families to Spitsbergen. Roads were built that allowed workers to live away from the mines themselves, and the company constructed barrackslike apartment complexes in the valley; rent for the homes was part of the wage agreement. It was 1997 before Store Norske separated out the rental of apartments or homes from employment at the mine and spun off its travel agency, lodging, and dining hall operations.

Today, Store Norske is still the big dog in town, although the district governor of Svalbard oversees municipal functions. The company owns 775 square miles of land in Svalbard at six main locations. (Manhattan in New York is about 33 square miles; the entire state of Rhode Island is about 1,233 square miles.)

The Russian mining operations, established in pre-Bolshevik times, became more extensive in the 1930s and 1940s under the Soviet Union. The largest mine was at Barentsburg, with another at very remote Pyramiden and the original mine at Grumant.

At its peak, Pyramiden had about 1,000 inhabitants and Soviet propaganda made it seem like a worker's paradise with the most northerly indoor swimming pool in the world (and the most northerly bust of Vladimir Lenin). Today, after the collapse of the Soviet Union, there are only a few dozen workers remaining, mostly engaged in salvaging equipment for use at Barentsburg.

In the summer of 1996, a Russian airliner crashed into Mount Opera near Longyearbyen; the Vnokovo Airlines Tu-154 was carrying 143 people, mostly Russian and Ukrainian miners and their families from Moscow, and was due to land on the island and pick up a load of workers heading off for a break. A year later, a fire at Barentsburg killed twenty-three miners.

In half a century of mining at the Norwegian outpost at Ny Ålesund, at least eighty miners died in gas explosions and other accidents; the mine was closed in 1963 after an explosion killed twenty-one miners. The remaining structures are used for a Norwegian scientific research station.

And just a month before my visit, one miner died and ten others were hospitalized after a drill broke through into an old section of the remote Svea mine filled with methane gas.

Dozens of coal mines have been started and abandoned on Spitsbergen over the years. Just two are now actively worked: the Russian mine at Barentsburg and a Norwegian operation at Gruve 7 just outside of Longyearbyen. Between the two of them, the mines extract about 600,000 tons of coal per year, twice the output of mines on the mainland of Norway.

Some of the coal is used right in Longyearbyen to fire the electric plant just outside town; the same plant also produces steam that is piped above ground to heat homes, businesses, and offices in the valley. The remainder is shipped to European markets for energy production and other uses.

The coal seam in the Longyear Valley sits within a mountain, "layered like the filling of a layer cake," according to Store Norske; it varies between about one and two yards thick. More recent mining at the Svea seam south of Longyearbyen is within a deposit as much as five yards thick.

The narrow seams were originally worked by hand. Now, most of this work is done by specialized mechanized diggers including a monsterlike device called a continuous miner that bites into a stope of coal with a rotating wheel of teeth that feeds back into a conveyor belt.

Coal kibbs climb a hillside in Longyearbyen.
Photo by the author

Hang a Left at the Needle

With only the crudest of instruments, early explorers like Hudson had to rely on the rough charts drawn by those who went before them, including Barents. When the weather cooperated, Hudson or one of his mates could take a reading of the height of the Sun and its relation to known stars and estimate their latitude; the best means they had to determine longitude was to look for landmarks on the shore or for distinctive features of islands.

(Think of the great waves of emigrants who crossed the U.S. southwestern desert, scanning the horizon for Ship Rock in what is today New Mexico. In that case, they were on sand looking for a rock that looked vaguely like a ship; in Hudson's case, they were on a ship looking for a rock, but you get the idea.)

In the Far North, one of the best known was Bear Island (Bjørnoya) due south of Svalbard at 74°45' North, 19° East, about halfway between the archipelago and the mainland of Norway, and

A landmark in the Barents Sea: Bear Island.
Photo by the author

specifically its southern end: the home of the singular hill that was called Mount Misery (Miseryfjellet) and the even-more unusual 260-foot-tall needle in the sea called Sylen, Norwegian for awl.

When the island was found by Barents in 1596, he named it Bear Island, a good name for a place that then—and now—is home to many more polar bears than humans. In 1603, the explorer Stephen Bennet also saw the island and thought he was entitled to give it a name; he called it Cherie's Island after Sir Francis Cherie, one of his financiers at the Muscovy Company.

From John Playse's journal of Hudson's first voyage:

July 31, 1607. This night we had a hard gale of wind from the southeast by east. The next morning at four o'clock we were opposite Cherie's Island, to windward of us by 15 miles. Knowing we were near, we kept a careful lookout for it, and the weather being clear, we saw it; a very ragged land on the water side, rising like haystacks.

101

The pounding of the surf and the grinding of ice have carved the island in fantastic shapes at one end, and near flat at the other. The 68-square-mile island is about 12 miles long, and is dotted with some 700 lakes. Mount Misery has three summits of about 1,600 feet in height.

Coal was first found in 1609; and the island was visited from time to time by Norwegian and Russian whaling and hunting expeditions, but the first permanent settlers—coal miners—arrived about 1916.

Bear Island was annexed by Norway in 1915, and three years later 1918 a weather station was established. With the exception of several years during World War II, there have been a few lonely souls stationed on Bear Island ever since to fly the flag and provide scientific information. In 2005, the observation post had nine inhabitants; five scientists, a cook, and three technicians.

The rough island has no natural harbor; supply ships arrive in June and again in September, and freight is brought ashore in small boats. The island also serves as an emergency landing and refueling station for helicopters going to and from Svalbard or performing rescue operations in the Arctic Sea.

There is very little to protect the station from the severe weather, and the island's namesake bears are said to be regular visitors during the dark winter; the other permanent residents are arctic fox. The bird cliffs at the south end of the island are considered mustsees for serious twitchers; the cliffs are noted as the home of huge colonies of Brünnich's guillemots.

We sailed out of Longyearbyen in the early evening under a cloudy but still bright sky. The next afternoon I sat on the verandah of my suite on the *Silver Cloud* reading some of the research material I had picked up in Spitsbergen. The choppy sea had been empty all day, but suddenly a few curious gulls squawked noisily along the port side of the ship and I looked up.

There, coming into view, was an unmistakable signpost in the sea: a long mountainous table of an island punctuated by a remarkable sharp spike at one end. I knew immediately what it was from the descriptions in the journals of expeditions of Barents, Bennet, and Hudson: we were passing Bear Island.

Generations of sailors knew the signpost that could have been erected here. North leads to Svalbard and the North Pole. South will bring you to Trømso and the top end of Norway. Due east will bring you to the middle of Novaya Zemlya. And a westward course leads to Greenland.

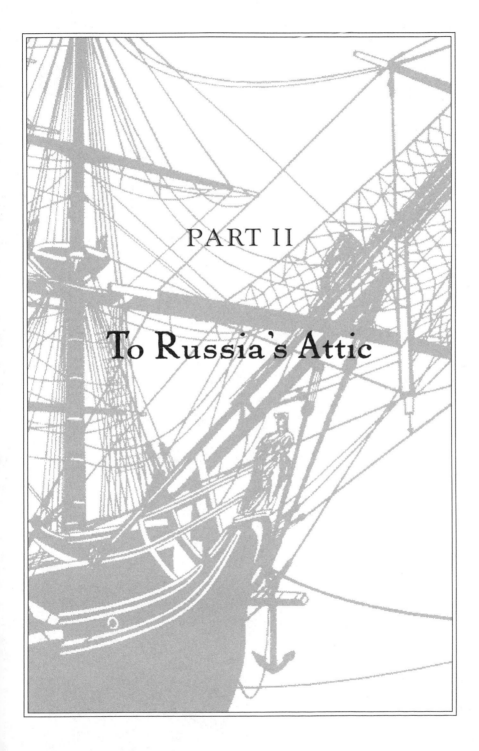

PART II

To Russia's Attic

CHAPTER 7

Voyage Two: Unicorns, Mermaids, and Unrest

A SECOND VOYAGE OR EMPLOYMENT
OF MASTER HENRY HUDSON
FOR FINDING A PASSAGE TO THE EAST INDIES
BY THE NORTHEAST:
WRITTEN BY HIMSELF

Their names employed in this action as follows: *Henry Hudson*, the master and pilot; *Robert Juet*, the master his mate; *Ludlowe Arnall; John Cooke*, boatswain; *Philip Stacie*, carpenter; *John Barns; John Braunch*, cook; *John Adrey, James Skrutton, Michael Feirce, Thomas Hilles, Richard Tomson, Robert Raynar, John Hudson*, and *Humfrey Gilby.**

In 1608, Henry Hudson was given a second chance by the Muscovy Company, with the same basic instructions: find the Northeast Passage to China. This time the plan called not for a trip across the North Pole, but instead a course along the coast of Norway to the remote Russian region of Novaya Zemlya and beyond.

Nova Zembla, as the Dutch and British styled it, or Novaya Zemlya as its Russian proprietors prefer, is another "new land." It is,

---

* Book three of *Purchas His Pilgrimes* (London, 1625), by Samuel Purchas.

NASA image of Novaya Zemlya in winter,
solidly frozen in to the east and barely
approachable from the west.
*Jacques Descloitres, MODIS Rapid Response Team,
NASA/GSFC.*

of course, anything but new. The hilly land is a continuation of the Ural Mountains on the mainland, which are among the planet's oldest peaks. The Urals mark the unofficial border between Europe and Asia at the western edge of Siberia.

The 600-mile-long crescent-shaped Novaya Zemlya extends north and northeast from the mainland, dividing the Barents Sea from the Kara Sea. The two pieces of land, either together or separately, are among the largest islands in the world.

Novaya Zemlya actually consists of two major islands—Severny (Northern) and Yuzhny (Southern)—separated roughly in the mid-section by the narrow Matochkin Strait that runs from the tiny settlement of Lagernyy on the Barents Sea east to the relatively larger

Matochkin Shar on the Kara Sea. The northern island has many glaciers, whereas the southern is mostly tundra. There are also a number of other minor islands in the archipelago. The thirty-mile gap between the bottom of the main southern island and Vaygach Island is officially the Kara Strait and unofficially on some maps, the Northeast Passage.

The explorer Willem Barents mapped the west coast of the main islands in 1596 and rounded the northern tip to winter on the east coast. The Muscovy Company used Barents's incomplete chart in planning Hudson's voyage.

Matochkin Strait is exactly the sort of passage that Hudson and other explorers of the time were constantly looking for: a passageway through a continent or island. Hudson's rough charts reported that earlier explorers had found strong currents from a waterway midway through the island.

Back to the *Hopewell*

Once again, Hudson was given the *Hopewell.* When he set sail in 1608, he had only three returnees from his first voyage on the *Hopewell*: John Cooke, his boatswain; James Skrutton; and his son John. Hudson's new mate was Robert Juet, an old salt—age about fifty—and according to a letter Hudson wrote to the geographer Richard Hakluyt, a man "filled with mean tempers."

Hudson's view of Juet was to prove of significant portent for this and the last two voyages he made; by most evidence, Juet was a near-constant instigator or participant in unrest and eventually an encouragement to mutiny. According to one account, which may have been based on unpublished or lost fragments of Hudson's private notes or an interview the captain gave to Hakluyt, Juet was locked away in his tiny private quarters with some friends when an Anglican priest came onboard near London to bless the ship and its crew. The captain and his mate were at odds before the *Hopewell* had even set sail.

Juet, along with Hudson, was one of the few men aboard who could read and write, and Samuel Purchas apparently had a copy of a separate journal he kept on the 1608 voyage but did not publish it; if there was such a private accounting, it has been lost.

An Unpleasurable Cruise to Novaya Zemlya

The *Hopewell* set out at the end of April. Hudson himself was keeping the journal, and his entries were spare for the first month, although he reported it to be "searching cold" and that the crew was ill. Conditions got worse once the ship neared the top of Norway; if there had been any hope of finding an Arctic summer, it seemed to end in June, when the ship sailed into ice.

> *April 22, 1608.* We set sail at St. Katherines, and fell down to Blackewall.
>
> *May 25, 1608.* All this day was clear weather and searching cold. . . . Then my carpenter was taken sick . . . and three or four more of our company were inclining to sickness, I suppose due to the cold.

The *Hopewell* had passed the Lofoten Islands off the coast of Norway the day before. Over the following week, the ship sailed into snow and gales. On June 3, Hudson sighted North Cape, the northernmost point of Norway. The carpenter recovered from his illness but next the cook and another member of the crew took sick.

> *June 9, 1608.* In latitude 75°29' we entered into ice, being the first we saw in this voyage; our hope was to go through it. We held our course between northeast and east northeast . . . until four in the afternoon at which time we were so far in and the ice so thick and firm ahead . . . that we had endangered us. We returned the way we had entered, with a few rubs of our ship against the ice.

For the next week, the *Hopewell* fought to make progress in the Barents Sea against unfavorable winds, fog, ice in the water, and frozen shrouds on the mast. On June 15, in the Bering Sea off the top of Norway somewhere between Murmansk and Novaya Zemlya, the monotony was broken.

According to Hudson's matter-of-fact report, several members of the crew spotted a mermaid who swam alongside the ship and "looked earnestly" at them.

June 15, 1608. Latitude at noon is 75°07'.

This morning, one of our company looking overboard saw a mermaid, and calling up some of the company to see her. One more came up, and by that time she was come close to the ship's side, looking earnestly on the men. A little after, a sea came and overturned her. From the navel upward, her back and breasts were like a woman's (as they say that saw her), her body as big as one of us, her skin very white, and long hair hanging down behind, of color black. In her going down they saw her tail, which was like the tail of a porpoise, and speckled like a mackerel. Their names that saw her were Thomas Hiles and Robert Rayner.

Sailors have spotted mermaids for thousands of years, often after they have been away from female companionship for a long, long time. In warmer waters, the creature has sometimes been identified as the extremely uninviting manatee or the dugong; both are members of the *sirenia* family, which derives its name from the legend of the sirens of the sea blamed for luring ships into harm's way. In the Arctic, the men may have been looking at a comely seal.

In the 1984 film *Splash*, Daryl Hannah played a much more attractive mermaid; in the story, she emerges from the water—the Hudson River—to assume temporary human form.

Hudson had three possible courses once he reached Novaya Zemlya. One was to hook around the northern end of the island, another was to find a passage through the strait that was reported to divide the large island, and a third was to drop down to the southern end and pass between Novaya Zemlya and the mainland.

In any case, the plan then called for a continuation along the coast of Siberia all the way east to the Bering Strait that does indeed lead from the Chuckchi Sea between Russia and Alaska and into the Pacific Ocean.

One of the underlying theories for this expedition was a belief

that beyond the River Ob in western Siberia was warm water, an unsubstantiated rumor in a territory that was barely known to the outside world.

Other "evidence" that this was the passage to Asia was a report
that a six-foot-long tusk found on Vaygach Island at the southern tip
of Novaya Zemlya was from a unicorn. According to conventional
wisdom, these creatures were well known to exist in the Orient.

The tusk was almost certainly from a narwhal, an Arctic marine
mammal that grows to about twenty feet in length; the males have
a twisted ivory tusk. The unicorn theory pops up in various books
of theories and justifications including *A Discourse Written by Sir
Humphrey Gilbert, Knight to Prove a Passage by the North-West to
Cathay and the East Indies,* which were collected by Hakluyt.

June 20, 1608. Fair, warm weather. . . . Here, we heard bears roar on
the ice, and we saw upon the ice and near unto it an incredible number of seals.

June 23, 1608. In the morning, thick fog, the wind at north northwest. From midnight until four o'clock this morning, we sailed northeast five leagues [seventeen miles], and then we were among the ice.

Eight o'clock . . . it cleared up, and we had ice ahead of us. . . . Our
shrouds were frozen. . . . This afternoon we had some snow.

We saw the sun at the lowest, north northeast, his height 7°15'.
[Our latitude was] 74°18'.

Far offshore of Novaya Zemlya and only about halfway up its
length, Hudson abandoned his attempt to reach the northern tip of
the archipelago. He began to steer south in hopes of finding a passage through the Kara Strait between the southern end of the south
island and Vaygach Island, just off the coast of Siberia.

June 25, 1608. We had little wind till noon . . . err it began to fall. We
were in the latitude of 72°52' and had ice on our larboard, and our
hope of passage was gone this way by means . . . of the abundance
of ice.

June 26, 1608. We had sight of Nova Zembla four or five leagues [fourteen to seventeen miles] from us, and the place called by the Hollanders, Swart Cliffe, bearing off southeast.

June 27, 1608. We being two miles from the shore, I sent my mate Robert Juet and John Cooke my boatswain on shore, with four others, to see what the land would yield that might be profitable and to fill two or three casks with water. They found and brought aboard some whales' fins, two deer's horns, and the dung of deer and they told me they saw grass on the shore of the last year, and young grass come up amongst it.

It was very hot on the shore, and the snow melted apace, they saw the footings of many great bears, of deer, and foxes. We saw two or three companies of morses near us swimming.

There was a cross standing on the shore, much driftwood, and signs of fires that had been made there.

June 28, 1608. At four o'clock in the morning our boat came aboard, and brought two dozen of fowle, and some eggs, whereof a few were good, and a whale's fin. And we all saw the sea full of morses, yet no signs of their being on shore. And in this calm, from eight o'clock last evening till four this morning we were drawn back to the northward, as far as we were the last evening . . . by a stream or tide.

The footings reported by Hudson are the prints of large animals. In the sea, the men saw morses: walruses.

The ship was caught in a northward current and slack wind. Rather than risk the chances of losing an anchor or its cable—a serious threat to the continuation of the voyage—they decided to tow the *Hopewell* with its small rowboat. It had to be hard labor, but Hudson found it an "encouragement to my company."

June 29, 1608. We had many morses in the sea near us, and desiring to find where they came on shore, we put to with sail and oars, towing in our boat and rowing in our bark to get about a point of land from whence the land did fall more easterly, and the morses did go that way.

At two o'clock this afternoon we came to anchor in the mouth of a river where lyeth an island in the mouth . . . There drove much ice out of it with a stream that set out of the river or sound, and there were many morses sleeping on the ice.

June 30, 1608. At the island where we were rode lyeth a little rock whereon were forty or fifty morses lying asleep. I sent my company ashore to them, leaving none aboard but my boy. . . . By means of their nearness to the water they all got away save one which they killed, and they brought his head aboard.

July 1, 1608. This morning I sent my mate Everet and four of our company to row about the bay to see what rivers were in the same and to find where the morses did come on land, and to see a sound or great river in the bottom of the bay which did always send out a great stream to the northwards against the tide that came from thence.

I found the same in coming in from the North to this place. [Because] of the great plenty of ice, the hope of passage between Newland and Nova Zembla was taken away.

My purpose was by the Vaygats to pass by the mouth of the River Ob, and to double that way the North Cape of Tartaria, or to give reason wherefore it will not be.

The Cape of Tartaria is at the top of the Taymyr Peninsula in central Siberia. It is separated from the south island of Novaya Zemlya by a passage that leads from the Kara Sea to the Laptev Sea—this is the body of water marked as the Northeast Passage on some modern maps.

With no particular evidence or experience to prove his theory, Hudson was expecting that he would find the passage there free of ice and be able to continue on to the Strait of Anian (the Bering Strait).

At about the same time, the English explorer John Smith was establishing and consolidating the settlement at Jamestown in Virginia on behalf of the Virginia Company. Hudson and Smith were aware of each other's efforts, exchanging letters and also consulting with Hakluyt.

In a journal published in 1612, Smith described some of the wildlife he ran into in Virginia. "Their bears are very little in comparison of those of Muscovia and Tartaria," he wrote.

Looking for Anything of Value

The voyage was not going well, but Hudson once again tried to find a silver lining in the dark cloud that enveloped the expedition. He hopes that "by the plenty of morses we saw here to defray the charge of our voyage."

And he suggests that the sound where the *Hopewell* is currently anchored, with its swift stream that keeps it clear of ice, might one day prove to be a through passage to the east of Novaya Zemlya, superior to the plans to go down under to Vaygach. From this we can assume he had entered a short distance into Matochkin Strait from the Barents Sea.

> July 2, 1608. At six o'clock this morning came much ice from south-ward driving upon us, very fearful to look on. But by the mercy of God and His mighty help, we being moored with two anchors ahead with veering [letting] out of one cable and heaving home the other, and sending off with beams and spars, [we] escaped the danger.

After fending off the ice with every tool at their command—anchors and lines, beams and spars, luck and grace—on the next day the *Hopewell* weighed anchor and set sail to run into the river or sound.

Hudson may have traveled as much as twenty-one miles into the strait, about a third of its length. We now know that the sixty-mile-long strait between the Northern and Southern islands of Novaya Zemlya is frozen over for most of the year and less than a third-of-a-mile wide and shallow at its midpoint.

> *July 4, 1608.* We weighed and set sail . . . and passed over a reef. Then we saw that the sound was full [of ice]. . . . A very large river from the north-eastward free of ice and a strong stream coming out of it. . . . We all conceived hope of this northerly river or sound. . . . [T]hen the wind veered more northerly and the stream came down so strong that we could do no good on it. We came to anchor and went to supper, and then presently I sent my Mate Juet, with five more of our company in our boat with sail and oars to get up the river. Be-

ing provided with victual and weapons for defense, willing them to
sound as they went. And if it did continue still deep, to go until it did
trend to the eastward or to the southwards and we rode still.

July 5, 1608. At noon our company came aboard . . . having had a
hard route, for they had been up the river six or seven leagues
[twenty-one to twenty-four miles]. . . . They then went ashore and
found good store of wild goose quills, a piece of an old oar, and some
flowers and green things which they found frowing.

We set sail . . . with sorrow that our labor was in vain; for had this
sound held as it did make show of, for breadth, depth, safeness of
harbor, and good anchor ground, it might have yielded an excellent
passage to a more easterly sea.

Generally, all the land of Nova Zembla that . . . we have seen is to
a man's eye a pleasant land; much main high land with no snow on
it, looking in some places green and deer feeding thereon.

It's an "a-ha" moment, or at least an opportunity for Hudson to re-
flect on the situation in which he finds himself. As modern Arctic
travelers now realize, there are multiple sources for the ice that is all
around: freshwater floes breaking off of glaciers and rivers, sea ice
formed by the extreme cold of winter, and even bergs that have
come from the polar ice barrier.

It is no marvel that there is so much ice in the sea toward the Pole,
so many sounds and rivers in the lands of Nova Zembla and Newland
to engender it; besides the coasts of Pechora, Russia, and Groenland,
with Lappia, as by proofs I find in my travel in these parts.

By means of which ice I suppose there will be no navigable passage this way.

Pechora (or Pecora) is another name for the mainland of Russia
west of the Ural Mountains below Novaya Zemlya; Lappia is Lapland, or Finland.

July 6, 1608. This place upon Nova Zembla is another then that which
the Hollanders call Costing Sarch, discovered by Oliver Brunel and
Willem Barents' observation doth witness the same. It is laid plot by
the Hollanders out of his true place too far north, to what end I know

not, unless to make it hold course with the compass not respecting the variation.

It is as broad and like to yield passage as the Vaigats, and my hope was that by the strong stream it would have cleared itself but it did not. It is so full of ice that you will hardly think it.

Variations on a Compass Theme

As I've noted, sailors of Hudson's time were able to measure their latitude—the distance up from the equator or down from the geographic North Pole—but could only make estimates of the longitude east or west of the prime meridian.

One instrument that was of some value was a compass, which could show the ship's bearing in relation to the magnetic pole. A compass, though, could not by itself be used to account for the drift of a vessel in currents or wind. And then there was one other important bit of information: the compass variation from true North.

Compass variation occurs because the magnetic North Pole is not in the same place as the geographic North Pole at 0°0'.

People had noticed that certain types of metals could be made to orient themselves in a predictable direction as early as 1090 in China. Italian scientists performed experiments in the twelfth and thirteenth centuries, and by the fourteenth century devices were appearing on ships.

Christopher Columbus carried a compass with him on his voyages in the mid-fifteenth century, and made some of the first formal notations of variations between where the compass needle pointed and where star observations said it should be oriented.

In 1608, as Hudson sailed to Novaya Zemlya, the magnetic North Pole was located on the west side of Melville Island in Canada's Elizabeth Islands about 800 miles from the geographic North Pole, midway between Greenland and Alaska. In the four centuries that have followed, the magnetic pole has wandered as far away as Prince of Wales Island, about 1,500 miles below true North.

The magnetic pole moves because it consists of a massive ocean of molten iron more than 1,850 miles below the earth's surface. It is always in motion, at varying rates of speed from about seven to twenty-five miles per year; scientists say that in the past century it has been moving north toward the geographic pole at the low end of its speed chart, about seven miles per year. Today, the magnetic pole has moved back toward true North, completing a U-shaped migration to end up to the east of Melville Island, about 600 miles below the geographic pole.

If you are situated directly below the magnetic pole and line up with the geographic pole, then your compass reading will be accurate. North is north. However, if you are east of the magnetic pole—say at Spitsbergen or Novaya Zemlya—the compass needle will be deflected to the left or west of the geographic pole. The amount of variation (also called deflection) varies depending on your location and the distance from the geographic pole.

In the United States, if you are near Chicago, the magnetic deviation is near 0°; magnetic north is geographic north. If you move east to the mouth of the Hudson River at New York City, magnetic north is about 14° west of true North. Over in the Aleutian Islands of Alaska, the compass would point about 15° east of true North.

A reading taken at the north or top end of Novaya Zemlya has a magnetic deviation of near 0° because the geographic pole and the magnetic pole are aligned with each other.

Abandoning the Second Voyage off Russia's New Land

In all, Hudson spent about a month or so at Novaya Zemlya, searching for the strait that ran between the two or a way around the 600-mile-long land mass. It was there, just like the charts said, but it was probably frozen over and indistinguishable from the surrounding land.

His search of the land seems to have occurred within a large sound that runs from about 71°0' to 71°30' on the inland side of the island of Ostrov Mezhdusharsky, which sits just offshore of the main south island of Novaya Zemlya.

His voyage to the North was impossible because of ice, and go-

118

ing the other direction did not get him to the bottom of Novaya Zemlya and Vaygach Island at its southern extreme. He never reached the narrow strait between the bottom of Vaygach and the mainland of Siberia—the Northeast Passage; had he ventured that far, he might have found it choked with ice.

On about July 12, Hudson began to sail west away from Novaya Zemlya, and on July 27, in a cold rain, they had to light their first candle, the first time they had seen a bit of night since May 19. They passed east of the Lofoten Islands of Norway again on July 30, but they could not see them.

> *August 7, 1608.* I used all diligence to arrive at London and therefore I now gave my company a certificate under my hand, of my free and willing return, without persuasion or force of any one or more of them.

There seems little doubt that something significant happened between July 6 and August 7 as the *Hopewell* sailed away from Novaya Zemlya and back toward England. The *master* of a ship does not ordinarily have to state for the record that he returned to his home port "without persuasion or force" by his crew. In fact, it sounds like exactly the opposite.

> For at my being at Nova Zembla, the sixth of July, void of hope of a Northeast Passage (except by the Vaigats, for which I was not fitted to try or prove), I therefore resolved to use all means I could to sail to the northwest. Considering the time and means we had, if the wind should friend us, as in the first part of our voyage it had done, and to make trail of that place called Lumley's Inlet, and the Furious Overfall by Captain Davis's, hoping to run into it a hundred leagues [345 miles], and to return as God should enable me.
>
> But now, having spent more than half the time I had, and gone but the shortest part of the way, by means of contrary winds, I thought it my duty to save victual, wages, and tackle by my speedy return and not by foolish rashness, the time being wasted, to lay more charge upon the action than necessity should compel. I arrived at Gravesend the six and twentieth of August.

Hudson does not lose the opportunity to make the point that he would have preferred to get out of Novaya Zemlya as quickly as he could and sail 3,000 miles west across the Atlantic to upper Canada and then venture 300 or so miles into the Furious Overfall.

But instead, he gives his company a certificate attesting to his free and willing return to London. It will forever reside in the historical record as the report of a captain who held shaky reign as the master and commander of his own ship.

CHAPTER 8

The Forbidden City

Novaya Zemlya is Russia's frigid, almost empty, and barely inhabitable attic. There were few if any people living there in 1608 when Henry Hudson sailed along its northern coast, and there may be even fewer there today.

For the first 350 years or so after early European explorers visited the archipelago, Novaya Zemlya remained cold and barely touched. But during World War II the surrounding waters were a killing zone for German air and naval forces attacking Allied supply ships. And in the cold war that followed, it became a notorious hotspot as a major Soviet nuclear weapons test site and dumping ground for nuclear reactors and radioactive waste.

According to the Russians, there is now a native population of about 100 in a pocket of the 35,000 square miles of ice and tundra. They are the Nentsy, a nomadic people who fish and hunt within the Arctic Circle from northern Norway to Siberia. (They are related to the Sami of Lapland and northern Scandinavia.)

Today, Vaygach Island at its bottom is known under its Russian name as Ostrov Vaygach. As we have seen, for hundreds of years the passage between the southern end of Vaygach and the mainland of Russia has been known as the Northeast Passage. That is, of course, the reason why Willem Barents, Hudson, and many others attempted to sail through those waters.

This particular version of northern navigation held the theory that there was clear water across the top of Russia all the way to the

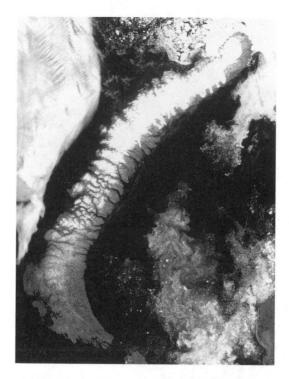

NASA image of Novaya Zemlya in mid-summer.
Jeff Schmaltz, MODIS Rapid Response Team, NASA/GSFC

Bering Strait. Nearly all the expeditions sooner or later ran into impenetrable ice.

Novaya Zemlya, New Land, Newfoundland, and Newland

It has always been a conceit of explorers that they "discover" new lands when they venture beyond the published charts. But, of course, Christopher Columbus did not discover the Americas—they were there before he arrived—and Hudson and other explorers of his time did not discover any new land, either.

That didn't stop mapmakers from applying that label in places all over the globe.

The Russian name for the archipelago between the Barents and Kara seas is **Нóвая Земля́** (Novaya Zemlya), meaning "New Land." The English and Dutch Latinized the name to Nova Zembla.

When Hudson sailed for Svalbard, his charts called that place Newland. When he would later enter into Hudson Strait, he sailed along the coast of Canada's Newfoundland. That part of the world, below the strait that Hudson would sail into in search of the Northwest Passage, was most likely given the Latin name Terra Nova by the Italian navigator Giovanni Caboto (sailing for the British as John Cabot) in 1497. The English later called it Newfoundland and the French dubbed it Terre-Neuve. They all mean the same: New Land.

And there's another Nova Zembla, this one off the northeast coast of Baffin Island in Canada's Nunavut Territory in the Davis Strait at 72°2' North latitude, 74°8' West longitude; this obscure little island is at almost the identical latitude as Novaya Zemlya in Russia, which runs from about 70°5' to 76°97' North latitude, at about 60° East longitude.

The Canadian island of Nova Zembla lies just fifty miles south of Bylot Island, named for Robert Bylot—a member of Hudson's crew on his fourth and final voyage and an observer of the mutiny that led to his death.

Russia's Attic

Murmansk is the largest city north of the Arctic Circle and Russia's only year-round port on its northern border; it is kept ice-free by the North Atlantic Drift ocean current, a remote branch of the Gulf Stream. Murmansk, on the Kola Peninsula, is near Russia's border with Finland and Norway. It was first developed as a port in 1899, and a railway was built to link it to Petrograd (now St. Petersburg) in the heart of Russia in 1917.

Joseph Stalin established the Soviet Fleet of the Northern Seas in 1933; it was renamed the Northern Fleet four years later. During World War II, naval vessels from Murmansk were involved in escorting Allied supply and relief ships to the Soviet Union. Convoy after convoy sailed from the United States and Canada to Murmansk; by one estimate, the United States sent 15,000 aircraft, 7,000 tanks, and 15 million pairs of boots to the Soviet Union through the port. Many of the convoys were attacked by German ships, and Murmansk itself was bombarded.

During World War II, a large number of U.S. and Allied merchant ships and naval escorts bringing supplies and armaments to the Soviets were trapped in the eastern entrance to Matochkin Strait—the narrow passage between the Northern and Southern islands of Novaya Zemlya—by German forces. In one period from June to July 1942, at least sixteen ships were sunk and a number of others were damaged near the settlement of Matochkin Shar.

After World War II, with the dawn of the cold war, Murmansk and the Northern Fleet became the heart of the Russian nuclear submarine program and eventually the largest of the Soviet Union's fleets, surpassing the Pacific Fleet. It was home to about two-thirds of the nation's nuclear subs.

The Northern Fleet also used facilities at Arkhangel'sk and Severodvinsk at the southern end of the White Sea, but both of these ports are ordinarily icebound for much of the year. For that reason, the Soviet Union designed and operated some of the largest icebreakers in the world including several nuclear-powered vessels to maintain a channel up to Murmansk and from there to the open sea.

Although the Soviet Union was extremely secretive about its surface and submarine operations in the area, U.S. and other cold war opponents did their best to spy on the area. We know of satellite surveillance; there was almost certainly spying by submarine and aircraft.

One advantage for intelligence collection in this area involves "choke points" in the ocean that funnel vessels into a relatively narrow passage. Russian ships going out to sea had to head for the North Cape of Norway, for Svalbard, or for Bear Island (Bjørnoya) to its south. Moving farther toward the west, the vessels had to pass through the Greenland-Iceland-Norway Gap.

After the breakup of the Soviet Union, the size of the navy was reduced and much of its equipment fell into disrepair. The industrial

base of Murmansk went into decline; local industries including shipyards, textile mills, and fisheries closed or were downsized.

In 2006, Russia operated seven nuclear-powered civilian vessels:
six icebreakers and one container ship. These ships are operated by
a "private" company but owned by the state.

The most modern of the ships, the *Yamal* (the *End of the Earth*),
was begun during the Soviet era and completed in 1992 under the
Russian brand of capitalism. The 23,445-ton, 490-foot-long *Yamal* is
one of the most powerful vessels of its size; two nuclear reactors
produce steam for six turbines, generating 75,000 horsepower. The
Arktika-class ships are confined to the Russian North because they
require cold sea water to cool the generating system.

Besides keeping open ports that connect to nickel foundries and
other industries on the Kola Peninsula, in years past the icebreakers
have also been offered as transportation to the North Pole for
wealthy tourists, a source of hard currency from foreigners. In 2005,
two-week voyages aboard the *Yamal* from Murmansk to the North
Pole were priced from $16,000 to $21,000 per person. For that price,
they throw in a helicopter and Zodiac tour.

In recent years, the nuclear icebreakers have—in the kindest
terms—begun to show their age. The Russians have made various
patches and repairs aimed at extending the operational lifetime of
the ships beyond their original planned twenty-five years in service.

The icebreaker *Lenin* was the world's first nuclear-powered civilian ship when it was commissioned in 1959. Experts believe that the
ship suffered a catastrophic failure of some sort—perhaps even a
meltdown of one of its reactors—in 1966 or 1967. Some reports said
a number of crewmen were killed—perhaps as many as thirty—and
others sickened. The ship was literally too hot to handle for several
years but somehow was returned to service in 1970 and continued
in the fleet until 1989. The *Lenin*'s three original reactors, along with
most of the ship's fuel, was dumped into Tsivolko Fjord in the Kara
Sea just off the east coast of Novaya Zemlya.

Meanwhile, a "new" icebreaker is expected to join the fleet, eventually. The keel of the *50 Let Pobedy* (the *50th Anniversary of Vic-*

tory) was laid in 1989 and the hull was launched in 1993, but the ship completely missed the 1995 commemoration of the end of World War II because of a lack of funding from the Russian government. It also missed the sixtieth anniversary in 2005. The uncompleted ship suffered damage in at least two shipyard fires in November 2004 and again in October 2005.

Wanna be the first tourist to go for a trip on that ship?

The Nuclear Wasteland

Novaya Zemlya came to be a nuclear wasteland through a combination of unique circumstances.

First of all, it is about 500 miles from Russia's northernmost port, Murmansk. After helping keep Russia alive and supporting the fight against Germany in World War II, Murmansk became the home of the heart of the Soviet Union's nuclear submarine fleet in the cold war.

The remoteness of Novaya Zemlya also made it an attractive place for nuclear testing and a dumping ground for decommissioned nuclear-powered naval vessels and nuclear waste; it was far away from major population centers and well within the security cocoon of the government.

And then there is the question of the quality and safety of the nuclear fleet itself. At best, submarines and icebreakers are difficult to build, operate, and maintain; nuclear-powered vessels especially so. The U.S. Navy has lost two nuclear submarines to accidents; in 1963 the *Thresher* sank off the coast of New England, and in 1968 the *Scorpion* was lost in the mid-Atlantic.

At worst, there is a reasonably well-documented history of incidents, accidents, and disasters in the Russian Northwest. All this became even more worrisome as the Soviet Union went into decline and as the new Russian Federation allowed many of the ships in the fleet to fall into disrepair.

At least three Soviet nuclear submarines sank in the Barents Sea and a fourth was intentionally scuttled in the Kara Sea off Novaya Zemlya. The most recent, in August 2000, was the *Kursk*, which suf-

126

fered an on board explosion and sank about eighty-five miles east of Murmansk. The *Kursk* was a young vessel, the last of the giant Oscar II–class submarines designed in the Soviet era; it was named after a city in the interior of southwestern Russia. The largest attack submarine ever built, the supposedly unsinkable vessel (it had a double hull) was about 500 feet long and 4 stories high.

Despite rescue efforts, all 118 crew and officers died in the sinking. The *Kursk* was eventually raised and brought back to a Russian scrap yard.

Not so the *Komsomolets*, which sank on April 7, 1989, about 100 miles southeast of Bear Island. This one-of-a-kind submarine (its hull was made of titanium) was supposedly able to dive deeper and cruise faster than any other undersea vessel. When fire broke out in a compartment near the stern, it quickly spread throughout the sub, and the pressure caused the hull to fracture. *Komsomolets* sank in about a mile of water, and forty-two crew and officers were killed; most of the handful of survivors were seriously injured.

The wreck of the *Komsomolets* has been visited several times. A 1992 examination found cracks along the entire length of the hull and possible breaches in the cooling pipes for the reactor. Although the Russians claimed there was "insignificant" radioactive contamination, later examinations found a large hole in the forward torpedo compartment and in 1994 plutonium was found to be leaking from one of two nuclear torpedoes still in the compartment.

In 1995 and 1996, some of the fractures in the hull were sealed, and the Russian government declared the operation a success, saying that further contamination was not expected, at least for the next ten or twenty years. Which may mean that the area between Bear Island and Hammerfest at the top of Norway—a prime fishing area and home to millions of birds that scatter throughout the Arctic and other parts of Europe—may be in danger of serious nuclear poisoning in the next decade.

According to the Bellona Foundation, a relatively nonideological Norwegian environmental study group, the situation is not much better in and around Murmansk. In the aftermath of the cold war, the group says, there are about a hundred nuclear submarines tied up and out of service; at least half of them are believed to still have nuclear fuel in place. Nuclear waste and decommissioned fuel from a number of vessels is said to be stored on nine poorly maintained ships in Murmansk, the nearby Severomorsk naval port or at the Severodinsk shipyard near Arkhangel'sk in the White Sea.

And then there are the five known nuclear dumpsites east of Novaya Zemlya, the current resting place of seventeen nuclear reactors, according to Bellona. As mentioned earlier, the icebreaker *Lenin*'s three reactors and more than half of the ship's fuel were dumped at Tsivolko Fjord. Two empty but still radioactive reactors were dropped not far away in Techeniya Fjord in about 100 to 125 feet of water in 1988. The decommissioned submarine *K-27*, still containing two experimental liquid metal reactors, was scuttled in 1981 at Stepovogo Fjord in about 150 feet of ocean. The area to the west of the islands—toward Norway—was also used as a dumping ground; seventeen out-of-service nuclear reactors are believed to have been dumped in the Barents Sea, and at least seven of them are believed to have contained spent fuel.

The Nuclear Test Site

After World War II, Novaya Zemlya was given its first significant human assignment: it became the Soviet Union's northern test site for nuclear weapons.

Three sites were part of the testing range that covered more than half of the land mass. At least forty-two underground nuclear explosions were conducted there, as well as a number of air-dropped devices including the Tsar Bomba, the largest thermonuclear bomb ever tested. There were also three known underwater explosions.

The Russian Federation signed the Nuclear Test Ban Treaty in 1996 and completed its ratification in 2000; however, the international agreement does not go into effect until all forty-four nations identified as having existing or potential nuclear facilities do the same.

As of early 2007, the United States had signed the treaty but not ratified it in Congress. That puts the United States in the company of countries like Iran and China, which have failed to ratify the agreement. Countries that have completely ignored the test ban treaty include North Korea, India, and Pakistan—each of which have demonstrated that they already possess a nuclear arsenal.

If it makes you feel any better, a number of countries not included in the required forty-four nations have voluntarily signed and ratified the treaty. Thus, we are presumably safe from nuclear fallout from tests conducted by nations including the Cook Islands, Fiji, Haiti, and the Vatican.

In recent years, Russia has continued to use the facility for what it has described as subcritical testing of separate components of nuclear ordnance. And the area has been considered as the location for a burial site for liquid and solid wastes from nuclear submarines and power plants, a Russian equivalent to the U.S. plans for Yucca Mountain in Nevada.

Studies conducted in the late 1980s by Johnny Skorve, a senior scientist at the Norsk Utenrikspolitsk Institutt (NUPI; Norwegian Institute of International Affairs) in Oslo, Norway, indicate some of the reasons why the Soviets may have found Novaya Zemlya to their liking as a test area.

His examination of commercial and declassified military satellite images of the area showed 85 to 90 percent of the pictures of the region were cloud-covered. One reason for these clouds is Novaya Zemlya's location in an area where slightly warm water from the Gulf Stream mixes with the cold water of the Barents Sea.

Beyond that, Skorve said, much of the test site area was constantly in shadow or poorly illuminated by the Sun because of the extreme northern latitude and the rough terrain. This limited the opportunities for images from Sun-synchronous orbits of the Landsat and SPOT satellites to a single daily pass around 10:00 A.M.

The NUPI study located the northern nuclear test site on the southern coast of the Matochkin Strait that divides the two Novaya Zemlya islands. The test area is snow-free for only three months in a typical year, with August as the warmest month.

According to Skorve, the mountain ridge that keeps the zone in continuous shadow and thus out of view of optical sensors on satellites was used for a number of nuclear tests; these sensors and satellites detected tunnels into the mountains and explosion craters. One particular satellite image collected in 1966 showed a path broken through the frozen surface of the strait by an icebreaker and evidence that heavy equipment had been hoisted from vessels onto the ice and driven to the tunnel entrances.

A Scientist's View

I spoke with John Pike, an expert on defense, space, and intelligence policy in the United States who now runs a group called GlobalSecurity.org. Pike, a familiar face on network and cable news on the subject of weapons of mass destruction and space issues, had previously been the director of space policy for the Federation of American Scientists.

"Novaya Zemlya was the primary high-yield nuclear test range for the Soviet Union," Pike told me. "It was not the first place they tested nuclear weapons, but when the weapons they were testing outgrew their other test ranges, this is where they got off to."

Is Novaya Zemlya a poisoned place? "It is not a tourist attraction," Pike said. "But basically the tests they were conducting there were either high-altitude air bursts or underground tests." That sort of air burst testing would not cause a great deal of nuclear fallout in the area, he said.

"You certainly get fallout from any above-ground test, but you get a lot less from an air burst than you do from a surface burst," Pike said. "What you are mainly worried about is when the fireball touches the ground. When that happens, you have a lot of material that is irradiated or that gets mixed in with fission products and then is sucked up into the air and blows away.

"But if it is a high-altitude air burst, the fire ball never touches the ground. You would have some fallout from the bomb casing, but the physical volume of it would be quite small relative to what you would get with a surface burst and that was basically why they moved their testing to Novaya Zemlya so that it would be out in the middle of nowhere and whatever fallout you did get directly from the bomb would not fall in populated areas."

Pike's organization did make public some of the details of a 1996 trial against a former Soviet navy captain who was arrested for publicizing nuclear hazards from poorly maintained vessels.

The Soviet physicist Andrei Sakharov, who went from designing nuclear weapons to becoming one of the regime's most outspoken advocates for human rights and a Nobel Peace Prize laureate, gave some of the details of the biggest bang at Novaya Zemlya, the Tsar Bomba (the Emperor Bomb) of 1961 at one of the chilliest times of the cold war.

This weapon is believed to have been the largest nuclear weapon ever used. The design of the device was for a 100-megaton explosion, but for testing some of the components of the bomb used lead instead of uranium, which reduced the yield to a mere 58 megatons or so. The use of the dummy load also made the test a very "clean" one in terms of fallout; if the full charge of uranium had been in place, this single explosion would have added 25 percent to the total amount of fission fallout since the invention of the A-bomb.

Russophiles point out that calling the spectacular weapon Tsar Bomba is in keeping with Russian traditions of making huge, showy creations just to demonstrate that they can. The Tsar Kolokol and the Tsar Pushka—the world's largest bell and cannon, respectively, at the time they were made—are on display at the Kremlin in Moscow. The bell, more than 200 tons, broke in 1737 before it was ever rung. The 40-ton cannon, made in 1586, was never fired.

The Northeast Passage Fulfilled?

The North Pole ice pack changes from year to year because of ordinary climatic variations; there seems little doubt that its size has shrunk in recent decades because of global warming. Some scientists say that it is in the process of pulling far back enough from the coast of Siberia to permit fulfillment of Hudson's first assignment: a year-round, or nearly year-round Northeast Passage.

In 2000, an oceanographer who sailed on the icebreaker *Yamal* to the North Pole told the *New York Times* that the ship found a mile-wide patch of open water at the top of the world. The captain had to sail six miles away from the geographic pole to find ice thick enough to allow its passengers to get off the ship and claim bragging rights for being at least that close. Since 2000, the ice at the North Pole has come and gone with seasonal variations.

Scientists and maritime experts now say that as the polar ice barrier recedes and coastal ice diminishes, the Northeast Passage may finally open as a shipping route. The lane would go up past the top of Norway and hug the coast of northern Russia, between the bottom of Novaya Zemlya and Vaygach Island (exactly the route Hudson hoped to sail) and then continue across Siberia to the Bering Strait between Russia and Alaska.

Blame it on global warming as more and more scientists do, or on the eons-long cycles of ice ages and warming trends. But measurements by some scientists show that the Arctic icecap has shrunk by as much as 3 percent in the past ten years and that the ice is only half as thick as it was half a century ago. At that rate, a passage across the top of Russia from Europe to Asia may be open within the next decade, and some experts see a year-round ice-free route by the end of the twenty-first century if not sooner.

The other major change, of course, is the thawing of Russia's unwillingness to allow foreign vessels to transit near its coastline. With the end of the Soviet Union, capitalism—in the form of charges for use of its ports including Murmansk, icebreakers, and other services—is trumping military secrecy.

The appeal of the Northeast Passage today is the same as it was in 1608 when Hudson tried to go through, and for earlier expeditions by Willam Barents and Sir Hugh Willoughby. Passage across the top of Europe to Japan would be much shorter (about twenty-two days for 7,000 nautical miles) than the present southern lanes that go through the Suez Canal (thirty-five days and 11,000 nautical miles) or the even longer routes that cross the Atlantic to the Panama Canal or go around Cape Horn at the bottom of South America.

It was the opening of the Suez Canal in 1869 that made the Northeast Passage seem less attractive; the emergence of the Soviet Union, including the presence of its Northern Fleet in the area, seemed to close off that route entirely. Ironically, with the cold war now over, a route near Russia is regarded as a safer passage than having to go through the Suez Canal in the politically unstable Middle East.

The Zembla Factor

The idea of a deadly, cold wasteland, almost inaccessible, became a fixture of Western literature within a century of Hudson's voyages to Spitsbergen and Nova Zembla. It was a frozen mirror to ideas like Utopia (imagined by Sir Thomas More in 1515), and later Xanadu (Kubla Khan's kingdom as put forth by Samuel Taylor Coleridge in 1797).

Nova Zembla persists in the cultural DNA of writers and readers today.

The satirist Jonathan Swift placed the antihero of one of his biting essays there in 1710, just a bit more than a century after Hudson's visit. In "The Battle of the Books: A Full and True Account of the Battle Fought Last Friday between the Ancient and the Modern Books in Saint James's Library," he wrote of a "malignant deity called Criticism," who dwelt on top of a snowy mountain in Nova Zembla.

Swift, never one for subtlety, had Criticism in a den full of half-devoured books and surrounded by "Ignorance, her father and husband, blind with age," as well as her mother Pride, her sister Opinion, and her children Noise, Impudence, Dullness, Vanity, Positiveness, Pedantry, and Ill-Manners.

Alexander Pope, who wrote about serious religious, political, and philosophical issues in poetic form, had the geography of the Far North on his mind in his "Essay on Man, Epistle II," published between 1732 and 1734.

> *Ask where's the North? At York 'tis on the Tweed;*
> *In Scotland at the Orcades; and there,*
> *At Greenland, Zembla, or the Lord knows where.*

In 1848, ten years after the French writer Léonie Thévenot d'Aunet published letters about her voyage to the Arctic, the English romantic writer Charlotte Brontë published her best-known work, *Jane*

Eyre. That book begins with the narrator telling of a dreary November day spent studying a book about birds, a volume she did not care for, except for the sections about the solitary rocks and promontories of the coast of Norway and beyond:

> Nor could I pass unnoticed the suggestion of the bleak shores of Lapland, Siberia, Spitzbergen, Nova Zembla, Iceland, Greenland, with "the vast sweep of the Arctic Zone, and those forlorn regions of dreary space,—that reservoir of frost and snow, where firm fields of ice, the accumulation of centuries of winters, glazed in Alpine heights above heights, surround the pole, and concentre the multiplied rigours of extreme cold." Of these death-white realms I formed an idea of my own: shadowy, like all the half-comprehended notions that float dim through children's brains, but strangely impressive.

The American author Nathaniel Hawthorne, best known for narratives like *The Scarlet Letter* and *The House of the Seven Gables*, found use of the North as an extreme in the short story "The Snow Image," published in 1851. "The difference betwixt the atmosphere here and the cold, wintry twilight out of doors, was like stepping at once from Nova Zembla to the hottest part of India, or from the North Pole into an oven," he wrote.

The French and then the world's imagination was captured by Jules Verne with his series of books that imagined a wondrous future: *Voyage to the Center of the Earth, From the Earth to the Moon,* and *Twenty Thousand Leagues under the Sea.*

In Verne's *Twenty Thousand Leagues*, published in 1869, the memorable Captain Nemo's fantastic voyage ended with a northward dash. The narrator, the fictional marine biologist Professor Pierre Aronnax, asks: "Would it touch at Spitzbergen, or on the shores of Nova Zembla? Should we explore those unknown seas, the White Sea, the Sea of Kara, the Gulf of Obi, the Archipelago of Liarrov, and the unknown coast of Asia?" To answer the question, the submarine *Nautilus* ends up surfacing in the Lofoten Islands of northern Norway, which as it turns out is due west of Nova Zembla or due south of Svalbard.

In a nod to Verne, the world's first nuclear submarine was given the name *Nautilus*. On August 3, 1958, the U.S. vessel made the first undersea passage to the North Pole. Departing Pearl Harbor on July 28, the sub completed its transpolar voyage when it arrived in Portland, England, on August 12.

Nova Zembla has surfaced in numerous other works over the years, including stories by Salman Rushdie. In 1998, it became the heart of a word coined by the British author William Boyd in his novel *Armadillo*.

Boyd asks:

> What is the opposite of Serendip, a southern land of spice and warmth?
> Think of another world in the far north, barren, icebound . . . Zembla. Ergo: zemblanity, the opposite of serendipity, the faculty of making unhappy, unlucky and expected discoveries by design.

The former *New York Times* word maven William Safire began his analysis of the word *zemblanity* by noting that the Russians were believed to be conducting nonnuclear tests at a secret laboratory on Nova Zembla. "Now this site of testing of nonnuclear explosives at a nuclear facility has given birth to zemblanity, the inexorable discovery of what we don't want to know," Safire writes.

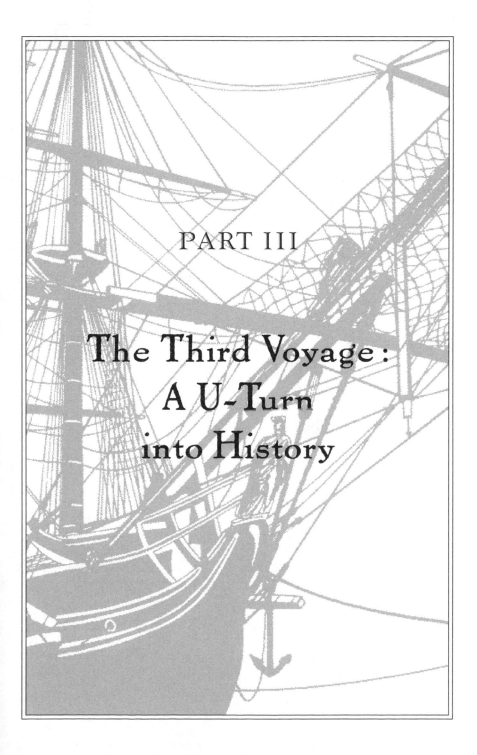

PART III

The Third Voyage:
A U-Turn
into History

0   500 Miles

0   500 KM

Parallel scale at 45°N 90°W

After Hudson abandoned his third attempt to get across the top of Europe to Asia, he turned his ship around and sailed west across the Atlantic to the North American coast. The *Half Moon* proceeded as far south as Virginia before heading for New York and the Hudson River.

CHAPTER 9

An English Captain
on a Dutch Ship

The Muscovy Company did not offer Henry Hudson another contract. Even if he may have had family connections, business is business. Hudson's first two voyages in search of the Northeast Passage could hardly be considered financial successes.

Were they unsure of his leadership skills? Did the hints of earlier uprisings by his crew mark him as a bad captain? Did some of his officers report mismanagement? Or was the company simply unwilling to spend good money after bad, convinced of the lack of an easy course through the Northeast Passage and unsure of the prospects of a Northwest route?

The investors in the Muscovy Company did not receive any direct benefit from Hudson's trips with the *Hopewell*, although a substantial and profitable whaling and walrus trade developed almost immediately as a result of his reports from Svalbard and Novaya Zemlya.

Hudson applied for a new assignment several times but was rebuffed or delayed. So he began to seek freelance work from the French and the Dutch, two seafaring nations just across the Channel from England.

Like the English, the Dutch were looking for a short and safe route that did not put their interests at risk from Spanish and Portuguese forces and their allies including Muslim pirates at sea and on land in Africa and Asia, and from Spanish forces in the Caribbean and Central America. At the same time, the Dutch and French were also looking for trading areas not within the sphere of influence of the British.

Hudson was anxious to get back to sea. He had no other trade and was not a wealthy man; he needed a contract.

Through letters, personal entreaties, and the professional grape-vine that existed among the planet's explorers and ships' captains, Hudson put out the word that he was available for hire. He was con-tacted by the Dutch, and through an intermediary he began discus-sions with the French and Henry IV; when word of the French connection became known, the Dutch pounced.

Exit the Spanish Armada, Enter the Dutch

Europe's almost constant wars and conflicts had taken another turn by 1609, in part because of the end of the Anglo-Spanish War that lasted from 1585 to 1604. (Later flare-ups would occur in 1664 and again in 1727.)

The war that coincided with Hudson's era, like many conflicts, arose out of disputes that included money and religion. In the latter part of the sixteenth century, Spain sought to consolidate and enforce its monopoly on trade with the Americas: principally in Florida, the Caribbean, the Gulf of Mexico, and Central America.

A cold war between the powers began about 1569 when English privateers including Sir John Hawkins and later Sir Francis Drake made raids on Spanish ships and colonies in the New World. Queen Elizabeth gave secret support to the "Sea Dogs" and made some per-sonal investments in their pillaging businesses.

On the religious side, the Spanish and English were at odds over the 1587 execution of Mary Queen of Scots, a Catholic. Mary had been held in captivity for nineteen years by Elizabeth after she fled Glasgow in the wake of an uprising by Protestant lords in Scotland; she was finally executed after Elizabeth's ministers blamed her for a series of Catholic plots against the English monarchy.

And just for good measure, the Spanish were also unhappy with aid given by Britain to Protestant rebels in the Netherlands, a region controlled by Spain.

Besides his efforts as a privateer, Hawkins was also one of the pioneers of the European slave trade, buying slaves in West Africa and selling them in the West Indies; again, Elizabeth was said to be one of his financial backers. In 1568, Spanish ships attacked Hawkins's fleet of six vessels in San Juan de Ulúa harbor in Veracruz, Mexico, destroying four of them. The ships commanded by Hawkins and his cousin Francis Drake were the only ones to escape. Hawkins went on to help finance some of Drake's explorations, mostly staying on land as a shipbuilder and treasurer of the navy.

The first major battle of the war was a victory for English forces at Cádiz in 1587. The port in southwest Spain, part of Andalusia, may be the most ancient city in western Europe, dating back to the Phoenician walled city of Gadir, built about 1100 B.C. Cádiz has been a place of great historical note for most of its existence; it was the base Hannibal used to launch his conquest of southern Iberia.

Over the centuries, it was ruled by the Phoenicians, the Carthaginians, the Romans, the Visigoths, and the Moors before it became a Spanish commercial center in the thirteenth century. Christopher Columbus sailed from there on his second and fourth voyages, and as a result of Spain's conquests in the New World, Cádiz became the home port for the treasure galleons bringing home plunder. It was those galleons, and the naval vessels protecting the port, that drew British raiders.

At the same time, King Phillip II of Spain was drawing plans for an assault on England including a massive fleet of some 130 ships and about 30,000 sailors and soldiers from Spain and the Netherlands. The goal was to invade England, remove Protestant Queen Elizabeth from the throne, return control to the Roman Catholic Church, and clear the way for the Spanish to defeat the Dutch rebels.

In April 1587, Drake led an attack on Cádiz that destroyed some of the gathering Spanish fleet there and delayed the invasion for a year. In July 1588, the Spanish Armada was spotted by a larger English fleet, including vessels that had been designed and improved by Hawkins.

The first skirmishes between the ships took place off Plymouth and the Isle of Wight below southern England. But the big battle took place near Calais, France, where the Spanish Armada anchored in hopes of meeting up with the large army that was supposed to sail from the Netherlands.

The English fleet was under Lord Howard, but he gave tactical command to Drake. The turning point in the battle is generally thought to be the night when Drake rigged six gunpowder-filled, burning ships on a course that steered them directly into the Spanish fleet at anchor.

A succession of battles went strongly in England's favor and by the end of August the remaining ships sailed away in disarray, heading north up the Channel, around Scotland and Ireland and into the North Atlantic. There, the remnants of the great armada sailed directly into a fierce hurricane off Ireland, a meteorological oddity: one of the northernmost hurricanes ever recorded.

Many of the remaining ships were wrecked on the beaches of Ireland; some of the crews were killed by English armies, while others were given shelter by Irish Catholics. By the end of the summer, only about half of the original 130 ships were able to return to Spain.

Although Elizabeth considered the battle (which saved her throne) a great triumph, the English were unable to gain any significant victories in the years to come. It did, though, cement the Church of England's Protestantism as the state religion. And Spain was nearly bankrupted by the war and the disruption of its commerce.

A weakened Spain finally recognized the end of its rule over the Low Countries (which today include the Netherlands, Belgium, Luxembourg, and parts of France and Germany). After decades of revolt and a declaration of independence, Spain recognized the Republic of the Seven United Provinces in the Netherlands in 1609 just five days after Hudson departed on his third voyage—this time under the Dutch flag.

The Dutch Merchant Nation-State

This time Hudson's employer was the Dutch East India Company (De Vereenigde Oost-Indische Compagnie), known by its Dutch initials as the VOC. The founders of the VOC, a group of Dutch merchants and trading companies, secured a charter in 1602 from the newly independent republic that gave it a monopoly on trade to the East. Its primary goal was to take over the lucrative trade in spices.

The charter specifically stated that it would conduct its business by travel to the East around the Cape of Good Hope at the bottom of Africa, or to the West by crossing the Atlantic and sailing below Cape Horn at the bottom of South America. But there was nothing that prevented the VOC from also conducting trade through northern passages.

The most important distinction accorded the VOC was that its charter gave it nearly all the powers of a nation-state: it could colonize or enslave nations, wage war, or sign peace agreements. This was very different from the Muscovy Company, which was strictly a commercial enterprise.

And the VOC had much greater resources than the English when it began; it had more than 40 ships in its fleet, about 600 cannons, and in excess of 5,000 sailors under contract. (By its peak in 1669, the VOC was the richest private company ever established, a global superpower with more than 150 merchant ships, 40 warships, and 50,000 employees including a private army of 10,000 soldiers.)

The VOC's offshore headquarters was in Batavia on the island of Java, now know as Jakarta, Indonesia. From there, the company ran operations in the Spice Islands (the Moluccas and the Banda Islands) and elsewhere. Its rule in Banda was particularly brutal, displacing or killing much of the local population and using slave labor to create a nutmeg industry there.

(On December 26, 2004, the provincial capital of Banda Aceh was the closest settlement to a major underwater earthquake; the resulting tsunami killed more than 127,000 people in Indonesia alone and perhaps 150,000 more elsewhere on the shores of the Indian Ocean.)

Hudson Strikes a Deal

Among the intermediaries Hudson met was Emanuel van Meteren, the former Dutch consul in London; he was also the English representative of the VOC. Van Meteren eventually offered an all-expenses-paid trip to Amsterdam.

The officers of the VOC were skeptical about the chances for success on a Northeast Passage and even less certain about a Northwest route. There was, however, a standing reward by the Dutch States-General in the amount of 25,000 guilders to any captain or organization that could discover a way to Asia by a Northeast route above Russia.

However, the French, who were already involved with early forays into upper Canada, were more sympathetic to Hudson's preference to explore the Northwest. James Lemaire, a Dutch navigator living in France, visited Henry IV and recommended he hire Hudson.

Here was an instance where the course of history could well have been changed if only the French had acted a bit quicker, or if Hudson had not been so anxious to sign a contract—any contract—regardless of his belief in its chance of success.

The Dutch offered first. The VOC had plenty of money and ships; Hudson appealed to them because he had recent experience in voyages in search of the Northeast Passage, even if they were not successful. He had proven himself able to navigate to the high northern latitudes and had managed to return with his ship and crew. Even though he had not brought back any profits, his knowledge and charts were valuable.

But having met with Hudson, the VOC delayed signing an agreement. Again, we don't know why; it may have been because of a similar lack of success by Willem Barents in the Far North or it may have been doubts about Hudson. But apparently, once the VOC learned that Hudson was also seeking a deal with the French, it quickly put forth its offer.

The Dutch had no problems signing an English subject to captain one of their vessels; Hudson would later find out that the British were not as happy. By 1609, there had already been small-scale skirmishes between the developing Dutch ventures and the English including battles (and piracy) over whales in the Far North, treasures from the Spice Islands, and other matters of commerce.

It was not unusual for would-be explorers to put their services out to bid. As noted earlier, Christopher Columbus was an Italian who sailed for the Spanish (and is known in some parts of the world and in some histories as Cristóbal Colón). Sebastian Cabot was a Venetian or Italian (born Sebastiano Caboto) who sailed for the English, as did his father Giovanni Caboto (John Cabot). Giovanni da Verrazano was an Italian sailing for the French.

In any case, the deal was straightforward and simple; a copy was reprinted by the historian Samuel Purchas in book three of *Purchas His Pilgrimes.*

Contract of the
DUTCH UNITED EAST INDIA COMPANY
with
HENRY HUDSON
January 8, 1609

On this eighth of January in the year of our Lord one thousand six hundred and nine, the Directors of the East India Company of the Chamber of Amsterdam of the ten years reckoning of the one part, and Mr. Henry Hudson, Englishman, assisted by Jodocus Hondius, of the other part, have agreed in manner following, to wit: That the said directors shall in the first place equip a small vessel or yacht of about thirty lasts burden, with which, well provided with men, provisions and other necessaries, the above named Hudson shall about the first of April, sail, in order to search for a passage by the North, around by the North side of Nova Zembla, and shall continue thus along that parallel until he shall be able to sail Southward to the latitude of sixty degrees. He shall obtain as much knowledge of the lands as can be done without any considerable loss of time, and if it is possible return immediately in order to make a faithful report and relation of his voyage to the Directors, and to deliver over his journals, log-books and charts, together with an account of everything whatsoever which shall happen to him during the voyage without keeping anything back; for which said voyage the Directors shall pay to the said Hudson, as well for his outfit for the said voyage, as for the support of his wife and children, the sum of eight hundred guilders; and, in case (which God prevent) he do not come back or arrive hereabouts within a year, the Directors shall further pay to his wife two hundred guilders in cash; and thereupon they shall not be further liable to him or his heirs, unless he shall either afterwards or within the year arrive and have found the passage good and suitable for the Company to use; in which case the Directors will reward the before named Hudson for his dangers, trouble and knowledge in their discretion, with which the before mentioned Hudson is content. And in case the Directors think proper to prosecute and continue the same voyage, it is stipulated and agreed with the before named Hudson, that he shall make his residence in this country with his wife and children, and shall enter into the employment of no one other than the Company, and this at the discretion of the Directors, who also promise to make him satisfied and content for such further service in all justice and equity. All without fraud or evil intent. In witness of the truth, two contracts are made hereof of the same tenor and are subscribed by both parties and also by Jodocus Hondius, as interpreter and witness. Dated as above.

The contract, in Dutch, was signed by Dirk van Os, J. Poppe, and Henry Hudson, with Jodocus Hondius as witness. Hondius, who acted as the interpreter for Hudson, was a well-known mapmaker and engraver. The Flemish Hondius had lived and worked in London and become acquainted with Hudson.

It is worth noting that the contract used the name Henry Hudson and the captain signed it in that way; the Dutch spelling of Henry as Henryk or Hendrick was applied by others.

The contract was very demanding of Hudson, and rather modest in its benefits. The pay of 800 guilders was worth about $320 at the time, not a huge amount of money but nevertheless significant enough to entice Hudson. The contract also promised about $80 more to his family if Hudson was to fail to return home safely within a year's time. At the same time, his wife, Katherine, and sons were required to move to Amsterdam and live there, in a way serving as hostages to ensure his return to The Netherlands.

The ship they offered, the *Halve Maen* (*Half Moon*), was a modest vessel; its stated size of thirty lasts is equal to about sixty tons in capacity. The re-creation of the vessel that sails on today's Hudson River is not much larger than four Greyhound buses parked two abreast.

And the contract was very specific in its assignment: although at the end of his second voyage Hudson had all but declared himself a disbeliever in the prospects of a Northeast Passage, that was exactly what the VOC had in mind. He was to "search for a passage by the North, around by the North side of Nova Zembla, and shall continue thus along that parallel until he shall be able to sail Southward to the latitude of sixty degrees."

The contract was thus saying that Hudson was expected to voyage, as he had before, from Europe up the length of Norway, along the North side of Novaya Zemlya (the side that is all but completely frozen in for most of the year), then continue above Siberia and finally hook southward through what we now know as the Bering Strait between extreme eastern Russia and Alaska.

Hudson could not have been happy with his assignment or hold a very high estimation of its chances of success.

CHAPTER 10

Voyage Three: London to New York, via Novaya Zemlya

Henry Hudson's voyage up the grand river that bears his name in New York is his most famous accomplishment. But like all four of his commands, it wasn't where he had planned to go in the first place.

His instructions from the VOC were very specific: go to Novaya Zemlya and nowhere else. The Hudson River in New York is definitely somewhere else.

On this voyage, most of the logbook was kept by the troublesome mate Robert Juet, with only a few existing fragments by Hudson himself.

The *Half Moon* departed Amsterdam on March 25, 1609, with a crew of sixteen, and headed north following the coast of Norway past the North Cape and into the White Sea. And as Hudson had to expect, almost immediately they were hammered by wind, extreme cold, and snow.

THE THIRD VOYAGE OF
MASTER HENRY HUDSON
TOWARD NOVA ZEMBLA; AND AT HIS RETURNE, HIS PASSING FROM
FARRE ISLANDS TO NEW-FOUND LAND, AND ALONG TO FORTIE-FOURE

Degrees and Ten Minutes, and thence to Cape Cod, and so to Thirtie-three Degrees; and along the coast to the northward, to fortie-two degrees and a halfe, and up the river neere to fortie-three degrees.

Written by Robert Juet, of Lime-house

March 25, 1609. We set sail from Amsterdam and by the seven and twentieth day we were down at the Texel.

Because it is a journey usually known, I omit to put down what passed till we came to the height of The North Cape of Finmarke, which we did perform by the fifth of May. On which day we . . . found it to be 71°46'.

So far, so good, on a journey "usually known." Hudson had been in the neighborhood twice in the past two years, and Juet on at least one voyage with him and perhaps on other journeys. The area was also known to explorers including Willem Barents.

The lack of detail may be innocent, but it may also mask some serious problems aboard ship; when the journal picks up again on May 19, the ship is south of its earlier position at the North Cape at the top of Norway. Who made the decision to turn around just six weeks into the voyage? How could Hudson go against the doubly specific instructions of his contract to go to Novaya Zemlya and nowhere else?

When Hudson returned from his voyage, he landed not in the Netherlands, where his financial sponsors were and the home port of the ship, but in England. He was placed under what amounted to house arrest by the British—something we'll explore later on. In the meantime, he sought out Emanuel van Meteren, the former Dutch consul in London who had helped bring Hudson and the VOC together. Van Meteren published the book *Historie der Nederlanden* in 1614 and in that work he filled in more of the story.

Van Meteren wrote that Hudson showed him his original logbook, charts, and notes—documents not available to us now. He tells us that as the *Half Moon* moved up the coast of Norway and into the still-lingering winter of April and May, a mutiny arose.

It began with quarrels and fights between the mixed English and

Dutch crew; the sailors from Holland were quite accustomed to sailing in the extreme heat of the East Indies and the Spice Islands and not at all comfortable in the ice and snow of Scandinavia.

Thomas Allibone Janvier, a very prolific but little remembered writer of the late nineteenth and early twentieth centuries, contributes some more detail to the story of Hudson in books about the founding of New York published in 1894 and 1903, and in *Henry Hudson: A Brief Statement of His Aims and His Achievements*, which was released in 1909.

Janvier quotes from van Meteren's *Historie*. He says that Hudson found the northern coast of Novaya Zemlya as choked with ice as it had been the year before and lost hope of proceeding through it. According to van Meteren—with the assumption that he was reporting what he had been told by the captain himself—Hudson laid before the crew two propositions.

> The first of these was, to go to the coast of America to the latitude of forty degrees. This idea had been suggested to him by some letters and maps which his friend Captain Smith had sent him from Virginia, and by which he informed him that there was a sea leading into the western ocean to the north of the southern English colony [Virginia]. Had this information been true (experience goes as yet to the contrary), it would have been of great advantage, as indicating a short way to India.
>
> The other proposition was to direct their search to Davis's Straits. This meeting with general approval, they sailed on the 14th of May, and arrived, with a good wind, at the Faroe Islands, where they stopped but twenty-four hours to supply themselves with fresh water.

Janvier points out that from time to time van Meteren's account of the voyage changes from third person to second person. The use of "we" may well mean that he was transcribing directly from Hudson's log, although we cannot be sure because that document is missing.

Janvier writes: For my own part,

> I believe that Hudson did precisely what he had wanted to do from the start. The prohibitory clause in his instructions, forbidding him to

go upon other than the course laid down for him, pointedly suggests that he had expressed the desire—natural enough, since he twice had searched vainly for a passage by Nova Zembla—to search westward instead of eastward for a water-way to the Indies.

As van Meteren states, authoritatively, he was encouraged to search in that direction by the information given him by Captain John Smith concerning a passage north of Virginia across the American continent—a notion that Smith probably derived in the first instance from Michael Lok's planisphere, which shows the continent reduced to a mere strip in about the latitude of the river that Hudson found; and that he very well might have conceived to be confirmed by stories about a great sea not far westward (the Great Lakes) which he heard from the Indians.

Either way, Janvier says, Hudson took advantage of the ice and the mutiny to fulfill his own goal of sailing westward.

He was equal to the emergency when the mutiny came, and so controlled it that—instead of going back, defeated of his purpose, to Holland—he deliberately took the risk of personal loss that attended breaking his contract and traversing his orders, and continued on new lines his exploring voyage.

It is indicative of Hudson's character that he met that cast of fate against him most resolutely; and most resolutely played up to it with a strong hand.

To this theory I would add the comments of other modern historians and experts on Hudson, who point out that regardless of the terms of the contract, the VOC officers were almost certain to have placed onboard the *Half Moon* a supercargo—a company representative to look after their financial interests. It is likely that Hudson received permission from the supercargo to seek another route without returning first to Amsterdam.

May 19, 1609. Close stormy weather with much wind and snow and very cold. . . . We found our height to be 70°30' and we had sight of Wardhouse.

According to Richard Hakluyt in *Principal Navigations, Voyages, Traffiques, and Discoveries of the English Nation,* Wardhouse was a castle standing on an island two miles off the mainland of Finland, the easternmost land subject to the king of Denmark at the time.

Three days later, May 22, the *Half Moon* was off Zenam or Senjen Island, 162 miles west southwest of the top of Norway. Perhaps just to emphasize their rough seas, Juet continues with his reports of violent storms: gusting weather with hail and snow.

> *May 26, 1609.* A great storm at the north northeast. . . . We steered away southwest before the wind with our fore-course abroad, for we were able to maintain no more sails. It blew so vehemently, and the sea went so high . . . that it would have dangered a small ship to lie under the sea. So we skudded seventy leagues [242 miles] in four and twenty hours.

The ship is near the Lofoten Islands, midway up the mainland of Norway. We next hear from Juet when the *Half Moon* reaches a somewhat safe haven at the Faeroe Islands north of the United Kingdom and considerably west of a straight route south to the ship's home port in Amsterdam.

> *May 30, 1609.* In the morning we turned into . . . Stromo, one of the Islands Faero. . . . As soon as we came in we went to rummage, and sent our boat for water and filled all our empty casks.
> *May 31, 1609.* In the forenoon our master, with most of his company, went on shore for a walk. . . . Then we set sail.
> *June 2, 1609.* At noon we steered away west southwest, to find Busse Island, discovered in the year 1578 by one of the ships of Sir Martin Frobisher, to see if it lay in her true latitude or no.

On June 3, the search for Busse Island continued but Juet reported they could not find it. That is probably because it did not exist; Busse was placed on nautical charts in 1578 during Frobisher's voyage on the *Emmanuel.* It was even claimed to have been explored and mapped in 1671 by another captain, Thomas Shepard.

Busse appears on some maps as late as the eighteenth century; some mapmakers supposed it to have sunken into the sea, like Atlantis. Busse may have been a fata morgana—a marine optical illusion.

June 11, 1609. This day we had change of water, of a whitish green, like . . . the ice water to the northwest. We found our [latitude] to be 51°24'.

June 15, 1609. We had a great storm and spent overboard our foremast.

The ship's position of 51°24' puts Hudson on a westerly course from Europe at roughly the same latitude as London and St. John's, Newfoundland, in Canada.

The *Half Moon* was sailing into the conveyor belt that carries icebergs from the east side of Greenland down to the bottom of that land mass and then up and into Baffin Bay—to the oncoming water of the Furious Overfall. There, the ocean current makes a U-turn to become the Baffin Island Current, which carries huge chunks of ice south along the continental slope of North America, the coast of Labrador and Newfoundland from Hudson Strait to the Grand Banks, and sometimes even farther south until they reach the warmer waters of the Gulf Stream.

Modern scientists estimate that about 40,000 medium to large icebergs calve off the glaciers of Greenland each year, and about 400 to 800 of them are taken by the current to the vicinity of St. John's, Newfoundland. It was one of these growlers that caused the sinking of the *Titanic* in April 1912 at about 41°46' North 50°14' West off Cape Race, Newfoundland. The stream of bergs usually continues into early summer, and occasionally a large piece of ice will make it much farther south; in 1926, a large iceberg was spotted just 150 nautical miles north of Bermuda.

For the next few weeks, the *Half Moon* battled the high seas and winds that are typical of the North Atlantic. Having lost the foremast and its sail, Hudson was forced to use the cumbersome and large main sail and jury-rig with other gear. On July 1, they were in sight of Newfoundland.

July 3, 1609. This morning we were among a great fleet of French-men . . . fishing on the bank but we spoke with none of them. At noon our latitude was 43°41'.

July 8, 1609. [The wind] fell calm and we caught 118 great cods. . . . After dinner we took 12 and saw many great schools of her-ring.

July 13, 1609. At six o'clock we had sight of the land and saw two sails on head of us. The land by the water's side is low land and white sandy banks rising full of little hills.

The *Half Moon* was at 43°25', off Cape Sable, Nova Scotia. The ship made several attempts at approaching land but ran into shoals, mist, and fog.

July 17, 1609. [Today] was all misty so that we could not get into the harbor. At 10 o'clock two boats came off to us, with six of the sav-ages of the country came out to us, seeming glad of our coming. We gave them trifles and they ate and drank with us and told us there were gold, silver, and copper mines hard by us and that the French-men do trade with them which is very likely for one of them spoke some words of French.

July 18, 1609. Fair weather, we went into a very good harbor. . . . The river runs up a great way. . . . We went on shore and cut us a foremast, then at noon we came aboard again and found our latitude to be 440°01'. . . . We mended our sails and fell to make our foremast.

On Hudson's previous two voyages, he had not reported sighting any "savages" nor contact with other Europeans. Here in mid-July, though, the *Half Moon* meets a fleet of French fishermen and natives who were already accustomed to trading with the outsiders.

Landfall was in George's Harbor at the mouth of the St. George River in Maine. The next day, still at anchor, they took the ship's boat ashore to look for fresh water and also found a shoal and harvested thirty-one lobsters. The surly Juet records a comment that seems out of place: "The people coming aboard showed us great friendship, but we could not trust them."

July 20, 1609. In the morning our scout went out to catch fresh fish . . . and returned in two hours bringing 27 great cod with two hooks and lines. In the afternoon we went for more lobsters and caught 40. Then we espied two French shallops full of the country people come into the harbor, but they offered us no wrong, seeing we stood upon our guard. They brought many beaver skins and other fine furs which they would have changed for red gowns. For the French trade with them for red cassocks, knives, hatchets, copper, kettles, trivets, beads, and other trifles.

Again, for reasons not explained, the entry for July 24 reports that "we kept a good watch for fear of being betrayed by the people, and noticed where they kept their shallops." The next day, though, Hudson and his men were the betrayers.

July 25, 1609. In the morning we manned our scout with four muskets and six men and took one of their shallops and brought it aboard. Then we manned our boat and scout with 12 men and muskets and two stone pieces or murderers and drove the savages from their houses and took the spoil of them as they would have done to us. Then we set sail and came down to the harbor's mouth and rode there all night.

A "murderer" was a small cannon carried aboard the *Half Moon*; useful only at short range, it was intended to clear the deck of intruders. Why did Hudson and his men steal a shallop (a small boat) and rob the natives? If there had been an incident or a provocation, there is no mention of it in the journal. The *Half Moon* sailed away from Maine, never to call there again.

August 3, 1609. Very hot weather. In the morning we had sight of land and steered in, thinking to go around to the northward of it. So we sent our shallop with five men to sound in by the shore and they found it deep . . . and they went on land and found goodly grapes and rose trees and brought them aboard.

The crew had landed near the tip of Cape Cod, which had been discovered by Captain Bartholomew Gosnold in 1602. Gosnold was also the first European to chart the offshore islands of Nantucket (given its name by Wampanoag Indians, long departed) and Martha's Vineyard (named by Gosnold for his daughter, who died in infancy, and his mother-in-law).

Today, the month of August on the cape and the islands is prime tourist season with hot temperatures and high humidity; at the time Hudson passed by, somewhere in the hold of the *Half Moon* were the clothing and other supplies loaded for the intended trip to frozen Novaya Zemlya and Siberia.

August 4, 1609. [Today] was very hot. . . . We heard the voice of men call. We sent our boat on shore thinking they had been some Christians left on the land, but we found them to be savages, which seemed very glad of our coming. So we brought one aboard with us and gave him meat and he did eat and drink with us. Our master gave him three or four glass buttons and sent him on land with our shallop again. And at our boats coming from the shore he leapt and danced and held up his hands and pointed us to a river on the other side for we had made signs that we came to fish there.

The people have green tobacco and pipes, the bowls of which are made of earth and pipes of red copper. The land is very sweet.

For the next several days, the ship proceeded carefully around the tip of Cape Cod, watching for the many shoals that build up there. On August 6, the *Half Moon* moved away from Cape Cod and passed to the south of Nantucket, well offshore of what is today the popular tourist beach at Surfside; Juet remarks on the numerous shoals on the south shore of the island, a condition that more than 400 years of captains in the area have come to know well.

In following days, the ship stayed offshore, sailing generally south down the coast of North America; at several points progress was hindered by storms and by what we now know to be the Gulf Stream, which moves northward up the coast.

On August 17, the ship approached Chesapeake Bay; it seems apparent that Hudson had charts and maps that showed where his friend Captain John Smith had established Jamestown in 1607 (and met Pocahontas). However, Hudson did not come in very closely to the settlement; that might have been because his vessel was Dutch and not English and could well have been regarded as an unfriendly visitor.

August 18, 1609. At four o'clock in the morning we weighed and stood into the shore to see the deeping or shoaling of it. . . . But toward noon the wind blew northerly with gusts of wind and rain. So we stood off into the sea again all night.

This is the entrance into the King's River in Virginia where our Englishmen are.

The ship went back out to sea and continued farther southeast along the coast. A storm arose on August 21 that drove the ship farther off course; a large wave broke on the foresail and split it, and the ship's cat "ran crying from one side of the ship to the other, looking overboard, which made us to wonder, but we saw nothing."

There is a long history of cat-related superstitions among sailors; they were said to be able to both summon up a storm and ward it off. And as a side benefit, they helped keep down the rat population that afflicted many vessels.

By August 24, the *Half Moon* was offshore of Cape Hatteras, North Carolina, and was able to resume its northerly course. Two days later the ship was off the bar of Virginia again; with unfavorable winds, the anchor was set and the *Half Moon* waited on the shoals.

On August 28, Hudson was alongside Delaware Bay, an area that had not been explored by Europeans. He sailed into the bay, hoping that ahead lay China, "but we found that the bay shoaled and we soon had 10 fathoms and the sight of dry sand between the channels. So we were forced to go back."

Juet goes on to offer some friendly advice to future mariners, part of the paper trail to justify the ship's movements: "He that will thoroughly explore this great bay must have a small pinnace that draws no more than four or five feet of water and must take soundings ahead of him. The northern land is full of shoals, and we were among them, for one time we struck."

Juet does not say that Hudson or his crew set foot on land there; a year later, the bay received its name from Samuel Argall, in honor of his financial backer, Lord De La Warre (Sir Thomas West), the governor of Virginia. De La Warre never visited Delaware Bay.

Back out to sea, the *Half Moon* proceeded north. On August 30, the ship was offshore of Hereford Inlet, New Jersey, and on September 2 it entered the outer reaches of the great New York harbor near Sandy Hook, New Jersey.

> *September 2, 1609.* We saw a great fire but could not see the land. . . . From the land which we had first sight of, until we came to a great lake of water, as we could judge it to be, being drowned land which made it to rise like islands.
> We had a great stream out of the bay.

Once again, Hudson was attracted by the great outflow of a waterway. This could be the strait that leads through the American continent to Asia.

Juet observes that "this is a very good land to fall with [make a landfall], and a pleasant land to see."

> *September 3, 1609.* At three o'clock in the afternoon we came to three great rivers. So we stood along to the northernmost, thinking to have gone into it, but we found it to have a very shoaled bar before it. . . . We cast about to the southward and found two fathoms, three fathoms, and three-and-a-quarter, till we came to the southern side . . . then we had five and six fathoms. . . . We saw many salmons, and mullets, and rays. The height is 40°30'.

CHAPTER 11

Up the Hudson River

Henry Hudson's charts called the waterway the Great River of the Mountains, which was pretty close to what Giovanni da Verrazano had named it in 1524: the Rio de Montagnes. The Iroquois called the river Cohatatea, while the Mohicans and Lenapes gave it the name Mahicanituk, meaning "Ever-Flowing Waters."

In 1611, Dutch settlers also called the river the Mauritius, in honor of Prince Maurice of Nassau, and the River of the Manhattees. For political reasons, it was also called the North River because it demarked the northernmost extent of Dutch claims in North America and to distinguish it from the South River, which the English called the Delaware River.

The river would not be called Hudson's River for another half-century, and over time the possessive dropped away to become the Hudson River. The lower river, below the tip of Manhattan and out to sea, is still referred to as the North River on today's maritime charts.

The Raritan River enters from the west, dumping into the bay between South Amboy and Perth Amboy, New Jersey. The Arthur Kill—actually a side channel of the Hudson that marks the western side of Staten Island and drains Newark Bay and the Hackensack River—also enters the harbor at Perth Amboy. The main channel of the Hudson exits into the Atlantic through the Narrows between Brooklyn and easternmost Staten Island; today, the gap is crossed by the majestic Verrazano Narrows Bridge.

Lower New York Bay presents a grand vista, as much as four-and-a-half miles wide at Gravesend Bay. If that name sounds familiar, remember that Hudson's first voyage began and ended near Gravesend on the Thames, and the second voyage also finished there. The New York name could have been derived from that same port on the Thames; Gravesend was the only one of the original six towns in Brooklyn that was a British settlement.

Another possibility, considered less likely, points to a Dutch name, s'Gravensande, which means "The Count's Beach" and could have been a nod to the early Dutch provincial governor William Kieft.

September 4, 1609. This day the people of the country came aboard of us, seeming very glad of our coming and brought green tobacco and gave us of it for knives and beads. They go in deer skins loose, well dressed. They have yellow copper. They desire clothes and are very civil. They have great store of maize or Indian wheat, whereof they make good bread. The country is full of great and tall oaks.

September 5, 1609. Our men went on land there and saw great store of men, women and children, who gave them tobacco at their coming on land. So they went up into the woods and saw great store of very goodly oaks and some currants.

This day many of the people came aboard, some in mantles of feathers and some in skins of diverse sort. Some women also came to us with hemp. They had red copper tobacco pipes and other things of copper which they did wear about their necks. At night they went on land again, so we rode very quiet, but durst not trust them.

The People Come to Meet Hudson

These interchanges apparently took place along the south side of Staten Island and nearby Monmouth County in today's New Jersey. The narrow river between two islands may have been Arthur Kill; the open sea was most likely the broad outer harbor of New York that lies on the other side of what is now called Verrazano Narrows.

This was the start of a series of ambiguous exchanges with the natives. At one moment the Native Americans seemed peaceable and interested in trade, and in the next entry Juet reports that the crew does not trust them. And then one of the crew is murdered, and the crew of the *Half Moon* kidnap several of the locals in retribution and for protection.

September 6, 1609. Our master sent John Colman, with four other men, in our boat over to the northern side to sound the other river being four leagues [fourteen miles] from us. They found . . . at the north . . . very good riding for ships and a narrow river to the westward between two islands.

The lands they told us were as pleasant with grass and flowers and goodly trees as ever they had seen and very sweet smells came from them. So they went in two leagues [seven miles] and saw an open sea and returned.

As they came back they were set upon by two canoes, the one having twelve, the other fourteen men. The night came on and it began to rain so that their match went out. They had one man slain in the fight, which was an Englishman named John Colman with an arrow shot into his throat, and two more hurt.

It grew so dark that they could not find the ship that night, but labored to and fro on their oars. They had so great a stream that their grapnel* would not hold them.

September 7, 1609. At 10 o'clock they returned aboard the ship and brought our dead man with them, whom we carried on land and buried and named the point after his name, Colman's Point. Then we hoisted in our boat and raised her side with waist-boards for defense of our men.

September 8, 1609. The people came aboard us and brought tobacco and Indian wheat to exchange for knives and beads and offered us no violence. So we fitting up our boat did mark them to see if they would make any show of the death of our man—which they did not.

Imagine the scene: the men had buried one of their own the day before, killed by a native's arrow, and on this day others came aboard to trade. Juet says they marked the visitors—watched them

---

* A grapnel is a small boat anchor.

very closely—to see if those who were on the ship showed any knowledge of the murder. What would they have done if somehow they had discerned a hint of guilt?

September 9, 1609. In the morning two great canoes came aboard full of men, the one with their bows and arrows, the other in show of buying of knives to betray us, but we perceived their intent.

We took two of them . . . and put red coats on them, and would not suffer the other to come near us. So they went on land and two other came aboard in a canoe; we took the one and let the other go. But he which we had taken got up and leapt overboard. Then we weighed and went off into the channel of the river and anchored there all night.

Uneasy with the intent of the natives, the crew of the *Half Moon* explored the outer reaches of the bay for the next few days to take soundings. The ship moved into the Narrows, near today's Coney Island and Gravesend in Brooklyn.

The ship began to move up the Hudson, anchoring the next night in the vicinity of today's Yonkers, and on September 14 the *Half Moon* moved thirty-six miles north. Sometime on that day they entered into the area of Tappan Zee, where the river suddenly opens up from about a mile wide to three miles across. The rocky palisades on the west side of the river and the lush green forest on the east side (later to be the home of Washington Irving's Sleepy Hollow) give the impression of a major strait. Today we know the water is salty at least sixty miles inland and tides extend all the way up to Troy.

At some point, a glimmer of hope must have crossed Hudson's mind; was this the entrance to a great crossing of the North American continent that would come out on the other side in China?

September 12, 1609. We turned into the river two leagues [seven miles] and anchored. This morning . . . there came eight and twenty canoes full of men, women and children to betray us but we saw their intent, and suffered none of them to come aboard.

September 14, 1609. The morning being very fair weather, the wind southeast, we sailed up the river 12 leagues [forty-one miles]. . . .

The river is a mile broad; there is very high land on both sides. . . .
The river is full of fish.

September 15, 1609. [With the wind from the south] we ran up into
the river 20 leagues [seventy miles], passing by high mountains. We
saw a great many salmon in the river. . . . This morning our two savages got out of a porthole and swam away. After we were under sail
they called to us in scorn. At night we came to other mountains which
lie from the river's side. There we found very loving people and very
old men.

As the *Half Moon* moved farther north, with the Catskill Mountains on the west and the distant Berkshires to the east, once again
the ship was met by natives willing to trade. It is possible that some
of these nomadic tribes had met with French traders who had come
down from Canada, or knew from others of the presence of unusual
visitors in the region.

Sometime on September 14 or 15 the dream of a wide or widen-
ing passage through the continent must have been shaken if not
ended. The river begins to bend a bit to the northwest after the Tappan Zee and then back to the northeast in the shadow of Bear
Mountain; its width drops sharply from three miles to less than a
mile and then in the valley below today's U.S. Military Academy at
West Point it makes almost a horseshoe bend and becomes more
shallow.

September 16, 1609. In the morning our boat went again to fishing
but could catch only a few by reason their canoes had been there all
night. This morning the people came aboard and brought us ears of
Indian corn, pumpkins, and tobacco, which we bought for trifles.

September 17, 1609. As soon as the sun was up, we set sail and
ran up six leagues [twenty-one miles] higher and found shoals in the
middle of the channel and small islands but seven fathoms of water
on both sides. Toward night we borrowed so near the shore that we
grounded, so we laid out our small anchor and heaved off again.
Then we borrowed on the bank in the channel and came aground
again. While the flood [tide] ran we heaved off again and anchored
all night.

On September 18, 1609, Hudson went ashore at the invitation of a local chief for a feast. Based on Hudson's calculation of his latitude, the *Half Moon* was near the town of Catskill, about forty miles south of today's Albany, New York. Some historians have added up the stated miles in the journals and think he may have been as much as thirty miles farther north, near present-day Castleton.

A fragment of Hudson's own journal exists for this part of the voyage:

In latitude 42°18' I sailed to the shore in one of their canoes, with an old man, who was the chief of a tribe consisting of 40 men and 17 women; these I saw there in a house well constructed of oak bark, and circular in shape.

There lay near the house for the purpose of drying, enough to load three ships, besides what was growing in the fields. On our coming into the house, two mats were spread out to sit upon, and immediately some food was served in well made red wooden bowls; two men were also despatched at once with bows and arrows in quest of game, who soon after brought in a pair of pigeons which they had shot. They likewise killed a fat dog, and skinned it in great haste with shells which they had got out of the water.

They supposed that I would remain with them for the night, but I returned after a short time on board the ship. The land is the finest for cultivation that I ever in my life set foot upon, and it also abounds in trees of every description.

The natives are a very good people, for when they saw that I would not remain, they supposed that I was afraid of their bows, and taking the arrows, they broke them in pieces, and threw them into the fire.

Reaching the Navigable End of the River

On September 19, the *Half Moon* proceeded another six miles farther up the river where the crew found shoals. Somewhere in the vicinity of today's Albany, most likely just south of the city but possibly a bit farther up the river toward Troy, Hudson stopped the northward passage of his ship. Over the course of the next three days, he sent the ship's small boat up the river to take soundings.

The descriptions seem to fit the area around Peebles and Green islands between Troy and Waterford, an area that is considered the end of the natural navigable channel of the Hudson River. At Waterford today, small vessels can head west into the Erie Barge Canal; at Troy, ships can go through Federal Lock to enter the Champlain Canal, which continues north to the lake.

Peebles Island, at the place where the Mohawk meets the Hudson River, was at one time the site of a Mohican village. During the Revolutionary War, a small fort was erected there. In the 1930s, Sanford Cluett built a shirtmaking factory there and developed the "Sanforized" technique to reduce shrinkage of cotton material; fabric was prestretched so that it would shrink to its proper size when first washed. His company, Cluett Peabody & Co., became famous for Arrow brand shirts.

September 20, 1609. Our master's mate with four men went up with our boat to sound the river, and found two leagues [seven miles] above us but two fathoms water and the channel very narrow

September 21, 1609. We determined yet once more to go farther up into the river to try what depth and breadth it did bear, but much people resorted aboard so we went not this day. Our carpenter went ashore and made a fore-yard.

And our master and his mate determined to try some of the chief men of the country whether they had any treachery in them. So they took them down into the cabin and gave them much wine and Aqua Vitae that they were all merry.

One of the men had his wife with him which sat so modestly as any of our country women would do in a strange place. In the end, one of them was drunk . . . and that was strange to them for they could not tell how to take it. The canoes and folk went all on shore but some of them came again and brought strips of beads (some had six, seven, eight, nine, and ten) and gave him. So he slept all night quietly.

September 22, 1609. In the morning our master's mate and four more of the company went up with our boat to sound the river higher up. The people of the country came not aboard till noon, but when they came and saw the savages well they were glad. So at three o'clock in the afternoon they came aboard and brought tobacco and more beads and gave them to our master and made an oration and showed him the country all around.

Then they sent one of their company on land, who presently returned and brought a great platter full of venison, dressed by themselves, and they caused him to eat with them. They made him reverence and departed all save the old man that lay aboard.

This night, at 10 o'clock, our boat returned in a shower of rain and found it to be at an end for shipping to go in. For they had been up eight or nine leagues [twenty-eight to thirty-one miles] and found but seven foot water and unconstant soundings.

And thus ended the *Half Moon*'s voyage up the Hudson River. One of the mysteries of the trip: if the ship's boat had indeed gone as far north as Juet reported, the crewmen should have reached Cohoes, where the Mohawk River tumbles over a 65-foot-high cliff; the waterfall is 1,300 feet wide and would seem hard to miss. However, the area is also prone to fog, and the waterfall is set back nearly half a mile from the Hudson River and hidden by rapids.

At noon on September 23, Hudson turned the *Half Moon* around and began heading south back toward the mouth of the river . . . and toward the natives who had been less than hospitable when he first arrived.

September 23, 1609. We went down two leagues [seven miles] to a shoal that had two channels, one on the one side and another on the other, and had little wind whereby the tide layed us upon it. So there we sat on ground the space of an hour till the flood came. Then we had a little gale of wind at the west. So we got our ship into deep water and rode all night very well.

September 26, 1609. In the morning our carpenter went on land with our master's mate and four more of our company to cut wood. This morning two canoes came up river from the place where we first found loving people, and in one [of] them was the old man who had [been] lying aboard of us. . . . He brought another old man with him which brought strips of beads and gave them to our master and showed him all the country there about as though it were at his command.

So he made the two old men dine with him, and the old man's wife; for they brought two old women and two young maidens of the age of sixteen or seventeen years with them who behaved very modestly. . . . At one o'clock they departed down river, making signs that we should come down to them for we were within two leagues of where they dwelt.

September 27, 1609. We set our fore topsail [but] our ship would not flat* . . . and ran on the . . . bank at half ebb. We laid out anchor to heave her off, but could not. So we sat from half ebb to half flood, then we set our foresail and main topsail and got down six leagues [twenty-one miles].

The old man came aboard and would have had us anchor and go on land to eat with him, but the wind being fair we would not yield to his request. So he left us, being very sorrowful for our departure.

At five o'clock in the afternoon the wind came to the south southwest. . . . We anchored. Then our boat went on shore to fish right against the ship. . . . They took four or five and twenty mullets, breams, basses and barbils.†

Each day, as the ship moved south in the Hudson River Valley, natives came aboard or alongside to trade corn, other food, and skins for trinkets and knives. On September 30, the *Half Moon* anchored near the present location of Peekskill, which Juet called "a very pleasant place to build a town on. The road [the channel] is very near, and very good for all winds save an east northeast wind. The mountains look as if some metal or mineral were in them. For the trees that grow on them were all blasted, and some of them barren with few or no trees on them."

October 1, 1609. In the morning we weighed at seven o'clock with the ebb, and got down below the mountains, which was seven leagues [twenty-four miles]. . . . The people of the mountains came

*Take its heading.
†Catfish.

aboard us, wondering at our ship and weapons. We bought some small skins of them for trifles.

This afternoon one canoe kept hanging under our stern with one man in it, which we could keep from . . . [and he] got up by our rudder to the cabin window and stole out my pillow, and two shirts, and two bandoliers. Our master's mate shot at him and struck him on the breast and killed him. Whereupon all the rest fled away. We manned our boat and got our things again. Then one of them that swam got hold of our boat thinking to overthrow it. But our cook took a sword and cut off one of his hands and he was drowned.

October 2, 1609. At break of day we weighed, the wind being at northwest, and got down seven leagues. Then the flood was come strong, so we anchored.

Then came one of the savages that swam away from us at our going up the river with many other, thinking to betray us. But we perceived their intent, and suffered none of them to enter our ship. Whereupon two canoes full of men, with their bows and arrows shot at us after our stern. In recompense whereof we discharged six muskets and killed two or three of them. Then above a hundred of them came to a point of land to shoot at us.

There I shot a Falcon* at them and killed two of them whereupon the rest fled into the woods. Yet they manned off another canoe with nine or ten men which came to meet us. So I shot at it also a Falcon and shot it through, and killed one of them. Then our men with their muskets killed three or four more.

So they went their way, within a while after, we got down two leagues [seven miles] beyond that place, and anchored in a bay clear of all danger of them on the other side of the river.

We saw a very good piece of ground and hard by it there was a cliff that looked of the color of a white-green, as though it were either copper or silver mine, and I think it to be one of them by the trees that grow upon it. For they be all burned and the other places are green as grass. It is on that side of the river that is called Mannahata.

We saw no people to trouble us.

*A light cannon.

The *Half Moon* was now back at Manhattan Island at anchor and on watch against attack. On October 3, they were hit by a storm and the ship ran aground on mud. The next day, under fair weather, the ship finally came out of the river and into the great mouth of the bay. By midday, they brought in the ship's boat and set the mainsail, spritsail, and topsails for the voyage out into the ocean.

October 5, 1609. We continued our course toward England, without seeing any land by the way, all the rest of this month of October. And on the seventh day of November, being Saturday, by the grace of God we safely arrived in the range of Dartmouth, in Devonshire.

What's wrong with this picture? The *Half Moon* was a Dutch ship, under Dutch financing, and Henry Hudson—though a British citizen—was under contract to the VOC to return the vessel to Amsterdam. (And there was the not inconsequential issue that the contract for the voyage had been so very specific about the plan: go to Novaya Zemlya in search of the Northeast Passage and go nowhere else.)

CHAPTER 12

From a Tear of the Clouds to a Flooded Grand Canyon

The Hudson River begins as a cold trickle of snowmelt on the southwest flank of Mount Marcy, the highest mountain in New York state. It ends at the mouth of the great harbor of New York City. But what we see with our eyes today is just a small piece of the picture.

In the history books, it is written that Henry Hudson sailed the entire navigable length of the river that would one day bear his name, about 150 miles from Manhattan to just short of Albany. And that much seems true.

But the full length of the river is closer to 315 miles that we can see, and at least 440 miles when you trace its ancient original path, which runs south and southeast from the high peaks of the Adirondacks near Canada to a drowned landscape a few hundred miles from Bermuda in the Atlantic Ocean.

New York's harbor, one of the greatest deepwater ports in the world and one of the reasons why the United States grew to become a global military and financial superpower, was carved by the freezing, melting, retreating, and advancing of huge glaciers that once covered much of the northern part of North America.

Over a period of hundreds of thousands of years, at least four waves of glaciers flowed south from Arctic and subarctic Canada—the same place where Henry Hudson would die in search of the

Northwest Passage—and then retreated. The frozen river of ice acted like a giant bulldozer, digging a deep trench to the sea and carving and rounding off the high peaks of the Adirondacks and the lesser mountains of the Catskills and filling in valleys.

Thinking in Glacial Time

The earth's great ice age began a million or so years ago; the last major ice sheet in North America spread its furthest about 20,000 years ago and finally retreated up into the Arctic just 6,000 years ago.

A glacier is almost always in motion one direction or another; its description as a frozen river is a helpful image. Glaciers are mostly built in huge snowfields at high elevations; aided by seasonal warming or fluctuations in temperature over longer periods of time, the effects of gravity work to compact and move downhill the rivers of snow. As the glacier advances, it picks up soil, rock, and huge boulders broken off mountains and bedrock in the valleys it creates.

The Hudson River Valley, upstate New York, and most of New England was sculpted by the movement of the glaciers. Walk through New York with a geologist and you'll be pointed to evidence of the ice age at almost every turn: piles of mixed clay, sand, and gravel are *till* left behind as a moraine on the surface. Depending on the topography, narrow, twisting ridges called eskers may have been formed. And dotted through upstate New York and into Canada are small rounded hills like upturned breasts of long-vanished giants; they're called drumlins.

Environmentalists of today can express all the concern they want about the effects of global warming; I don't disagree with their concerns at all. But it's all but impossible to speak with a geologist or climatologist about the concept of significant and permanent change that occurs over the period of a few years, a few decades, or even a few hundred years. Their calendar is measured in the tens and hundreds of millions of years.

They conjecture about global conditions in the early Proterozoic Age of 2.5 billion years ago. And they really warm to the Cryogenian period of 600 to 800 million years ago, when sea ice may have covered the ocean from the poles to the equator.

And then the most recent ice age began about 40 million years ago with cycles of glacial advances and retreats on time scales in the range of 40,000 to 100,000 years. We emerged from that period about 6,000 years ago; some say 10,000 years, but what's a few millennia among experts?

The Drowned River

And so back to the view of the Hudson River as we see it today: the river from its source once extended another 150 miles to the Atlantic Ocean.

When the ice age was at its peak, the water level of most of the world's oceans was much lower. Manhattan, a few miles inland from the point where Hudson (and Grovanni da Verrazano before him) found the river, was at one time about 150 miles inland.

The advancing glacier carved out a deep trench in the rocky surface, an East Coast equivalent of the Grand Canyon. Naval cartographers have mapped the Hudson River Gorge way out into the Atlantic. As far out as 125 miles southeast from New York City, the ancient river bed lies in a canyon that is 7 miles wide and 4,000 feet below the surrounding ocean bottom.

When the glaciers retreated and melted, the water went into the oceans and raised the sea level; Manhattan became prime property near the ocean with a magnificent port.

Heading up the River

Today, the Hudson River is part outflowing river and part tidal estuary all the way up from New York City to Troy, just above Albany; because the river becomes markedly shallow and narrow above that point, Troy has the highest tides on the Hudson, an average rise of 4.7 feet.

From Troy 145 miles south to the mouth of the river at Manhattan, the total drop is just five feet. A number of tributaries enter the river from both east and west sides; the most significant below the Mohawk River is the Walkill, which merges with the Hudson at Kingston.

For much of the year, salt water from the Atlantic flows upriver with the tide as far as Newburgh and sometimes beyond; in the spring when there is heavy runoff from melting snow in the mountains, the freshwater-saltwater line is pushed closer to Manhattan and is usually located near Tappan Zee.

Every time I pass through or over Tappan Zee, I try to imagine Hudson's dreams. He had sailed into a great bay in hopes that it was a strait through the great American continent that would lead to Asia. This location is one of the widest places on the river, more than three miles across and still salty.

The Great Cataract

At one time, Cohoes Falls was considered one of the great sights of the United States. Though not nearly as dramatic as Niagara Falls near Buffalo, the Cohoes Falls were at first more easily accessible to visitors from New York and Europe: straight up the Hudson River to its top at the Great Cataract of the Mohawk.

The falls are a broad table of rock; at peak periods in the spring and early summer the Mohawk River is swollen by snow melt, and as much as 32,000 cubic feet of water tumbles each second over a 75-foot drop. (By comparison, before about half the flow is diverted to hydroelectric plants, an average of 200,000 cubic feet per second heads toward the American Falls and the Canadian Horseshoe Falls at Niagara. The drop there is about 176 feet from the top of the rock to the river level, although the water at the American Falls crashes into a jumble of broken rock just 70 feet down.)

Early European visitors to Cohoes described the great beauty of the broad falls. Today, however, you have to use your imagination to factor out the spectacularly ugly iron railroad track that blocks the direct frontal view of the cataract and the century-old mills that still stand alongside. A portion of the flow of the river itself is taken above the falls for the city of Cohoes water supply, some of the water is diverted into the Erie Barge Canal to help maintain its level, and still more water is diverted for small hydroelectric and water power plants.

In 1804, the Irish poet Thomas Moore visited the area and sent a report to his mother in Ireland: "I was to see the Coho Falls . . . and was truly gratified. The immense fall of the river over a natural dam of thirty or forty feet high, its roar among the rocks and the illuminated mist of spray which rises from its foam were to me objects all new, beautiful and impressive."

Moore's poem, "Lines, Written at the Cohoes Falls of the Mohawk River," begins:

> *From the rise of morn till set of sun*
> *I have seen the mighty Mohawk run,*
> *Oh! I have thought, and thinking sighed*
> *How like to thee, thou restless tide!*
> *But urgent as the doom calls*
> *Thy water to its destined falls,*
> *And the last current cease to run!*
> *Oh may my falls be as bright as thine!*

In 1831, however, a group of American engineers and investors received a state charter permitting them to put a private dam across the Mohawk and build canals to supply water power to mills. The first wooden dam lasted only a few months, washed away by an ice floe. In 1839, a more substantial structure of timber, stone, and concrete and about 1,500 feet wide was installed. At least ten diversion canals were also dug. By the late nineteenth century, there were various tourist attractions at the falls as well, including an inn and an open trolley car that crossed directly over the top of the falls.

The village of Green Island still derives much of its power from a hydroelectric plant at Cohoes Falls; residents pay some of the lowest electric bills in New York. In 2006, local officials were battling with state authorities for the right to put in a new, larger plant; its chief competitor was a private Canadian company. The existing 38.8 megawatt plant has not changed greatly in nearly a century.

A group called Friends of the Falls was organized in hopes of returning the Cohoes cataract to near its original state by using less of its water for hydroelectric production. In late 2005 Chief Jake Swamp, a former head of a tribe in the Mohawk Nation in the Six Nations Iroquois Confederation, met with the group to share some of the oral history of the falls.

According to Swamp, Hiawatha—a local native made famous by the writings of Henry Wadsworth Longfellow—had visited the area as a young man and was challenged to climb out onto a leaning tree overhanging the falls as a test of his strength and ability to bring peace to the local tribes.

The word *Cohoes* is believed to be derived from the Iroquois *Cahhoos*, meaning "a canoe falling," or the Mohawk *Ga-ha-oose*, meaning "ship-wrecked canoe."

Either way, the name seems attached to an event that occurred not long after Hudson and the *Half Moon* were nearby. In 1655, the Dutch explorer Adriaen Van der Donck wrote the book *Description of New Netherlands* and reported:

> In the area of the great falls of the Macques Kill [Mohawk River] which the Indians name the Cahoos Falls . . . an occurrence of this kind took place here in our time. An Indian whom I have known accompanied by his wife and child with sixty beaver skins descended the river in his canoe in the spring when the water runs rapid and the current is strongest. . . . This Indian carelessly approached too near the Falls before he discovered the danger, and notwithstanding his utmost exertions to gain the land, his frail bark with all on board was swept over by the rapid current and down the Falls; his wife and child were killed, his bark shattered to pieces, his cargo of furs damaged. But his life was preserved.

Monsters and Giants

Another claim to fame for the area is one of the oldest artifacts of the state of New York. In September 1836, workmen digging an excavation for Mill No. 3 of the Harmony Mills, on Mohawk Street in Cohoes above the falls, unearthed the well-preserved bones of a mastodon; the creature was found buried beneath sixty feet of peat, twigs, and loam, probably deposited in the area by the Mohawk River.

Mastodon americanus thrived in the Pleistocene or ice age, roaming over much of the planet for a million years. Their sudden disappearance may have been related to climatic change: the same great ice age that covered much of New York state to a depth of two miles and created the Hudson River.

The Cohoes mastodon, a male, was estimated to have weighed between five and six tons and been nearly nine feet tall; his tusks were four-and-a-half-feet long.

The bones were at first kept at Harmony Mills; in later years, they were exhibited in Troy and at a county fair before they were finally given to the state. A restoration of the mastodon and the original bones are on display in the lobby of the New York State Museum in Albany; a replica is shown at the Cohoes Public Library, between a pair of Tiffany windows.

Modern scientists have confirmed the creature's species, but at the time there were some claims that the bones were a hoax. It was a time when small fortunes were being made on the basis of bogus curiosities. One of the most famous was the Cardiff Giant, a ten-foot-tall stone man "discovered" in 1869 in Cardiff, New York, about 100 miles west of Albany near Syracuse.

The giant was said to have been found by workers digging a well. The owner of the property began charging visitors fifty cents, and thousands made the journey before he sold it for $37,500 to a group of businessmen, who moved it to Syracuse and placed it on display. There, scientists declared it an obvious fake, but that did not deter the showman P. T. Barnum, who offered to pay $60,000 to lease the giant for a few months to show it at his museum in New York. When he could not reach an agreement, Barnum had a replica made and put that on display to great success.

It was eventually discovered that the Cardiff Giant was the invention of the tobacconist George Hull, who commissioned the creation of the statue after an argument with a Methodist minister who said the words of the Bible were meant to be taken literally, including the statement that the earth at one time was home to giants.

The phony Cardiff Giant is today at the Farmer's Museum in Cooperstown, New York; Barnum's replica of the fake is in the collection of a private museum in Farmington Hills, Michigan.

The Adirondack Empire

When many people envision the state of New York, they think of the concrete canyons and the asphalt streams of Manhattan, its most famous and powerful city. But the green heart of the Empire State is the Adirondack Park. Nearly half of the 6 million acres of land in the park is owned in perpetuity by the people of New York and the remainder is private but closely controlled.

The park is the largest publicly protected area in the contiguous United States, greater in size than Yellowstone, Yosemite, Everglades, and Grand Canyon National Parks combined. The district is about the size of Vermont, larger than New Hampshire, New Jersey, Massachusetts, or Connecticut and dwarfing the relatively tiny states of Hawaii, Delaware, and Rhode Island.

The extraordinary ecological treasure was created by the state legislature in 1885 largely because of the efforts of wilderness explorer and writer Verplanck Colvin, who was one of the first to survey the Adirondacks. He had been hired in 1872 by lawmakers to find out what they had up there in the dense forest and steep hills.

Colvin made use of his annual reports to the legislature in Albany to warn against unregulated and unchecked logging and mining. "Unless the region be preserved essentially in its present wilderness condition, the ruthless burning and destruction of the forest will slowly, year after year, creep onward," he reported. "Vast areas of naked rock, arid sand and gravel will alone remain to receive the bounty of the clouds, unable to retain it."

And in one of his surveys, Colvin put poetry to his description of a tiny puddle on the flank of Mount Marcy. "Far above the chilly waters of Lake Avalanche, at an elevation of 4,293 feet . . . is a minute, unpretending tear of the clouds—as it were—a lonely pool shivering in the breezes of the mountains, and sending its limpid surplus through Feldspar Brook to the Opalescent River, the well-spring of the Hudson."

Lake Tear of the Clouds is unofficially the source of the Hudson, although other nearby ponds and rivulets contribute.

Even in the heart of the Gilded Age, when many of the nation's great fortunes were made in harvesting the developing nation's seemingly endless supplies of timber, ore, and other natural resources, New York state set aside commerce in favor of environment. The Adirondack Park is not pristine—there are some roads, a few mines and logging camps, and some scattered resort towns. But you can hike or drive for miles and not see another person.

Colvin was very much an environmentalist, although that term had not been invented yet. He was unusually adept at creating alliances among naturalists and business interests in the developing financial and trading capital of New York City as well as places like Albany and Buffalo that were benefiting from the use of the Hudson River and the Erie Canal as a highway into the heartland.

His main warning was that heavy logging and development of the Adirondacks would reduce the snowpack that supplied the water for the rivers that fed the canal, and this environmental argument was embraced as an economic necessity by important business interests.

In 1894, Colvin helped beat back attempts to weaken the laws that created the park. New York's constitution was amended to include the following provision: "The lands of the state, now owned or hereafter acquired, constituting the forest preserve as now fixed by law, shall be forever kept as wild forest lands. They shall not be leased, sold or exchanged, or be taken by any corporation, public or private, nor shall the timber thereon be sold, removed or destroyed."

The words still stand in the New York State Constitution and still protect the park.

Whirligigs and the Making of a President

I traveled into the park from its southwestern border on a late summer afternoon, a day when a hint of the coming winter was in the air. Just short of the town of Otter Lake, we crossed over the Moose River, one of two waterways of that name I passed in search of Hudson's bones.

New York's Moose River is a very different place from the muddy and forlorn Moose River that separates Moosonee from Moose Factory Island in James Bay, but it trumpeted its own warnings of the presence of humankind.

Old Forge is one of the old resort towns grandfathered into place within the Adirondack Park, a short but jarring stretch of ticky-tacky motels, gift shops, and pancake houses in a clearing of the tunnels of pine trees that leads into the park. A place called "A Touch of Ritz" had its front yard filled with spinning plastic whirligigs, on sale at end-of-season closeout prices. Old Forge is the opposite of Colvin's dreams, but the fact that it is a contained blight in a huge park is comforting.

Another of the first champions of the park was young Theodore Roosevelt. Born in New York City to a situation of wealth, Roosevelt spent his early years as an ardent "naturalist" conducting explorations of the little-known woods and forests of northern New York near the Canadian border. Among his first published writings, produced at age sixteen, was "The Summer Birds of the Adirondacks in Franklin County, N.Y."

At Harvard, he turned his goals to politics and was elected in 1882 at age twenty-four as a state representative. After posts in New York City as president of the Police Board, and in Washington as assistant secretary of the navy, he returned to Albany as governor from 1898 to 1900. In 1901, he was elected vice president under William McKinley.

On September 7 of that year, McKinley was shot by an anarchist in Buffalo. Roosevelt, who was on a fishing and hunting trip on Lake Champlain, came to the city and stayed a few days by the president's side. When McKinley seemed to be recovering, Roosevelt left to join

179

a family vacation at the rustic Tahawus Club in the heart of the Adirondack Park.

A week later, McKinley took a turn for the worse, and a special train was dispatched to the end of the line in North Creek. A messenger was sent by wagon to the Tahawus Club, but found that Vice President Roosevelt was hiking on Mount Marcy; a second messenger went to find him on the trail.

On the night of Friday, September 13, 1901, Roosevelt left the club on a thirty-five-mile buckboard wagon trip to the hamlet of Tahawus and on to North Creek; it took more than six hours to complete the journey over rough roads made slippery and muddy by rain.

Driving along Route 28, along a particularly dark and empty stretch of road, I came across a marker erected in 1908: at this lonely spot, at 2:15 A.M., September 14, 1901, Theodore Roosevelt became president after McKinley's death in Buffalo. Roosevelt would not know it, though, until three hours later when he finally met up with the train at North Creek. He would be sworn in the next day after paying his respects to McKinley's family in Buffalo.

The Accidental Land Baron and the Trial of the Century

John Brown made his fortune in Providence, Rhode Island, before, during, and after the American Revolution as an early pioneer in the China trade, and, like many other businessmen in coastal New England, as a slave trader. The son of Captain James Brown, he was one of the "four brothers" who were among the wealthiest merchants of early Providence and the founders and patrons of Brown University.

In 1798, Brown sent one of his sons-in-law, John Francis, to New York City to sell a valuable shipload from the Orient. Francis received $200,000 for the shipment, a substantial amount of money at the time. But somehow he returned to Providence not with the money but with a mortgage—actually, a second mortgage—on 210,000 acres of untouched and all-but-unknown land in the Adirondacks.

Almost predictably, the holder of the first mortgage defaulted and the land (about one-third the size of the entire state of Rhode Island) came into Brown's hands. He hired surveyors and laid out a tract with eight townships with temperate and hopeful names: Industry, Enterprise, Perseverance, Unanimity, Frugality, Sobriety, Regularity, and Economy.

Brown paid for the construction of a twenty-five-mile-long wagon road carved out of the forest following an old Native American trail and subsidized a few dozen farmers to move to the area around Economy; a dam and grist mill built at the bottom end of a pond in there would later become the settlement of Old Forge. The farms quickly failed due to the extreme winters and remoteness of the area; shortly after Brown's death in 1803, the experiment ended.

Another son-in-law, Charles Frederick Herreshoff, decided to try to make a business on the huge tract of land; according to a family biography, Herreshoff and his wife, the former Sarah Brown, could not sustain themselves in the manner to which they had hoped to be accustomed to in Providence on their share of Brown's estate.

In 1811, Herreshoff brought 300 Merino sheep to upstate New York. He built a home near Thendara, just west of today's Old Forge. He also opened an iron mine and built a forge.

The mine was not profitable and wolves enjoyed the sheep. In 1819, Herreshoff failed at a suicide attempt that would have buried him alive in the mine; he did succeed in a second attempt, killing himself with a gun. By 1825, the mine, the gristmill, and the forge were closed and the property was mostly abandoned.

Today, there's still a stub of the former wagon trail, Brown's Tract Road, branching off of Route 28 near Thendara and heading toward the Moose River Settlement.

The next time the area came into the news was in 1906, when Chester Gillette drowned Grace Brown in Big Moose Lake. The "trial of the century," at least the one that occurred six years into the twentieth century, was an international sensation.

The facts of the case were laid out in a month-long trial; the transcript and Gillette's appeal of his conviction read like a script from *Law and Order.*

Gillette met Brown in 1905 when they both worked at a skirt factory in Cortland, New York. They were of uneven social status:

Gillette was a prep school graduate and the factory was owned by his uncle. Brown was a farmer's daughter. They kept their relationship secret from coworkers and most of their friends and family.

In 1906, Brown became pregnant; testimony from some of her acquaintances said she was extremely upset at her situation and by various accounts she held suicidal thoughts, feared for her own life, or expected Gillette to marry her. In any case, she and Gillette headed off on a trip to the Adirondacks—into John Brown's Tract—and checked into the Glenmore Hotel in Big Moose.

The hotel owner rented them a rowboat and they headed out into the lake; neither returned. Brown's body was found the next day, and Gillette was arrested in the hamlet of Inlet ten miles away. The prosecution argued that Gillette had tried to rid himself of his unfortunate problem by hitting Brown on the head with a tennis racket.

Gillette took the stand in his own defense, and at first claimed that she had slipped and struck her head (leaving a tennis racket–shaped cut); later, he changed his story to say that Brown had committed suicide.

The courthouse in the town of Herkimer was packed with reporters dispatching daily stories based on the testimony, which included Brown's love letters. A *New York Times* reporter wrote, "Pathetic letters written by Grace Brown to Chester Gillette in the month before her tragic death, when she was waiting at her home for him to come and marry her, were the feature of to-day in the trial of Gillette for the murder of the girl. The people in the packed courtroom and the prisoner wept when they were read."

A November 27, 1906, article was headlined:

DOCTORS SAY BLOWS KILLED GRACE BROWN;
Testify That She Did Not Drown, As Gillette Asserted
SKULL AND FACE BEATEN
Tennis Racquet Could Have Caused Injuries Which Were
Inflicted Before the Body Entered Waters

Gillette was found guilty in what is considered one of the first American murder convictions based entirely on forensic and circumstantial evidence. On March 30, 1908, he was executed in the electric chair at the state prison in Auburn; a final *Times* article says a clergyman who attended him in his last moments implied that he heard a confession of the murder.

The sordid tale, only slightly disguised, was the subject of Theodore Dreiser's 1925 novel *An American Tragedy*. The book, with sex outside of marriage, a murder, and an execution, was banned in Boston in 1927. It was made into a movie under the book's title in 1931, a version Dreiser disapproved of; a remake more to his liking, *A Place in the Sun*, was produced in 1951 starring Montgomery Clift and Elizabeth Taylor.

Echoes of Another Northern Mining Town

Past Old Forge and Raquette Lake is the hamlet of Blue Mountain Lake, nearly at the geographic center of the Adirondack Park. In 1881, Frederic Durant built one of the largest and most extravagant mountain hotels in the East at Prospect Point along Blue Mountain Lake.

Durant was a nephew of the railroad tycoon Thomas C. Durant, who made his fortune with the construction (and the creative financing) of the Union Pacific Railroad; the Union Pacific was the westward line that competed to lay the most tracks until it met up with the eastward Central Pacific Railroad in 1869.

The younger Durant's Prospect House was the first hotel in the world with an electric light in every room; the design for the wiring and generating plant was personally overseen by Thomas A. Edison. The six-story hotel had 300 rooms, a bowling alley, a shooting gallery, a telegraph office, and its own orchestra.

Guests traveled by rail as far as the tracks could take them and then transferred to stagecoach and finally to a boat to get to Prospect Point. Among those who roughed it in great luxury were some of the nation's wealthiest families, including the Astors, Mellons, Roosevelts, Vanderbilts, and Whitneys. Colvin and his surveying crew also stayed at the hotel when they sought a break from the wilderness.

Heading north to the base of Long Lake and then east, I came to the town of Newcomb, population about 544, and about 265 miles due north of lower Manhattan in New York City. A small bridge carries Route 28N over a crystal-clear, fast-running stream about a foot deep over a rocky bottom. A sign read: HUDSON RIVER.

Looking upstream, I saw the high peaks of the Adirondacks that so inspired Colvin, Roosevelt, and all the others who have made it this far into the park. To the east of the meandering stream is the 5,344-foot-high Mount Marcy; to its right is Skylight Mountain and at left Redfield Mountain, each just a few hundred feet shorter than Marcy.

Native Americans from one of the tribes of the Iroquois Confederation called the highest peak Tahawus, meaning "He who splits the sky." Marcy forms the north-south divide between the Hudson and St. Lawrence watersheds.

In the shadow of Marcy, at the end of a long and lonely rough road through pine canyons alongside the bubbling stream called the Opalescent River and abandoned railroad tracks and bridges, is the ghost town of Tahawus. The settlement, originally called McIntyre after one of the early miners, was begun in about 1826, when iron ore was discovered along the banks of the upper Hudson River— more of a stream here—at the base of the hills.

By 1838, McIntyre included a blast furnace and forge, saw mills, and a number of dams on the Hudson and other nearby streams to provide power for the mills. Ore was hauled by wagon and later by railroad from the remote Upper Works at McIntyre and additional facilities at Newcomb called the Lower Works. In 1845, David Henderson—another of the original miners—was killed in an accident when he was searching for new locations for power dams on a stream closer to the peaks; since then, that rivulet has been known as Calamity Brook.

In 1856, a spring flood destroyed all the dams on the upper Hudson. At the same time, an unknown impurity found in the ore lessened its value and made it difficult to raise new investment to reconstruct the dams. The Upper Works closed in 1857.

In the 1870s, the naturalist movement led to a different sort of development. The Preston Ponds Club was built just outside of the mine site; it later became the Adirondack Club and eventually the Tahawus Club.

The long-abandoned mine was reopened during World War II, when it was realized that the impurity in the iron ore was titanium, a strong and lightweight metal that was used in making aircraft components. In another form, titanium dioxide, the element is used in the manufacture of white paint.

The mine was purchased by the National Lead Company in 1941; in 1963, the company moved the entire population of Tahawus out of the mining area and down to Newcomb. Operations continued until 1989, and the final train of ore departed the area two years later.

I drove to the end of the road, marked by a padlocked gate. Proceeding on foot a half mile farther, I found the ghost town, which is dominated by a sixty-foot brick chimney and a processing plant with a metal-sheathed conveyor belt. The blast furnace, built in 1854 and powered by the flow of Hudson River water, is one of the last remaining such structures in the world.

It had been just a few months after I had returned from another mining town at one of the ends of the world, Longyearbyen in Spitsbergen, and even though the setting could not have been more different, the echoes of dormant mechanical monsters were the same.

The Source of the Hudson

Between Tahawus and Mount Marcy, a dozen or so brooks, streams, rivulets, and ponds tumble down the south and west faces of the high peaks. Between and among them the Hudson River is born.

Colvin declared Lake Tear of the Clouds as the source and that's as good as any starting place. The little pond sits at 4,322 feet above sea level, about 1,000 feet down from the peak of Mount Marcy. The outlet of the pond is Feldspar Brook; the Feldspar and Calamity brooks flow toward Henderson Lake and out of that body of water comes the upper Hudson River. Just below Tahawus another stream—the Opalescent River—comes down from Mount Marcy and joins the Hudson.

The Hudson River near Newcomb after Calamity Brook
and the Opalescent River join the stream.
Photo by the author

Not far from Aiden Lair, a stagecoach inn where Vice President
Theodore Roosevelt changed horses on his mad dash to Buffalo to
assume the presidency, the Hudson heads west about ten miles into
Newcomb before beginning its mostly southern journey.

The Hudson River drops an average of sixty-four feet per mile in
its first fifty miles, over small waterfalls and through shallow rapids
as it heads toward the communities of North River, North Creek, and
Riparius. The stretch from Riparius (the word itself refers to the
banks of a river) to the Glen, about eight miles, is a class-three
whitewater rapids—enough to daunt most amateurs.

Near Warrensburg, the Hudson is joined by the Schroon River, the
outlet of Schroon Lake, which is also fed by waters coming down
from the area of the high peaks. At Hadley, the Sacandaga River en-

ters from the west and the Hudson River begins to take on the appearance of a significant waterway.

At Corinth, the river heads due east for about twelve miles, passing through Moreau Lake—basically a wide stretch of the flowing river—before reaching Hudson Falls near Glens Falls. Here, the river tumbles over a falls of about fifty feet and then turns due south for the rest of its journey to New York City and the Atlantic Ocean.

But as Hudson and his crew found when they ascended to a point somewhere just south of Albany, the river above that point is shallow and impossible to navigate for large ships. At Cohoes, the Mohawk River—the largest of all the tributaries to the Hudson—enters from the west.

It is at that point, in the nineteenth century, that the Erie Canal was dug to follow the path of the Mohawk to Buffalo and beyond. At about the same time, the Champlain Canal was created to link up with Lake Champlain between New York and Vermont to compete with Canadian trading and shipping interests farther north on the St. Lawrence River.

CHAPTER 13

The River Polluted

How did a pristine trickle of melted snow from Lake Tear of the Clouds in the Adirondacks become the headwaters of the United States' longest Superfund site?

The answer lies in the rush to industrialization in the nineteenth century. The Adirondacks were protected from significant degradation through the efforts of people like Verplanck Colvin and Theodore Roosevelt.

Leaving the forests and streams of the Adirondacks close to their natural state helped keep ships afloat in the Hudson River below Albany and in the Erie Canal that was dug east to west. And a regular flow in upstate rivers allowed the harnessing of that water to power vast mills and factories that were built along the waterfalls on the upper Hudson and on the lower Mohawk.

The banks of the Hudson from Waterford north to Glens Falls, and the Mohawk west from Cohoes were once lined with huge mills that made use of the flowing water to rotate machinery or to spin turbines to generate electricity. The same water also served as a very convenient disposal system for effluent from the plants.

So, too, did dozens of cities and towns see the Hudson and Mohawk rivers as a convenient way to flush away sewage. From the upper reaches all the way to New York City, the end of the sewer system was often a pipe that dumped into the river.

Trapping crabs in the Hudson River at Bear Mountain.
Photo by the author

Edison and General Electric Arrive

In 1887, Thomas A. Edison moved his Edison Machine Works to Schenectady; at its peak during World War II, the factories employed 40,000
people. About half of the entire working population of the city worked
for "The G. E.," as they called it. The two small original machine shops
were still standing in 1949 when the vast Schenectady Works of the
General Electric Company spread over a 600-acre campus with more
than 240 buildings.

Schenectady is nestled into a large bend of the Mohawk River,

189

which also serves as part of the modern Erie Barge Canal. A few miles due west, near Waterford, the river hooks toward the south and over Cohoes Falls on its final plunge into the Hudson River; just ahead of the falls, the canal branches off into the famous Waterford Flight of locks, which has the largest drop (or lift) of any canal in the world over its short distance. In a distance of just a mile and a half, a "flight" of five locks raise or lower boats 165 feet.

The General Electric Research Laboratory, nicknamed the "House of Magic," was the first large-scale industrial laboratory in the country dedicated to research in pure science. Other divisions brought to Schenectady by Edison included three broadcasting stations. WGY-AM was one of the first commercial radio stations in the nation; it began operations in 1922 and in October of that year it presented the first broadcast of baseball's World Series, won by the New York Giants over the New York Yankees. In 1928, General Electric launched W2XB with the first regularly scheduled television broadcasts; the station continues as WRGB.

Edison's empire began with the Electric Light Company in 1878. There followed the General Electric Company (GE) and a long stream of consumer and industrial products that required effective electrical insulation products. GE moved from shellac and gutta percha (a hardened resin from the tree of the same name, originally found in East Asia including the Malay Peninsula) to the development of phenolic resins, the precursor of many modern plastics.

GE's first plastics plants were in various parts of Massachusetts, but by 1949 there was also production in Schenectady and at a facility in Waterford. In 1953, a company researcher discovered polycarbonate resin, and the company marketed it as Lexan; that extremely durable plastic is a mainstay of modern manufacturing for products from bottles and glasses to iPods.

Another major need for a company manufacturing electrical devices was cooling and insulating chemicals for use in large transformers and motors. GE set up plants in Glens Falls and Hudson Falls, north of Waterford along the Hudson.

And in the aftermath of World War II, as GE was converting many of its factories back from military products to consumer items, it was asked to design and operate a government-owned atomic power research laboratory at the Knolls, a former country estate near Schenectady. Although GE apparently had some plans to work on civilian generating systems, the resulting Knolls Atomic Power Laboratory instead concentrated on the development of nuclear-powered reactors for U.S. Navy submarines.

The Smell of Jobs

I once worked as a newspaper reporter in a small Ohio town that was dominated by a paper mill. The odor from the factory, especially on a humid summer day, was almost unbearable. I once described it as smelling like a dog that had rolled in sauerkraut and fireplace ash; the part that you couldn't smell made your eyes tear and your chest ache.

The mayor and the chamber of commerce, though, had a different description: they called it "the smell of full employment."

Around Fort Edward, Hudson Falls, and Glens Falls, the GE factories were full of polychlorinated biphenyls (PCBs), which have no discernible odor. Radioactivity from the Knolls laboratory is invisible and also odorless. In Waterford, though, where my wife grew up, residents recall the sharply acrid smell of silicone wafting down river from the plant.

Today, GE's facilities in upstate New York are much reduced; many of the jobs have moved to less-expensive workforces in the Sunbelt or overseas. More than 20,000 jobs have departed from the Schenectady Works in the past two decades; just a few thousand remain at a turbine factory. In Waterford, the GE Silicones plant is still the largest employer in the town, with 1,500 jobs, although that is less than half of its peak level. The Knolls Atomic Power Laboratory is now operated by Lockheed Martin, with 2,600 employees in Niskayuna and West Milton.

But GE is hardly forgotten in the Hudson River Valley, principally because of the things it left behind: massive pollution of the Hudson River with PCBs and silicone and a legacy (mostly still secret) of radioactive releases along the Mohawk.

A warning against eating fish caught
in the Hudson near Waterford.
Photo by the author

In its *GE 2005 Citizenship Report*, the company states: "We are currently involved in 87 sites on the Superfund National Priorities List. At many of these sites, GE's involvement is very small. We have sole responsibility at just eight. We have reached agreements with federal and/or state regulators at almost every site about the right way to proceed." On its face, this statement is correct, although there are some holes in the agreements with federal and state regulators that are big enough to run a river through.

Did GE Bring Good Things?

It is the legacy of the PCBs that have made the greatest impact on the upper Hudson, and places as far away as New York City to the south and the Canadian Arctic to the north. PCBs are manmade chemicals that do not exist in nature. The first PCB-like products were discovered in about 1865; Monsanto began manufacturing them in the United States in 1929 and GE was its largest customer.

For all the twentieth century, Monsanto was the only U.S. manufacturer of the compound; the company has its own pollution problems including allegations of massive dumping of PCBs into a creek and landfill at a factory in Anniston, Alabama.

PCBs are chlorinated oils with some very specific and valuable properties: they are not flammable, have a high resistance to electricity, and are extremely stable even when exposed to heat or pressure. This made PCBs near-perfect compounds for use as insulators and coolants in electrical transformers and capacitors; in many instances, fire codes required the use of the chemical.

A number of different mixtures of PCBs were commercially produced in the United States and elsewhere. Many were known under the trade name of Aroclor, often with a number attached that indicated the compound's approximate percentage of chlorine by weight. According to a report from an agency of the U.S. Department of Health and Human Services, for example, Aroclor 1254 is a form of PCB in which chlorine constitutes 54 percent by weight.

Other places PCBs were used included fluorescent light ballasts, carbonless copy paper, compressors, and certain plasticizers, pigments, and adhesives.

It is the stability of PCBs that made them so enticing to manufacturers; that same property is the reason why they are such a danger to the environment. Simply put, PCBs that are spilled on the ground, dumped in a landfill, or discharged into a river have an almost permanent consequence.

Some ecologists also believe that PCBs that are deposited on tidal flats of the Hudson River twice a day evaporate into the atmosphere and are carried away by the winds to be redeposited by rain or snow in places that have no direct relation whatsoever to the original pollution: places such as Hudson Bay in the Canadian subarctic and Spitsbergen above Norway, where polar bears have been found to carry the chemical.

PCBs work their way up the food chain into fish, birds, and humans in a process called bioaccumulation; the chemical builds up in the fatty tissue of animals. The larger the animal, the greater the concentration.

Up to this point, ecologists and accused polluters are mostly in agreement. It is also generally agreed that GE dumped about 1.1 million pounds of PCBs and related substances into the Hudson River from factories in Hudson Falls and Fort Edward from 1947 to 1977; discharge of PCBs into a waterway was not made illegal until 1978, when the federal Environmental Protection Agency (EPA) instituted a ban.

The argument comes with the next two claims:

1. That PCBs represent a serious health hazard to humans and other creatures

2. That the tons of PCBs dumped into the Hudson and currently sitting on the river bottom should be dredged up and hauled away

The biggest source of PCBs from GE operations was its factory in Hudson Falls. There, in an old mill building known over the years as the Fenimore Mill, the Fenimore Sulphite Mill, and then the Union Bag and Paper Factory, GE manufactured electrical capacitors from 1952 until 1976. A similar operation had begun at a GE plant in Fort Edward in 1947.

The Hudson Falls plant is on a bluff above the east bank of the Hudson River. At the north end of the eight-acre site is the Bakers Falls Dam, which is part of a hydroelectric facility installed in the early 1900s at a natural waterfall on the river. The original name of the village was Baker's Falls, named for Albert Baker, who arrived from New York City in 1768, before the American Revolution, and installed a small dam and water-powered sawmill at the falls.

Below the GE plant, on the banks of the river, is the abandoned Allen Mill. Deep beneath the factory was a 150-year-old tunnel that carried water through raceways to power turbines in the mill and a tailrace tunnel to discharge water back into the river. Sometime in the distant past, the tunnel had been closed off with a wooden gate.

According to various environmental groups, over the course of twenty-four years of GE's operation at Hudson Falls, PCBs were not properly stored or disposed. Spills from operations went into porous shale on the property.

In 1991, the forgotten wooden gate on the buried tunnel beneath the Allen Mill finally gave way. A flood of PCBs and other toxins that had trickled down through the shale were suddenly released into the Hudson River.

According to some environmentalists and scientists, PCB levels in some of the hotspots of the upper Hudson increased by 100 times over the course of a few months. The release had come from a pool of chemicals that had built up in a mill that wasn't GE's, just one of dozens of sources—obvious and hidden—for the pollution of the river.

After a consent agreement with the state of New York, GE spent about $165 million on cleanup, wells, pumps, and water purification on just the land around its Hudson Falls plant and the Allen Mill.

Up and down the river state and federal environmental agencies and independent groups have found small hotspots at barrel cleaning and refurbishing companies, transformer repair shops, and casually maintained or undocumented landfills and dump-yards.

Other actions, natural and human, contributed to make the situation worse. According to a timeline prepared by the Clearwater environmental group, a few of the significant events include:

- In 1973, the Fort Edward Dam was removed from the upper Hudson River, releasing a large amount of PCB-contaminated sediment that had built up behind the structure.

- An EPA study in 1974 found high levels of PCBs in Hudson River fish, and the U.S. Food and Drug Administration set a safety threshold of 5 parts per million in fish for human consumption.

- In 1976, Congress passed the Toxic Substance Control Act banning the manufacture of PCBs and prohibiting all uses except in totally enclosed systems.

- Also in 1976, the New York State Department of Environmental Conservation closed the Hudson River commercial fishery, making it illegal to fish in the upper Hudson from the Fort Edward Dam to the Federal Dam at Albany and warning individuals about the dangers of eating fish from the river.

- In April 1976, the worst local flood in a century flushed large amounts of polluted sediment down the river.

- And on September 8, 1976, GE announced it would no longer dump PCBs into the Hudson River from its plants in Hudson Falls and Fort Edward. The company agreed to spend $1 million on PCB research and $3 million to monitor pollution levels in the river; in return, the state agreed not to blame GE for PCBs in the river.

- In 1977, Monsanto ended all production of PCBs.

- On September 8, 1983, the EPA updated its Superfund National Priority List, adding forty miles of the upper Hudson River as a polluted waterway.

Silicone and Radioactivity

General Electric Silicone Products remains as the largest employer in Waterford and all of Saratoga County, a mostly rural economic backwater. The sprawling plant sits along Hudson River Road, about a mile and a half above town.

GE's *2005 Citizenship Report* states that the company paid New York State $300,000 in 2003 as a result of issues related to wastewater discharges, spill containment, and hazardous waste management. The company said it has instituted a multimillion upgrade to its treatment and containment facilities.

According to CorpWatch, an environmental and business watchdog group in California, GE has paid hundreds of thousands of dollars in fines in the past decade, plus additional spending to improve local emergency response capabilities. The group said that the EPA has cited GE for more than two dozen violations when toxic chemicals were unreported or underreported.

Among the chemicals involved, according to CorpWatch, were dimethyl sulfate, chlorine, trichloroethane, ammonia, and toluene. All these chemicals are on one or another state, federal, or environmental watchdog list of suspected or recognized carcinogens or toxic chemicals. Some, such as dimethyl sulfate, are believed to be more dangerous in airborne release, while others may be more toxic if taken in through drinking water or in fish or mammals eaten as food.

Very little is known with any certainty about the Knolls Atomic Power Laboratory in Niskayuna, just east of the city of Schenectady. The secure facility sits on 170 acres of land within a buffer zone of several thousand acres, extending 4,200 feet along the Mohawk River a few miles from the Cohoes Falls and its entrance into the Hudson River.

According to a Web site about the Knolls plant maintained by Lockheed Martin, "We safely operate two prototypes of submarine nuclear propulsion plants," and the facilities maintain, support, and enhance the mission capability of Los Angeles–class submarines, Ohio-class ballistic missile submarines, and Virginia-class submarines.

An October 2005 report by the EPA gave Knolls mostly good grades for its current operations. Inspectors noted that the facility did produce various hazardous wastes and radioactive materials, but that there was no disposal of these substances on site; tankers and barrels of the material are taken away to other licensed disposal operations.

There were some areas of localized soil contamination including PCBs, heavy metals, and volatile organic compounds with some effects on local groundwater, but the EPA says it appears that today, what happens in Knolls stays in Knolls . . . or is trucked away.

That much is on the record; most of the rest is in the form of allegations by former employees in local and national news coverage and in an Academy Award–winning documentary.

In a January 1, 1991, article in the *New York Times*, headlined QUESTIONS RAISED ABOUT THE SAFETY OF NAVAL REACTORS, the reporter Matthew L. Wald quoted federal officials and GE executives, who ran the site at the time, as saying that the facility had an excellent safety record and no serious operating problems. However, they said, all records about possible incidents at the plant were classified.

Wald interviewed two former employees who said there had been several mishaps with reactors at the site, including one in which a reactor was shut down for two years after an accident in which radioactive material got into a cooling system. There was also serious concern about the fact that the naval reactors, land-based operating equivalents of submarine-power plants, did not have emergency cooling systems to deal with serious problems.

Allegations in the *Times* article included the discovery of radioactive materials in office lighting fixtures, under a parking lot, and in a building in Schenectady where GE had tested technology to produce fuél for nuclear bombs. According to Wald, the building was later used as a food-distribution warehouse.

In 1992, the filmmaker Debra Chasnoff's documentary, *Deadly Deception: General Electric, Nuclear Weapons, and Our Environment*, received an Academy Award. The film accuses GE of mishandling the cleanup of the Hanford Nuclear Reservation in Washington state and poisoning workers with asbestos and radiation at the Knolls plant in Schenectady.

Deadly Deception includes interviews with survivors and relatives of both facilities, with regular repetition of the advertising jingle, "GE: We bring good things to life." It was commissioned and produced by Infact, a Boston-based group opposed to nuclear weapons and other issues.

Infact, now known as Corporate Accountability International, alleges that in the early 1950s the Knolls Atomic Power Laboratory routinely dumped water contaminated with cesium-137, strontium-90, uranium, and plutonium into the Mohawk River.

The PCB Problem

I've not come across any reasonable scientist or businessperson who suggests that drinking a glass of PCBs on ice would offer a health benefit, or even be merely harmless. At least one politician made that offer, though.

However, there have been many who have said that the claim that PCBs are deadly toxins or carcinogens is not true, or greatly exaggerated. Many of those who dispute the dangers of PCBs, of course, work for companies that have a major financial interest in avoiding lawsuits and cleanup costs.

According to a toxicological profile published by the Agency for Toxic Substances and Disease Registry, a federal public health agency of the U.S. Department of Health and Human Services, "The preponderance of the biomedical data from human and laboratory mammal studies provide strong evidence of the toxic potential of exposure to PCBs." Among the studies cited by the agency were the Yusho incident in Japan, where residents consumed contaminated rice oil, and the Yu-Cheng incident in Taiwan, in which a population ate contaminated fish.

The agency reports that health effects associated with exposure to PCBs in humans and animals include liver, thyroid, dermal, and ocular changes, immunological alterations, neurodevelopmental changes, reduced birth weight, reproductive toxicity, and cancer. The profile also cites studies that evaluated cancer mortality in workers exposed during capacitor manufacture and repair. "Based on indications of PCB-related cancer at several sites, particularly the liver, biliary tract, intestines, and skin (melanoma), the human studies provide suggestive evidence that PCBs are carcinogenic."

Before discharge was outlawed in 1978, PCBs regularly entered the atmosphere, water, and soil during the manufacturing process. They could also be spilled during transport or as the result of leaks of fires in transformers, capacitors, and other electrical devices.

On February 5, 1981—after the manufacture of PCBs was ended but while they were still in wide use—an electrical fire broke out in the basement of the new State Office Building in Binghamton, New York, about 140 miles west of Albany. The extreme heat in the small equipment room caused a rupture in a seal on a large transformer, and about 180 gallons of PCB oil leaked out and was vaporized.

The building's own ventilation system distributed much of the smoke throughout the eighteen-story structure; automatic systems opened vents on the roof that drew the toxins upward, and the situation was made worse when firefighters opened the door to the mechanical room. Among the chemicals distributed in the cauldron of heat and smoke were PCBs as well as 2,3,7,8 trichlorodibenzo-p-dioxin. This form of dioxin, used in the Vietnam War as the Agent Orange defoliant, is considered among the most toxic chemicals to humans.

At least 482 office workers, as well as firefighters and rescuers, were exposed to the mixture. The building was sealed up within a cocoon of plastic sheeting and workers were forbidden to reenter to recover items from their desks.

A few months later, Governor Hugh Carey*—a politician renowned for shooting from the lip—complained about the delay in reopening the building. He offered "to walk into Binghamton or any part of that building and swallow an entire glass of PCBs." While his staffers cringed and reporters scribbled, Carey went on: "You've got to take PCBs in quantities, deadly, over a long period of time and probably be pregnant, which I don't intend to become, and then you get PCB contamination."

As it turned out, the cleaning of the building took thirteen years; when it reopened in 1994, the state had paid $53 million to regain use of a structure with an original price tag of about $17 million.

Will GE Take Away Bad Things?

Although GE is conspicuous by its size and the spread of its factories and types of products in the upper Hudson River region, it is by no means the only company cited by state and federal agencies for mishandling or misreporting toxic chemicals.

To its credit, GE has not completely run away from responsibility for its involvement in various discharges, spills, and releases from its plants and laboratories along the Hudson and Mohawk rivers. It has, though, fought long and hard to limit the amount of money it has to spend, especially when it comes to dealing with what remains of the 1.1 million pounds of PCBs it let loose into the upper Hudson River.

---

*In the interest of full disclosure, I worked as a speechwriter for a member of Governor Carey's cabinet at the time. I was not involved in Carey's PCB comments; I was among those who cringed.

The federal Superfund law makes polluters, not taxpayers, responsible for the costs of cleaning up designated toxic hotspots. By 2000, the EPA had moved from relatively modest projects to close outflow pipes and cover and seal off landfills to a much more extensive (and expensive) dredging of the polluted sediment in the Hudson River.

Besides arguing against the EPA Superfund ruling, GE also tried to present an environmental argument against the dredging: scooping up the contaminated river bottom would put more PCBs into the river than leaving them in place, the company said.

In 1998, President Bill Clinton's EPA administrator Carol Browner assailed the company for its delays in a hearing before a committee of the New York State Assembly. She quoted comments made earlier that year by Jack Welch, the chief executive officer of GE, during the annual shareholder's meeting.

"G.E. would have the people of the Hudson River believe, and I quote, 'Living in a PCB-laden area is not dangerous,'" Browner said. "Well, you know something? The science tells us the opposite is true."

Steven Ramsey, the vice president for environmental programs at GE, told the *New York Times* that the company had a long list of independent studies it believed showed no link between PCBs and cancer in humans and that other studies questioned any connection to other health effects.

The company launched a newspaper, radio, and television campaign in the Albany area seeking to make the point that dredging was environmentally irresponsible; it wasn't the cost, GE said. By some estimates, GE spent at least $60 million in 2000 not on cleaning up the river but on advertisements and public relations efforts to try to avoid dredging.

Dredging the Hudson

GE was joined by a relatively small and select number of individuals and groups in objecting to the idea of dredging the upper Hudson to remove PCBs in the sediment; some had connections to the company and others apparently had come to that point of view on their own. There was a great deal of support for the plan from most of the environmental groups in the river valley.

The deciding vote, and the only one that had the force of law, came from the EPA. In 2002, the EPA issued its Record of Decision, an official order to GE to dredge the upper Hudson to remove PCBs in the sediment.

GE continued to object to parts of the plan, but in October 2005 it finally entered into a consent decree with the EPA and the U.S. Department of Justice to undertake what may be the largest environmental cleanup project in history, dredging forty-three miles of the Hudson River from Hudson Falls to Troy over a six-year period and at an estimated cost of $700 million. In theory, the dredging of the upper Hudson is supposed to begin sometime in 2008.

Within weeks of the agreement, a new controversy arose when an expert from NOAA, produced a memo for the EPA that questioned whether GE truly intended to dredge some of the worst parts of the river or whether it intended to attempt to cover them over with a "cap" of clean sediment; the NOAA memo was obtained by the environmental organization Riverkeeper, which leaked it to the *New York Times*.

GE's 2006 fiscal year revenues were about $157.2 billion; record earnings the year before from continuing operations totaled $18.3 billion. Besides its industrial divisions, GE also owns NBC Universal, which includes the NBC television network (*The Tonight Show*, *The Today Show*, *Law and Order*, and *ER*) and Universal Studios film production and theme parks.

CHAPTER 14

The Conscience
of the River

The first settlement house in the United States, a center to help new immigrants and the working poor, was founded in 1886 on New York's Lower East Side. Its first building was on Forsyth Street, about a mile from the Hudson River docks, where ferries unloaded new immigrants arriving from Europe through Ellis Island.

University Settlement was a combination of a private social welfare agency, a school, a community center, and a public bath and health facility. It became the model for more than 400 other agencies in gateway cities around the nation.

Alumni included the songwriters George and Ira Gershwin and the politicians New York mayor Abe Beame and U.S. senator Jacob Javits. Eleanor Roosevelt taught dance at the settlement, a somewhat disturbing image. Her husband, Franklin D. Roosevelt, called the settlement "a landmark in the social history of the nation."

In 1910, University Settlement was given a gift of eighty undeveloped acres on the slopes of Mount Beacon, about seventy-five miles up the Hudson River; a year later it established a summer camp for underprivileged kids. It was there, in the summer of 1961, that I met the folksinger Pete Seeger; I was eleven years old; and the three weeks I spent there established for life my political views, my taste in music, and my connection to the river.

Seeger, whom poet Carl Sandberg called "America's tuning fork," sang for the campers at University Settlement Camp all that summer in the year he was indicted for contempt of Congress by a near-unanimous vote of the House of Representatives. The charge stemmed from a 1955 hearing before the House Committee on Un-American Activities at which he was asked questions about his involvement with the American Communist Party as a young man. A year later, Seeger as well as the playwright Arthur Miller and six others were cited for contempt of Congress.

In March 1961, he was found guilty by a federal court jury on all ten counts of an indictment charging him with refusing to answer questions by the committee. The conviction was unanimously reversed a year later by the U.S. Court of Appeals. He was at the camp in 1961; the next year he split his summer between camp counselor in Beacon and working with the civil rights voter registration movement in the South.

His father was the noted musicologist Charles Seeger, and Pete unapologetically credits him with getting him involved with the American Communist Party in the 1930s, a connection that continued into the 1950s. "I still call myself a communist," Seeger told the *New York Times* in 1995, "because communism is no more what Russia made of it than Christianity is what the churches make of it. But if by some freak of history communism had caught up with this country, I would have been one of the first people thrown in jail."

But at Camp Beacon we just knew him as Pete, the guy who led the nightly campfire in songs of labor organizers such as "Which Side Are You On?" and "Joe Hill," civil rights anthems such as "We Shall Not Be Moved," and his own classic songs of love and protest such as "If I Had a Hammer" (written with the fellow Weavers singer Lee Hays), "Turn, Turn, Turn," the musical version of the Old Testament's Ecclesiastes 3:1–8 ("To everything there is a season and a time for every purpose under Heaven"), and "Where Have All the Flowers Gone?"

I went on as a young adult to protest the Vietnam War and the military draft, and my sense of social justice has remained more or less as it was in those summers at camp. And Seeger and the extended family of singer-songwriter-protestors he inspired has served as the soundtrack of my life: Bob Dylan; Joan Baez; Judy Collins; Peter, Paul and Mary; Arlo Guthrie; the Byrds; and so many more.

A View of the Hudson

Seeger sang for the campers at University Settlement off and on for more than thirty years; he still lives on a mountainside near Beacon with his wife, Toshi, his windows and lawn looking out over the Hudson. I caught up with him forty-four years after I left his campfire.

"After World War II my wife and I were living in Greenwich Village," Seeger told me. "Her parents had three floors and a basement for one hundred dollars a month. Then we had two little babies and I didn't know how to raise them on the sidewalk in New York.

"As a matter of fact, from age three on I thought cities were a big mistake. I remember looking out my parents' apartment one winter and seeing a traffic jam and saying cities are stupid. Why does anybody live in the city? It's too crowded, too dirty, too noisy, and I was really a nature nut. I thought everybody should live in the country.

"Right now I think that if there is a human race here in a hundred years it may be the people in the cities who will save us. People in the cities have to learn to live together whether they are of the same ethnic group or not.

"In a small town you say, 'Oh isn't it nice to be here; we all are of the same group.' In the city you've got to ride on the subway with people of a hundred different backgrounds or more.

"Anyway, we looked around where my grandparents lived (in Connecticut) and it was all too expensive. A real estate agent showed us an old farm in Dutchess County. I remember a big barn, a big house, ten acres with a brook and woods and they were asking five thousand dollars. We couldn't afford it.

"The agent said, 'What can you afford?' I said, 'Maybe some land.' And they found me some land overlooking the Hudson, halfway between the town of Beacon and Cold Spring. And we have lived here now fifty-six years."

Pete and Toshi bought seventeen acres for $1,700 and built a cabin for $900. The house looks out across the Hudson at New Windsor on the western shore.

"My philosophy has been that the world is going to be saved by people who fight for their homes. I am a great believer in the concept coined by the Rockefeller Institute environmental activist Rene Dubos in the 1970s: 'Think globally, act locally.' "

Like most of the people I interviewed for this book, Seeger was quick to make a connection between his head and heart and a nearby river. Among his songs: the hopeful "Sailing Down My Golden River," which glorifies the prospect of "Sailing down my golden river, sun and water all my own, yet I was never alone."

We talked about the sparkling river below his cabin. "Rivers have an interesting symbolism. They are a joining together of many small streams and they gain a new character as they grow. The small stream goes trickle, trickle, jump, jump. The river tends to be more placid; it moves slowly but very powerfully.

"Throughout history people have had an attraction to rivers. We know that the first cities of the world were along the Tigris and Euphrates and probably in China along the Yangtze."

As the United States developed, Seeger said, most of the early settlements were also along the rivers. "You could get water to drink and cook and wash with, and get fish and shellfish to eat. And then commerce came along."

It was commerce, of course, that ended up polluting and even poisoning some of the great rivers—the Hudson is a prime example. Upstream paper mills, chemical plants, and hundreds of thousands of toilets emptied into the river, and by the middle of the twentieth century the Hudson was dying.

And so Seeger wrote another song, the wistful "Sailing Down My Dirty Stream" (sometimes sung as "Sailing Up My Dirty Stream"), an anthem of the defenders of the river:

Sailing down my dirty stream
Still I love it and I'll keep the dream

That some day though maybe not this year
*My Hudson River will once again run clear.**

The song observes that down the valley 1 million toilet chains find the Hudson such a convenient place to drain. "And each little city says, 'Who, me? Do you think that sewage plants come free?' "

About the same time Seeger put his beliefs and music toward the Hudson he led the creation of the Clearwater environmental group. In 1966, with the river carrying a cargo of raw sewage, toxic chemicals including PCBs, and other pollutants, Seeger and others announced plans to "build a boat to save the river."

Three years later, the *Clearwater*, a 106-foot wooden sailing sloop designed in the style of eighteenth- and nineteenth-century Dutch sailing sloops, was launched on the river. The next year, *Clearwater* sailed to Washington, D.C., to seek the attention of the federal government. Together with the musician Don McLean ("American Pie"), Seeger held a press conference and an impromptu concert in a congressional office building, highlighting the plight of the Hudson River and the need to protect U.S. waterways. More than seventy members of Congress attended.

"Back in the days when we first thought of Clearwater, many people said 'You can't turn back the clock. The Hudson is filthy and there is no way you can clean it up,' " Seeger told me. "But we dreamers said, 'Who knows what we can do?'

"At the time, I was singing songs against the Vietnam War. Some of the conservative people said the group would never go anywhere if Seeger is connected with it. So I resigned as chairman. I was just a figurehead but I got them to agree in return that people who paid their ten dollars to become a member of Clearwater would also once a year get a chance to vote on the board of directors; up until then the board of directors just reappointed itself.

"And so the following year, when the boat was actually sailing, it was the young people who tipped the scales and voted to call the

*Copyright Pete Seeger, 1961, 1964.

Early morning sea smoke rises on the Hudson River.
Photo by the author

boat *Clearwater* rather than *Heritage*, which was what some of the conservative members wanted to call it. And within a few years we changed the charter to say the purpose of the *Clearwater* was to clean up the Hudson.

"And most people said, 'Well how can you do that? You have to get the powers that be to do that.'

"I called on old left-wing tactics. We assailed Washington and got to roaming the House Office Building. I had with me a pie chart of the federal budget showing how much goes for this and how much goes for that. And I said, 'Here is how much goes for the environment.' It was a tiny little sliver, less than one percent. And I flung the pie chart like a Frisbee off into the audience in disgust.

"Two years later when [Richard M.] Nixon was having his sled followed by a lot of wolves, we figured he would throw a bone to one of them to get it off his tail. And he started making nice noises about the environment and so the water pollution amendments of 1972 passed."

Those "amendments" were technically the Federal Water Pollution Control Act Amendments of 1972, much better known as the landmark Clean Water Act. Suddenly, the idea of cleaning up the Hudson did not seem an impossible, frivolous dream; Clearwater was joined by other groups up and down the river, including Scenic Hudson.

"We didn't expect any great revolution to come along, but we said 'keep pushing, who knows?' I had a bumper sticker for many years that said, 'If the people lead, eventually the leaders will follow,' " Seeger said.

The River Keepers

Henry Hudson's 1609 log of his voyage up the river from Manhattan to the shoals and rapids near Cohoes and Waterford speaks of clean water teeming with fish and shellfish. Birds patrolled overhead and other animals fished from the shore.

Three hundred and fifty years later, much of the river was dead. And those who chose to eat what fish or birds remained to be caught were ingesting PCBs and other toxic chemicals.

"In the days before the Clean Water Act, the Hudson actually caught fire on numerous occasions, down south in the New York City area near the Jersey Kill and the refineries," said Andy Mele, the former executive director of Clearwater.

"We have many photographs of flammable deposits of tars and oils right on the surface and lots of dead fish the length and breadth of the river," he told me.

The Hudson was literally a running sewer, an extension of the outflow pipes of factories and plumbing systems from above Glens Falls all the way down to New York City 200 miles south.

Mele said that most of the attention was applied to the sexier forms of pollution, things like petroleum compounds, benzene, toluene, ethylene, and truly frightening threats like PCBs and dioxin. "They are the ones that send chills up and down people's spines," Mele said, "but the everyday pollution which was causing a good deal more harm was shit."

Metropolitan centers from Albany to Poughkeepsie and Kingston to Manhattan were growing like crazy. "Everybody's plumbing had to go somewhere," he said, "and where that went was the river and the bay."

Sewage is rich in phosphorus and nitrates, both of which are key nutrients. As one example, algae growth ballooned out of control, Mele said. At the same time, all the biological matter in the water sank down to the river bottom, creating a pool of bacterial activity.

"Bacteria are net consumers of oxygen and what you wound up with were zones that were hypoxic—deficient in oxygen—for ten or fifteen miles or longer around Albany and fifteen or twenty miles around New York City and spreading right out into the Hudson canyon out of New York Harbor.

"The river was biologically dead except for bacteria," said Mele. The Hudson was at its worst in the 1960s, he said.

The Hudson River Fishery

"During World War II and into the late 1940s, Hudson River shad were booming," Mele told me. "They didn't taste bad and the catches were just unbelievable.

"About 1949, around the time I was born, the shad population crashed and it never fully recovered. And they are not likely to re-cover, either. Sturgeon was fished right through the sixties.

"There was a robust economy built around those two species. I heard from one of the last of the sturgeon fishermen that the last year it was legal to fish for sturgeon you could make $50,000 har-vesting the roe. I spoke to another guy who said he put four kids through college on shad."

Shad are unusual among freshwater fish in New York; like salmon, they are anadromous: they spend most of their lives in the saltwater ocean and only return to fresh water to reproduce. They migrate up large rivers like the Hudson in huge spawning runs.

At the time Hudson sailed up the river, the fish probably went well above Albany toward Glens Falls. In more recent times, though, they have mostly been blocked from passing any farther than the

Federal Lock between Troy and Waterford, which marks the navigable end of the Hudson River.

The Changed Shoreline

"Many early texts refer to the city of Hudson as the head of navigation on the river," Mele said. "And yet Albany was up there thriving away. Sloops and the early steamers could certainly make it, but it was wicked tricky navigation.

"There were lots of shoals and sandbars. It must have been stunningly beautiful, just rich with tidal wetlands. But then once the Erie Canal was built and the steamboats came along and started competing with the railroad, in roughly 1850, everybody started screaming for more canalization.

"By the start of the twentieth century, thirty percent of the river's surface area had been filled in to straighten up the river into how we see it today."

But the biggest impact on the river came from industrialization and the growth of cities along its banks.

"In the early and mid-1960s, America's twenty-year love affair with modern chemistry was in full bloom and companies like Monsanto and Westinghouse and General Electric and many others were just cranking out chlorinated hydrocarbons and plastics. The space program was demanding all sorts of new materials, and these companies were making silicone, urethane, and all this stuff that we take for granted today.

"The economy of the river had shifted from resource extraction. That had been the primary goal in Hudson's day: what can we hack out of the soil? They were looking for iron and coal.

"There are potholes in every rock face around the Hudson Valley cut by guys with pickaxes prospecting for coal. They actually found it in one or two places but never in marketable quantities. They cut blue stone. They took cement. They took clay and made bricks out of it. They clear-cut the Hudson Valley at least twice, for firewood and for home construction."

The first energy revolution, of coal and steam, gave way to the second: oil and the internal combustion engine. Mele, as a dutiful environmentalist, called it "infernal combustion." He did readily admit to owning a car, although after our interview he was headed to the train station to catch a more-efficient afternoon express from Poughkeepsie to New York City.

Uncontrolled Industry

"In the first half of the twentieth century, we had all of these fuels and chemicals derived from fossil fuels loose in the environment with no sense of what the downside might be," Mele said. "Most of these companies might have had a vague sense that this stuff was sort of nasty, but they just put it in drums and buried it or dumped it into the river, and it just went away. There were no environmental laws."

There was, however, a federal law called the Rivers and Harbors Act of 1899 that had gradually come to be interpreted by the courts to cover things like pollution; it said no one could put any foreign object into navigable waterways. Environmentalists began to use the law against polluters.

"In the mid-sixties, during the Vietnam protest era and that whole cultural upheaval, long-haired and bearded kids took sterile mayonnaise jars into canoes and began to paddle the waterways of America to capture stuff pouring out of industrial outfall pipes," Mele said.

One of the things that propelled the environmental movement was the fact that people who discovered sources of pollution were able to sue companies and collect as much as half of any penalty that was assessed.

"And so industry ultimately went to Washington and begged to be regulated to get the kids with the canoes off their backs," he said. "And so it wasn't just the environmentalists and the tree huggers; everybody wanted regulation. And so they came up with the Clean Water Act."

Up and down the river valley, groups began to come together to try to save the Hudson.

"You had a group like Scenic Hudson, which was essentially trying to preserve the visual character of the valley; [their first big issue was] fighting the Storm King pump storage plant," Mele said. "The Hudson River Fisherman's Association, which later became Riverkeeper, coalesced around the power plant fish kills and other things that were hurting the fish.

"And Clearwater was built around this notion of the folksinger Pete Seeger. I sometimes think of the boat as a time machine; it gives an alternate view of reality. *Clearwater* has tall white sails and a beautiful hull and the idea was that people would come down to the river again and [decide] that we all should take care of it. If they had done feasibility and economic studies, the boat would never have been built."

Has the Hudson Been Saved?

In the nearly four decades since the launching of the *Clearwater* and the signing of the Clean Waters Act, the amount of chemicals and inorganic pollutants going into the Hudson has been reduced dramatically. That's the good news. But when I asked Mele, "If the river was at its worst, at a Ten, in the 1960s, where is it now?," he surprised me with his answer.

"It's about a twelve now," Mele said. "There is still a lot of sewage in the water but it is not as much of a problem as it used to be. The Clean Water Act required the construction of sewage treatment plants, but they are aging and crumbling and overwhelmed and their design is faulty because they use combined sewer overflows. The calculations are that in Manhattan, if one-tenth of an inch of rain falls, ten percent of the sewage goes into the river untreated.

"Ironically, the problem today is zebra mussels," Mele said. "They came in the ballast water from tankers from the northeast Mediterranean region. They first colonized the Great Lakes and gradually moved into the canal system. They have just totally taken over the fresh water reaches of the river.

"Fortunately, they don't do well in salt water, so they have stopped just north of Haverstraw. But there are so many billions and billions and billions of these wretched little animals that they are siphoning and filtering the entire volume of the river every two or three days."

The barnacle-like mussels—usually an inch or less in size—look like small clams with a yellow or brown D-shaped shell with dark and light-colored stripes, and were first found in 1988 in the Great Lakes. They are the only freshwater mollusk that can firmly attach itself to solid objects including ship's hulls, rocks, docks, and water intake pipes. They function like insatiable vacuum cleaners, sucking in nearly all the nutrients in the river; in some areas, according to Mele, the biomass in the river has been reduced by 90 percent.

"We are beginning to see that shad and stripers going out of the river for their first year in the North Atlantic are at seventy-five or eighty percent of their typical pre–Zebra Mussel body weight, which means that there is essentially a famine going on. And there is not a damn thing we can do about it," Mele told me.

Nearly forty years after the birth of the environmental movement in the Hudson Valley and the passage of the Clean Water Act, and after tens and hundreds of millions of dollars spent on improving water treatment, ending discharge of dangerous chemicals, and mitigating the effects of mistakes of the past, the Hudson is worse off today than it was in the 1960s?

"It is very hard to grapple with," Mele said. But it is also a mostly natural thing, part of a cycle of change that sometimes has nothing to do with insults by humans and sometimes only partly the result of civilization. The Zebra Mussel is not the first invasive species in the Hudson Valley.

"The carp is an alien species. The water chestnut is an alien," Mele said.

But back to the Zebra Mussel, the ironic strangler of the Hudson today: "It is a lost cause," Mele said, "unless over time there develops a bacterium or some sort of natural parasite or predator that has an affinity for Zebra Mussels.

"Natural selection and evolution occurs through opportunistic mutation; hopefully, some opportunistic mutation will occur and will take out and reduce the mussels to a more manageable number. But currently they are so prolific; if you look at their population graphs, there are these huge spikes followed by big crashes. The big crashes come when they just breed themselves out of house and home until there is literally no food left for them. It is just insane.

"But even then, some survive. Maybe there are a couple of years off, but then they are right back."

And even more ironic, there has been evidence of what Mele called an awful game of tit for tat. Ships filling with ballast water from the Hudson have taken one of the local residents back to the Black Sea, and it has decimated that ecosystem: comb jellies, inch-long jellyfish from the river, are now overwhelming the ecosystem and have destroyed sardine and anchovy fisheries, according to Mele.

It is, of course, something that has gone on for as long as humans have been trading with each other. The Spanish conquistadors conquered much of the Americas not with the sword but with disease; our friendly unwanted neighbor the cockroach came over in the bedding of Hessian soldiers during the American Revolution.

"From a pure-water quality perspective, the Hudson has improved to about a Four or Five," Mele said. "It is still just as turbid, though. One of the things Europeans did when they got here was bring their style of architecture. Native American Onondaga oral histories tell us that the river ran clear enough that you could see fish in it. Native Americans used what we now call 'slash and burn' agriculture. They ddin't tear open the land; they just would poke a stick in the ground and plant stuff. But we tear open large areas of land, and every time it rains huge amounts of soil go into the river."

An Environmentalist Looks at GE and PCBs

I asked Mele to weigh in on the controversy over dredging PCBs from the upper Hudson. There was no equivocation in his answer.

"It is not safer to leave it in there," Mele said. "Every day there is a measurable environmental impact from leaving it there. Every year another five hundred pounds of PCBs washes over the Federal Dam at Troy. It enters the estuary and enters the food web of marine mammals and the people who eat them, including some of the people living in the Hudson River cities. PCBs are New York's most notorious export.

"There are twelve square miles of tidal wetlands in the Hudson River estuary that are wetted and dried twice a day with the rise and fall of the river. Each time they are dried out, more PCBs evaporate into the atmosphere. We also happen to be right smack under an atmospheric upwelling zone. This stuff is sucked up and separated. Part of it goes north. Part of it goes south.

"The stuff that goes north gets condensed and attached to water droplets and comes down in the form of snow and rain. As a result, fish and marine mammals are highly contaminated. Polar bears up north are showing up with withered reproductive organs. The Inuit have breast milk that is so hot you wouldn't be allowed to go anywhere near it if it was a food product on the shelf of a grocery store.

"Every day that we do nothing there is a measurable environmental impact. GE has just delayed and delayed endlessly. They have created all sorts of junk science. The science does not hold up and is not credible."

An Environmentalist Waxes Poetic

At the risk of straying away from science and closer to New Age mysticism, I asked Mele if during his work he ever let his mind travel back to the 1600s to think of the river as the way it was when Hudson and his crew first saw it.

"Absolutely," he said. "I view the Greek philosopher Heraclitus as sort of the father of chaos theories. He said something to the effect of this: 'You can dip your toe in the river twice, but you are never putting your toe in the same river.' It is a very metaphysical statement and very much in keeping with the chaos theory.

"One of the great charms for me about the Hudson River is the fact that if you wiggle your finger in it some day a little infinitesimal particle of energy might lap up against a piling in Africa. It is like a highway to the rest of the world.

"The power and the majesty of the Hudson River is about that link to the world," Mele said. "It is about its rich biological complexity and then the sort of ebbing and flowing of various natural tragedies and triumphs."

"It is like Charlemagne and Alexander the Great and those kinds of huge seismic forces washing back and forth under the water. Unknown, unheralded the Zebra Mussels come and tear things up; prior to that the striped bass was almost locally extinct, and now it is burgeoning in huge numbers.

"The shore of the river no longer looks the way it did for Hudson but you can certainly imagine it. And when you are out on an old boat you can allow yourself to slip into a feeling that you are in a different place and you have stuck your toe into a slightly different river and you have gone back a couple of hundred years. To me it feels great. I am very conscious and very aware of it, and I know a lot of other people are."

So New Age it was.

CHAPTER 15

The *Half Moon* Sails Again

I met Chip Reynolds on a blustery day in June as crew and volunteers were preparing the *Half Moon* for its summer of sailing on the Hudson; the ship was tied up alongside a concrete pier at one of Albany's water treatment plants just north of the Capitol building. Tall, thin, and serious with a wry undercurrent, Reynolds has a bit of John Cleese in his face and mien. He is the director of the New Netherland Museum in Albany and the master of the organization's ship.

"We are looking at our replica of the *Half Moon*," Reynolds said. The ship was at the upper range of size for what the Dutch called *jaghtes*, a shortening of the word *jaghtschip* (chasing ship). The modern term *yacht* is derived from the same word.

Jaghtes were fast-sailing, highly maneuverable ships that ordinarily would be in the East India trade, sailing from Amsterdam in the company of *fluitschips* (flyboats) and frigates and larger cargo ships to Batavia, modern-day Jakarta, Indonesia.

"The yachts were the fast trading vessels," Reynolds told me. "Neither these nor the larger cargo ships would go out individually to make sales. They would sail in convoys for protection and security. When they were sailing in convoy, these would typically be in the lead or they would carry messages ahead. And once they were in the Spice Islands, they would do the interisland trade because they were more maneuverable and could move around more quickly than the larger ships.

The replica *Half Moon* moored at Albany.
Photo by the author

"And also you didn't have as much exposure," Reynolds said. "If one of these was taken, you didn't lose everything. You would lose a small portion."

The Dutch Trading Fleet

Reynolds said smaller yachts in the Dutch fleet around the time of Henry Hudson's voyage would have been perhaps fifty to sixty tons in size, tonnage being a measurement of capacity, not weight. The *Half Moon* was just over 100 tons. Fluitschips and frigates could be upward of 400 tons and required larger crews.

"Some of these yachts would have just stayed down there in the Spice Islands and traveled around trading. The *Half Moon* was just one of dozens of yachts that the East India Company had in con-

219

The reconstructed *Half Moon* prepares
for a season on the Hudson River.
Photo by the author

struction on the waterfront in the early 1600s. When the East India
Company decided to provide Hudson with a vessel, this was one
that was under construction, so they just provided it to him."

(Some historians believe the *Half Moon* may already have sailed
on trading voyages, perhaps to the Spice Islands, before Hudson
was given command in 1609.)

These ships were mostly built to sail to the hot climes of Batavia and the Spice Islands, and yet Hudson was dispatched in the *Half Moon* to sail to Novaya Zemlya and the Arctic. I asked Reynolds if the Dutch took this into account in any way.

"I doubt it," he said. "Remember that to get to Indonesia they had to go around the Cape of Good Hope. So, they knew they were going to be sailing into tough conditions no matter what. There is no evidence to indicate that there would have been different construction practices for vessels going to the Far North. It was just off the shelf."

Dutch shipbuilding had evolved toward the construction of freighters, a trend that accelerated once the Netherlands was able to break free of Spanish rule.

"Look at the evolution of shipbuilding technology," Reynolds said. "You go from the late 1400s when the Spanish and Portuguese galleon style was common; those tended to have a lateen rig, and they did not have much cargo capacity. They were mostly sailing in coastal routes."

(A lateen rig hangs a triangular sail from a spar that crosses an upright mast. The design is believed to have come from the north coast of Africa.)

"When [Christopher] Columbus came across, the Portuguese were going around Africa and others were looking at crossing the Atlantic and coming this way. The Basques were coming across to do fishing off the coast of North America.

"As the whole oceanic trade began to expand, ships had to get larger in order to get the economy of scale to do that kind of sailing," Reynolds said. Vessels needed more space to carry the commodities—spices or fish or the stuff they would steal from other ships. And they also needed more substantial vessels to weather ocean storms and carry sufficient provisions to stay at sea longer.

"By the time you got to the late 1500s, especially for the Dutch ships, you can see a change from the hull form where the bow had a much finer entry. The *Half Moon* had a very bulbous bow; it was big and beefy and broad."

Reconstructing the *Half Moon*

The replica of the *Half Moon* that now sails the Hudson was built near Albany in 1989. Just as we don't know exactly what Henry Hudson looked like, historians have never found maritime plans for the ship. That is most likely because the *Half Moon* was nothing out of the ordinary; it was one of dozens or hundreds of similar jaghtes built by the Dutch at the time.

The replica was based on plans, paintings, and descriptions of other ships of the time with the addition of a few details gleaned from logs, journals, and registration papers filed in Holland.

Though it is thought to be authentic in appearance, today's *Half Moon* was constructed with some modern materials mixed in with old designs. For example, the wood is sealed with epoxy and the frame and beams are made of laminated and sealed wood. The rigging is made of synthetic rope with a stainless-steel core; the sails are also made of synthetic material. Down below is a small diesel engine that is available for auxiliary power; Reynolds points out that it is of little or no use in maneuvering when the ship is moving very slowly because the propeller—obviously a modern and nonauthentic component—sits behind the rudder.

The replica has six major sails on three principal masts, a total of more than 2,700 square feet of fabric held aloft. The longest dimension of the ship is its length from its beak to the poop deck (the most forward level surface to its aftmost planking) of about eighty-five feet. The *Half Moon*'s beam or width is just 17.3 feet at its broadest on the top deck. And its draft, the depth of the ship that sits below the waterline with a full load aboard, is about 8.5 feet.

There are three major upright masts. Closest to the bow is the foremast, raked slightly forward. Near the middle of the ship is the mainmast. Just ahead of the cabin at the stern is the mizzenmast, which is raked slightly to the aft or stern. There is also a bowsprit that sticks out toward the bow of the ship over the figurehead.

The helmsman steers the ship from a position just in front of the mizzenmast; ships of this period did not use a wheel but instead a whipstaff, which was a heavy piece of wood that passed through a hole in the deck to a pivot point below. The staff was horizontally linked to the end of the tiller and from there the rudder. Standing in front of the whipstaff, the helmsman pushes it to the right to move the tiller to the left; in turn, the tiller pushes the rudder to the right and aims the bow of the ship in the intended direction.

Of course, as any sailor will tell you, and as Captain Reynolds emphasizes, the fact that the ship is pointed on a particular heading does not mean it will sail in that direction. The direction of the wind, the influences of currents and tides, and the matter of how close the captain is attempting to sail into an oncoming wind all have an effect.

Ahead of the whipstaff is a human-powered capstan that is used as a winch to raise and lower sails, gaffs, and anchors; another capstan is directly below so that the crew can turn it without being on the exposed deck or to allow double-teaming with two levels of men.

The main deck runs the length of the ship including the open area between the mizzenmast and foremast as well as the enclosed officer's cabin at the stern. At the stern of the ship, above the officer's cabin, is the captain's cabin; the roof of that small cabin, and the highest platform on the ship other than on the masts, is the poop deck.

The cabin at the front of the ship, just short of the foremast, is called the forecastle and on the 1989 replica of the *Half Moon* this area includes the stove for the galley.

One level down from the main deck is the 'tween deck or orlop deck; the Dutch called this the *tusschendek*. This low-ceilinged area includes the tiller and capstan near the stern and the anchor cable at the bow. In between is storage space, several small cannons, and makeshift hammocks and beds for the crew. Four of the ship's small defensive cannons, two on each side, are positioned here; two others sit at the stern.

The lowest level of the *Half Moon* is the hold, a surprisingly capacious area divided into areas that stored barrels in some compartments and sacks and loose materials elsewhere.

Reynolds said that when he took command he had worries about some of the design elements of the replica; he was especially concerned about the possibility of taking on water through the open gun ports on the orlop deck during a severe heel. As such, standard operating procedure on the vessel in unprotected waters calls for caulking the ports closed.

In 1996 on his first trip with the ship, Reynolds reported, the ship was hit broadside by a sudden squall on the Hudson River, a storm where peak winds reached fifty knots—about fifty-seven miles per hour. The *Half Moon* was unable to quickly point into the wind or fall off, so it took the full force broadside. The sturdy little ship survived to sail another day.

Rigging Today's *Half Moon*

Most of us can get lost very quickly when a seaman begins to describe sail and rigging design—even more so when you're dealing with a 400-year-old Dutch ship. Reynolds stood on the dock and pointed out some of the features of the *Half Moon.*

"In the fore of the ship you have the bowsprit, which is the yard sticking forward at an angle out of the beak. Beneath that would be hanging a spritsail; it is on the square yard and the sail hangs down from that bowsprit.

"These ships did not carry jibs the way we think of them today. You don't see jibs coming into play for another hundred years after this. The point of this is that these vessels suffered weather helm, which means that if you let go of the whipstaff or the tiller, you have to compensate for the natural heading of the ship by pulling the helm up into the wind.

"Let's say we are heading toward that far shore over there," Reynolds said, pointing east across the Hudson toward the town of Rensselaer, "and the wind is coming in from our left. We would have to force the ship to turn to the left, into the wind, in order to sail straight. That weather helm is offset by putting more sail farther forward which is what that bowsprit is all about, and later the jib.

"The farther forward, the more leverage you get and more turning effect you get per area of sail. A tiny little sail would have an enormous effect on the steering of the ship because it is so far out there. That's why you had these really long bowsprits."

"On the foremast you have a topsail, which is a square sail set from the top; the top is the basketlike affair mistakenly referred to as the crow's nest. It is a top, or in the Dutch terminology, the *mars*. The topsail yard is above the mars.

"And they even had one element that we could add to this: a spritsail top mast. Just as we have these topsails on the mainmast and the foremast, we could have another little topsail that would be on the very tip end of that bowsprit. What that does is move sail area far forward and that balances the ship by causing it to fall off the wind."

Even in modern naval architecture, Reynolds said, the goal is to have a ship that once its sails are set will stay close to being balanced—meaning that when you let go of everything, it will naturally steer up into the wind.

"This is a major safety factor. If you find yourself at sea in a storm and you lose your steering, you want the vessel to just slowly wind vane up into the wind so that it will just lie ahull."

When a ship lies ahull, it drifts without the effect of the sails. However, Reynolds said, if a ship falls off (turns away from the direction of the wind), its sails become full with air and the ship's stern is exposed.

Inside the *Half Moon*

"There was no formal method of design at the time of the original *Half Moon*," Reynolds said. "These ships were built to rule of thumb. They didn't have a naval architect making a picture that they followed. The shipwrights laid out a keel; they put down a plank that starts out at the bow and comes all the way back to the stern. Then they would lay another plank on top of that and then they put in some little pieces of wood to hold those planks together.

"And then so on until they get to the point where it is high enough up that they can put in the first futtocks [curved timbers that form the frame]. Finally, they make the planks fit to the frame. It is skin-first construction, as opposed to frame-first.

"They would specify the tonnage of the ship they wanted to build, and once they had that tonnage, they knew the keel length. Once they had the keel length, then they had the breadth, and once they had the breadth they had the depth. Everything goes as a ratio off these measures."

These were not fast ships; the VOC didn't much care about speed for the sort of cargo it would be carrying. The 10 or 15 percent disadvantage caused by the yacht's broad bow was more than offset by the value of a larger cargo capacity.

Sailing the replica *Half Moon* today is like participating in an archaeological experiment, Reynolds said. "When I first saw depictions of these very crowded anchorages in London and Amsterdam and other European ports, I said to myself that has to be a fanciful construction of the artist, because you just couldn't pack that many ships in there.

"Since then I have sailed in crowded conditions with the *Half Moon,* tacking and maneuvering the vessel through clam fleets in Long Island Sound where the clammers have been maybe fifty feet apart. That has given me firsthand experience to say when you have someone who knows how to sail this ship, and an experienced crew, you can do it."

Even to an amateur, it is apparent that the small ship has a lot of sail and a rather puny rudder. I asked Reynolds about maneuvering.

"The principal control is from the sails," he said. "This rudder is greatly restricted in its swing compared to modern ships. If you're on a modern ship—any of the ships that come into the port of Albany or tug boats or small sailing sloops—you are going to find at least thirty-five degrees of swing to each side; some will go over to forty or fifty degrees. Our rudder might go thirteen degrees to each side. So, when we are full over we are still only one-third of the way over relative to a modern vessel."

Though the rudder is small, Reynolds said, it is nevertheless important in keeping the vessel balanced: like a trim tab on a modern ship (and the aeronautical equivalent on a plane). "When we tack, we can't just shove the thing over, because then it acts like a brake," he said.

"We have reached nine or ten knots under sail alone, from the mouth of the Chesapeake Bay up into New York Harbor in optimum conditions."

The key, Reynolds said, is to find wind strong enough to drive the ship but not so powerful as to make the seas so rough that it will pitch (front-to-back movement), roll (side to side), or yaw (twist). Any of these movements can reduce the forward motion.

"The ideal would be to have flat water and a wind speed of thirty knots, but you don't get that in the ocean," Reynolds said.

The *Half Moon* Makes a Cameo

"Since I have been on," Reynolds said, "the farthest we have gone is near the Virginia–North Carolina border. I went there because that's where Hudson went; he didn't land there, but he sailed into that vicinity and started making his trip back up the coast."

The replica *Half Moon* had traveled to Virginia to make a cameo appearance in *The New World*, a movie released in 2006 set within the story of the first encounter between European and Native American cultures at the time of the founding of the Jamestown settlement in 1607, including a version of the Pocahontas story.

The *Half Moon*, under the command of Captain Reynolds, stood in for one of the original Jamestown vessels, the *Susan Constant*, in a scene proceeding up the James River and the Chickahominy River toward the first landing. Filmmakers gave the ship a makeover in darker colors, and hid all signs of modern adaptations made to the vessel.

The trip to Virginia and other sea trials gave Reynolds a good appreciation for the capabilities of the vessel. "It handles very favorably," Reynolds told me. "In the open ocean we have been out in a full gale for thirty-six hours and I felt more secure on this than I have on nineteenth-or early twentieth-century square-rigged sailing ships where the topsides are lower. On those ships, they are longer and sleeker but in similar conditions the decks would have been awash with green water.

"On the *Half Moon*, we have these very high topsides. We have bulwarks that are all the way around so when we were out in the middle of this storm I did not even have the crew don their life jackets. We were really secure. In comparable conditions on a more modern vessel I would have rigged jack lines and had people wearing life harnesses.

"Now because we are higher up, you feel the motion a lot more when you are moving. But it is a stable ship. Just to give you a feel for this, when I was standing on the quarter deck back [near the stern], I was looking up at the waves that were coming in on us [at the bow]."

From One Captain to Another: Hudson's Sailing Ability

In the journals of Hudson's voyages in the waters near Spitsbergen, Novaya Zemlya, and Greenland, there are notations about times when they were overwhelmed by the seas and were forced to drop all sails.

"That was standard procedure for dealing with storms in those days," Reynolds said. "Once you got up to about gale-force winds, the seas become really gray and the motion of the ship is tremendous.

"Remember, they did not have the same level of understanding of meteorological conditions we do, and they didn't have weather forecasts. Conditions on the ship would get miserable for the crew and there would come a time when the best thing to do was just stop and lie ahull.

"We have done that in our *Half Moon*," Reynolds continued. "It sounds absurd in this day and age to just strike all the sails and lie there, but actually that is a very effective tactic in these vessels. Or you can set an anchor, and even if you can't reach the bottom you set a couple of anchors at the bow and it causes the ship to lie with the bow into the wind. And as the waves are coming on, you ride up and over them just like that."

On Hudson's 1609 voyage—the one that took him from England to Novaya Zemlya to the Hudson River—Robert Juet writes about setting anchors off the coast of Virginia.

"My first thought was, 'Who in their right mind would set anchor out in the ocean?' But now having the benefit of experience on this vessel and knowing more about the technologies of the seventeenth century I can see how that is a very effective tactic."

And then there came time for Hudson to maneuver his rudimentary, broad-bowed, understeered vessel up the river from Manhattan on a waterway that includes strong tides, changing currents, shifting winds, and a few sharp changes of direction.

"The *Half Moon* handles extraordinarily well on the river," Reynolds told me. "It's actually more effective on the river. The tidal currents going up and down give you a tremendous boost."

Reynolds said that as he read the journal section that dealt with crossing the Atlantic, he was surprised to find that they seemed to recognize what today we know to be the Labrador Current.

"At first I thought, that really isn't happening," Reynolds continued. "How could they measure a half-knot current with the instruments they had in their day?"

But sailing the replica of the *Half Moon*, Reynolds said, he found that the countervailing force of the current can make a difference in the degree to which the ship can point up into the wind.

"If you are sailing along with even a half knot of current trying to make your way into the wind, you are going to be able to point up to a certain level," Reynolds said. "If the current is favorable, you can go up a little higher; if the current is countervailing, you are going to be down from that a little bit. And it is a recognizable amount."

The difference might be more than five degrees from the intended heading, enough for Hudson and his men to recognize something like the Labrador Current out in the open ocean. And on the Hudson River, the current is one to two knots with the ebb and flow of the tides; the speed of the current increases with the melting of the winter snows and during periods of rain.

"On most of the rivers in the mid-Atlantic, you can ride these currents for a considerable distance," Reynolds said. "If you catch the start of the flood going up and pace yourself, you will be able to ride that current right up the river. The same can happen when you go back down.

"When you take maximum advantage of the ebb and flood currents, not only do you point a little bit better into the wind but [also] you increase your speed over the ground."

Making the Connection to Captain Hudson

"One of the very first trips that I took on the *Half Moon* had me traveling to and from the Chesapeake Bay in the same time of year Hudson did," Reynolds said. "I have to admit that when I reached the mouth of the Delaware and realized it was virtually the day Hudson was there it had a big impact on me.

"I looked out and realized I was seeing exactly what he would have seen. I was taking soundings and I was worried about the same Hen and Chicken shoals that he was measuring. You would have to be a pretty shallow person to not feel a sense of connection.

"But apart from the New Agey part of it, it really does give me insight as to what Hudson must have been thinking as he was traveling through there and measuring the depth of water," Reynolds said. "And I do feel that on the Hudson River there have been many times when we have been anchored at a location where Hudson would have been anchored at the same time of year. You see things and you feel things.

"We tied up to the dock at West Point one time in early October, which would have been within weeks of when Hudson had passed there on his voyage," Reynolds said. "I woke up early; the water was still warm and the air was cold and crisp and there was not a breath of air.

"I was watching the fog as it was developing off the water and rising up and you begin to get a little circulation pattern; it was as if there were these little ghosts surrounding us, dancing up and down from the water. With a modern mind we can understand things like convection, but there was another part of me looking at it through Hudson's eyes and thinking what an amazing and remarkable natural phenomena this was."

CHAPTER 16

Hudson's Obscure Monuments

The late years of the nineteenth century—the Gilded Age—was a time when the rich got very rich and the United States' great cities began to think in grand terms. The 1893 Columbian Exposition in Chicago had created a fabulous celebration of industry and economic power—the "White City." The New York Public Library, a beaux arts masterpiece, was begun in 1897.

In that same year, Ulysses Grant's tomb—which is still the largest mausoleum in North America—was dedicated on a bluff above the Hudson River at 122nd Street, with more than a million people participating in a parade and ceremony. The Soldiers and Sailors Monument, a memorial to the Civil War dead, was completed in 1902 at Eighty-ninth Street and Riverside Drive.

In 1901, Theodore Roosevelt was summoned from Mount Marcy near the source of the Hudson River for a mad dash to Buffalo to assume the presidency after William McKinley succumbed to an assassin's bullet. (He was shot at another grand World's Fair, the Pan-American Exposition in Buffalo.) Roosevelt, who was larger than life in most everything he did, used the "bully pulpit" to propel U.S. influence in the world, including the assumption of the Panama Canal project in 1904.

And in 1905, a group of New Yorkers began to make plans to commemorate the tercentennial of Henry Hudson's voyage up the river in 1609. At the head of the first group was Robert Roosevelt, uncle of the president.

At the same time, a separate group decided to hold a celebration of the centennial of steam navigation on the river in 1907, and the Robert Fulton Memorial Association was formed. Its original leader was General Fred D. Grant, son of the former president and general now entombed in upper Manhattan.

The two commemorative groups were soon brought together as a joint commission, and they made plans for celebrations and monuments for what became known as the Hudson-Fulton Celebration. The chosen time was the week beginning September 20, 1909; whether intentional or not, that date corresponds with the moment when Hudson finally gave up on proceeding farther north in the river and prepared to turn around and sail back toward Manhattan.

The Fulton portion of the event was chiefly the re-creation of a replica of the steamship.

The Hudson committee's plans were much grander. The biggest project was to be the Hudson Memorial Bridge, spanning Spuyten Duyvil Creek at the top end of Manhattan to connect to the Bronx and Westchester. It was estimated to cost about $5 million.

The original plans called for the central steel span to be 825 feet long, just 15 feet shorter than the longest similar bridge in the world, a steel arch over the gorge at Niagara Falls. The roadway would stand 170 feet over the creek.

The city of New York was expected to pay for the bridge, but the memorial commission proposed to raise funds from the public for the construction of "some suitable monument" to Hudson on a knoll at the southern end of the bridge approach.

The grand bridge envisioned by the memorial committee was delayed; to begin with, the Municipal Arts Commission objected to the design for masonry arch decorations on the approaches, saying they were out of context with the forested cliffs of the area. In any case, the city failed to come up with the money.

Instead, the group turned its attention to three other projects: a re-creation of the *Half Moon*, a party on the river from Manhattan to Albany, and the erection of a monument to Hudson.

The First Replica of the *Half Moon*

The original idea had been to build the *Half Moon* in New York, but the sponsors quickly gave that up when they received an offer from the people of Holland to contribute a replica.

In 1908, just as in 1989, the builders had no original plans from which to work. Researchers scoured the archives of the Amsterdam and Zealand chambers of the VOC for details of the ship's size and type and based their design on other ships of the time. One of the sources was a set of plans believed to be for the *Hope*, which is thought to be a sister ship to the *Half Moon*.

Construction of the ship began using oak beams, which had been recovered from a Dutch navy yard; the wood had been submerged for more than a century. The keel was laid on October 29, 1908, and the ship was launched on April 15, 1909; the cost was estimated at about $40,000.

The replica was loaded aboard the steamship *Soestdyk* of the Holland-America Line and transported from Rotterdam to New York, where it was put back in the water at the Brooklyn Navy Yard. On September 25, 1909, the *Half Moon* left the yards and entered the Hudson River for its part in the celebration.

In the Dutch re-creation of the ship, the *Half Moon* had a figurehead of a red lion with a golden mane; the ship's bow was painted green with red and yellow ornaments of sailor's heads. The main body of the ship was painted brown, but the high poop deck at the stern was sky blue with white clouds; on the stern was a yellow crescent moon with a "man in the moon" figure within.

Finally, above the windows of the captain's cabin were standards and symbols including the arms of Amsterdam and the Seven Provinces and the monogram of the Amsterdam chamber of the Dutch East India Company—the initials VOC. An ornate lantern hung from the stern.

Other details included a carved wooden post or bitt, in the shape of the head and shoulders of a man; a pulley built into the post held some of the halyards that were used to hoist the yards up the mast.

On ships of the time, this was called the "knight-head" or "silent servant."

The 1909 replica was similar, although apparently slightly smaller, than the 1989 version. The "heavy guns" in the earlier replica were about 800 pounds each, and the orlop deck included the necessary tools and accessories for the weapons including rammers, sponges, ladles, matchsticks, and extractors. Also hung on the wall were pikes for close-up battle.

The forecastle included three brass tablets with Dutch homilies and platitudes of the sort your grandmother might have made in needlepoint. According to 1909 accounts, the plaques read: HONOR THY FATHER AND THY MOTHER, DO NOT FIGHT WITHOUT CAUSE, and GOOD ADVICE MAKES THE WHEELS RUN SMOOTHLY.

The captain's cabin was quite small, just five-feet-three-inches high; there were two windows at the stern and one on each side. The Dutch stocked their replica with items including pewter plates and utensils, various navigational instruments, and a replica of Hudson's contract with the VOC.

The *Half Moon* was sailed up the river by its Dutch crew. It was accompanied by the reconstruction of Robert Fulton's *North River Steam Boat*, the first steamer on the Hudson. The two vessels made a slow passage from Manhattan to Troy, stopping for ceremonies at almost every town and village along the way. There was also a series of motorboat races on the river; powered small craft were still a novelty on the Hudson.

The Hudson Monument

Although the city of New York had agreed to donate land for a memorial to Hudson, nothing happened until after the celebration was completed. At the New York City Hall, I studied a stack of yellowing documents belonging to the art commission.

According to the handwritten forms, final approval was given December 14, 1909, to the Hudson Monument Association for a commemoration given as a gift to the city. It was described as "a column built of Milford granite surmounted by a statue in bronze of Henry Hudson, with bas reliefs on opposite sides of the base or pedestal."

The column was to be located in a new park that would be part of the nonexistent Hudson Memorial Bridge, near West 227th Street in Spuyten Duyvil.

The commission gave final approval to the column and a preliminary okay for the statue and reliefs. The proposed sculptor for the statue was Karl Bitter of West 77th Street in New York.

Ground was broken for the column in late 1909. According to reports of the day, four children were enlisted to use silver shovels for the event; they represented the Weckquaesgeek Indians, who occupied northern Manhattan, the Dutch, the English, and early-twentieth-century Americans. The column was to be 100 feet in height, and the supposed elevation of the plot of land was 200 feet above sea level, which conveniently added up to 300, as in the tercentennial of Hudson's voyage. The Doric-style column, though, was not completed until 1912, and there was no statue to place at its top.

Bitter, who was born and trained in Vienna, immigrated to the United States in 1889 and quickly became one of the best-known and most successful artists of the late nineteenth and early twentieth centuries. He worked on pieces for the World Columbian Exposition in 1893 and was the director of the Pan American Exposition in Buffalo in 1901.

Bitter had completed several plaster models of Henry Hudson by 1912 when funds ran out. On April 9, 1915, when exiting a performance at the Metropolitan Opera in New York, he was struck by a car that jumped the curb; he died several days later.

Among his remaining works is the Pulitzer Fountain (also known as "Pomona" or "Abundance"), just east of New York's Plaza Hotel on Fifth Avenue. Other works in New York City include ornaments and sculptures at the Metropolitan Museum of Art and the U.S. Customs House and the famed Astor doors at Trinity Church in lower Manhattan.

It was not until 1935 that the combined powerhouses of Mayor Fiorello H. La Guardia and New York's master government builder Robert Moses put the projects—the bridge and the statue—back on track. Work on the sculpture was resumed by Bitter's assistant, Karl Gruppe. Born in Rochester, Gruppe was the chief sculptor for the New York City Department of Parks from 1934 to 1937. Among Moses's many titles was Parks Commissioner, although his most powerful position may have been his chairmanship of the Triborough Bridge Authority, which shaped much of modern New York with bridges and highways.

Moses acquired the land where the approaches for the Hudson Bridge had been planned and named it Henry Hudson Memorial Park. The land runs along Independence Avenue in the Bronx between Kappock Street and West 227th Street, about a quarter-mile inland from the river. The bridge was completed in December 1936; the monument was finally dedicated on January 6, 1938.

Gruppe's statue shows Hudson dressed in foul weather gear, legs spread as if balancing himself on a rolling deck. The work stands about

One of Karl Gruppe's models for the Hudson Memorial in New York.
Photo by the author. Sculpture from the Collection of the City of New York

eighteen feet tall and is difficult to see detail from the park; in the ensuing years, the forested area of the lower Bronx has been filled in with apartment blocks. Sailing up the Hudson, you can barely see the top of the column and the statue.

More easily examined are the bas reliefs on the north (upriver) and south sides of the base of the column. The southern sculpture shows Hudson receiving his commission from the VOC; the other side is a tableau that shows an armed Dutchman in a ruffled collar trading trinkets for furs with three Native Americans.

The Hudson Memorial statue pokes its head up between apartment buildings
in the Bronx.
Photo by the author

While studying the art commission documents at New York City
Hall, I literally stumbled across a bronze statue in the hallway. The
plate at its base read: HENRY HUDSON BY KARL GRUPPE. It was a small-
scale version of one of the prototypes for the monument that sits at
the top of the column in the Bronx. The face of Henry Hudson did
not particularly resemble the portrait that hangs in the Governor's
Room two floors below, but there is no reason why it should. They
are both artists' conceptions.

The *Half Moon* Comes to Cohoes

The commemoration was considered an artistic success but a financial failure. On October 11, 1909, the *Half Moon* was turned over to

the Americans; part of the agreement with the Dutch gave the ship in perpetual trust to the people of New York.

For a period of time, the vessel was maintained by the Palisades Interstate Park Commission on the west bank of the Hudson before the deteriorating ship was moved to Rondout Creek near Kingston. In 1924, it was towed up river to Cohoes, near where Hudson's crew ended their exploration.

I spoke with Walt Lipka, an enthusiastic amateur historian who filled in some of the details of how the replica came to reside in a riverside park in Cohoes and its sorry demise.

Daniel Cosgro, the mayor of Cohoes in 1924, held sway over a block of votes that was important in state politics. He cashed in some of his chips by petitioning the legislature for ownership of the replica. According to Lipka, Cosgro even threatened to take back the Cohoes mastodon bones if the *Half Moon* wasn't delivered.

The ship was brought ashore south of the historic Van Schaick Mansion, where a park was prepared to hold it as an exhibit. Before the ship was even installed, vandals attempted to burn it down, but Lipka said the ship was so water-logged it didn't catch fire.

The gambrel-roofed Van Schaick Mansion, at the junction of the Hudson and Mohawk rivers, was built between 1735 and 1755 by Anthony Van Schaick on part of the "Half Moon" land patent held by the family. The patent, granted to Goosen Gerritsen Van Schaick and Philip Pieterse Schuyler in 1665, included all the land lying between the two rivers, including the town of Waterford and the islands that divide the "sprouts" of the Mohawk into the Hudson.

The house was used as a military headquarters during the American Revolution; Benedict Arnold was among the generals who met at the house to plan the battle of Saratoga. In preparation for the battle, 5,000 Continental soldiers were garrisoned on the grounds; the Polish volunteer Thaddeus Kosciusko oversaw the construction of breastwork defenses on Peebles Island at the same time.

The *Half Moon* was put in a small pond in East Side Park in 1925, and some repairs were undertaken to make it into a historic, or at least touristic attraction, Lipka said. City parks personnel gave tours, and records show visitors from around the state, nation, and foreign places.

But the vandals also made regular visits. A December 20, 1932, article in the *Cohoes American* reported the sixth fire at the ship that year, a major blaze that generated flames visible across the city and in Troy on the other side of the river. The ruins of the ship were removed soon after. Today, a circular depression in the grass marks the former location of the pond and the *Half Moon*.

The Orange, White, and Blue

The official flag of the city of New York commemorates the Dutch and the Native Americans, but not Hudson.

The flag has three vertical bars: blue, white, and orange—the colors of the flag of the United Netherlands in 1625. Floating in the white bar is the city seal, a complex combination of symbols. A central shield is quartered by an X-shaped saltire cross that is made up of four sails of a windmill. In the top and bottom quadrant is a beaver. The left and right segments each hold a barrel of flour.

The shield is supported to the left by a Dutch sailor. In his right hand he holds a "plummet"—a lead ball on a chain used to take depth soundings. To the right is a Native American holding an empty bow. They both stand on a horizontal laurel branch.

The windmill and flour represent the early industry of the city; the beaver comes from the original flag of New Netherland, and more important, from the lowly rodent that made huge fortunes in Europe for the early traders in the New World.

At the top of the seal is an American eagle. Below the laurel, the original version of the seal and flag bore the date 1664, commemorating the capture of New Amsterdam by the English (and the adoption of the name New York for the city). In 1997, the date on the seal was changed to 1625, commemorating the original founding of the city by the Dutch.

And finally, a ribbon half-circles the bottom of the seal: it reads SIGILLUM CIVITATIS NOVI EBORACI, a Latin phrase meaning "Seal of the City of New York."

The Weathervane

When the current *Half Moon* is not at its occasional moorings just below the Capitol in Albany, its presence is still noted by the extraordinary weathervane at the State University Plaza. The immense building itself, at the foot of State Street, was designed by the architect Marcus T. Reynolds to resemble the Nieuwerk annex of the Cloth Guild Hall, a huge Flemish gothic structure in Ypres, Belgium.

The building was constructed as the headquarters of the Delaware and Hudson Railroad. It is covered with ornate carvings and statues. A portal at the base of the main tower includes the name and coat of arms of Henry Hudson; nearby is the salamander symbol of Francis I of France, who sent a land expedition to the Albany area before the Dutch landed.

Other names and families of note memorialized on the building include the Van Rensselaers, the Livingstons, and the Schuylers. There's also a coat of arms for the railroad, and several carvings of beavers—one of the most important items of trade in the region. Just for good measure, tucked under the gable at the top of the main tower is a version of Michelangelo's "The Thinker."

Reynolds was one of the most important architects of the early twentieth century in Albany. Besides the Delaware and Hudson, and *Albany Evening Journal* buildings, he was also responsible for the famed Gideon Putnam Hotel in Saratoga Springs as well as more than a dozen other notable buildings in the capital city.

According to the State Education Department, the weathervane is the largest such working device in the country: it is nearly seven feet long and nine feet high, and weighing in at 400 pounds. It was also designed by Reynolds and installed in January 1915 as the building neared completion. The gold leaf weathervane, which is visible from the river and much of downtown Albany, depicts the *Half Moon* under sail.

CHAPTER 17

The Hudson Through Modern Eyes

The Hudson remains a busy river, although the mix of traffic has changed greatly since the *Half Moon* came north in 1609, followed by other Dutch and then English explorers in sailing vessels.

Within five years of Henry Hudson's trip, there was a Dutch trading post at Fort Orange on Castle Island near Albany, and a permanent settlement was made there in 1624. The next year New Amsterdam was established at the mouth of the river and famously "purchased" from the natives in 1626; soon after the English took over in 1664 it was renamed New York in honor of the Duke of York.

By 1783, river ports like the town of Hudson became home ports for major whaling fleets that sailed in waters as distant as the South Pacific.

The first commercial steamboat service on the river began August 17, 1807, when Robert Fulton's experimental boat departed New York; it arrived in Albany a mere thirty-two hours later (including an overnight stop). The vessel, variously called the *Clermont*, the *North River Steamboat*, and the *North River*, continued until the onset of ice that winter.

Robert R. Livingston, Fulton's powerful partner, had convinced the New York State Legislature to grant a twenty-year monopoly on the use of any steam-powered vessel. This exclusion delayed the expansion of service on the river—which has shores in both New York and New Jersey at its lower end—until the U.S. Supreme Court intervened in 1824, setting some of the rules for interstate commerce. By 1840, there were more than a hundred steamboats on the Hudson.

In 1825, with the completion of the first version of the Erie Canal, the Hudson River became something of the sort of passage to the Northwest that early explorers had envisioned: barges with grain, coal, and other commodities could travel from as far away as the Great Lakes to meet up with waiting cargo ships at Albany or at other warehouse and transshipment ports like Kingston. Freighters heading the other way would bring finished goods from New York and Europe to the nation's interior via the canal.

The privately financed Delaware and Hudson Canal connected the river at Rondout near Kingston some 108 miles west to the coal fields near Honesdale, Pennsylvania. Coal was offloaded at Rondout and shipped down to New York or up to Canada until 1898, when the Delaware and Hudson transformed itself into a railroad company.

Other traffic on the river included vessels carrying ice harvested and stored in the winter and then transported to the hot cities in the summer. Towns along the Hudson also brought to market bricks, cement, iron, and agricultural products.

By the mid-nineteenth century, the river was regularly traveled by luxurious vessels that connected New York to Albany and intermediary ports; the queen of the valley was the Hudson River Day Line. The ships offered cabins, formal dining rooms, and entertainment. The company's last run was on September 13, 1948, when its elegant vessel the *Robert Fulton* went downriver from Albany.

Today, barges of fuel oil and gravel come up the river, in the company of midsized freighters picking up huge turbines and modern equipment manufactured by General Electric and other companies near the Hudson. Ice breakers keep the upper river clear in the winter.

Farthermore, a handful of vessels still carry passengers up and down the river in season. The *Clearwater* and the replica of the *Half*

Moon make day trips in the summer; in the fall, some major cruise ships travel part of the way up the river from New York on "leaf-peeper" tours. And also on the Hudson are the ships of a one-of-a-kind cruise line with a mouthful of a name: American Canadian Caribbean Line (ACCL).

Among the ACCL's yearly trips are journeys from the company's base in Rhode Island that round the corner at the Battery and enter into the Hudson near the Statue of Liberty and proceed upriver all the way to Waterford. One itinerary hooks a left into the Erie Barge Canal across to Oswego and then north and back east through the St. Lawrence Seaway to Quebec City: It is a grand tour of some of the most historic and important waterways on the east coast of North America.

A Modern Captain on the Hudson

At age twenty-eight, Mike Valenti is a young man in an old business; he has been on the river and out to sea for nine years. As a master of one of the small ACCL cruise ships, he is one of a small group of modern-day Hudson River ship captains.

I sailed with Valenti on the *Grande Caribe*, an unpretentious custom-built 100-passenger ship; the vessel was launched from the Rhode Island shipyards of the iconoclastic designer Luther Blount. Among its features are a shallow draft, a narrow beam, and a pilot house that can be retracted from the top deck to make the ship low enough to squeeze below dozens of overhanging bridges that make the Erie Barge Canal unusable by more conventional vessels.

We talked about the Hudson River as it is today; Hudson would still recognize it, although he would surely be taken aback by the skyscrapers of Manhattan and the condos of New Jersey. And for its entire length, from Manhattan to Albany, the river has been channeled and dredged to allow reliable navigation.

"The ship channel follows the deepest water," Valenti said. "And that's where the swiftest currents are; they can run a good two-and-a-half knots in either direction."

The ocean brings two high tides, two low tides, and two periods of slack or no tide in roughly a twenty-four-hour span. Today, tidal charts and computer programs can tell a captain the predicted currents and water levels with great precision, Valenti said, although every once in a while there is a significant deviation from the prediction. In October 1991, for example, the "perfect storm" that caused problems all through the U.S. Northeast also brought record high tides up the Hudson River.

The river runs north with the incoming flood tide and south with the receding or ebb tide. For most of the river, this means that vessels will either gain a few knots as they travel under sail or under power, or will have to fight against the tide and lose some speed or burn more fuel. At the places where the river bends, the tide can move a vessel to one side or the other, although that same swift current tends to keep the channel deep at those locations.

When Hudson's *Half Moon* sailed up the river in 1609, it ran aground a number of times on shoals in the middle of the river or on bars near its edges; this despite the fact that the flat-bottomed ship had a draft of just over six feet. Today, the river is dredged and maintained by federal authorities, and the controlling depth—the shallowest section of the marked channel—is thirty-two feet, with some areas offering much more water beneath the keel.

As I sailed on the river, I tried to imagine Hudson and Robert Juet's appraisal of the waterway. As they passed by the sites of today's Dobb's Ferry and Irvington, the river suddenly opens up to roughly double the width of the lower passage. Did they slap each other on the back or hoist a tankard of stale beer, convinced that they were indeed in a strait that would cross the continent?

The narrowest point on the river below Albany is near Bear Mountain just above Peekskill; it's called the Race. Heading north, at a place called Stony Point, the river bends to the right for about three miles, then to the left at Jones Point for another three miles and then back to the right at Anthony's Nose (the present location of the Bear Mountain Bridge). In that stretch of water are the swiftest currents on the Hudson.

And to make things worse, this is one of several places on the river where from a mile or so away the river seems to come to an abrupt end at the base of a mountain; the sharp bends are not visible until you are much closer.

At the Race during a flood tide, the river runs about two knots faster than the typical one-and-a-half knots elsewhere on the river; with a receding or ebb tide, a boat has to fight against a current running that much faster.

A few extra knots of current is not insignificant for a sailing vessel, especially in a narrow stretch where the river is less than 2,000 feet wide. "I would imagine you would have to do quite a bit of tacking in that kind of situation," Valenti said. "He would have had his hands full."

The river makes another jog just below the U.S. Military Academy at West Point. Heading north, the Hudson makes an S-turn. Just before the turn is a location called "World's End," which is charted as the deepest place in the Hudson at 202 feet. At the S-turn, the rocky Constitution Island juts out from the eastern shore; early Dutch mariners' logs noted that this was a particularly difficult stretch of the river because the wind is often channeled straight on the nose of oncoming ships.

During the Revolutionary War, Continental forces made use of the narrow channel, the current, and the oncoming wind to attempt to erect a barrier against British ships heading up the river. A heavy iron chain atop a boom of heavy logs was placed across the river from West Point to Constitution Island in 1778; although fleets had passed by the year before, the chain was never tested.

I made a trip to the military academy and stopped at Trophy Point, a spectacular overlook that shows the narrowing river and the S-curve. Some of the cannons, guns, and other trophies on display are enclosed within a fence made of surviving two-foot-long links from the 1778 chain.

If Hudson and Juet had their doubts at the Race, they might have felt better a few miles north when the Hudson opens up again near Beacon.

Dangers in the River

Although today's Hudson River is dredged, with a deep channel marked all the way up to the Federal Lock that marks the end of the navigable river and the entrance to the Erie Barge Canal heading west and the Champlain Canal heading north, there are still places where an inexperienced boater can run into trouble. In many places, shoals exist on either or both sides of the river.

"Going aground on the Hudson a half dozen times back then, before it was charted and mapped, is not too bad," Valenti said. "As you navigate today, on any given weekend you can hear yachtsmen giving calls to sea tow to get them off a mud flat."

Valenti said the area north of Castleton to Albany—the place where Chip Reynolds believes the original *Half Moon* ended its journey—has many islands and marsh land that extends into the river. "It's not like the Caribbean where you can navigate by the water color, because whether it is two feet deep or one hundred feet deep it looks the same," he said.

The *Half Moon* on the Hudson

I asked Captain Reynolds of the replica *Half Moon* to think about Captain Hudson making a trip up the unknown and uncharted river in 1609.

"Here's a guy with vast experience and extensive knowledge for his time," Reynolds said. "That guy is not going to see the Tappan Zee and jump to the conclusion [that he has found the Northwest Passage], because there are plenty of other places that look the same.

"Why didn't he think that he could go through the continent on the Delaware? Because they sounded there, and they saw that it was too shallow for shipping to get through.

"Hudson was a guy who was very much driven by the evidentiary nature of his findings. When you come up into the Tappan Zee, it is wide open, but you can see from one end to the other and know that it is going to narrow down. And if you are taking soundings,

The Hudson bends in an "S" near West Point.
Photo by the author

once you get over to the west side of the Tappan Zee the water is shallow. You are only in two fathoms of water.

"But what he was doing was evaluating what he finds [and looking for] an opening that is worth pursuing," Reynolds said. "So he continues on up. Hudson comes to Croton Point, where the river narrows because of the peninsula there, but just past it [it] opens up again at Haverstraw Bay. He keeps going.

"When you are above the Hudson Highlands, above the Catskills, you start to see more flat land," Reynolds said. "There are a few mountains off in the distance but the geography and the terrain is changing. You are starting to see a lot more sedimentation in the river, sandbars, and evidence of flooding. This is telling you that you are not really passing through a continent; you are getting near the headwaters of a river."

The river narrows again near Stony Point, just below Bear Mountain. And now the river passes through a stretch where it is very re-stricted, but deep with a strong current; the mountains are higher and closer to the water. Couldn't Hudson have concluded that this was the end of the line?

No, said Reynolds, not if you are aware of other great passages such as the Straits of Magellan at the bottom of South America, or the Bosporus strait between Europe and Asia. The Bosporus, for example, is as wide as two miles in some places and as narrow as a third of a mile in others. "These are places where there is a huge volume of water moving through a constricted opening," Reynolds said, "but still allowing for major passage between bodies of water."

And so, in Reynolds' reconstruction of Hudson's thinking, he presses on. From Newburgh on up to above Poughkeepsie there is a long, straight, and relatively narrow reach, but the water is still very deep: at least ten to fifteen fathoms, or sixty to ninety feet. Hudson may have worried that he was running up an embayment toward the headwaters of a river, but there was not sufficient evidence for him to completely rule out the possibility of a strait.

"But by the time they got above Saugerties and to Athens, there must have come the point where they began to really think more about the possibility of a dead end," Reynolds said. By the time the Half Moon reached near where the Normanskill enters the Hudson near Selkirk—about eight miles south of Albany—the sandbars become more extensive and nearly reach from bank to bank.

The modern-day shoreline for much of the Hudson has changed from the way it was in the 1600s because of development, dredging, and channeling of the river. The places where it has changed the least are in places where the waterway is hemmed in by rocky hills and mountains, places such as the Palisades, the Hudson Highlands, and around Poughkeepsie. But from Troy south to Coxsackie and even below, the river has bulkheads and artificial walls or fills that have been put in to narrow the river and create a navigable channel.

The *Half Moon*'s Northernmost Anchorage

No one knows for certain where the *Half Moon* stopped its north-ward exploration of the river. Various historians and civic boosters declare the spot to be at Albany, at Waterford, and even at the town a few miles farther north of the Waterford shallows that calls itself Half Moon.

Reynolds guesses the location was not even all the way to present-day Albany. He pointed downstream a few miles to a set of smokestacks and below that to Henry Hudson Park across from the town of Castleton-on-Hudson, where several tributary streams enter the Hudson, dumping silt into the river and causing the formation of sandbars.

In Reynolds' mind, then, it is somewhere around Selkirk and the Normanskill that Hudson came to anchor and stopped his northward sailing on the *Half Moon*. He sent the small sloop up the river to explore and report back to him.

"He was coming up here without any knowledge of what the bottom was like; almost certainly he was running his sloop ahead to take soundings," Reynolds said, "because if their ship went hard aground and they couldn't get it off again, they would have been out of luck. They had no replacement to come get them."

Why not Waterford, as some people believe? "Not a chance," Reynolds said. "The river gets too narrow. And if you read the journal's description of what was going on with the sloop as it was traveling upstream, they do not describe Cohoes Falls. There is no mention of it. They also do not mention the myriad of islands and heavy currents that come out of the confluence of the Mohawk and the Hudson.

"Once you get up above Troy, you start hitting a maze of islands that leads you into the area around the mouth of the Mohawk," Reynolds continued. "It is so dramatic that if the *Half Moon* had been closer to it, or if the sloop had gone up there, there would have been some mention of that.

"They do talk about hitting extensive shoals, and that is the principal indicator that says, 'We can't go farther than this, because with those shoals you are not going to get shipping traffic to go up there. It is going to be small boats only."

With all the little islands in the river near Troy, wouldn't it have been possible that the *Half Moon*'s scouts in the little sloop could have passed Cohoes without seeing the falls and the entrance of the Mohawk River?

"You could be right," Reynolds said. "They could have been in a position where they couldn't see the falls. But what you do see is the current of water that is coming into the Hudson from the side; it is so strong that it is unmistakable. Even though they were traveling at a dry time of the year, as perceptive as these guys were about the conditions around them I think they would have noticed it."

In any case, Reynolds said, by the time they got near Albany they had to know that it was pretty likely that they had not found a passage through to the other side of the continent and on to Asia.

"They are hitting these sandbars and that makes them a little uneasy and the river is getting narrower. They don't want to risk the ship any further so they send the sloop ahead," said Reynolds.

The crew rowing the sloop—without Hudson, who remained on the ship—were probably wondering why they were wasting their efforts on the river. It's possible, Reynolds said, that their journal—which gives very little detail of exactly where and why they stopped heading north—reflects the fact that by this time the crew was not quite as dedicated to the task as Hudson was.

"I am not presenting that as my argument," Reynolds said. "It is equally plausible that the guys going up the river were very thorough in their searching. They just started finding the shallow waters, and that told them that even if the river went all the way through, large ships couldn't make it."

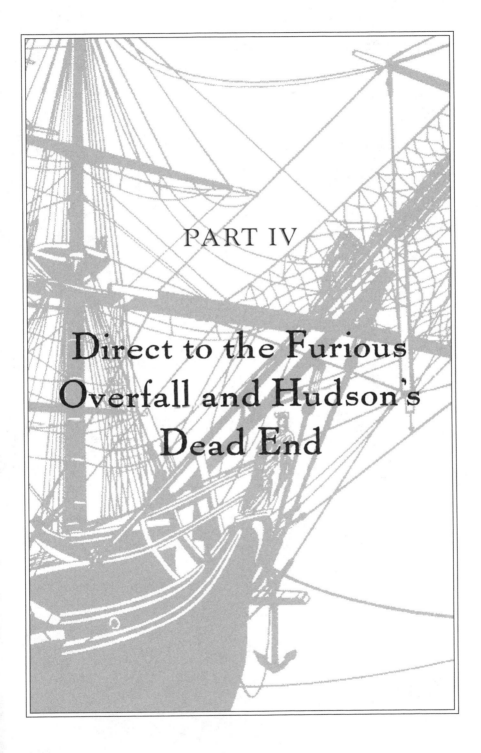

PART IV

Direct to the Furious Overfall and Hudson's Dead End

Hudson's fourth and final voyage took him into Ungava Bay in northern Quebec and then up and around the Nunavik Peninsula and into Hudson Bay and eventually the dead end of James Bay, where he and his crew were forced to spend the difficult winter of 1610–11.

CHAPTER 18

Voyage Four: Hudson Sets His Own Course—One-Way to Northern Canada

Henry Hudson returned from his voyage up the North River without finding a passage to China, but the information in his charts and logbooks was of great interest to his Dutch employers and the English government. The *Half Moon* and its documents were seized by the British when the ship landed in England instead of its Amsterdam home in October 1609.

Once again, there are not clear answers to the questions of why Hudson did not bring the ship directly back to its owners, whether he handed over all the papers or held on to some, or whether the Dutch received all the logs and charts once the ship was finally released to their custody more than six months later.

Although it was not uncommon for captains to sell their services to foreign enterprises, Hudson and the English among his crew were forbidden from leaving England or accepting employment by the Dutch, French, or other powers.

In any case, Hudson sought English backing for a fourth voyage. The Muscovy Company was out of the picture, but some of the individual investors in that company and others were now interested in trying to find the Northwest Passage and willing to give Hudson another chance.

The primary source of funds for Hudson's last trip was a syndicate that included Sir Thomas Smythe, a wealthy merchant and investor in the VOC; Sir Dudley Digges, son of the celebrated navigator Sir Thomas Digges; John Wolstenholme, the collector of customs for the port of London; and a bit of royal money and imprimatur from Henry Frederick, the Prince of Wales.

Digges and Wolstenholme would be commemorated by the naming of a pair of landmarks at the entrance to Hudson Bay; it was somewhere near Cape Wolstenholme and the Digges Islands that seeds of the final mutiny against Henry Hudson seemed to have been planted.

To Sea on *Discovery*

The ship he was given was the *Discovery*, a vessel that had already been an important part of Arctic exploration. And it was a ship's name that would go on to great fame in other centuries and in other seas.

The *Discovery* had previously been commanded by George Weymouth in 1602 on an expedition financed by the Muscovy Company; the goal was the Northwest Passage across the top of Canada. Over time, the *Discovery* would make six known voyages to the area.

Fragments of Hudson's journal—beginning in London in April 1610 and ending abruptly on August 3 near Cape Wolstenholme—survive. The men who would mutiny against Hudson and some others almost certainly destroyed the missing portions.

We can read an incomplete journal by Abacuck Prickett, a "passenger" who survived the journey and presented a sketchy account of the mutiny to authorities when the *Discovery* returned in 1611. Some of the testimony of the survivors before the Admiralty Court inquiry was also collected and published.

Hudson's and Prickett's writings were collected and published by Samuel Purchas in his 1625 book *Purchas His Pilgrimes*.

We'll begin with Hudson's journal, which is intriguing for the mysteries it raises.

An Abstract of the Journall of Master Henry Hudson, for the Discoverie of the North-west Passage, begun the seventeenth of Aprill, 1610 ended with his end, being treacherously exposed by some of the Companie.

April 17, 1610. The seventeenth of April 1610 we break ground and went down from Saint Katherine's Pool, and fell down to Blacke-wall, and so plyed down with the ships to Lee.

On board the *Discovery* were twenty-two men and two ship's boys: Henry Hudson, captain; Robert Juet, mate; John King, quartermaster; William Wilson, the original boatswain; Robert Bylot, leading seaman; Edward Wilson, surgeon; Thomas Woodhouse; Arnold Ludlow; Michael Butt; Adam Moore; Syracke Fanner; Philip Staffe, carpenter; Bennett Matthew (or Matheus), cook; Sylvanus Bond; John Thomas; Francis Clements; Michael Perse; Henry Greene; Adrian Motter; John Williams, gunner; Master Coleburne (or Colbert); Abacuck Prickett; John Hudson, ship's boy; and Nicholas Syms, ship's boy.

Despite his troublesome nature, for the third time Robert Juet is brought aboard by Hudson. Staffe, Ludlow, Perse, and young John Hudson had also sailed with him before. Abacuck Prickett was listed as a "passenger" but may have been aboard to look after the interests of one of the backers of the voyage; Prickett had been a manservant for Dudley Digges. Coleburne was more obviously assigned as a representative of the financial interests behind the voyage.

The *Discovery* was seen off by a distinguished committee that included Prince Henry, the geographer Richard Hakluyt, Smythe, and Digges. The prince and Smythe made their final farewells to Hudson in the master's cabin aboard ship.

Six days into the voyage, while the *Discovery* was near the mouth of the Thames, Hudson discharged Coleburne and put him on a small boat headed back to London. Hudson wrote that he sent with him "my letter to the Adventurers, importing the reason wherefore I so put him out of the ship."

The contents of the letter Hudson sent to his financial backers are not known. We can only assume that Hudson disagreed with suggestions or orders from the company man. Putting Coleburne off after the ship had set sail, though, allowed Hudson to proceed without having to deal directly with his financial backers about the matter.

On May 5, the ship reached the top of Scotland near the Orkney and Shetland islands. On May 8, they sighted the Faeroe Islands and three days later arrived at the eastern shore of Iceland, proceeding south to pass beneath.

After waiting for favorable winds and stocking the ship with food and water, on June 1 the *Discovery* put out to sea from a harbor on the west side of Iceland at or near the Arctic Circle.

It appears that Hudson—navigating almost exclusively by latitude and compass—was right where he wanted to be. He had found his landmarks in the sea: the Orkneys, the Shetlands, the Faeroes, and Iceland.

From Iceland, he worked his way due west and found Greenland. When he picked his way through the ice down to the bottom of Greenland—the world's largest island, and a place marked on the rough charts of Martin Frobisher as the "Land of Desolation"—he was at a latitude that was almost a straight line across to Captain John Davis's Furious Overfall, the entrance into subarctic Canada now known as Hudson Strait.

> *June 15, 1610.* We were in sight of the land in latitude 59°27′ which was called by Captain John Davis "Desolation." . . . And then running to the north-westward until the twentieth day we found the ship in 60°42′ and saw much ice and many ripplings or overfalls, and a strong stream setting from east southeast to west northwest.

A eureka moment. From desolation to ripplings, overfalls, and a strong current running to the northwest. Northwest, as in the passage to China.

At this moment, Hudson and the crew of the *Discovery* were near the top of Newfoundland at the eastern end of what would be known as Hudson Strait. If they had continued due west, they would have entered directly into Hudson Bay. Instead, the *Discovery* headed north to the rugged coast of Baffin Island near Cape Elizabeth, losing two weeks to variable winds and heavy ice.

There are few entries in Hudson's journal during this two-week period, but Prickett's private notes said that at this time "some of our men fell" sick, and there were signs of problems.

On July 5, "troubled with much Ice in seeking the shore," the *Discovery* is along the bottom of Resolution Island, which lies off the east end of Baffin Island's Meta Incognita Peninsula. The decision was made to head south to get out of the ice, and the *Discovery* entered into Ungava Bay.

Along the east shore of the bay, a place of treacherous shoals and huge tidal changes of as much as fifty feet and more, Hudson spotted land, a "Champaigne Land" worth celebrating.

July 8, 1610. Here we saw the land . . . covered with snow, a Champaigne Land, and called it Desire Provoketh. We still plied up to the westward, as the land and ice would suffer, until the eleventh day, when fearing a storm we anchored by three rocky islands in uncertain depth . . . and found it a harbor insufficient by reason of sunken rocks one of which was next morning two fathoms above water. We called them the Isles of God's Mercies.

The flood commeth from the North, flowing eight [fathoms] the change day.

Hudson's matter-of-fact journal includes a tide report: the sunken rock they found alongside them one night was two fathoms (twelve feet) above the surface of the water. The next morning, they measured the full tidal flood at eight fathoms, or forty-eight feet.

Desire Provoketh is believed to be Akpatok Island, the largest land mass in Ungava Bay, about 28 miles long and 14 miles wide and topped by a flat plateau 500 to 800 feet high. It was probably a good thing that Hudson and his men did not attempt to land there; it is very difficult to approach by sea because of sheer cliffs that reach down to the water and there were reports from later explor-

ers that the small band of natives who lived there practiced canni-
balism.

Hudson moved southward toward the bottom of Ungava Bay,
"but found ourselves embayed with land and had much ice." And so
the *Discovery* went back up north into the strait, sailing this time
along its southern shore past the Inuit gathering place of Salluit.
When they spotted land once again on August 1, they named it Hold
With Hope.

August 2, 1610. We had sight of a fair headland on the northern shore
six leagues [twenty-one miles] off, which I called Salisbury's Foreland.
We ran from them west southwest for fourteen leagues [forty-eight
miles] in the midway of which we were suddenly come into a great
and whirling sea whether caused by meeting of two streams, or an
Overfall, I know not.

Thence sailing west and by south seven leagues [twenty-four miles]
farther, we were in the mouth of a strait . . . and had no ground at one
hundred fathoms. The strait being there above two leagues [seven
miles] broad.

August 3, 1610. We put through the narrow passage, after our men
had been on land, which had well observed that the flood did come
from the north. . . . The head of this entrance on the south side I
named Cape Wolstenholme, and the head on the northwestern shore
I called Cape Digges.

After we had sailed with an easterly wind, west and by south ten
leagues [thirty-four miles] the land fell away to the southward and the
other isles and lands left us to the westward. Then I observed and
found the ship at noon in 61°20 minutes, and a sea to the westward.

Cape Wolstenholme is on the northernmost tip of the Ungava
Peninsula, near the point where the land falls away and the vast
Hudson Bay appears. Digges Islands are to the west and within
Hudson Bay. In Hudson's journal and on many maps, they are indi-
cated as a single island, but they actually have a channel that passes
north to south through them, and on modern charts they are called
Digges Islands.

These are the last known words written by Henry Hudson. It is reasonable to assume that Hudson continued to keep his journal; it is also reasonable to assume that one or another of the mutineers sought to remove written evidence of the captain's record of events that transpired after August 3, 1610.

CHAPTER 19

Prickett's Journal:
Sanitized for His
Protection

T he *Discovery* was by no means a luxury cruise ship, but Abacuck Prickett was listed in the manifest as a passenger; most historians assume he was aboard to keep an eye on the financial investment of the backers. His status as neither an officer nor a member of the crew may have saved his life in James Bay. His journal most likely also spared him (and a few others) from the gallows when they returned to London.

Prickett maintained a personal journal for the entire voyage, and it was published in 1625 as part of Samuel Purchas's collection of papers of early explorers. Although some of his comments place blame on members of the crew, it is not unreasonable to assume that he was very careful not to become too much of a threat to the dangerous men around him.

His journal fills in some of the gaps of knowledge including elements missing from the early pages of Henry Hudson's notes and events that occurred after the captain's journal comes to an abrupt end.

Prickett did not always give us the dates of his notes, and he did not use latitudes to more precisely fix his locations. But he had more of an author's eye, pointing out such things as the eruption of Mount

Hekla on Iceland and reporting some of the grumblings and then the outright mutiny of the crew.

A LARGER DISCOURSE OF THE SAME VOYAGE AND THE SUCCESSE THEREOF, written by ABACUK PRICKET

We began our voyage for the northwest passage the seventeenth of April, 1610.

Thwart of Shepey, our Master sent Master Colbert back to the owners with his letter.

We raised the Isles of Westmonie where the King of Denmark has a fortress. . . . But in our course we saw that famous hill, Mount Hecla, which cast out much fire, a sign of foul weather to come in short time.

We left Iceland astern of us and met a main of ice which did hang on the north part of Iceland and stretched down to the West, which when our Master saw he stood back for Iceland to find a harbor which we did on the Northwest part . . . where we killed a good store of fowl.

From hence we put to sea again, but neither wind nor weather serving, our Master stood back for this harbor again but could not find it, but fell with another to the south of that, called by our Englishmen Louise Bay where on the shore we found a hot bath and here all our Englishmen bathed themselves. The water was so hot it would scald a fowl.

Prickett adds a tiny detail to the removal of Master Coleburne from the *Discovery*, saying that he was put ashore across from the Isle of Sheppey, which is at the mouth of the Thames—the last piece of English land Hudson was to touch, presumably far enough away from London to prevent Coleburne or his employers from preventing the captain from setting off on his crossing.

His notes on the crossing of the North Atlantic include mention of a sighting of the Isles of Westmonie (today these are the Vestmann Isles on the southwest coast of Iceland), the erupting Mount Hekla, and a thermal spring at Louise Bay on Iceland that is hot enough for a bath or to scald a fowl.

Hekla, Iceland's most active volcano—nicknamed the "Gateway

to Hell"—has erupted many times in modern history, most recently in 2000; Prickett would have been aware of a major event in 1597 recorded by other explorers in the area.

The First Mountain of Ice

Near the end of June, the *Discovery* entered into the Davis Strait toward Hudson Bay and Prickett reports that the crew saw its first major iceberg.

> From the Desolations our Master made his way Northwest, the wind being against him . . . but in this course we saw the first great island or mountain of ice.
>
> On the west side of [Davis] Strait, our Master would have gone to the north of it but the wind would not suffer him, so we fell to the south of it into a great rippling or overfall of current. . . . Into the current we went and made our way to the north of the west till we met with ice which hung on this island.
>
> Wherefore our Master casting about, cleared himself of this ice and stood to the South, and then to the West, through store of floating ice. . . . In this our going between the ice we saw one of the great islands of ice overturn which was a good warning to us not to come nigh them, nor within their reach. . . . The next day we had a storm, and the wind brought the ice so fast upon us that in the end we were driven to put her into the chiefest of the ice and there to let her lie.
>
> Some of our men this day fell sick. I will not say it was for fear, although I saw some small sign of other grief.

Something happened here in early July and in the coming weeks; Prickett hints at fear and discord and later reports Hudson was in despair. The *Discovery* is tacking back and forth in Hudson Strait and Ungava Bay, dodging icebergs, and dealing with difficult winds and a tide that drops and rises as much as fifty feet twice a day.

> Our course was as the ice did lie, sometime to the North, then to the Northwest, and then to West, and to the Southwest, but still inclosed with ice. Which when our Master saw, he made his course to the

South, thinking to clear himself of the ice that way, but the more he strove the worse he was and the more enclosed until we could go no further.

Here our Master was in despair, and as he told me after he thought he should never have got out of this ice but there have perished.

Therefore he brought forth his Card and showed all the company that he was entered above a hundred leagues further than ever any English was and left it to their choice whether they would proceed any further: yea, or nay.

Prickett reports that the despairing captain calls a meeting of the crew and shows them his card—the rough and incomplete nautical chart he had, probably based on Captain George Weymouth's brief foray into the region in 1602—and allows them to vote whether to continue.

This may be the most important clue—ambiguous though it is— to the story of Henry Hudson. Why does the captain waiver? Why does he allow his men to vote on their direction? Is this the management style of a commanding leader?

We tend to think of stern autocratic ship captains such as William Bligh of the *Bounty*, Edward Teach (better known as the pirate Blackbeard), and great fictional figures such as Captain Ahab of Herman Melville's *Moby Dick* and Lieutenant Commander Philip Francis Queeg of Herman Wouk's *The Caine Mutiny*.

Viewed through modern eyes, it is hard not to think that what seems like weakness on Hudson's part could have been interpreted by the crew as giving them free rein to take control of the ship without being asked again. But it is also true that this was a small ship, privately financed and not under military control, and for all intents and purposes as far away from headquarters and help as the *Apollo* astronauts were when they traveled to the Moon.

And then there is also the possibility that Prickett's report was sanitized for his protection. Was there a direct challenge to Hudson's command at this point? Did Hudson ask for a vote, or was he the witness to a decision made by his crew?

In any case, Prickett reported that after many words to no purpose, the men voted to continue their exploration in the cold and unforgiving waters of Ungava Bay. They had no idea that the worst was yet to come. And Hudson was to face his final mutiny.

> Some were of one mind and some of another, some wishing themselves at home, and some not caring where . . . but there were some who then spoke words which were remembered a great while after.
>
> There was one who told the Master that if he had a hundred pounds, he would give fourscore and ten to be at home. But the Capenter made answer that if he had a hundred he would not give ten upon any such condition. . . . After many words to no purpose, to work we must on all hands to get ourselves out and to clear our ship. After much labor and time spent, we gained room to turn our ship in, and so little by little to get clear in the sea. . . .
>
> We continued our course to the northwest and raised land to the north of our course . . . and coming nigh out, there hung on the easternmost point many islands of floating ice and a bear on one of them which from one to another came towards us till she was ready to come aboard. But when she saw us look at her she cast her head between her hind legs and then dived under the ice.

Prickett paints a portrait of a torturous period of weaving back and forth in Ungava Bay in search of a passage through the ice and to the west. At various times, the ship anchored itself to large floes of ice to move with them in the current. When the *Discovery* finally made it near the top of the bay and Hudson Strait, it was driven back south by a storm, and once again we have Prickett's report that the captain was "loath at any time that we should see the North shore."

> To the North and beyond this lies an island that to the east has a fair head and beyond it to the west other broken land which makes a bay within, and a good road may be found there for ships. Our Master named the first Cape Salisbury. . . .
>
> We fell into a rippling or overfall of a current which at the first we took to be a shoal, but the lead being cast we had no ground. On we passed still in sight of the South shore. . . . Our Master took this to be a part of the [mainland] but it is an island. . . . This island has a fair head to the East and very high land which our Master named Digges

Cape and the land on the south side . . . makes another cape or headland, which our Master named Wolstenholme's Cape. . . .

Our Master sent the boat ashore with my self in charge and the carpenter . . . and others to discover to the West and Northwest . . . but
we had further to it than we thought for the land is very high and we
were overtaken with a storm of rain, thunder and lightning.

Exploring Digges Islands proved very difficult for the party because of the steep hills. They found a great waterfall, many birds,
and sorrel and scurvy grass (arctic cress), which some sailors knew
to look for as a source of vitamin C.

Passing along we saw some round hills of stone like grass cockes*
which at the first I took to be the work of some Christian. We passed
by them till we came to the south side of the hill; we went unto
them . . . and I turned off the uppermost stone and found them hollow within and full of fowls hanged by their necks. . . .

Our Master in this time came in between the two lands and shot
off some pieces to call us aboard, for it was a fog. We came aboard
and told him what we had seen and persuaded him to stay a day or
two in this place, telling him what refreshing might there be had. But
by no means would he stay, not pleased with the motion.

So we left the fowl and lost our way down to the southwest. . . .
Now we came to the shallow water wherewith we were not acquainted since we came from Iceland. . . . In this our course we had
a storm and the water did shoal. . . .

Our Master sent the boat ashore to see what that land was and
whether there were any way through. They soon returned and showed
that beyond the point of land to the south there was a large sea.

Hudson Revives Old Matters

It is at this point, after passing between Digges Islands and Cape
Wolstenholme, that Hudson's journal ends. The captain's account—
the pages that survived the voyage—does not include mention of a
vote about whether to proceed with the voyage.

*Haystacks.

We have only Prickett's journal, a brief note by Thomas Wood-house, and the testimony of the others from this point forward.

According to Prickett, a few days after the *Discovery* made its way out of the bay, Hudson fired Robert Juet as mate and Francis Clements as boatswain.

> Some two or three days after our coming into the bay and going out, our Master took occasion to revive old matters and to displace Robert Juet from being his Mate, and the Boatswain from his place, for words spoken in the first great Bay of Ice. Then he made Robert Bylot his Mate, and William Wilson our Boatswain.

After demoting his top two officers, Hudson proceeds to push on into Hudson Bay, but rumblings among the crew continues. And according to Prickett, Hudson made a series of ill-conceived orders that endangered the crew.

He commenced to sailing up and down the length of Hudson Bay and into James Bay and back up again. Hudson Bay and its extension into James Bay together encompass nearly 600,000 square miles of water, an area about equal to the combined land masses of the seagoing nations of southern Europe: France, Spain, Italy, Portugal, and Greece.

> Up to the North we stood, till we raised land, then down to the South, and up to the North, then down again to the South. And on Michael-mass Day [September 29] came in and went out of certain lands which our Master sets down by the name of Michaelmasse Bay.
>
> The weather being thick and foul, we came to an anchor . . . and there lay eight days in all which time we could not get one hour to weigh our anchor. But the eighth day the wind beginning to cease, our Master would have the anchor up, against the mind of all who knew what belonged.

Against the mind of all who knew what belonged . . . open or at least barely hidden dissent against the decision making of the captain. And then a swell of the sea throws the men off the capstan—

NASA image of Hudson Bay at top, and James Bay at bottom, in April 2002 as the ice was beginning to recede northward.
Jacques Descloitres, MODIS Rapid Response Team, NASA/GSFC

the vertical drum with wooden spokes that was used to raise and lower the anchor and other heavy equipment on the ship—hurting some of the crew.

Well, to it we went, and when we had brought it a peak, a sea took her and cast us all off from the capstan and hurt [many] of us. Here we lost our anchor, and if the Carpenter had not been, we [would] have lost our cable too. But he, fearing such a matter, was ready with his axe and so cut it. . . .

We came to our westernmost bay of all, and came to an anchor nearest the north shore. Out went our boat to the land that was next us; when they were near it, our boat could not float to the shore it was so shallow, yet ashore they got.

Here our men saw the footing of a man and a duck in the snowy rocks and wood. . . . Being at anchor in this place, we saw a ledge of rocks to the south of us, some league in length. It lay north and south, covered at a full sea, for a strong tide sets in here.

At midnight we weighed, and stood to go out as we came in, and had not gone long but the Carpenter came and told the Master that if he kept that course he would be on the rocks. The Master conceived that he was past them, when presently we ran on them and there stuck fast twelve hours. By the mercy of God we got off unhurt, though not unscarred.

So as October arrived and winter approached, the *Discovery* struggled against the elements in the dead end at the bottom of James Bay. The men were distrustful of Hudson, cold, hungry, and fearful of the coming winter.

Prickett worries about a labyrinth without end.

We stood up to the East and raised three hills, lying north and south. We went to the furthermost and left it to the North of us, and so into a bay where we came to an anchor. Here our Master sent out our boat with myself and the Carpenter to seek a place to winter in. And it was time, for the nights were long and cold, and the earth covered with snow.

Having spent the last three months in a Labyrinth without end, being now the last of October, we went down to the east to the bottom of the bay but returned [slowly]. The next day we went to the south and the southwest and found a place whereunto we brought our ship and hauled her aground, and this was the first of November.

It appears that the *Discovery* was sailing around the area of Waskaganish in the southeastern corner of James Bay. The ship probably passed across the mouth of the Moose River near present-day Moosonee before returning to the east coast. The actual wintering-over place has not been found, but some historians believe it was near where the Nottaway River or the Rupert River empties into Rupert Bay.

By the tenth thereof we were frozen in, but now . . . it behooved us to have care of what we had. . . . We were victualled for six months in good proportion. . . . If our Master would have had more, he might have had it at home and in other places.

What exactly was Prickett getting at here? Was he reflecting the crew's suspicion that Hudson had a secret stash of victuals hidden away?

Prickett also makes reference to Hudson's journal, perhaps to a section that did not survive the voyage. And then he tells of the first death of a member of the ship's company, and in doing so he begins to name some names of the troublemakers among the crew, reaching all the way back to an incident that occurred on Iceland the previous May.

Our Master took order, first for the spending of what we had and then to increase it, by propounding a reward to that that killed either beast, fish, or fowl as in his journal you have seen.

About the middle of this month of November died John Williams our gunner. God pardon the Master's uncharitable dealing with this man. Now that I am come to speak of him, out of whose ashes . . . that unhappy deed grew which brought a scandal upon all that are returned home. . . . Not to wrong the living, nor slander the dead, I will by the leave of God deliver the truth as near as I can.

You shall understand that our Master kept [in his house at London] a young man named Henry Greene, born in Kent of worshipful parents, but by his lewd life and conversation he had lost the good will of all his friends, and had spent all that he had.

This man our Master would have to sea with him because he could write well. . . . This Henry Greene was not set down in the owner's book, nor any wages made for him. He came first aboard at Gravesend, and at Harwich should have gone in the field with one Wilkinson.

Writing very carefully, as he would from this point forward—as if constructing testimony for a court—Prickett reports that Greene and the ship's surgeon, Edward Wilson, had an argument at Iceland, "which set all the company in a rage, so that we had much ado to get the surgeon aboard. I told the Master of it, but he bade me let it alone for he said the surgeon had a tongue that would wrong the best friend he had."

But according to Prickett it seems that Juet, the perennial trouble-maker, had to get involved and make things worse. In a drunken ramble, Juet tells the carpenter "that our Master had brought in Greene to crack his credit that should displease him." That is, Juet claimed that Greene had been brought aboard as Hudson's spy, an inside man to report on the private words of the crew.

According to Prickett, Hudson had become so enraged when he learned of Juet's accusation that he was prepared to sail 150 miles back to Iceland and send him home in a fishing boat; Prickett says he was talked out of this by the crew. None of this is included in the fragments of Hudson's journal that returned home with the ship.

Prickett's reference to Hudson's "uncharitable dealings" with the gunner apparently included special preference when it came to disposing of the dead man's gray cloth gown.

> So Henry Greene stood upright, and very inward with the Master, and was a serviceable man every way for manhood. But for religion he would say, he was clean paper whereon he might write what he would.
>
> Now when our gunner was dead, and as the order is in such cases, if the company stand in need of any thing that belonged to the man deceased then it is brought to the mainmast and there sold to them that will give most for the same. This gunner had a gray cloth gown which Greene prayed the Master to . . . let him have it . . . and no one else.

More strife: Prickett says that "out of season and time" the master ordered the carpenter to go and build a house on shore. Earlier, when it might have been easier to do that, the master refused to call for the work.

The carpenter tells Hudson that because of the snow and frost he "neither could, nor would" do the work. The captain went and brought the carpenter out of his cabin to strike him, "calling him by many foul names and threatening to hang him." The carpenter told Hudson he knew his job better than the captain and that "he was no house carpenter." A shelter was finally built, with much labor, but it was not to be of much use.

And more: Hudson had ordered that none of the crew go out on the land without a gun and another member of the crew with a spear. This was both for their protection against animals and "savages" and also as hunters for the ship's company. The day after the argument, the carpenter went on shore with Henry Greene, and somehow this so enraged Hudson that he took the gunner's gray gown from Greene and gave it to the new first mate, Robert Bylot.

It's hard not to think of Humphrey Bogart's fine madness as Captain Philip Francis Queeg in *The Caine Mutiny*. Hudson is showing signs of losing his marbles.

And then winter arrives in James Bay.

When Henry Greene saw, he challenged the Master . . . but the Master did so rail on Greene with so many words of disgrace, telling him that all his friends would not trust him with twenty shillings, and therefore why should he? As for wages he had none, nor none should have, if he did not please him well. Yet the Master had promised him to make his wages as good as any man's in the ship, and to have him one of the Prince's guard when we came home.

But you shall see how the devil out of this so wrought with Greene that he did the Master what mischief he could in seeking to discredit him, and to thrust him and many other honest men out of the ship in the end.

To speak of all our trouble in this time of winter which was so cold as it lamed most of our company, and my self does yet feel it, would be too tedious.

But I must not forget to show how mercifully God dealt with us in this time, for in the space of three months we had such store of fowl—partridges as white as milk—that we killed above a hundred dozen, and [we had all] the fish that came to the net.

The Spring coming, these fowl left us, yet they were with us all the extreme cold. Then in their place came diverse sort of other fowl, as swans, geese, duck, and teal [although] they were harder to come by.

Now in time these fowl were gone. . . . Then we went into the woods, hills, and valleys for all things that had any show of substance in them [no matter how vile]. The moss of the ground . . . which I take the powder of a post* to be much better, and the frog . . . was not spared.

But amongst the diverse sorts of buds, it pleased God that Thomas Woodhouse brought home the bud of a tree full of a turpentine substance. Of this our surgeon made a concoction to drink and applied the buds hot to those that were troubled with ache in any part of their bodies, and for my part I confess I received great and present ease of my pain.

About this time, when the ice began to break out of the bays, there came a savage to our ship. . . . The first we had seen in all this time. Our Master treated [him] well, and made much of him. . . . To this savage our Master gave a knife, a looking glass, and buttons; he received them thankfully and made signs that after he had slept he would come again, which he did.

When he came he brought with him a sled which he drew after him and upon it two deer skins and two beaver skins. . . . He had a script under his arm out of which he drew those things which the Master had given him. He took the knife and laid it upon one of the beaver skins, and his glasses and buttons upon the other and so gave them to the Master who received them. And the savage took those things which the Master had given them and put them up into his scrip again.

After the long hard winter, the crew of the *Discovery* makes its first contact with a native, most likely a Cree trapper. Though the men need food, the native seems to already have a sense of the developing industry of the bay; he barters animal skins for knives and trinkets.

The Cree of James Bay may well have learned of the ways of the Europeans from earlier explorers south and north of the bay. In 1534 and 1535, the French explorer Jacques Cartier had sailed on the St. Lawrence River at least as far west as the present site of Montreal. From 1576 through 1587, the English adventurers Martin Frobisher and Davis had explored Baffin Bay and Baffin Island.

The solitary native who met with Hudson may not have been

*Sawdust.
†A small bag.

happy with the captain's bargaining skills. After what Prickett describes as an unsatisfactory exchange, the native departs with what seems to be a promise that he would return.

Then the Master showed him a hatchet for which he would have . . . one of his deer skins, but our Master would have them both, and so he had, although not willingly. After many signs of people to the North and to the South, and that after so many sleeps he would come again, he went his way, but never came more.

Now the ice being out of the sounds so that our boat might go from one place unto another, a company of men were appointed by the Master to go fishing with our net. . . . The first day they went [they] caught five hundred fish, as big as good herrings, and some trout, which put us all in some hope to have our wants supplied . . . but these were the most that ever they got in one day.

Henry Greene and William Wilson, with some others, plotted to take the net and the shallop, which the carpenter had now set up. . . . But the shallop being ready, our Master would go in it himself to the south and southwest to see if he could meet with the people.

So the Master took the sieve* and the shallop and so much victual as would serve for eight or nine days and to the south he went. They that remained aboard were to take in water, wood, and ballast and to have all things in a readiness [when] he came back. But he set no time of his return for he was persuaded if he could meet with the people he should [obtain much meat from them]. But he returned worse than he went forth for he could by no means meet with the people, although they were near them, [although] they would set the woods on fire in his sight.

Being returned, he fitted all things for his return. First [he] delivered all the bread out of the bread room, which came to a pound apiece for every man . . . and delivered also a Bill of Return† to have . . . to show if it pleased God that they came home. He wept when he gave it unto them.

The boat and sieve went to work on Friday morning and stayed till Sunday noon, at which time they came aboard and brought fourscore [eighty] small fish, a poor relief for so many hungry bellies.

*Net.
†Receipt.

Finally, the *Discovery* was able to get out of its wintering place and back on James Bay. The ration of bread was gone, and Hudson broke out what he declared to be the remaining cheese: he produced five packages, but Prickett says that the crew had calculated on its own that there should have been nine.

And the machinations went on: Greene gave half of his ration of bread—which was supposed to last fourteen days—to another member of the crew and made him promise not to give it back to him until the following Monday. But Prickett says Greene then began to badger the man for his bread until he got it back. And Wilson, the boatswain, had eaten in one day his two weeks' ration and had become sick for two or three days.

The *Discovery* began sailing out of James Bay, which must have pleased the crew, but the general course may have concerned them: not due north, but northwest—as in a resumption of the search for the Northwest Passage.

In any case, on June 18 the ship got caught up again in ice still in the bay. There followed more discord and suspicion.

> The Master told Nicholas Syms that there would be a breaking up of [sea] chests and a search for bread and willed him if he had any to bring it to him, which he did, and delivered to the Master thirty cakes in a bag. This deed of the Master—if it be true—made me marvel what should be the reason that he did not stop the breach in the beginning but let it grow to that height as it overthrew himself and many other honest men. But there are many devices in the heart of man, yet the counsel of the Lord shall stand.

Something broke. Someone said the first word. Someone took the first step. And the final mutiny was on.

CHAPTER 20

The End of Hudson's Days

Escape from the winter quarters did not bring relief from dissent. According to Abacuck Prickett's account, on Saturday June 21 the ship was once again troubled by ice in James Bay, food was running low, and the first specific plans for mutiny were discussed.

With an eye on history, or at least on the gallows, Prickett reports what he heard and says that he advised the men not to "commit so foul a thing in the sight of God and man." But Prickett also does not stand in the way of the conspirators, at least not in the account he brought back with him to England.

Being thus in the ice on Saturday the one and twentieth of June at night, Wilson the boatswain and Henry Greene came to me lying in my cabin lame and told me that they and the rest of their associates would shift the company and turn the Master and all the sick men into the shallop and let them shift for themselves.

For there was not fourteen days victual left for all the company, at that poor allowance they were at . . . the Master not caring to go one way or other. And that they had not eaten anything these three days and therefore were resolute either to mend or end. And what they had begun they would go through with or die.

When I heard this, I told them I marveled to hear so much from them, considering that they were married men and had wives and children, and that for their sakes they should not commit so foul a thing in the sight of God and man . . . for why should they banish themselves from their native country?

Henry Greene bade me hold my peace, for he knew the worst, which was to be hanged when he came home, and therefore of the two he would rather be hanged at home than starved abroad. And for the good will they bear me they would have me stay in the ship.

Prickett casts himself as a would-be peacemaker, even to the point of claiming he would have been willing to join Hudson in the shallop. But he writes that the conspirators decided to allow him to return to England without taking part in the mutiny.

I gave them thanks, and told them that I came into her not to forsake her yet not to hurt myself and others by any such deed. Henry Greene told me then that I must take my fortune in the shallop. If there be no remedy, said I, the will of God be done.

Away went Henry Greene in a rage, swearing to cut his throat that went about to disturb them, and left Wilson by me with whom I had some talk, but to no good. He was so persuaded that there was no remedy now but to go on while it was hot, lest their party should fail them, and the mischief they had intended to others should light on themselves.

Henry Greene came again and demanded of him what I said. Wilson answered, "He is in his old song, still patient." Then I spoke to Henry Greene to stay three days in which time I would so deal with the Master that all should be well. So I dealt with him to forbear but two days, nay twelve hours; there is no way then, say they, but out of hand.

Then I told them that if they would stay till Monday I would join with them to share all the victuals in the ship and would justify it when I came home, but this would not serve their turns. Wherefore I told them, it was some worse matter they had in hand than they made show of, and that it was blood and revenge he sought, or else he would not at such a time of night undertake such a deed.

Henry Greene [with that] taketh my Bible which lay before me and swore that he would do no man harm, and what he did was for the good of the voyage and for nothing else, and that all the rest would do the like.

Henry Greene went his way, and presently came Juet, who because he was an ancient man I hoped to have found some reason in

278

him, but he was worse than Henry Greene for he swore plainly that he would justify this deed when he came home. After him came John Thomas and Michael Perse, as birds of one feather. But because they are not living I will let them go, as then I did.

Then came Motter and Bennett [Matthew], of whom I demanded if they were well advised what they had taken in hand. They answered they were, and therefore came to take their oath.

Now because I am much condemned for this oath, as one of them that plotted with them, and that by an oath I should bind them together to perform what they had begun, I thought good here to set down to the view of all how well their oath and deeds agreed. . . . You shall swear truth to God, your Prince and Country you shall do nothing but to the glory of God and the good of the action in hand, and harm to no man. That was the oath, without adding or diminishing.

Prickett says that he has exhausted his efforts to prevent the mutiny; now he prays that they at least not go forth in the dark but wait for morning.

And he reports some of the decisions made by the conspirators. Prickett says that he questions their decision to abandon the ship's carpenter, an important member of the crew; Philip Staffe is, according to Prickett, offered the chance to stay aboard the *Discovery*, but he chooses to bring his tools and stay with the captain.

Prickett says Staffe asks him to leave a marker at the top of Hudson Bay near the place where the crew had found the native storehouses for drying fowl if the *Discovery* makes it that far, and he promises to do the same if the bedraggled men in the shallop manage to sail the nearly 800 miles north to Cape Wolstenholme and Hudson Strait.

I called to Henry Greene and Wilson and prayed them not to go in hand with it in the dark but to stay till the morning. But wickedness sleepeth not.

For Henry Greene keepeth the Master company all night . . . and others are as watchful as he. Then I asked Henry Greene whom he would put out with the Master. He said the carpenter John King and the sick men.

I said they should not do well to part with the carpenter what need so ever they should have. Why the carpenter was in no more regard amongst them was, first for that he and John King were condemned for wrong done in the victual. But the chiefest cause was for that the master loved him and made him his Mate, upon our return out of our wintering place, thereby displacing Robert Bylot whereat they did grudge, because he could neither write nor read.

And therefore, said they, the Master and his ignorant Mate would carry the ship whither the Master pleased, the Master forbidding any man to keep account or reckoning, having taken from all men whatsoever served for that purpose.

It was not long ere it was day. Then came Bennett for water for the kettle. He rose and went into the hold. When he was in, they shut the hatch on him.

In the mean time Henry Greene and another went to the Carpenter and held him with a talk till the Master came out of his cabin. . . . Then came John Thomas and Bennett before him, while Wilson bound his arms behind him.

He asked them what they meant? They told him he should know when he was in the shallop.

Now Juet, while this was a doing, came to John King into the hold [where he] had got a sword of his own, and kept him at bay and might have killed him, but others came to help him and so he came up to the Master.

Then was the shallop hauled up to the ship side, and the poor, sick, and lame men were called upon to get them out of their cabins. The Master called to me [and I] came out of my cabin as well as I could to the hatchway to speak with him. Where, on my knees, I besought them for the love of God to remember themselves and to do as they would be done unto.

They bade me keep my self well, and get me into my cabin, not suffering the Master to speak with me. But when I came into my cabin again, he called to me at the horn, which gave light into my cabin, and told me Juet would overthrow us all. No, said I, it is that villain Henry Greene, and I spoke it not softly.

Now was the carpenter at liberty, who asked them if they [knew] they would be hanged when they came home. As for himself, he said, he would not stay in the ship unless they would force him. They bade him go, then. . . . I will, said he, [if] I may have my chest with me and all that is in it. They said he should, and presently they put it into the shallop.

Then he came down to me, to take his leave of me. [I tried to] persuade him to stay. [But] he was so persuaded by the Master that there was not one in all the ship that could tell how to carry her home.

Said he [the carpenter] if we must part. . . . he prayed me if we came to the Capes [Wolstenholme and Digges] that I would leave some token that we had been there, near to the place where the fowls bred. And he would do the like for us. And so, with tears, we parted.

Hudson Is Abandoned

And then came the moment that has become memorialized in John Collier's famed portrait that shows old man Hudson, his hand on the tiller of a small boat with his young son clutching his knee. In the background are mountainous icebergs, much larger than the sheet of ice that fills James Bay. Collier imagined the scene when he painted the picture in about 1860.

According to Prickett, the men were put into the shallop, which was tied to the stern of the *Discovery*. And then the little boat was cut loose.

Now were the sick men driven out of their cabins into the shallop. . . . In the meantime, there were some them that plied their work as if the ship had been entered by force, and they had free leave to pillage, breaking up chests and rifling all places. One of them came by me [and] asked me what he should do. I answered he should make an end of what he had done.

Now were all the poor men in the shallop, whose names are as follows:

Henry Hudson, John Hudson, Arnold Ludlow, Syrack[e] Fanner, Philip Staffe, Thomas Woodhouse or Wydhouse, Adam Moore, John King, Michael Butt.

The carpenter got a piece [a gun] and powder and shot, some pikes [spears], an iron pot with some meal, and other things.

They stood out of the ice, the shallop being [tied] fast to the stern of the ship and [when they were well out] they cut her [loose].

While the small shallop drifted not far from the *Discovery*, the men who remained aboard the ship took in the topsails and pointed the ship up into the wind so that it would stay where it was while they ransacked every corner of the ship.

> In the hold they found one of the vessels of meal whole, and the other half spent . . . We found also two firkins* of butter, some twenty seven pieces of pork, half a bushel of peas.
>
> But in the Master's cabin we found two hundred of biscuit cakes, a peck of meal, beer to the quantity of a butte.†

When the men came up from searching the ship, Prickett writes, the shallop was under its own sails and catching up to the *Discovery*. So the mutineers raised sails to speed away.

> They let fall the mainsail, and out with their topsails, and fly as from an enemy.
>
> Coming near the east shore they . . . stood to the west and came to an island and anchored. . . .Michael Perse killed two fowl and here they found good store of that weed which we called cockle grass in our wintering place. Here we lay that night, and the best part of the next day, in all which time we saw not the shallop, or ever after.

Good-bye Henry Hudson, his son, a few supporters, and the sick and lame: nine in all. The *Discovery*'s shallop and those aboard were never seen again.

The ship began to work its way northward toward Hudson Bay and Hudson Strait, running into what Prickett describes as the worst ice the crew has yet encountered.

> Now Henry Greene came to me and told me that it was the company's will that I should come up into the Master's cabin and take charge . . .I told him it was more fit for Robert Juet. [But Juet] said he should not come in it nor meddle with the Master's charts or journals.

*Small quarter-barrels.
†A large cask of as much as 108 imperial gallons.

So up I came, and Henry Greene gave me the key of the Master's chest and told me then that he had laid the Master's best things together which he would use himself when time did serve. . . . The bread was also delivered [to] me.

The wind serving, we stood to the northeast, and this was Robert Bylot's course, contrary to Robert Juet who would have gone to the northwest. We had the eastern shore still in sight and in the night had a stout gale of wind and stood before it till we met with ice into which we ran from thin to thick till we could go no further.

The ice lay so thick ahead of us, and the wind brought it after us astern, that we could not stir backward nor forward. We lay embayed fourteen days in worse ice than ever we met [before].

At last being clear of this ice, he raised four islands which lay north and south . . . and came to an anchor between two of the most northernmost. We sent the boat ashore to see if there were anything there to be had but found nothing but cockle grass, whereof they gathered.

Before we came to this place, I might well see that I was kept in the ship against Henry Greene's mind, because I did not favour their proceedings better than I did. Then he began, very subtly, to draw me to . . . search for those things which himself had stolen. And [he] accused me of a matter no less than treason amongst us, that I had deceived the company of thirty pieces of bread.

Now they began to talk amongst themselves that England was no safe place for them, and Henry Greene swore the ship should not come into any place till he had the King's Majesty's hand and seal to show for his safety. They had many devices in their heads, but Henry Greene in the end was their captain. . . .

We kept the east shore still in our sight, and coming thwart of the low land we ran on a rock that lay under water and struck but once. . . . We might have been made inhabitants of that place but God sent us soon off without any harm that we saw.

Back to Cape Wolstenholme

After a fractious voyage north that included arguments between Prickett and Juet over their location, the *Discovery* eventually reaches Cape Wolstenholme at the top of Hudson Bay. It was here they planned to harvest fowl and other meat for the voyage back home.

It was mid-July, though, and any native hunter would have told them the time to find birds there was mostly in the spring and fall. What few birds were there would most likely be small gulls instead of the larger and meatier geese.

As it turned out, there were natives in the area and something went terribly wrong: the crew of the *Discovery* may have been perceived as a threat or perhaps their attempts at bartering for food were objectionable.

We raised the capes with joy and [headed] for them and came to the island that lie in the mouth of the strait. But bearing in between the rocky isles we ran on a rock and there stuck fast eight or nine hours. It was ebbing water when we thus came on, so the flood set us afloat.

The next day being the seven and twentieth of July, we sent the boat to fetch some fowl, and the ship should weigh and stand as near as they could, for the wind was against us. They had a great way to row, and by that means they could not reach to the place where the fowl bred. They found good store of gulls, yet hard to come by on the rocks and cliffs. But with their pieces they killed some thirty and towards night returned.

Now we had brought our ship more near to an anchor . . . upon a reef or shelf of ground . . . and stood near to the place where the fowl bred, they could not find it again nor no place like it.

The eight and twentieth day, the boat went to Digges . . . for fowl . . . and being near they saw seven boats coming about the eastern point towards them. When the savages saw our boat they drew themselves together and drew their lesser boats into their bigger, and when they had done they came rowing to our boat.

The savages came to them, and by signs grew familiar one with another, so as our men took one of theirs into our boat they took one of ours into their boat. Then they carried our man to a cove where their tents stood . . . where the fowl bred.

Our boat went to the place where the fowl bred, and were desirous to know how the savages killed their fowl. . . . They take a long pole with a snare at the end which they put around the fowl's neck and so pluck them down. When our men knew that they had a better way of their own, they showed him the use of our pieces, which at one shot would kill seven or eight.

Our boat returned to their cove for our man and to deliver theirs. When they came they made great joy, with dancing and leaping and stroking of their breasts. . . . Our men came aboard, much rejoicing at this chance, as if they had met with the most simple and kind people of the world.

And Henry Greene, more than the rest, was so confident that by no means we should take care to stand upon our guard. God blinding him so that where he made reckoning to receive great matters from these people, he received more than he looked for.

The next day, the nine and twentieth of July, they made haste to be ashore . . . and weighed and stood as near to the place where the fowl bred as they could. And because I was lame, I was to go in the boat to carry such things as I had in the cabin . . . and so with more haste than good speed, and not without swearing, away we went: Henry Greene, William Wilson, John Thomas, Michael Perse, Adrian Motter, and myself.

When we came near the shore, the people were on the hills dancing and leaping. To the cove we came where they had drawn up their boats; we brought our boat to the east side of the cove, close to the rocks. . . . The people came and every one had somewhat in his hand to barter. But Henry Greene swore they should have nothing till he had venison, for that they had so promised him by signs.

Now when we came, they made signs to their dogs—whereof there were many like mongrels, as big as hounds—and pointed to their mountains and to the sun, clapping their hands. Then Henry Greene, John Thomas, and William Wilson stood hard by the boat head. Michael Perse and Adrian Motter were got up on the rock, gathering sorel.

Not one of them had any weapon about him, not so much as a stick, save Henry Greene only, who had a piece of a pike in his hand. Nor saw I anything that they had wherewith to hurt us.

Henry Greene and William Wilson had looking glasses, and Jew's trumps,* and bells which they were showing the people. The savages standing round about them, one of them came into the boat's head to me to show me a bottle. I made signs to him to get him ashore, be he made as though he had not understood me. Whereupon I stood up, and pointed him ashore.

*Jew's harps.

In the meantime, another stole behind me to the stern of the boat, and when I saw him ashore . . . I sat down again. But suddenly I saw the leg and foot of a man by me. Wherefore I cast up my head and saw the savage with his knife in his hand, who stroke at my breast over my head. I cast up my right arm to save my breast. He wounded my arm and struck me into the body under my right pappe.*

He struck a second blow which I met with my left hand, and then he struck me into the right thigh and [nearly] cut off my little finger of the left hand. Now I had got hold of the string of the knife and had wound it about my left hand, he striving with both his hands, to make an end of that he had begun.

I found him . . . weak in the grip . . . and getting hold of the sleeve of his left arm so bear him from me. His left side lay bare to me, which when I saw I put his sleeve off his left arm into my left hand, holding the string of the knife feast in the same hand. And having got my right hand at liberty I sought for somewhat werewith to strike him. Not remembering my dagger at my side, but looking down I saw it, and therewith struck him into the body and the throat.

While I was thus assaulted in the boat, our men were set upon on the shore. John Thomas and William Wilson had their bowels cut, and Michael Perse and Henry Greene being mortally wounded came tumbling into the boat together. When Adrian Motter saw this melee, he came running down the rocks and leaped into the sea and so swam to the boat . . . and Michael Perse took him in.

Now Michael Perse had got a hatchet, wherewith I saw him strike one of them. . . . Henry Greene cried, "Courage!" and laid about him with his truncheon. I cried to them to clear the boat and Adrian Motter cried to be taken in.

The savages . . . took to their bows and arrows, which they sent amongst us. Henry Greene was slain outright, and Michael Perse received many wounds and so did the rest.

Michael Perse cleared the boat and put it in from the shore, and helped Adrian Motter in, but in turning of the boat I received a cruel wound in my back with an arrow.

Michael Perse and Adrian Motter rowed the boat away, which when the savages saw they ran to their boats and I feared they would have launched them to have followed us, but they did not.

*Nipple.

Now when they had rowed a good way from the shore, Michael Perse fainted and could row no more. Then was Adrian Motter driven to stand in the boat head and wave to the ship, which at the first saw us not. And when they did they could not tell what to make of us, but in the end they stood for us and so took us up.

Henry Greene was thrown out of the boat into the sea and the rest were had aboard . . . the savage being yet alive [but] without sense. But they died all there that day, William Wilson swearing and cursing in a most fearful manner. Michael Perse lived two days after and then died.

Thus you have heard the tragical end of Henry Greene and his mates, whom they called captain, these four being the only lusty men in all the ship.

The poor number that was left were to ply our ship to and fro in the mouth of the strait, for there was no place to anchor . . . besides they were to go in the boat to kill fowl to bring us home, which they did although with danger to us all. For if the wind blew [and] there was a high sea, the eddies of the tides would carry the ship so near the rocks, as . . . feared our Master [Robert Bylot], for so I will now call him.

After they had killed some two hundred fowl, with great labor on the south cape, we stood to the east. But when we were six or seven leagues [twenty-one to twenty-four miles] from the capes the wind came up at east. Then we stood back to the capes again.

After this, the wind came to the west so we were driven to go away and then our Master stood for the most along the north shore till he fell into broken ground about the Queen's Foreland and there anchored. From thence we went to God's Mercies, and from thence to those island which lie in the mouth of our strait.

A Diet of Fried Bones

The birds they had harvested did not provide much sustenance. Prickett states that they rationed themselves to half a bird a day and ate them with a bit of the remaining meal onboard. They had to skin the birds because the feathers would not pull out. Robert Juet figured out a way to make use of the skin by burning off the feathers. "And as for the garbage, it was not thrown away," Prickett writes.

They continued on a course east southeast toward the Desolations, "from thence to shape our course for Ireland." The wind, though, was blowing against them and Juet persuaded the company to head for Newfoundland and look for other English explorers there in hopes that they would have food and supplies or might have left a store of supplies for others.

Instead, the ship sailed to the southeast, dropping down to about 57° of latitude, some 300 miles below the entrance to Hudson Strait, and there they found a favorable southwesterly wind. Prickett says that Juet came to him and asked him if he thought they should take advantage of this wind, and Prickett said he told him "it was best to go where we knew corn grew, and not to seek it where it was cast away or not to be found." In other words: take advantage of what was available.

Toward Ireland we now stood, with prosperous winds for many days together. Then was all our meal spent, and our fowl . . . dry. But being no remedy, we were content with the salt broth for dinner and the half fowl for supper.

Bennett our cook made a mess of meat of the bones of the fowl, frying them with candle grease until they were crisp. With vinegar put to them [they] made a good dish of meat. Our vinegar was shared, and to every man a pound of candles delivered for a week, as a great dainty.*

Now Robert Juet by his reckoning said we were within sixty or seventy leagues [207 to 241 miles] of Ireland, when we had two hundred. And sure our course was so much the longer through our evil steerage; for when our men became so weak that they could not stand at the helm but were [forced] to sit.

Then Robert Juet died for mere want, and all our men were in despair and said we were past Ireland and our last fowl were in the steep-tub.† So our men cared not which end went forward. . . . Some of them would sit and see the foresail or mainsail fly up to the tops, the sheets either flown or broken, and would not help it themselves or call to others for help which much grieved the Master.

*Delicacy.
†Pot.

Now in this extremity it pleased God to give us sight of land, not far from the place our Master said he would fall . . . which was the Bay of Galloway. . . . In the end there was a joyful cry, "a sail, a sail." . . . To the nearest we stood and called to him. His bark was of Fowey* and was at anchor fishing; he came to us and brought us into Beer Haven.

Here we stayed a few days and dealt with the Irish to supply our wants, but found no relief for in this place there was neither bread, drink, nor money to be had amongst them. Wherefore they advised us to deal with our countrymen, who were there fishing, which we did. But we found them so cold in kindness that they would do nothing without present money, whereof we had none in the ship.

In the end, we procured one John Waymouth, master of the bark that brought us into this harbor to furnish us with money, which he did, and received our best cable and anchor in pawn for the same. With this money, our Master . . . bought bread, beer, and beef.

Now as we were beholding to Waymouth for his money, so were we to one Captain Taylor for making of our contracts with Waymouth. . . . He took a bill for our cable and anchor and for the men's wages who would not go with us unless Waymouth would pass his word for the same. . . . Whereupon Captain Taylor swore he would press them [and] if they would not go he would hang them.

In conclusion, we agreed for three pound ten shillings a man to bring our ship to Plymouth or Dartmouth and to give the pilot five pound. But if the wind did not serve but that they were driven to put into Bristol, they were to have four pound ten shillings a man and the pilot six pound.

Omitting further circumstances, from Beer Haven we came to Plymouth and so to an anchor before the Castle. And from Plymouth with fair wind and weather without stop or stay we came to the downs, from thence to Gravesend where most of our men went ashore.

Master Robert Bylot . . . had me up to London with him and so we came to Sir Thomas Smith's together.

*Fowey is in Cornwall in southwestern England.

Did Prickett Tell the Truth?

Prickett's journal stands on its own, contradicted by no other complete report. It is reasonable to assume that he tried to polish his own apple as brightly as he could and protect most of the survivors, leaving the blame on the dead: primarily Greene and Juet. He also speaks to the reader: "This report of Prickett may happily be suspected by some as not so friendly to Hudson."

After all, Prickett reminds us, he returned with those who so cruelly exposed Hudson. Why is the reader to believe him? In answer, he says, he has attached the report of Thomas Woodhouse, one of those who died; Woodhouse, he says, points the finger at Juet.

"I have presented the evidence just as I had it. Let the Bench censure, hearing with both ears, that which both eyes they may see," Prickett writes.

Woodhouse's note fills in an important gap, an event that occurred September 10, 1610, more than a month after Hudson's journal abruptly ends. The letter was reprinted by Samuel Purchas.

The note concludes with a strange final paragraph that was almost certainly not written by Woodhouse; in Purchas's collection of documents, it is set off in italics from the rest of the note. But subsequent histories of the Hudson expedition over the course of 400 years have almost all dropped that typographic distinction.

A Note Found in the Deske of Thomas Wydowse,
Student in the Mathematickes, He Being One of Them
Who Was Put Into The Shallop

The tenth day of September, after dinner, our master called all the company together to hear and bear witness of the abuse of some of the company [it having been the request of Robert Juet] that the master should redress some abuses and slanders, as he called them, against this Juet. Which thing after the master had examined and heard with equity what he could say for himself, there were proved so many and great abuses, and mutinous matters against the master, and action by Juet, that there was danger to have suffered them longer. And it was fit time to punish and cut off farther occasions of the like mutinies.

It was proved to his [Juet's] face, first with Bennett Matthew, our trumpet, upon our first sight of Iceland, and he confessed that he supposed that in the action would be manslaughter, and prove bloody to some.

Secondly, at our coming from Iceland, in hearing of the company, he did threaten to turn the head of the ship home from the action, which at that time was by our master widely pacified, hoping of amendment.

Thirdly, it was deposed by Philip Staffe, our carpenter, and Arnold Ludlow, to his face upon the Holy Bible, that he persuaded them to keep muskets charged and swords ready in their cabins, for they should be charged with shot ere the voyage was over.

Fourthly, we being pestered in the ice, he had used words tending to mutiny, discouragement and slander of the action, which easily took effect in those that were timorous; and had not the master in time prevented, it might easily have overthrown the voyage: and now lately being imbayed in a deep bay, which the master had desire to see, for some reasons to himself known, his word tended altogether to put the company into a fray of extremity, by wintering in the cold.

For these and diverse other base slanders against the master he was deposed, and Robert Bylot, who had showed himself honestly respecting the good of the action, was placed in his stead the master's mate.

Also Francis Clements, the boatswain, at this time was put from his office, and William Wilson, a man thought more fit, preferred to his place. This man had basely carried himself to our master and to the action.

Also Adrian Motter was appointed boatswain's mate, and a promise by the master that from this day Juet's wages should remain to Bylot, and the boatswain's overplus of wages should be equally divided between Wilson, and one John King, to the owners good liking, one of the quarter masters, who had very well carried themselves to the furtherance of the business.

Also the master promised, if the offenders yet behaved themselves henceforth honestly, he would be a means for their good, and that he would forget injuries, with other admonitions.

These things thus premised Hudson's exposing, and God's just

judgments on the exposers, as Prickett hath related (whom they reserved, as is thought, in hope by Sir Dudley Digges his master to procure their pardon at their return), I thought good to add that which I
have further received from good intelligence, that the ship coming
aground at Digges Island, in 62°44', a great flood came from the west
and set them on float, an argument of an open passage from the
South Sea to that, and consequently to these seas. The weapons and
arts which they saw, beyond those of other savages, are arguments
hereof. He which assaulted Prickett in the boat, had a weapon broad
and sharp indented, of bright steel (such as they use in Java), riveted
into a handle of morse tooth.

Who wrote that last paragraph? In my copy of *Hudson the Navigator*, which was published in 1860, the entire passage is presented
as if written by Woodhouse. The same was repeated in Thomas Allibone Janvier's book of 1909, and most modern histories that reprint
the note do the same. But it makes no sense to me.

If Woodhouse was cast adrift in the shallop on June 21, 1611, then
he did not witness the attack on the others that took place at Digges
Islands on July 29.

Woodhouse was not likely to have offered a free pass in the form
of an explanation of why the mutineers spared Prickett ("in hope by
Sir Dudley Digges his master to procure their pardon at their return").
And he was not with the mutineers and others at Digges Islands, and
therefore he could not have offered "evidence" that the route to the
South Sea may indeed lay through Hudson Strait because Prickett's
attacker used a weapon similar to those in use in Java.

The most likely author of the final paragraph, appended to Woodhouse's note, was Purchas; it would have been an editor's commen-
tary, set off in italics. Other possibilities include a functionary of the
VOC, the sponsor of the voyage. Or the words might have been
added by an interested party during the course of the prosecution of
some of the survivors by the Admiralty Court.

I asked Chip Reynolds, the captain of the replica *Half Moon* and
the director of the New Netherland Museum in Albany his opinion
of what appeared to be a 400-year-old mistake in the written record.
He consulted his copy of *Purchas His Pilgrimes.*

"I think it was probably a note by Purchas that lost its identity and just got reprinted over and over again," he said.

On this small mystery of the story of Henry Hudson, then, I'm ruling in favor of separating the supposedly final paragraph from the Woodhouse note and considering it instead a four-century-old editorial comment.

A Final Accounting

Of the twenty-four men who set sail from London on April 17, 1610, aboard the *Discovery*, only eight would return alive to England.

The survivors were Abacuck Prickett, Sylvanus Bond, Robert Bylot, Francis Clements, Bennett Matthew, Adrian Motter, Nicholas Syms, and Edward Wilson. Perhaps the luckiest crew member was Master Coleburne, who was put ashore by Hudson only six days into the trip before the *Discovery* had even left the Thames.

Abandoned in the shallop were Henry Hudson, his young son John, Michael Butt, Syracke Fanner, John King, Arnold Ludlow, Adam Moore, Philip Staffe, and Thomas Woodhouse.

Killed in skirmishes with the natives were Henry Greene, Michael Perse, John Thomas, and William Wilson. John Williams died of natural causes before the onset of winter in James Bay. And Robert Juet, Hudson's bad apple, died of "mere want" just days before the *Discovery* made it back to England; it was a convenient death, removing the last of the conspirators—as identified by Prickett—from the ranks of the survivors.

CHAPTER 21

The *Discovery* Comes Home

When the *Discovery* returned to England without Henry Hudson and his son John, the captain's wife, Katherine, did what most modern wives would do: she asked for money. Oh, and a rescue mission would be nice.

The VOC did mount several trips back to Hudson Bay and James Bay the following year; they were going to be sending ships there anyway, so money was not an object. According to some accounts, captains were requested to keep an eye out for any signs of the two Hudsons.

When it came to compensating Katherine for the loss of her husband and son, though, things got a bit testy. According to company records, Katherine Hudson kept after the directors of the company for several years; she was referred to as a "troublesome and impatient woman" in documents.

She sought money and asked the company to give one of her surviving sons, Richard, a job on a ship sailing to the East Indies. When the company finally agreed on a financial settlement, Katherine was sponsored on her own business venture, traveling to Ahmadabad, India—a major industrial center known for its cotton mills—to purchase indigo and other items of trade. That much was apparently a success, but then she had to sue the VOC to get it to pay the cost of shipping the items back to England.

Katherine returned home in 1622 as a relatively wealthy woman, and was received at court; in her remaining two years of life, she unsuccessfully sought to have a monument to Henry Hudson erected in London. There still is no significant statue or other commemoration of Hudson in the British capital.

The *Discovery* Goes Back to Hudson Strait

In April 1612, three of the survivors went not to the gallows but instead back out to sea on a two-ship expedition financed by young Prince Henry (the Prince of Wales) and the Muscovy Company. Robert Bylot was engaged as pilot of the *Discovery*, accompanied by Edward Wilson and Abacuck Prickett. The second ship was the much larger *Resolution*.

The commander of the voyage was Thomas Button, a member of Prince Henry's court. Button was given specific instructions by the prince on how to properly command his crew and avoid mutiny; he also carried a letter from the prince's father, King James, to be given to the emperor of Japan when the ships made it through the passage and arrived in Asia.

The 1612 expedition was little more successful than Hudson's voyage. After passing through Hudson Strait, the *Resolution* landed men on Digges Islands, where they apparently tried to seize some canoes from the Inuit who were there; five crew were killed.

The *Discovery* and *Resolution* crossed over the top of Hudson Bay to its west shore and then sailed south. Like Hudson, the expedition was forced by the quick onset of cold weather to find a place to winter over. The vessels sought refuge in the mouth of the Nelson River, a place later named Port Nelson, about 175 miles south of modern-day Churchill in the province of Manitoba on Hudson Bay.

While the *Resolution* and *Discovery* were wintering over, Prince Henry unexpectedly died. Henry Frederick Stuart, the first child of James VI of Scotland and Anne of Denmark, was considered a highly promising heir to the throne; his father had been given the English Crown in 1603 (taking the name James I) after the death of Elizabeth I.

Henry was born in February 1594, and his midyear christening is said by some literary historians to have inspired William Shakespeare's *A Midsummer Night's Dream*. It must have been a heck of a party.

As a young man, Henry studied politics and maritime matters and showed a special interest in the English search for the passage to Asia.

In November 1612, Henry went for a swim in the Thames—probably not a good idea at any time of the year, especially in a time of plague—and came down with a fever. He died quickly, most likely from typhoid, although there were rumors his father might have poisoned him to remove him as a threat.

Free of the ice in the spring of 1613, the *Discovery* and *Resolution* went north and explored as far as they could in a waterway on the west side of Southampton Island. Eventually determining that it was too shallow to offer passage to Asia, Button exited what is now called Roe's Welcome Sound and began his return to England.

Button's journal of the voyage has been lost, but once again we are able to read the reports of others, from our old friend Prickett and another member of the crew. According to these accounts, Button gave his ship's name to Resolution Island, the first piece of land he came to off the eastern coast of Baffin Island. Later in the voyage, when he reached the western shore of Hudson Bay, he made a disheartening landfall at a place he called Hopes Checked.

In August 1613, on his way out of Hudson Bay, he made landfall west of the top of Nunavik. He named it Mansel Island after friend and supporter Sir Robert Mansel, now an important figure as the treasurer of the navy and one of the sponsors of the expedition.

The *Discovery* returned to Hudson Strait again in 1614 under William Gibbons on an unsuccessful exploration. Its final two voyages in search of the Northwest Passage took place in 1615 and 1616; the *Discovery* had been purchased by the explorer William Baffin, who served as mate to Robert Bylot.

The 1615 trip was much more directly headed west and northwest through upper Canada. The *Discovery* passed Salisbury and Nottingham islands at the western edge of the strait and continued on through the icy Foxe Channel as far as Southampton Island at the northern extreme of Hudson Bay. They entered into the aptly named Frozen Strait above Southampton and determined that there was no safe passage through that route.

Their 1616 voyage skipped Hudson Strait entirely. Instead, they sailed along the western coast of Greenland and well up into Baffin Bay, reaching to 77°45' North latitude before returning down the east coast of Baffin Island. Along the way, they gave name to Bylot Island on Lancaster Sound.

Although they did not know it at the time, they had actually found the entrance to the Northwest Passage. Later explorers would determine that—weather and ice permitting—the passage to the west coast of North America went between Bylot Island and Devon Island through Lancaster Sound.

Facing the Hangman's Noose

England's history of dealing with crime on the high seas—mutinies and piracy—was a model of inconsistency. The penalty was generally the hangman's noose, but the specificities of the law were often ignored.

In the case of pirates, many were given license as privateers when it suited British economic or political interests. In the instance of the mutineers against Henry Hudson, the survivors were apparently worth more alive than dead because of their knowledge of navigation in Hudson Strait. And, as I have noted, it was most convenient that the alleged leaders of the uprising—Henry Greene and Robert Juet among them—died in the New World or on their way back home.

Trinity House, which had been given a royal charter by Henry VIII in 1514 as protector of the safety of shipping and the well-being of mariners, declared that the returned survivors deserved to be hanged and began proceedings against them in the Admiralty Court. The money men behind the *Discovery*'s voyage under Hudson, though, were barely heard from.

Robert Bylot, who successfully brought the *Discovery* and the surviving crew home, was apparently given either a formal pardon or a wink-and-a-nudge free pass by Prince Henry or someone else in power. At least four and perhaps one or two others of the crew were briefly detained.

In any case, details of the late and half-hearted legal proceedings against the survivors were little explored for nearly three centuries. In 1909, Thomas Allibone Janvier—a well-known writer for *Harper's Magazine* and the author of many books on subjects including the Bohemian life of New York and travel in Mexico—wrote the book *Henry Hudson: A Brief Statement of His Aims and His Achievements: To Which Is Added a Newly Discovered Partial Record Now First Published of the Trial of the Mutineers by Whom He and Others Were Abandoned to Their Death*. There's a bit of hyperbole in the title and in Janvier's writing, but he did bring into print some incomplete documents that had been languishing in London archives.

He deals first with Prickett, noting that his sworn testimony and his unsworn personal journal are in agreement, which is not surprising and also does not prove the truth of either account. "Sworn or unsworn, Prickett was not a person from whom pure truth could be expected when, as in this case, he was trying to tell a story that would save him from being hanged," Janiver writes.

According to Janvier, almost immediately after the return of the survivors, five of them were brought before the masters of Trinity House in what amounted to a pretrial hearing. The summation of their testimony, Janvier reports, was this: "They all charge the Master with wasting [i.e., filching] the victuals by a scuttle made out of his cabin into the hold, and it appears that he fed his favorites, as the surgeon, etc., and kept others at ordinary allowance. All say that, to save some from starving, they were content to put away [abandon] so many."

The first to make a formal statement about the events in James Bay was Edward Wilson, the surgeon, in January 1612. Wilson stated that "the Master had bread and cheese and aquavite in his cabin and called some of the company whom he favored to eat and drink with him in his cabin, whereupon those that had nothing did grudge and mutiny both against the Master and those that he gave bread and drink unto."

Wilson said he was a mere bystander to the event; he was either not pushed to incriminate others or chose not to name names. He did, though, clear Sylvanus Bond, Nicholas Syms, and Francis Clements of involvement.

Tellingly, the next area of questioning of Wilson was whether he knew if the Dutch intended to pursue future voyages to the same area in search of the Northwest Passage. Wilson said he had no specific knowledge of that, but he had heard that some gentlemen and merchants of London were interested in returning.

Robert Bylot was examined by the court four years later, on February 7, 1616. His testimony is notable in its lack of specifics; from a distance of 300 years, it almost seems as if a prosecutor was helping Bylot lay out a case to avoid charges.

According to Bylot, there was "a discontent amongst the company of the ship the *Discovery* in the finding out of the N.W. passage, by occasion of the want of victuals, Henry Green being the principal, together with John Thomas, William Wilson, Robert Ivett [Juet] and Michael Pearse, determined to shift the company, and thereupon Henry Hudson, the master, was by force put into the shallop."

Bylot is later reported as testifying there was "no mutiny to his knowledge, until the said Greene and his associates turned the master and the rest into the shallop." And, he said, he and Prickett tried to persuade the mutineers not to go forward with their plan.

On July 24, 1618, more than seven years after the mutiny in James Bay, four of the men were arraigned in Southwark "for feloniously pinioning and putting Henry Hudson, master of the *Discovery* . . . into a shallop . . . without meat, drink, clothes or other provision, whereby they died." Charges against Francis Clements and Bennett Matthew were dismissed by the court; Edward Wilson and Abacuck Prickett were found not guilty.

End of case. There were trading routes and riches to be found.

All in a Name

The *Discovery* was an important name in maritime history. When Hudson made his fourth and final voyage as master, his ship already had been to the Arctic.

The ship that Hudson used had been commanded by George Weymouth in 1602 on an expedition financed by the VOC, the goal was the Northwest Passage across the top of Canada. Weymouth carried a letter from Queen Elizabeth I addressed to the emperor of China.

The *Discovery* may have been new or recently built when Weymouth first sailed. The small vessel, with a ship's company of about seventeen, sailed on May 2, 1602, from London through the Orkney Islands, then south of Greenland, and eventually made landfall in the New World at what they reported as the latitude of 62°30', which would be somewhere on the southern end of Baffin Island at the entrance to what was later known as Hudson Strait.

Weymouth then turned south but was blocked from entering the strait by ice and fog; instead, the *Discovery* headed north up the east coast of Baffin Island above the Arctic Circle to about 68°53'. There, Weymouth reported that the crew mutinied and the ship turned back to begin its trip to England. On their way out, they sailed a distance into Frobisher Bay and then into Ungava Bay; the *Discovery* returned to England in August.

Weymouth reported that "truely there is in three several places great hope of a passage, between the latitude of 62 and 54 degrees; if the fog does not hinder it, which is all the fear I have."

Although it is highly unlikely that an expensive asset like the *Discovery* would sit unused, the next confirmed voyage of the ship was with Hudson for his 1610 expedition to northern Canada. One of the three ships sent by the Virginia Company in 1607 to found the settlement at Jamestown was also named the *Discovery*, but that small, two-masted vessel would not seem to match the three-mast bark given Hudson in 1610. That ship was probably tied up on the James River when Hudson approached Jamestown onboard the *Half Moon* in 1609 but did not land.

Captain Cook's Voyages of Discovery

A century and a half later, Captain James Cook sailed on three of history's most famous explorations. His first voyage circumnavigated the globe, passing Cape Horn below South America and continuing on to Tahiti and the South Pacific; he became only the second known European to reach New Zealand, and in 1770 he confirmed the existence of the fabled southern continent of Australia. His ship, the *Endeavour*, continued along the eastern coast of Australia and passed across its top, touching New Guinea and then Batavia (Jakarta) in Indonesia.

In 1772, he commanded the *Resolution* on a circumnavigation at high southern latitudes, becoming one of the first explorers to enter within the Antarctic Circle. He discovered South Georgia and the South Sandwich Islands, and made landfall at Easter Island and Vanuatu.

His third and last voyage began in 1776, once again on the *Resolution*, in the company of a second ship named the *Discovery*. The goal was once again a passage between the Atlantic and Pacific.

After a stop in Tahiti, Cook became the first European to visit the Sandwich Islands (now Hawaii). He continued eastward to reach the west coast of Canada on Vancouver Island and then proceeded north up the coast near what are now modern-day Juneau and Anchorage and entered into the Bering Strait between Alaska and Russia, although he was unable to pass through because of ice and foul weather.

Cook returned south to the Sandwich Islands, where he became engaged in a dispute with some of the islanders; on February 14, 1779, Cook was clubbed and stabbed to death on the beach at Kealakekua Bay on the big island of Hawaii.

The *Resolution* and *Discovery* returned to England without Cook, just as the earlier ships of the same names returned without Hudson.

Two More *Discoveries,* Headed North and South

Britain's Royal Geographical Society converted an old whale ship named *Bloodhound* into a research vessel for an expedition to the Arctic from 1875 to 1876. It was renamed the *Discovery.*

In 1901, the same group built a new ship specially designed for cold-weather exploration. The Royal Research Ship *Discovery* was one of the last three-masted sailing vessels built in England; it also included a small engine and propeller.

On July 31, 1901, under the command of Captain Robert Falcon Scott, the *Discovery* set sail from London and arrived in Antarctica in January 1902. The ship reached its intended winter haven on Ross Island on February 8 and was quickly frozen in place; the expectation had been that the ship would be able to continue its exploration the next summer, but instead the *Discovery* was locked in the ice for two years.

Among his crew was twenty-eight-year-old Ernest Shackleton, who went on to fame with his own expedition (and rescue) in 1914–1916.

Although Scott conducted research and made an attempt to reach the South Pole, he received orders from his backers, delivered by a relief mission, to abandon the ship and return on a rescue vessel if he could not break out of the ice by the end of February 1904. Scott used explosives to break open a path through nearly twenty miles of ice to reach the open ocean; the *Discovery* returned to England in September of that year.

In another irony of history, the geographic society was short of funds when Scott returned, and the group was forced to sell the *Discovery* to the Hudson's Bay Company, which used it as a cargo vessel to haul supplies and trading items from London to Hudson Bay. The ship continued in that role until the outbreak of World War I, when it was appropriated to carry war supplies to Russia.

The Final Frontier

The most recent great ship to carry the name is the space shuttle *Discovery*, which entered service on August 30, 1984, as the third spacecraft in the fleet. As of early 2007, the *Discovery* had made thirty-three flights.

In naming the craft, NASA specifically referred to Hudson's and Cook's early ships.

The space shuttle is about 122 feet long, with a cargo bay about 60 feet long and 15 feet in diameter; it is roughly the size of Hudson's final ship.

CHAPTER 22

Into Hudson Bay
by Icebreaker

The *Ushuaia* had traveled from the bottom of the world to the top, at least as far as we were concerned; like lines of latitude and hours on the clock, the concept of a globe with a top and bottom is an invention of humans. In any case, the sturdy ship had come up from its home base in Tierra del Fuego at the southern end of Argentina to Ungava Bay near the entrance to Hudson Strait in Canada.

The ice-hardened vessel, built for scientific research, had been converted to carry adventuresome tourists on voyages to the Antarctic in the Southern Hemisphere summer. In 2005, the *Ushuaia* made a three-week trip up the east coasts of South America and North America from Mar del Plata near Buenos Aires to arrive in St. John's, Newfoundland, to fill its fuel tanks and provision for a Northern Hemisphere summer in the Canadian subarctic.

From St. John's, the ship had rounded the corner of Newfoundland and headed northwest, into the Labrador Sea and then through the Furious Overfall between Labrador and Resolution Island.

I met up with the ship as it bobbed at anchor in the Koksoak River, several miles away from the beach at Kuujjuaq in Ungava Bay. Henry Hudson, ever the deliberate and cautious captain, had sailed south into Ungava Bay toward Kuujjuaq before heading back north and then west into Hudson Strait.

The *Ushuaia* had been chartered by the Makivik Corporation for the inaugural season of the adventure travel company Cruise North. Makivik is an Inuit-owned company created in 1978 as part of the James Bay and Northern Quebec Agreement that redrew the governmental map and established—for better or worse—a set of business arrangements that opened up much of the area for development of hydroelectric power plants and other enterprises.

Besides construction, fishing, and transportation services (including two airlines, First Air and Air Inuit) Makivik now hopes to lure more tourists to the little-visited areas of Ungava Bay, Hudson Strait, Baffin Island, and Hudson Bay.

The *Ushuaia* was built in 1970 in Toledo, Ohio, as the *Researcher* for NOAA; it was renamed as the *Malcolm Baldrige* in 1987 in remembrance of a U.S. secretary of commerce, who died in a rodeo accident. At one time, the *Baldrige* was one of the most advanced oceanographic ships afloat, carrying a floating scientific laboratory and two room-sized state-of-the-art computers.

The reinforced steel ship, a class-1 ice-hardened vessel, is 278 feet long with a beam of 51 feet. In 1996, following a final around-the-world cruise, the *Baldrige* was decommissioned by NOAA. A few years later, the ship was bought by an Argentinean expedition tourism company. Renamed the *Ushuaia*, it was refitted to carry sixty-six passengers and thirty-eight crew. Its knife-edge bow and hull design permit it to operate in areas with ice as thick as six to eight feet; its heavy and powerful diesel engines rumble through the ship when it is under way.

The Cold War Is Gone, But Not the Cold

Kuujjuaq, which means Great River, is the largest community in Nunavik, with about 2,200 residents. Nunavik is the name given to Quebec's Arctic region, lying north of the fifty-fifth parallel, south of Hudson Strait, and between Hudson Bay to the west and Ungava Bay and Labrador to the east. Above Nunavik is Canada's Nunavut Territory, which extends all the way to the top of Ellesmere Island at 83° North.

Like many of the settlements in Canada's north, Kuujjuaq's history as a town is fairly short; a Hudson's Bay Company (HBC) post was established in 1830 on the eastern shore of the Koksoak River, and its presence drew regular visits from nomadic Inuit traders. There were also small bands of Montagnais and Naskapi in the area.

In 1942, the U.S. military built an air force base called Crystal 1 on the west shore of the river and step by step the community moved across the water to be closer to the facilities. The town still includes some old ribbed-steel Quonset huts and other military detritus.

Most of the cars in town have no license plates, which is a violation of provincial law, but the owners cannot obtain insurance. And in any case, there's nowhere to drive: the few gravel roads end just outside of town.

In Inuktitut, the literal language of the matter-of-fact Inuit people, Nunavik means "place to live." An Inuk (pronounced *ee-nook*) is a person, Inuuk refers to two people, and a group of three or more Inuk are the Inuit, which means "the people." Finally, the name of their language, Inuktitut, means "like a person."

They say, "Ay" for hello, and "Ah" to acknowledge someone's greeting. Why waste energy?

The one word you no longer hear, at least among the people, is the one the French invented for them, *Esquimaux*, or its English equivalent, Eskimo. The word may have come from a Montaignais phrase referring to a woman who laces snowshoes.

The Montaignais are an unrelated tribe, part of the Algonquian linguistic group that includes the Cree as well as more than two dozen other peoples who lived in the Northeast all the way down to New York and Massachusetts; the Mohicans and the Leni-Lenape that Henry Hudson encountered on the river from Manhattan to Albany were from this group.

Throughout my time in Ungava Bay, Hudson Strait, and Hudson Bay, I found the Inuit to be very direct, serious, and generous people—attributes that probably suit them well in their sometimes very severe land.

Coming into the North

My trip had begun at Pierre Elliott Trudeau Airport in Montreal. Way past the bustling lounges for Air Canada, Air France, British Airways, and the other big names was a generic set of gates for some of the local lines: Air Inuit, Air Creebec, and First Air.

The boarding lounge for First Air was nearly full, and nearly evenly divided among three groups. There were a few dozen Inuit families coming back from the big city with various packages: one boy held a live goldfish in a bowl and others carried boxes of food and supplies.

At the airline counter, I had run into a group of men dressed in camouflage outfits; they checked in enough guns, scopes, knives, and ammunition boxes to outfit a midsized nation's invasion force. The conversation was of caribou. "This going to be a new species for you?" an older hunter asked a young man.

And then there was another group of adventurous tourists—the passengers heading up north to rendezvous with the *Ushuaia* for a passage from Kuujjuaq through Hudson Strait and into the wake of Henry Hudson.

Our two-and-a-half-hour flight on one of First Air's superannuated 727 jets brought us to Kuujjuaq's airport. Little more than a remnant of the former U.S. base, the airport consists of one asphalt and one gravel airstrip and a hangar. Our bags were delivered from the plane by a front-end loader and placed in a pile in the parking lot: suitcases, rifle cases, and cases of junk food.

Kuujjuaq, about 30 miles upstream on the Koksoak, is only 230 miles away from the massive Hydro Quebec plants to the west on James Bay, but it is not connected to the grid. Electricity comes from a droning diesel generator in town.

Ungava Bay squabbles with the Bay of Fundy that lies between Nova Scotia and New Brunswick in Canada for the right to claim the highest daily tidal differential in the world; in parts of Ungava and on the Koksoak, the difference between high and low tide can be twenty feet. According to some scientists, the diversion of some of the rivers for the hydroelectric plants in the interior of the peninsula

307

has reduced the flow of water into the Koksoak, making it even more treacherous to mariners.

This was not the *Ushuaia's* first encounter with the tides on the Koksoak; two weeks earlier, on the ship's inaugural voyage for Cruise North, it had run aground on the muddy bottom of the river and been forced to curtail its trip and summon the Canadian coast guard for an inspection.

When we arrived, the ship lay anchored in the Koksoak about three miles from the gravel haul-out used as a harbor for supply barges. Our luggage was ferried out to the ship, and then it was our turn for a rough and windy trip across the river in one of the *Ushuaia's* fleet of semirigid inflatable rafts called Kiel boats.

The ship could not be confused with a luxury liner, but the accommodations were functional and simple. I had been invited aboard as a lecturer; I shared a tiny bunk-bed cabin with Bruce Qinnuajuak and his antique rifle. Qinnuajuak's title on the crew manifest was Bear Monitor.

And then we waited overnight for the flood tide to come into the river and put enough water in the Koksoak to allow the *Ushuaia* clearance to make its way north down the river and into Ungava Bay.

That night after dinner, the *Ushuaia's* rafts zipped across the river to the landing to pick up about a dozen teenage Inuit girls and a few even-more-shy boys from town; they entered the lounge to give a performance of traditional Inuit throat-singing.

The most famous throat singers are from Tuva near Mongolia. A link between the Inuit and some of the Asian peoples of Siberia and perhaps Mongolia is widely believed by many scientists and anthropologists; the coincidence of a somewhat similar form of musical entertainment is undeniable.

There are members of Inuit tribes, and related bands, across the entire northland from Greenland to Nunavut and northern Quebec all the way to Alaska. On the other side of the Bering Strait, bands of Inuit live on the Chukchi Peninsula at the northeastern corner of Russia.

The prevailing theory is that the ancestors of the Inuit crossed over a land bridge at the Bering Strait between Chukchi and Alaska about 12,000 years ago. If Henry Hudson had succeeded in sailing past Novaya Zemlya and along the coast of Russia to the Bering Sea on his second voyage in 1608, he would have floated over that ancient land bridge.

The Inuit form of throat-singing lies somewhere between song and chant, between noise-making and vocal aerobics. The literal-minded Inuit call it *Katadjak*, or "games in which one makes noises."

It began as entertainment for women and their children who were left behind when the men were out hunting and fishing. In its classic form, two girls stand with their faces just inches apart, grasping each other's elbows to hold them in tight. They are close enough to use the open mouth of the other person as a resonator for their sounds. It looks and sounds nearly orgasmic.

The singing sometimes has a name or a subject: seagulls at sunset, or a flock of geese. Other songs are repetitions of vowels and consonants or family names.

The competition consists mostly of seeing which one of the two can continue the longest without running out of breath or losing the tempo. The best of the throat singers have mastered a technique similar to the circular breathing used by some players of wind instruments: they can make sounds on both the exhale and inhale of breath.

Christian missionaries and priests sought to ban throat-singing as pagan, and it has only reappeared from its hiding place in the culture in the past few decades. Today, there are competitions in most of the major settlements and regional contests at fairs.

Each of the twenty or so songs we heard aboard ship and in other Inuit settlements we visited ended in the same way: one of the two girls would break down in giggles, signifying the end of the game.

The population of Kuujjuaq, and in all the Inuit territory, is quite young; about 65 percent are no more than twenty-five years old. Jessic Annanack, an Inuit woman serving as a guide on the *Ushuaia*, was number ten in a family of eleven children.

"We don't have holidays," Annanack said. "But today was a beautiful day near the end of the summer, and today we would gather all of our friends to go and pick blueberries."

Her description of an ad hoc holiday sounded almost identical to the one given me by Tove Eliassen in Longyearbyen in Spitsbergen thousands of miles and many cultures away. Eliasen had waxed poetic about the celebration of a beautiful moonlit Arctic night.

When darkness finally settled over Ungava Bay, well past 10:00 P.M., we moved onto the dark fantail at the stern of the ship to watch the skies. There is almost no light or industrial pollution, and the view of the far northern stars is spectacular. But the real show is more subtle: the ephemeral, wavering aurora borealis. The northern lights are in the skies all year long, all day long at high latitudes, but they are not visible until after sunset.

The display began as streaks of light, like glowing clouds in the night sky. The streaks slowly drifted about, like wisps of smoke in the wind; red and orange color moved in and out of the clouds with an occasional puff of green.

Annanack told me that parents warn their children not to pay attention to the lights in the sky. "If you watch them, they will come and crash on your heads," she said. "They can chop off your heads and bounce them like basketballs."

A more modern, and less violent piece of advice about the northern lights, she said, is this: move your jacket zipper up and down to shoo them away. I tried, but the lights kept coming back every night, always painted with a different brush.

Summer in Ungava Bay

Kuujjuaq sits astride the tree line in northern Quebec. Black spruce and larch fill some of the marshy valleys to the south; to the north few things grow more than a foot above the rocky surface. In August and September, the region is nearly overrun by the massive migration of the George River caribou herd.

There is no such thing as a native "home" in town; nearly all the houses are prefab designs shipped to the settlement by the provincial government or a tribal agency. But many of the houses also have a tipi in the side yard or backyard. The tipis are used to dry and smoke meat, for ceremonies, and as reminders of the nomadic lifestyle the residents have mostly given up for the stability of the little town.

The houses stood atop cinderblock or wooden pillars to keep them separated from the permafrost; without that gap, the heat from the house would soften the earth below and the structures would sink into mush.

The settlement's original name of Fort Chimo is said to be a corruption of the Inuktitut word *Saimuk*, which means "let's shake hands." The traders of the HBC apparently mistook the greeting for the name of the place.

Early the next morning we made a brief visit to Old Fort Chimo on the eastern shore of the Koksoak; only a handful of people still live there near the original trading post, cut off from the relocated modern settlement by the river.

A village cemetery is still visited by family members; some of the graves were decorated with flowers and a few had small carpets of coins. The last burial was in 1997. The very rough land has the look of a place enjoying a brief summer respite from six to nine months of tough winter.

As modern visitors—forewarned by naturalists aboard the ship—we knew that the glistening flecks of what looked like silver and gold in the stones was quartz and fool's gold. Early explorers had been less informed or more willing to suspend disbelief.

The brightest color on the tundra was the electric orange lichen on some of the rocks; lichen is a combination of fungus and algae, and the color indicates that the rock had been well fertilized with guano from overflying birds that had used it for target practice.

Diana Island and Quaqtaq

In mid-July 1610, Hudson passed an island covered with snow that somehow gave him hope in a time when his journal is filled with despair; he called the land "Desire Provoketh." Today, that is believed to be Akpatok Island, the largest island in Ungava Bay.

The *Ushuaia* anchored just west of Akpatok Island at the top of the western shore of Ungava Bay where it meets Hudson Bay. We were among the first tourists to ever wade ashore at the tiny settlement of about 310. Quaqtaq—pronounced like duck-talk, *kwok-tok*—means "tapeworm," not a very attractive tourist lure. It is among the most isolated places in all of Nunavik.

Quaqtaq sits at the top of a peninsula that marks the end of Ungava Bay and the start of Hudson Strait; Hudson called the land "Hopes Advance" when he finally exited the ice-choked bay at the end of July 1610. As far as we know, he never saw it again.

Archaeologists have found evidence that there has been seasonal occupation of the peninsula for as much as 3,500 years; the Thule people, ancestors of the Inuit, may have first camped there as early as 1400. The first semipermanent settlement came in 1927 when an independent trader set up a post nearby to deal with the Tuvaaluk Inuit, who came to the area for winter camping and hunting on the ice.

According to local stories, a beluga hunter who came to the area in about 1930 when it was known as Nuvukutaaq ("the long point") found live parasites in his feces. His literal-minded Inuit companions renamed the place as Quaqtaq and the discomfiting name has held.

Government services did not come to the area until the 1950s, after a measles epidemic killed eleven adults—about 10 percent of the population. The Quebec government installed a post office and a radio telephone in the 1960s. There are no roads that connect to other settlements.

Cape Wolstenholme and Digges Islands

We sailed past Cape Wolstenholme at the very top of the Ungava Peninsula in a fog bank swirled by sixty-knot winds. From time to time, the winds would open a view of the sheer cliffs at the cape, and then they would change direction and we would be back in a whiteout. It was August, a month later than when Hudson had passed by in 1610, and the water was still speckled with chunks of ice ranging from the size of a refrigerator to houses. It was a severely unpleasant place to be traveling, even in a sturdy ice-hardened expedition ship like the *Ushuaia*.

As we have seen, Hudson's journal ends abruptly on August 3, 1610, between Cape Wolstenholme and Digges Islands, even though he would survive until at least June 21 of the following year in James Bay before he was set out of the ship by the mutineers.

It was near Wolstenholme that Hudson turned away from the Northwest (the direction that the Northwest Passage would seem to trend) and instead turned left and south into Hudson Bay and eventually to James Bay. Here, Hudson fired Robert Juet as his mate and elevated Robert Bylot.

Past Cape Wolstenholme, the *Ushuaia* stayed near the coast; to our north was Digges Islands, which are two landmasses bisected by a strait into East and West Digges. The eastern chunk is fortresslike and nearly unapproachable, whereas the western piece has been visited over the centuries. Visitors have found rusted trinkets on West Digges and of course some have claimed them to be from Hudson's ship or from others who followed in the early seventeenth century.

West Digges Island holds some well-preserved Inuit ruins. It is also, along with Cape Wolstenholme, the site of one of the largest seabird colonies in Arctic Canada. Uncounted millions of thick-billed murres visit the cliffs of Digges and Wolstenholme.

Ivujivik: The Bay Where the Ship Came In

We broke out of the fog and the wind as we headed south into Hudson Bay. Brad Rhees, the expedition leader, worked the radio telephone to arrange a visit to Ivujivik. As it turned out, the first reception committee swam out to meet us: a pod of curious *tirilluk* (bearded seals).

The community sits within a small sandy cove, the only flat and low land between steep cliffs. The town's name means "churning and piling of ice along the shore." Offshore, the strong tides of the Hudson Strait and the returning currents out of Hudson Bay collide.

Ivujivik, just to the west of the top of the Ungava Peninsula, is about 500 miles north of Kuujjuarapik, 1,250 miles north of Montreal, and 435 miles northwest of Kuujjuaq. The community consists of 56 households with about 300 people.

As it is through much of the area, the Inuit practice communal welfare: a hunter who brings in a whale or a caribou or any other meat is expected to divide the catch into fifty-six pieces for distribution. (In the pragmatic modern world, that means fifty-six packages were brought to the community freezer. The hunters are also supported by cash payments from the band.)

Beluga whales pass through the strait in early July—a time when the waters are still filled with ice floes and bergs—and then return in late September. Hunters go out into the rough seas in small boats. Armed with rifles instead of wooden harpoons or spears, they shoot behind the whales to encourage them to move into the harbor. The goal is to force the creatures into shallow water, where they can be killed and dragged up onto the beach to be butchered.

The blubber—two inches thick over most of the body—is the most valued and quickest to be distributed. Various cuts of meat are put into the freezer raw, boiled, or dried.

Other staples in Ivujivik include arctic char, crabs, walrus, ringed seal, and bearded seal. Even though harp seals pass by in large groups just offshore, the locals draw the line here. My guide, Adamie Kalingo (this first name is a version of Adam from the Bible), a youth protection community worker, told me that this was a preference that seemed to apply in this little village only: "Since a long time ago—many, many generations ago—a harp seal was seen eating a human carcass, and it made us disgusted," he told me.

The residents did eat sculpin, Kalingo said, although this was a food mostly favored by women who liked its very oily flesh. I've seen sculpin, and personally I think I'd rather take my chances with harp seals. Sculpin are among the oddest looking fish in the sea with spiny heads and nasty prickles on their fins, and more: they have three sets of fins and hairy eyelash-like cirri above their eyes. If you've ever seen a clownfish in an aquarium, you've got an idea of a more handsome version of this creature.

The Arctic version of the sculpin, which lives in the deep waters from Ellesmere Island south into James Bay, east of Greenland, and in the Arctic Ocean around Svalbard, is able to live in waters as cold as 28 degrees, which is very close to the freezing temperature of seawater. Scientists say it does this by producing glycoprotein, a natural form of antifreeze that links a protein and a carbohydrate; a more familiar form of glycoprotein for most of us is egg white. The sculpin is ugly, spiny, and slimy, but good enough for the womenfolk.

The people I met in the little town of about 300 were happy to see a few dozen visitors from our ship walking around town; we visited the community center where groups of girls were working on throat singing for an upcoming competition. They broke down into giggles very quickly in the presence of outsiders.

Ivujivik itself would have ranked pretty high in an ugly contest. It had the feeling of a temporary town, like an outpost in Antarctica; the presence of the Argentinean *Ushuaia* anchored offshore added to the picture. The old ship was the most substantial construction in sight.

We made a pilgrimage to the local cooperative store for soda, candy, and other essentials; as it was in most of the native communities in the North, the band blocked the sale of alcohol at its store.

Like other Inuit towns, there has not been a historical town at this location. It had instead been a gathering place in the summer and later a trading post.

Kalingo is well wired into the community. He devotes much of his time to attempting to help young people avoid the despair that has led to a frightening suicide rate among the young.

Life is hard in Ivujivik, Kalingo said. You begin with a settlement of just 300 people and very little to do—a major investment in an indoor hockey rink has not proven a big draw, he said—and then consider the costs of isolation. An airplane ticket to Montreal costs about $1,500 each way, he said, and many of the relatively few students who do go south for higher education fail to complete their studies because of the expense and the distance from their families.

Ivujivik was among just a handful of communities that opposed the James Bay Treaty in 1974; it later consented, grudgingly. As with most other remote places in Quebec, villagers do not own the land under their homes; instead, they rent it from the province and from a government-recognized landholding authority.

The *Ushuaia* was not the first large ship to show up unexpectedly at Ivujivik. In 1610, Hudson and the crew of the *Discovery* sailed past Salluit and between Digges Islands and Ivujivik on the mainland.

To this day, the larger bay within which Ivujivik sits is called Saaqayaaq which means "the bay where the ship came in." The ship itself has a word of its own, too: Umiarraaluq, "a big boat with a sail."

According to Kalingo, the Inuit tell how a big sailing ship came into these waters from Ungava Bay. One night they stopped here, he said, and the next day a fight broke out. A big noise came off the ship, and a man in a kayak was killed.

"I heard this from a great hunter," Kalingo said. "And I will pass it down to my grandchildren."

Stalking Polar Bears on Mansel Island

Were we stalking a polar bear, or was he stalking us? I'm not certain, although Qinnuajuak, my cabin mate, made sure we stayed downwind of the bear patrolling the beach on Mansel Island. He held his rifle closer than usual as we walked.

We guessed that the bear was a male because at this time of the year, in August, the females would still be with their cubs. Unable to get out on ice floes to catch seals and fish, polar bears spend the summer a bit like some humans do: they laze about, grab whatever food they find lying around, and generally try to exert as little energy as possible. It's not quite like hibernation, and it happens only in the summer; in winter polar bears are on the hunt.

Mansel Island, called Puujjunaq by the Inuit, is the smallest of three substantial islands at the top of Hudson Bay. Like all the islands in Hudson Strait, Hudson Bay, and James Bay, it is governed by the territory of Nunavut. There are no permanent residents on the

1,300-square-mile island; there is a substantial caribou reserve, many Inuit sites, and more than a few polar bears.

We don't know if Hudson made a call at the island on his way down toward James Bay, or if the mutineers stopped there on their way back up and out of Hudson Bay the next spring. The *Discovery* did land at Mansel Island in 1613, under the command of John Ingram with Robert Bylot as pilot; they were once again in search of the Northwest Passage but had also been asked to keep an eye out for Hudson.

In 1912, the American explorer Robert Flaherty arrived in Cape Wolstenholme and just by chance he happened to witness the landing of a makeshift, leaky raft made of sealskin, inflated seal bladders, and whalebone. Aboard was an Inuit hunter named Comock along with his wife, their eleven children, and two dogs.

According to Flaherty's account, Comock and his family had gone hunting ten years before in search of a legendary island teeming with caribou and surrounded by walruses and seals and other food. They found themselves on Mansel, sixty miles west of Wolstenholme, marooned there as the only humans in one of the most difficult environments on Earth.

Flaherty had a rudimentary motion picture camera with him on his first meeting; he reshot the movie on a later visit (and developed the film in a makeshift darkroom he brought with him to the frozen North). The film he released in 1922, *Nanook of the North*, was an international sensation and created much of the images we have of Inuit life before the modern era.

Inukjuak: Golf in the High Latitudes

Meeko, age seventy-six, was the unofficial greeter for the village of Inukjuak on the north bank of the Innuksuak River. Not that the 1,200 or so residents there receive all that many visitors, but word of our imminent arrival had gotten through to Meeko, and she zipped on down to the beach on her all-terrain vehicle (ATV).

She shook the hand of each of the several dozen strangers who

Meeko, the unofficial greeter of Inukjuat.
Photo by the author

waded ashore from rafts and posed for pictures. She then headed up from the beach with one of the visitors perched uncertainly on the basket at the back of her ATV.

The Innuksuak River runs turbulent and fast at the village; turquoise water courses through rapids where the river meets the bay. Archaeologists have only begun to catalog and appraise many sites along the river, but indications are that the area has been used as a gathering place for thousands of years.

Inukjuak—the name means "the giant"—is home to about 1,200 people. In the spring, the ice between Inukjuak and the islands breaks up and rises into frozen mountains as the currents begin to move up toward the Furious Overfall. The handful of roads in the community go about three miles inland and come to an end.

South of the port are the Hopewell Islands, an intriguing name:

Hopewell was the name of Hudson's first two ships, from London to Svalbard in 1607 and to Novaya Zemlya in 1608. An English family name, it was used for several other notable ships that sailed to the Virginia colony later in the century. The islands were obviously given their name by one or another English explorer, which one is not certain. The northern group of islands includes Cox, Captain, Ward, McCormack, Morse, and Hopkins; while the southern group includes Frazier, Drayton, Leonard, Hotchkiss, and Bartlett.

The Inuit had come to trade at a Révillon Frères and then a HBC post established at the mouth of the river in the 1920s; it was not until the 1950s, though, that some of the natives began to make a permanent settlement there. In 1953, the Canadian government forcibly relocated about twenty families from Inukjuak and residents of several other Inuit villages to newly created communities 1,200 miles north in the High Arctic. It was an effort to strengthen the country's claim on the empty territories at places including Resolute Bay and Grise Fjord. One commentator called the families human flagpoles.

Although they were used to a nomadic life on the Ungava Peninsula, the Inuit from Inukjuak were not accustomed to the even more challenging conditions above Baffin Bay. It wasn't until 1996 that the Canadian government offered "reconciliation"—not an apology—to the displaced people, along with $10 million in a trust fund and direct compensation.

There are some rumblings about Hydro Quebec seeking to dam the Inukjuak River; the community is opposed. But the people are not against other changes. Eric Atagotaaluk, the president of the landholders council, showed me the community's newest recreational facility: a rough and casual sixteen-hole golf course. "We didn't have enough room for eighteen holes," he said.

They also don't have any grass; the fairways are made from sand and rock with a few toupees of plastic turf at each hole. There's not yet a country club to go with the Inukjuak Golf Course, but they have applied names to a few of the holes: the most difficult is called Tiger Woods, and others include First Hole, Last Hole, Gas Station, and Ditch.

There would seem to be some time available for leisure. About 40 percent of the population is unemployed and 20 percent is on welfare, Atagotaaluk said. There is a community hunt for caribou each August, and local fishermen harvest seals and walrus but not beluga whales; much of the meat is stored in the community freezer.

Blueberry Jam at Umiujaq

Heading south, we hugged the west coast of Ungava to stay between the mainland and the Nastapoka Island chain, which sounds like a stopover on the Lawrence Welk concert tour. There are more than 500 islands and islets in lower Hudson Bay and James Bay; the Hopewell-Nastapoka-Long Island group is the longest chain of islands in Canada, extending about 375 miles. Most of the islands are what geologists call cuestas, with a steep face on one side and a gentle slope on the other.

We may have been the first cruise ship to make a call at the tiny village of Umiujaq, population about 315. The settlement dates back only to 1985; it was established when plans for the diversion of the Great Whale River at Kuujjuarapik were being made by Hydro Quebec. Inuit whose traditional traplines and fishing areas were threatened by the project were offered new homes in the Richmond Gulf.

The Great Whale project is being blocked by native groups and environmentalists and may never happen, but the settlement remains. It was established at the base of a hill said to resemble an overturned *umiaq*, a walrus-skin Inuit boat; Umiujaq means "which resembles a boat."

We arrived as preparations were underway for the annual Blueberry Jam. Locals were spread out into the bush in search of blueberries (gatherers, not farmers). The collected berries were brought back to the municipal building to be shared among all the residents; most of the crop was put in the freezer for the winter. A prize would be awarded—not to the largest load or the best berries—but instead to the person who brings in a crop that is closest to a randomly selected weight.

Nearby, the waterfall of the Nastapoka River tumbles about 100 feet off the cliffs into Richmond Gulf; with typical Inuit pragmatism, it bears a name that means "place where water falls down and clouds rise up." The area is home to a significant population of peregrine falcons, eider ducks, and common loons.

Crossroads of the Bay

The *Ushuaia*'s turnaround was at the last community on the western coast of the Ungava Peninsula, near the line in the water where the Hudson Bay ends above and the James Bay begins below. It is also the border between the Inuit and the Cree territories; it is the only place in Quebec where both bands live side by side.

The split-personality settlement was built on a sand spit at the mouth of the Great Whale River, officially known on maps by its French name of Grande Rivière de la Baleine. The natives from the southernmost Inuit group call it Kuujjuarapik ("little great river"). The members of the northernmost Cree band in Quebec call the place Whapmagoostui ("where there are whales"). The Quebec government, which has little influence over the entire region other than the provision of certain services and payments under treaty agreements, has also tried to apply the name Poste-de-la-Baleine (Post of the Whale). English traders had called their post Great Whale River.

Thus, this one little place, population about 1,215, has four names for the settlement, four levels of government (Cree and Inuit local, plus token representatives of provincial and federal authorities), three names for the river, three police forces (Cree and Inuit departments, with provincial backups), and one Anglican church.

At 55° North latitude, Whapmagoostui-Kuujjuarapik is also the geographical boundary between the tundra of the south and the taiga of the north. There are no roads in or out of the community; it is accessible only by small plane and the very occasional visit of boats in July or August.

The Great Whale River runs east to west about 450 miles from Lake Bienville in the middle of the peninsula, draining some 16,500 square miles of nearly untouched land that is home to caribou, wolf, and other animals; the river near the bay attracts beluga whales and rare freshwater seals.

Archaeologists say that Cree and Inuit have moved through the region for nearly 3,000 years. Outsiders arrived in the eighteenth century; the HBC opened a trading post at Great Whale River in 1820 to buy furs and whale products.

An Anglican mission was established in 1882, followed by a Catholic mission in 1890. It was not until a few decades into the twentieth century that the Royal Canadian Mounted Police brought an outside government presence to the area.

The Outside World Moves In

As with Kuujjuaq on the other side of the Ungava Peninsula, Kuujjuarapik came into the modern era during World War II when the U.S. Army constructed a military base and airport. In 1948, the base became a Canadian installation and location of a cold war radar station, which was part of an early attack warning system; the Mid-Canada Line crossed eastern Canada from the Atlantic Ocean to Hudson Bay along the fifty-fifth parallel.

In some ways, the multicultured settlement was dealt a double blow by the Hydro Quebec project. In the original James Bay and Northern Quebec Agreement of 1975, there was the expectation that the Great Whale River would be one of the waterways that would be dammed and diverted to a hydroelectric plant; much of the hunting and fishing areas would have been submerged or reduced.

As part of the deal, the Inuit band (the Kuujjuarapik side of town) negotiated a clause that required the utility and the provincial government to relocate many of their people to the new community of Umiujaq about 100 miles north in 1985 so they could continue their traditional lifestyle. About 300 Inuit made the move; the governmental newspeak for the process was "relocalization."

At the same time, opposition to the diversion of the Great Whale River was growing. Activists from the area, together with environmentalists from Canada and the United States, lobbied in Montreal and Ottawa against the project. A group of Cree traveled to the United States and paddled a boat on the Hudson River to gain publicity for their cause. They focused on a proposed contract that would have brought James Bay hydroelectric power to Maine and New York.

Among the paddlers on the river and in the corridors of the state capital at Albany were Matthew Mukash, then the chief of the Whapmagoostui Cree, and Robert F. Kennedy Jr., representing the Natural Resources Defense Council and other environmental groups on the Hudson River.

In March 1992, then New York governor Mario Cuomo canceled a $12 billion, twenty-year contract to buy power generated by Hydro Quebec. The state assembly had already passed a bill blocking the state from buying power from a foreign nation without a full environmental assessment and the state senate was due to take up the legislation when Cuomo stepped in.

Hydro Quebec declared that New York's pullout would not be the end of the Great Whale project; a top official promised that power would be flowing from a new plant near Whapmagoostui by 2000. In 2006, the project was still on the shelf.

When I visited, the community seemed a bit like a place that had never been completed, especially on the Inuit side of town. Those who remained behind practice subsistence hunting of caribou, beluga whale, seal, arctic char, and other foodstuffs; some of the meat is sold or traded. There are also a handful of what the Inuit call *Qallunaat* (non-aboriginal outsiders; the word means "those who pamper their eyebrows"), who operate hunting and fishing expeditions for a small number of tourists who fly up to the village from lower Quebec.

A few weeks before my visit, I had placed a phone call to arrange for a place to stay. I was told to call a guy named Claude, who ran a small very basic bar near the airport and an even more basic hotel at the edge of town; from the outside it looked like a temporary warehouse.

When I came to shore from the *Ushuaia*, a local school bus driver took me up to the hotel, but it was shuttered and dark. Next, we dropped by Claude's bar, which was similarly closed on an early Sunday morning, with double padlocks over the front door and iron grates over the windows. I stayed on the bus for a few loops as the driver picked up some of the passengers from the ship who were heading for the airport. Suddenly, the bus skidded to a stop on the gravel road.

"There's Claude," the driver said.

Claude was driving a fire and rescue truck, apparently a third job. I told him I was ready to check into his hotel for the night, and he stared at me blankly for a moment. "We're closed," he said.

I reminded him that we had spoken by phone a few weeks earlier. After a few moments—during which I considered whether I would be spending the night battling mosquitoes on a bench down by the bay—Claude waved me into his truck and took me up to the hotel. He gave me the key to the front door and showed me how to turn on the lights for the building; I was the only guest in the hotel. That night I slept with my suitcase wedged against the door.

My goal in Kuujjuarapik was to meet with the Reverend Tom Martin, literally the big man in town. Walking the dirt roads of town, I flagged down a passing patrol car from the Kativik Regional Police, run by the Inuit tribe.

The driver turned out to be nineteen-year-old Chris Martin, son of the Reverend Martin; he was in his second year as a patrolman in the first Inuit police department in Canada. I rode as a guest in the backseat of the paddy wagon to Martin's house.

CHAPTER 23

The Man in the Middle

Tom Martin is a bear of a man, a presence large enough to be noticed anywhere, but especially when he is one of the few outsiders in the small community of First Nations people along the eastern shore of Hudson Bay.

The Reverend Martin is the minister at St. Edmund's Church, the Anglican Church in Whapmagoostui-Kuujjuarapik. Before I sat down with him, I attended Sunday mass, which was celebrated in Cree.

As there are at most religious ceremonies, there were many varying levels of attention, devotion, and formality. There were about 150 parishioners in the seats and a few dozen children running around, rolling wooden and metal toys on the floor, and drumming on the pews.

Some members of the choir and lectors wore Christian robes, while others were dressed in native shirts with long, beaded, and colored tails. Some of the parishioners were dressed in their Sunday finest: Western-style shirts and pants or frilly but modest dresses. But the majority of the congregation was dressed as if they were on their way to a big city mall: t-shirts, NHL jerseys, and jeans.

Although I could not understand the service, the rhythms and structure were familiar, including the call and response: "World without end, amen" in Cree. The collection plate was a fur hat; I tossed in a twonie, a Canadian two-dollar coin.

The Reverend Martin moved from big-city Toronto to the tiny settlement in one fell swoop in 1984. I met with him in his simple, modern home in town, a street above the church.

"Frankly, I had some marriage problems and my bishop in Toronto wasn't very keen about that kind of thing, and so basically he said 'you've got to go,' " Martin told me.

"By this time I was remarried. We looked at three or four different possibilities and this place came open and they arranged for us to come up and look around. The house they had for us to live in was basically a shack," he said. "When I saw that, I figured my wife would say no. But she had already decided this was the place for us.

"We came to the church on Easter weekend and there was a visiting bishop performing confirmations," Martin said, "and he introduced me to the congregation as the minister. And we said, 'Whoa, we haven't said anything yet.'

"Later on that afternoon, we had a meeting with some of the Crees, and one of them said through a translator, 'Thanks for coming. You are an answer to our prayers, because there has been nobody here for about four years.' And so after that kind of an introduction, how can you say 'No'?"

Though he had been born and educated in Toronto, Martin said he still had a feel for the outdoor life, and all of his previous parish work had been in small rural congregations. "Once you realize that it doesn't matter what language is spoken or what the culture is, a small town is a small town," he said.

They Called Him Jesus

Martin is six-feet-four-inches tall, and large in other dimensions as well. "Compared to your parishioners," I said, pausing for a moment. "I am a giant," he finished.

Martin said that a number of years ago when he was in a parish in southern Ontario he attended a commemorative ceremony for the Canadian martyrs, a group of eight missionaries who were martyred at the hands of one or another native tribe in New France and other parts of Canada and northern America in the seventeenth century. Among them was Jean de Brébeuf, who was known as the apostle of the Hurons; he was captured in 1649 and subjected to brutal torture before being killed. In the oral history, St. Jean de Brébeuf is spoken of as having the heart of a giant.

"I read some research that the Jesuits gave me, and I found out that in those days the average Indian was just under five feet and the average European was about five-and-a-half feet. We know this from archaeological evidence. Jean de Brébeuf was a man about my size, so no wonder he was considered to be a giant."

The focal point of St. Edmund's Church is the large, vivid mural on the back wall behind the altar. It seems a perfectly fitting backdrop for the multicultural milieu of the settlement: Jesus Christ walking on the Great Whale River.

Eddy Weetaluktuk, a noted native artist, was primarily responsible for the mural, which was first installed in an earlier church in the village. It's a remarkable piece of work integrating traditional Christian themes and images with local scenery and sensibilities.

(I was reminded of a painting of "The Last Supper" I had seen in the cathedral in Cuzco, 11,400 feet above sea level in the Peruvian Andes; there, a native artist had replicated the work of the great masters of Europe, although the skin color and facial features of the apostles were those of the indigenous people. On the table, instead of the traditional roast lamb, the main course was a cooked cuy (a guinea pig, which is considered a great ceremonial delicacy).

In the Kuujjuarapik mural, Jesus is a very tall man with Western features, a priestly white gown, blond hair, and a beard. He reaches out to Peter, emerging from the water. Peter has the face of an Inuk and wears an animal skin robe.

In the background are the cliffs of the far shore of the Great Whale River, the view out the window of the church where the mural was first mounted. "We do get whitecaps like that on the river," Martin told me. "The boat that is depicted in the picture was the community boat at the time."

Besides Peter in the river, there are eleven apostles—some in Inuit and others in Cree clothing—in the boat, which flies a Canadian flag. A chevron of geese passes by overhead, and closer to the water a pair of seagulls float on a wind current.

Jesus and the apostles at St. Edmund's Church in Whapmagoostui-Kuujjuarapik.
Photo by the author

When the Reverend Martin arrived in the settlement, he was more than just another unusual white man in the combined Cree and Inuit culture. "They looked at me and they called me Jesus," he said.

"There was a certain resemblance if you look at the picture in the church of Christ walking on the water," Martin said. "I have a lot of kids in town who still today look at me and call me Jesus."

Even 350 years after the arrival of the first white missionaries in the North, Martin's appearance in the settlement was a bit mystifying to some. "They were confused between the messenger and the message," Martin said.

St. Edmund's is the third significant Anglican church in the settlement. According to Martin, the original structure was an "iron church" that was imported from England. "Back in the days of the British Empire, they had a need for prefab buildings throughout the empire and you would go to a catalog and order one," he said. That church was brought over by ship and installed first at Moose Factory Island, then moved north to the mouth of the Little Whale River near the present location of Umiujaq, and then about 1880 was moved to Kuujjuarapik. The iron church was used until 1962.

A Book of Common Prayer

After more than twenty years in town, Martin seems well accepted and connected. Although he has not mastered the Cree and Inuit languages, he can read the syllabics in the prayer books—one for each culture—and relies on native ministers and lectors for translation. "I said to one man, I will learn some Cree," Martin said. "He said, 'no, no. I want to practice my English on you.' "

Neither culture had written languages at the time the first missionaries came to the North in the mid-nineteenth century. The Cree syllabary was created by Methodist missionaries near Moose Factory Island at the bottom of James Bay, and characters for Inuktitut followed later.

"One of my main subjects in theological school was the prayer book. And so even though the Cree and the Inuktitut prayer book are translations, I know where I am even though I don't know what the words are.

"Inuktitut is basically written the way it sounds. If you can understand the syllabics, then you can do a passable job, even though it might be slow.

"Cree is more like English in that in one context you pronounce a combination of signs in one way, but in a different context that same combination is pronounced differently. So for Cree you have to have an ear for the language."

In some ways, at least for the Anglicans (the largest local Christian denomination), Martin and the church is a bridge between the Cree and Inuit communities. Before the James Bay Agreement, he said, there had been one community in town with a single government and school. After the modern treaty was put in place, things became much more bureaucratic. "They drew a line down through the community that said, 'This is Cree and this is Inuit,' " Martin said.

"With that came two of everything: two police forces, two fire departments, two nursing stations, two radio stations, and two municipal organizations," he said. "The Inuit nursing station was on Cree land, and guess where the Cree nursing station was? Only the white man would do that."

The church, though, was in common for both peoples. "In my first few years here, I would have to stop and think which language I was supposed to be using at this time," Martin said.

At Christmas, Easter, and other important holidays, there are joint services conducted in both languages. And funerals—which usually touch the whole community—are usually bilingual.

Some of the native people are determined to maintain their differences and separation from each other, Martin said, but there is also a growing number of mixed marriages or cohabitation that produce children with parents from both sides of the community. "Those kids are crying out for appreciation of both cultures," he said.

A View of Two Cultures

"Part of Anglicanism is that from the very beginning the service had to be in the language of the people," Martin said. "But I think we did a lousy job of adopting the culture into the church. I think what happened in the past was that there was a great influx of missionaries who came in and really worked hard at this whole business of learning the language and presenting the tools for worship. The Bible and the prayer book were translated very quickly so that people could get right into it.

"But for instance, at the Cree service this morning, the prayer book was produced in 1918 and since then we have had one major revision. So, we are a little bit behind there.

"We did that first push in producing everything for the people then, but [we] haven't sustained it over the years," Martin said. "They did not get into the whole idea of bringing the culture more into the church."

Martin had presided over a Cree wedding the night before; I asked him if it was a ceremony that most Christians would recognize. "Definitely. Except for the language, that was a wedding you could have anywhere down south, with all the frills," Martin said.

Many of the native people are perfectly happy melding in elements of the outside culture when it suits them, just as shotguns and snowmobiles have supplanted bows and arrows and dog sleds.

"I am constantly saying to couples that they don't have to spend all that money on a wedding," he said. "At one time I reckoned that the average Cree wedding might cost twenty-five thousand to thirty thousand dollars, and it has gone up since then. I ask them, 'Why don't you wear traditional clothing?' It falls on deaf ears."

My near-circumnavigation around the Ungava Peninsula on the *Ushuaia* had been exclusively in Inuit communities in the even-more difficult environment to the North. Although I was received graciously by almost everyone I met, I told Martin it seemed to me that the Inuit were by nature much more intense than the Cree.

"That's pretty fair," Martin said. "The Cree have a good sense of humor and in many ways an earthy sense of humor. Some of the things that they laugh and joke about we would consider in our culture going too far. Very crude. But you sort of learn to go along with it. The Inuit have a different sense of humor.

"One of the big differences between the two groups is that the Cree are extremely family oriented. Family is very important and out of that comes a meaningful respect for elders.

"The Inuit tend to be very individualistic," Martin said. "Family is important but the individual, in my observation, is more important than the family. And therefore while they talk about elders being important, in reality they are less important.

"I won't say that one is good and one is bad. They are just different and you just have to recognize that."

Death Comes Too Early

One of the most troubling things I learned about the people of the North was the high rate of suicide among the Inuit, as much as six times greater than the rest of Canada. It was a subject that was on the minds of nearly all the community leaders and elders I met on my trip.

According to a study by the Canadian Psychiatric Association, in

2002 the death rate by suicide in Nunavik was about 82 per 100,000 people. Suicide and self-injury were the leading cause of death for Inuit under the age of forty-four. Few communities were untouched.

According to the association, the Inuit population in 2004 was the youngest in Canada. The birth rate was double that of the national average, and 39 percent of Inuit were under the age of fourteen.

This was not news to the Reverend Martin, and he worried about his unique bicultural community.

"Up until not even a year ago there were no suicides among the Cree," he said. "It was all Inuit. But unfortunately in the last year we began to have suicides among the Cree.

"We have been fortunate in this community that we have not had the suicide rate of some of the other communities," he said. "In some places, you can count on one a month."

I asked him why he thought this was happening.

"Partly, I think it is a breakdown of the family," he said. "Fathers and mothers are too busy doing their own thing and ignoring their kids. We are raising a couple of generations of very angry young people where the mother or father or both are out drinking or gambling or doing drugs. The kids have been raised in a vacuum."

There has to be at least one more piece to the puzzle, I said, because as an American I come from a country which is in many places no better at paying attention to our children. We have drugs, alcohol, and we have big-city problems, but not the suicide rate. In 2000, there were less than 11 suicides per 100,000 people in the United States; chillingly, though, the suicide rate among young Native Americans was much higher than among the general population.

It was clear that Martin was upset about what he saw; he chose to pull no punches.

"In some really northern communities some so-called Christians tend to be very judgmental," he said. "You are bad. Nobody wants you, and even God doesn't want you. And so people basically say, 'Why hang around? There is nobody interested in me.' "

Chris, Martin's police officer son, had joined us in the family living room. "I dealt with the first suicide we had in town," he said. "I think these people had been told, 'You are so bad God will never forgive you. You are going to hell.'

"I have dealt with about thirty people now who have attempted suicide," Chris said. "They told me the reason they were attempting suicide was because they have been told by everybody that they are going to hell anyway. Why should they wait around if they can just kill themselves and get it over with?"

The Reverend Martin said the highly judgmental brand of Christianity that is practiced farther north in the Arctic, the idea that there is no hope for those who have sinned, is certainly not what he preaches.

In the Far North, though, the communities are even more isolated than those of Nunavik. "They have nothing else to think about," he said. "And there isn't the ability to get up and move. You are stuck in a tiny community."

Martin's parish also includes the offshore Belcher Islands and the 750-person Inuit community of Sanikiluaq, which sit about 100 miles west of Umiujaq. As islands in James Bay, they are technically part of Nunavut; according to Martin, they are some of the most isolated places in that nearly barren territory.

"Some very wise nurses there told me that when people attempted suicide in Sanikiluaq they realized it was a ploy to get shipped out of town to a bigger hospital," Martin said. "All they wanted was a break from the community."

I offered Martin whatever anonymity he might want, but he was quite willing to stay on the record. In his opinion, much of the problem had its source in his own church.

"Within our own Anglican church there is a Pentecostal element, and they tend to have a great deal of emotionalism," Martin said. "It is a feel-good kind of thing. I can go and scream out my sins and [have] a catharsis.

"Now when I was a kid, I never went to church until I was eighteen," Martin said. "And when I was in high school, I used to laugh at the Roman Catholics in Toronto at the time. They would go to confession on Saturday so that they could go to mass on Sunday and then they could start all over again on Monday. Like a revolving door.

"And yet this is exactly what I see among some of my Anglican friends in the North," Martin said. "I am talking about three- and four-hour-long services at night."

Leaving your kids alone for four hours at a time to go to church— or to go to a bar or gambling—is a dangerous thing, Martin said.

At Church with the Crees

I sat down in a pew of the large church, as unobtrusive as I could hope to be. There were two white men among 300 or so Cree: me at the back taking notes and Tom Martin at the front conducting the service.

Martin introduced each part of the service in English, and one of the lay assistants would translate his words into Cree. For some of the prayers, Martin would lead the congregation, reading phonetic Cree from the translated Book of Common Prayer.

One little boy spent most of the service pushing a toy car up and down the center aisle. A couple of kids at the back wall were drumming on a rail. Others wandered in and out.

The Reverend Martin was somewhere between bemused and resigned: "The parents would sit there with their kids taking the place apart and not do anything," he told me later. "The Crees especially, and the Inuit, too, feel a kid has to grow up and experience life and learn by his mistakes. 'No' is not their vocabulary.

"You just have to grin and bear it," he said, "but occasionally it gets too much for me and I just say, 'Will somebody do something about those kids?' "

CHAPTER 24

In the Land of the Giants

Kuujjuarapik's airport sits at the top of a small hill above the beach. As I walked up the dirt and gravel road, I came closer and closer to a twin-engine plane that seemed poised to take off down the main street; it was only when I came very close that I realized there was actually a runway running the other direction. The gate in the chain link fence was wide open.

Along with the airport terminal—a leftover from a World War II military building—everything in town seemed prefabricated or bolted together, a modern equivalent of the Wild West where everything was brought in by wagon train or made from leftovers. No roads reach Kuujjuarapik; everything has to come in by barge or land at the airport.

I entered the tiny terminal to board my morning plane to Radisson and followed other passengers into a security screening room. There, a female security guard hand-searched every piece of luggage, including paper bags of blueberries heading south. After carefully examining the contents of a local man's suitcase and waving him through, the guard turned and gave him a kiss because he was going away for two weeks. Then she took away a pair of tweezers from the carry-on of the Anglican bishop of Nunavik.

On Air Inuit, there were no preflight instructions; there were no seatback tables to raise anyway. We taxied away and took off.

The Twin Otter, a sturdy, powerful high-wing twin engine airplane, was more like a well-used bus with aluminum floors and minimal padding on the seats. Aboard were ten Cree and Inuit, me, and two white pilots in military-like flight suits.

Soon after takeoff from Kuujjuarapik, I spotted the first trees of any size I'd seen in more than a week; the town, like Kuujjuaq on the other side of Nunavik, sits astride the tree line. Within the forest were thousands if not millions of lakes, from tiny pools to major bodies of water.

A Cree who got on the plane with me stared intently out the left side window as the plane headed south. Noticing me watching him, he said: "I want to see my hunting lands."

Europeans often remark about the great emptiness they see flying over the midsections of the United States; those of us who live on the coasts have been known to call the vast open plains and unpopulated forests "flyover country." If Montana or Wyoming are empty, then interior Nunavik is a black hole. It is a spectacular world of rivers, rapids, streams, lakes, marshes, and green forest in the warm months, and a symphony of white snow and ice for the rest of the year. There are no roads, no villages, no power lines, and nothing else to remind you of human life. The deserts of the United States and the wide open spaces of Alberta seem, by comparison, urban metropolises.

Things changed quickly as we began our descent into the La Grande Airport at Radisson, the home of Hydro Quebec. The company calls the region Le Pays des Géants (the Land of the Giants).

The Hydro Outpost

Radisson is the only French Canadian settlement in all of Nunavik. It was built to support the initial construction of the massive Hydro Quebec development on the La Grande River in the 1970s; by 1978, at the peak of the project, there were 2,000 people in the community and another 8,000 workers at temporary camps.

The instant village had an Olympic-sized indoor swimming pool, a gymnasium, a curling rink, and a ski hill. "There was one huge cafeteria where they served six thousand meals in an hour-and-a-half," said Eric Hamel, one of Hydro Quebec's public relations rep-

A signpost in Radisson.
Photo by the author

resentatives. "In 1978, at a good breakfast, they cooked six hundred dozen eggs, seven hundred pounds of bacon, and fourteen thousand pieces of toast," he said.

Hamel came to Radisson in 1975 as a twelve-year-old; his family moved to the North when his father's construction company became involved in the Hydro Quebec project hauling building equipment and then turbines, transformers, and other devices for the dams and power plants.

"My father was in charge of some of the big trucks that came up on the new Route de la Baie James—the James Bay Road," Hamel said. The road had been specially built to accommodate the weight and width of the vehicles.

Included in the fleet were ninety-six-wheel flatbeds and another specialty transport they called the "Titanic." The vehicles had wheels that could turn with the curves of the road; the heaviest of the loads included 300-ton transformers. Nothing could pass them when they were on the move.

"My dad's job included calculating how they could go up hills with these loads," Hamel said. The work continued all year long, including the winter, when the road would be covered with snow and ice from Mattagami 380 miles north to Radisson; the convoys would move at about six miles an hour and take about six days to make the one-way trip.

For the initial power station, the trucks hauled twenty-four huge transformers plus sixteen turbines. Before the James Bay Road was completed, and during construction, a rough airport at La Grande was served by huge Hercules transports and Boeing 737 airplanes, landing on gravel and snow runways. That airport was made permanent to serve the La Grande 1 and 3 and the Robert-Bourassa power plants, and it was there I landed on my flight south from Waskaganish. Hydro Quebec maintains its own schedule of charter flights from Montreal to bring workers in for shifts at the dams and power plants.

The cost of infrastructure—the road, airport, support facilities, and the like—was about $1 billion. But even that pales beside the total cost of the 8 power stations, 10 dams, 285 dikes, and diversions in the La Grande complex: $23.8 billion. Even in Canadian dollars that's a huge expenditure.

The James Bay Road was opened to the public in 1980; besides permitting access to Radisson, spur roads would eventually allow road access to isolated communities on James Bay itself, including Chisasibi, Eastmain, and Waskaganish.

Today, Radisson is home to just 400 people, plus 120 transient workers for Hydro Quebec—a modern version of the migratory life of the Cree and Inuit. "We call them 'eight-six workers,'" Hamel said. "They are eight days on, six days off when they go home to their families in the south of Quebec."

The cost of living in Radisson is high, just as it is in any remote place where gasoline and food have to be trucked a few extra hundred miles; Hamel estimated things cost about 25 percent higher than they do to the south. The two local grocery stores include exotic items like bananas for a dollar apiece. They also stock an international showcase of beer and wine; unlike many of the Cree and Inuit towns, alcohol is readily available.

Hamel attended school in Radisson through the third year of high school and then went off to Quebec City to study civil engineering at Université Laval; he returned to work as a powerhouse tour guide in 1995 and moved on to the public relations department. "I prefer transmitting information," he told me.

"I have a little weekend camp," Hamel said, "and I go there whenever I have time because the summers are short. We go fishing for walleye and lake trout."

Ironically, in the heart of the hydroelectric empire, Hamel's isolated camp is off the grid. It is powered by a solar panel and a backup gasoline generator.

The Project of the Century

The La Grande hydroelectric facility swims in a sea of superlatives: the world's largest work site took twenty-five years to complete in one of the most remote and unforgiving places on the planet. How big? The affected territory spreads over more than 135,000 square miles, larger than all of New England plus New York State.

Under Quebec legislation passed in 1971, the James Bay territory is defined as the land lying between the forty-ninth and fifty-fifth line of North latitude, bordered to the west by James Bay and the Quebec border, and to the east by the dividing line of the James Bay and St. Lawrence River watersheds.

To the Quebec government and its partners in the Hydro Quebec, it was the "project of the century." To the Cree, many of whom still lived a nomadic hunter-gatherer lifestyle in the north country, it was more like an uninvited and permanent change to uncounted thousands of years of traditions and practices.

Work on the project began in 1971 when the provincial government—led by the charismatic, bull-nosed premier Robert Bourassa—

enacted special legislation to create the Société d'énergie de la Baie James (The James Bay Energy Corporation). The legislation predated the accord between the province and the residents of the area—the James Bay and Northern Quebec Agreement—which was not signed until 1975.

One reason for the lag in time was that the various Cree bands had no central government or political apparatus; there was no one to make an agreement with until Quebec forced the issue. It was in many ways a repeat of the situation in 1905, when Canadian government officials, accompanied by private trading groups such as the Hudson's Bay Company, [HBC] came into the North and created a leadership for remote native bands so that a treaty could be enacted.

Before the first shovelful of earth could be moved, engineers needed to find a way to transport huge pieces of equipment and thousands of workers to a place without roads; until 1971, much of the interior of the territory was untouched except for isolated traplines, camps, and trails carved by the natives and followed by the *coureurs des bois* (runners of the woods), who took the overland fur trading route from French settlements along the St. Lawrence River. A handful of temporary campsites along James Bay and Hudson Bay had dealt with English and French traders who came in by ship.

The work began with the creation of helicopter landing sites and then small airstrips to bring in surveyors, and then followed construction of a 450-mile-long road through wilderness, peat bogs, and taiga forest. There were rivers and streams everywhere; contractors took advantage of the frigid winter to haul heavy equipment across frozen rivers before bridges could be built. The road, from Mattagami—the northernmost outpost of French Canadian society and the end of the existing road and rail system in Quebec—proceeded north to the work site on the La Grande River that would one day be called Radisson. "We use round numbers: it cost $450 million to build 450 miles in 450 days," Hamel said.

Construction began on the first generating station, La Grande 2, in the winter of 1973. The final plant in the system, Laforge 2, was commissioned in December 1996. A few months earlier, the Quebec National Assembly voted unanimously to change the name of La Grande 2 to the Robert-Bourassa complex, honoring the former premier, who had died a few months earlier.

The reason that the Hydro Quebec project come into being is because of the huge flow of water in the James Bay region. From its source at Lac Naococane to its mouth on James Bay, the La Grande drops 550 meters (nearly 1,800 feet), and the original average flow of water was 61,500 cubic feet per second. To bring even more water to the generating stations, the plan also called for construction of reservoirs and diversion channels for other rivers.

Hydro Quebec diverted 90 percent of the water in the Eastmain River and 87 percent of the flow of the Opinaca River, changing their direction to flow north instead of west. And on the other side of Nunavik at the headwaters of the Koksoak River, engineers took about 41 percent of the Caniapiscau watershed and made the water flow to the east. The result nearly doubled the flow of the remade La Grande.

There are eight power plants on the river. La Grande 1 is the station closest to James Bay; completed in 1994, it was the first run-of-river station and the largest concrete structure in the complex. The largest and most productive plant is Robert-Bourassa, which was completed in 1981 after eight years of work. Up the river just a bit is La Grande 2A.

Farther inland is La Grande 3 and La Grande 4, and deep into the wilderness are three more plants: Laforge 1, Laforge 2, and Brisay, which serves as a regulator for flow of water from the Caniapiscau reservoir at the eastern end of the system.

Hydro Quebec built five major reservoirs. Measured by maximum area of water, the largest is the Caniapiscau at 1,650 square miles. The Réservoir Robert-Bourassa is 1,095 square miles, and La Grande 3 is slightly smaller at 935 square miles. The two smallest—still substantial bodies of water—are the Opinaca (400 square miles) and La Grande 4 (295 square miles).

The Eastmain River dam was completed in 2005, and impound-

The La Grande 1 hydroelectric plant near Radisson.
Photo by the author

ment began in November of that year. More than 1,000 workers labored on the power plant, which is expected to be finished by the summer of 2007.

The water from the Eastmain River will be gathered in a twenty-two-mile-long reservoir. After passing through the turbines, the water will be returned to the river to flow into the Opinaca reservoir and then into Robert-Bourassa reservoir. This branch of the Hydro Quebec system will thus use the same flow of water at three generating stations: Eastmain 1, Robert-Bourassa or La Grande 2A, and La Grande 1 before flowing into James Bay. Most of the flow of the Eastmain River, though, will no longer pass through the Cree settlement of Eastmain.

I asked Hamel about the Great Whale project, which would divert the waters of that river away from Whapmagoostui-Kuujjuarapik and into the La Grande system; Hydro Quebec was forced to pull back from that plan in 1992 when environmentalists were able to convince New York state to cancel a contract to purchase power. Choosing his words carefully, Hamel gave the company line: "The Grande Baleine is a project, but it is on ice for now."

Shades of Gray

The hydroelectric plants of James Bay generate deeply conflicted feelings for many people.

The Cree and other native peoples mourn the loss of their traditional way of life as rivers are diverted and traplines displaced. But some realists appreciate the flow of money and jobs that the hydroelectric plants have brought into the region.

Environmentalists decry the diversion of rivers and other alterations to the natural ecosystem, including the release of mercury in flooded territories. But many will admit a strong preference for "clean" hydroelectric power generation over burning oil, gas, or coal.

I had the same sort of ambiguous feelings as I toured the fantastic structures in the land of the giants. The dams, spillways, and generator halls are among the grandest human creations I have seen: like skyscrapers, cruise ships, and space shuttles. And yet it was jarring to see them scarring the earth in a place otherwise untouched by humans.

To its credit (and as required by law), Hydro Quebec has devoted a great deal of effort to mitigating the effects of its presence in the North.

Hamel pointed out a number of scenic overlooks—the French call them *belvederes*—and other efforts by Hydro Quebec to at least pay notice to the natural environment as it had existed before the rivers were diverted and the dams installed. In some areas, dikes were installed to create marshland for hunters. Other land features were restored to allow for migration by land animals; indeed, as Hamel and I drove across a dike, we spotted a large caribou swim across a reservoir and then scamper up the bank and down into a valley alongside one of the power plants.

One of the key provisions of the James Bay and Northern Quebec Agreement of 1975 was the mapping of the territory into categories.

Category 1 includes the native communities themselves; mostly Cree around James Bay and mostly Inuit around Hudson Bay.

Category 2 land is held in reserve for the native population (mostly Cree in James Bay) for fishing, trapping, and hunting. Some of the traditional traplines were preserved as part of the agreement; in places where the reservoirs drowned the land, new areas were set aside in this category. Hamel said Hydro Quebec installed a boat ramp to James Bay and a thirty-one-mile-long road to provide access in the La Grande region.

Category 3 is considered public land; anyone with a Quebec fishing or hunting permit can go on the reservoirs or the land. Some species are managed with quotas.

As I toured with Hamel, we stopped in a section above the Robert-Bourassa complex where a long dike helps channel water to the dam. "We are in Category Two lands," Hamel said. "We planted this area with herbs so that goose come and rest here in the spring and the autumn. And the Cree come and hunt. It is one of the sites where we incorporated the materials from the construction to build nice places."

As much as proponents of hydroelectric energy production like to talk about the process as "clean," the fact is that one of the major unintended consequences of dams and diversions is a significant increase in the amount of mercury released into the water and the food chain; above certain levels, mercury is toxic to humans and many other forms of life.

The mercury is released into the environment as part of a natural process that begins when plants are flooded and decompose; they release mercury absorbed from the ground. Hydro Quebec cites scientific studies that say the mercury release has a thirty-year effect.

In the first ten years after the flooding of a reservoir, the local flora decomposes and releases mercury. The mercury transfers itself in the form of methylmercury and is absorbed by fish; some of the fish are eaten by humans and some are eaten by birds or mammals, which are in turn eaten by humans. In the initial years after flooding, mercury concentrations as much as five times higher than natural levels were found in lakes and streams.

After a ten-year buildup of mercury, levels gradually subside over the next twenty years.

"After thirty years, you go back to the way it was at the beginning," Hamel said. "We have detailed studies before, during, and after the reservoir and we still measure it today. Every year we go fishing to see where we are in the cycle."

The research and monitoring extends to the human inhabitants of the region. Scientists study hair samples from Cree and sports fishermen—including Hamel—to determine the amount of mercury in the system.

Cree and outsiders were advised not to fish in the reservoir in the first ten years after it was flooded, while mercury was increasing; Hydro Quebec located and monitored other sites deemed safe for fishing.

One of the most notorious incidents in the history of the Hydro Quebec project occurred in early October 1984, when an estimated 10,000 migrating caribou drowned as they were attempting to cross the Caniapiscau and Koksoak rivers about sixty miles upriver from Kuujjuaq on Ungava Bay. The animals were swept over waterfalls or carried away by what was claimed to be an unusually high flow of water.

Hydro Quebec later asserted that the rivers were running high because of abnormally high rainfall, not as the result of the construction work for its hydroelectric plants. Some native groups disputed that, saying that too much water was released from a new dam that was built to form the headwaters of the La Grande waterway.

The province dispatched a fleet of helicopters and cargo planes to remove most of the carcasses; permafrost near the drowning area made it impossible to bury the animals where they were found. Hydro Quebec was asked to construct barriers to force migrating herds to cross at safer locations. An incident of this magnitude has not happened again.

Caribou, which are large awkward animals related to reindeer, can grow to 700 pounds or more; they subsist mainly on lichen. The animals that died were part of the George River herd—perhaps 400,000 in size. The herd is the biggest in North America and among the largest in the world.

In the Heart of the Machine

We drove across the top of one of the dikes that led to the 532-foot-high dam that holds back the huge reservoir above the Robert-Bourassa power plant. Hamel unlocked several gates and then we came to the first of two guards in trucks parked to block the road; they were a recent addition to the security perimeter around the Hydro Quebec facilities.

For a period at the start of the summer of 2005, all access by tourists to the La Grande power plants and dams was shut down after a Montreal television reporter managed to bluff his way into one of the buildings.

We reached the entrance to the power plant, a huge steel door in the side of a hill that looked a bit like Superman's Fortress of Solitude, which come to think of it, was described in the comic books of my youth as carved into the rock face of an ice-covered mountain in a desolate Arctic wasteland.

In any case, the door was big enough to accept a midsized ship, or sixteen massive generators hauled in by double-width trucks at the time of construction. Each of the generators, without their casings and piping, is about forty-five feet wide and eighty feet high.

The exterior door opened to let us in and then closed behind us to form an airlock between the outside world and the slightly pressurized machinery hall. When the inside door opened, we crossed over to drive on the left side of the road in keeping with traditional traffic patterns inside mines that call on drivers to hug the left wall very tightly.

We drove a few hundred feet through the massive service tunnel and parked; we were met by a security guard whose sole purpose was to keep her eyes on me at all times. Armed only with my notebook and pen, we entered into a stunning cathedral that combined high-tech and Jules Verne. The walls of the hall were rough granite, like a journey to the center of the earth. The floor was polished and clean enough to eat off if I could have smuggled lunch into the facility.

The largest underground generating station in the world, some 450 feet underground, the Robert-Bourassa machine hall extends a third of a mile, about 1,600 feet or a bit more than five football fields in length and more than 100 feet wide. The ceiling is nearly fifty feet overhead; beneath my feet the generators sit in a chamber that deep again.

A hundred feet away was a second room of nearly the same dimensions: the surge chamber, a granite cavern that sits between the output draft tube of the generator and the tailrace tunnel that returns the water to the La Grande River. The surge chamber is designed to protect the generators anytime they start up or stop suddenly; the water rises in the chamber instead of flowing back toward the turbines.

A 2,000-foot-long tunnel connects the Robert-Bourassa powerhouse to the neighboring La Grande 2A generating hall, where there are six additional generators. The combined annual generating capacity of the two plants is 37 billion kilowatt hours. That's the equivalent of a year's supply of electricity to 3.4 million typical U.S. households.

The air itself felt charged. I heard and felt the low-frequency rumble of incoming water surging through the penstock from the reservoir built up behind the dam; a high-frequency whine came from the sixteen generating units in the hall. The room was deserted except for Hamel, the guard, and me; most of the monitoring is done from remote stations including company headquarters in Montreal.

More than 3 million cubic yards of rock was excavated for the powerhouse, access and service tunnels, and the surge chamber. The excavated materials were used to build retaining structures and roads.

There was one more must-see in Le Pays des Géants: the incomparable Giant's Staircase. Ten huge steps, each about 100 feet wide and 40 feet high, were carved out of the rock to serve as an emer-

The Giant's Staircase at the La Grande dam.
Photo by the author

gency spillway to release water from the Réservoir Robert-Bourassa in case of excessive water level or a problem with the dam or powerhouse; engineers based its dimensions on their estimate of a once-in-10,000-year flood.

The staircase is so huge that it is very difficult to gauge its scale. Hydro Quebec painted a human-sized stick figure at the base; it is almost impossible to spot.

A Village in the Stream

Most of the construction work for the hydroelectric facilities was far away from human settlements. One exception was the village of Fort George, which was moved from its original location on Governors Island at the mouth of the La Grande River where it reaches James Bay.

Fort George was established by the HBC as a trading post in the early part of the nineteenth century. Hydro Quebec's plans to more than double the flow of river worried some residents; after a 1978 referendum, a new community called Chisasibi was built on the mainland nearby.

New houses began to arrive on barges in 1981. Many of them were installed in circles, as if they were tents surrounding a central point.

The village of 4,000 people has a fully staffed hospital, which is more than Radisson can offer. The local school system serves about 1,000 students, a large number for a small settlement.

Hamel and I had a farewell lunch at the Chisasibi community center. I had hoped for something unusual, caribou steak or arctic char with a side of bannock, perhaps. Instead, the food was basic cafeteria fare; most of the entrees were offered with poutine, a frightening French Quebec favorite: fries swimming in gravy.

CHAPTER 25

The Disquiet of the Braves

Chief Robert Weistche is angry, proud, sad, and cautiously hopeful. Sitting along the south shore of the Rupert River, we talked about the people and community of Waskaganish at the bottom of James Bay.

This may have been the place where Henry Hudson and the crew of the *Discovery* spent a cold and hungry winter from 1610 to 1611. Today, it is still an isolated, troubled place—the first and only road to the outside world was opened in the summer of 2001.

The sixty-five-mile-long unpaved road to Waskaganish is a spur off the James Bay Road. Hydro Quebec and the provincial government put in the road as the power company began plans to divert much of the flow of the Rupert River away from Waskaganish and into the power generation system already established farther north.

Although Waskaganish has finally been connected by road to the rest of Canada, the disquiet and sadness among some of the members of the Waskaganish band of the Cree Nation is building. Members of the Cree Nation and many environmentalists are divided, not united, by the prospect of the Rupert River project, which may begin in 2007 and is scheduled for commissioning by 2011.

If completed, the Rupert diversion will include 4 new dams, 75 dikes, and diversion bays that will flood about 134,000 square miles.

On the one hand, the river is deeply intertwined with the history and culture of the Cree, and environmentalists also recognize it as one of the planet's last remaining wild and nearly uncontaminated rivers. On the other hand, the hydroelectric plants bring income and a small number of jobs to an area that has had neither and—by some measures—hydroelectric generators are a cleaner alternative to the burning of fossil fuel.

For these reasons, you will find Cree who support the Hydro Quebec plan and those, such as Weistche, who are determined to fight it to the end. Also, you will find environmentalists who prefer hydroelectric plants to almost any other alternative, and you will find those who weep at the coming loss of a great natural resource.

It was the broad, fast-flowing river that may have drawn Hudson into a somewhat protected cove in 1610, and it was the river—rich with fish and surrounded by birds and wildlife—that made it a gathering place for nomadic Cree.

The presence of the Cree and the access route afforded by the river made it attractive to the Hudson's Bay Company (HBC). Pierre-Esprit Radisson and Médard Chouart des Groseilliers, established the HBC's first post in Canada in 1670 along the banks of the waterway, and they named it after their royal sponsor, Prince Rupert. They called the post Rupert House.

The HBC would go on to set up a network of posts at the mouths of most of the major rivers flowing into James Bay (including the Albany, Moose, Rupert, and Eastmain) and a depot for loading and off-loading larger vessels on Charlton Island west of Rupert House. The Cree would later call the trading post on the Rupert River under a native name, Waskaganish, meaning "little house," to differentiate it from the larger store at Eastmain.

The 1,800 or so full-time and seasonal residents of Waskaganish come from families with traditional hunting territories that extend deep into the Rupert, Broadback, Nottaway, and Pontax watersheds. Another 400 or so live off the preserve but come in from the bush from time to time.

Storm Clouds over the Rupert

Weistche met me along the banks of the Rupert. A line of rain showers had passed through a few hours earlier as my plane had landed at the tiny airport; next came a full rainbow over the river, and then dark clouds began to scud across the hills that framed the water.

In an elaborate series of phone calls that worked their way up through friends, acquaintances, and associates in the weeks leading up to my visit, I had arranged to meet Weistche for an interview. As I had found with other arrangements I had made with Cree and Inuit, the concept of an appointment on a particular day at a specific time was a bit outside of their ordinary way of life.

After I had checked into my room at the Kanio-Kashee Lodge along the river, just steps away from the original location of the HBC's Rupert House, I called the chief to confirm our interview. He told me he had other things to do; perhaps he could see me in a week or so when he expected to be back from a trip into the bush.

I was there just for that day and the next, and so I pushed him for a bit of time, and he relented: he told me to meet in twenty minutes along the river. The interview began awkwardly and stiffly and went south from there for a while.

He told me that Cree ancestors had probably been in the area going back several thousand years; archaeologists and scientists believe that the water level in the bay had once been much higher, probably lapping against a terrace of rock on a distant hill, where they had found some remains.

In more recent times, dating back to when Henry Hudson may have visited, local bands would have come to the mouth of the river seasonally. "There might have been several gathering places around here on the bay, or on the shore line in front of the Hudson's Bay building down by the lodge," Weistche said. "They used to call that area Kanio-Kashee, which means a sandy outcrop of land, and this might have been a nice place for camping in the summer months."

Waskaganish, like most of the Cree and Inuit villages I visited, had a mixture of modernity and vestiges of the old ways. Modern

A trilingual stop sign in Waskaganish.
Photo by the author

touches included pickup trucks, snowmobiles, and cookie-cutter houses. There were also tipis and other traditional homes and shelters, and trilingual stop signs in English, French, and Cree.

I asked Weistche how successful the elders were in keeping alive the native culture; he didn't sound very hopeful. "There seem to be a smaller number going out in the camps now," he told me. "A lot of the older trappers are the main carriers of tradition."

Above us to our left was an old Anglican church and graveyard, each in a condition somewhere between historic relic and derelict. To our right were the boarded up offices and stores of some of the HBC's operations, in similar condition. And between us and the river, the ground was strewn with plastic bottles, junk food wrappers, and other modern garbage.

I asked Weistche whether what we saw around us was a contradiction of his people's oft-expressed respect for the land and the wa-

An old Anglican church and cemetery in Waskaganish.
Photo by the author

ter. He was not happy with the question; in fact, he came close to walking away from the interview. But once he began to answer, a great deal of the modern story of the Cree came into focus in a way it hadn't before.

"This is our community, and there are a lot of things that are not really a part of our culture but are part of our way of life today," Weistche said. "When you look around the community as an outsider, you really notice those things because you are coming from an environment that is usually quite pristine and well maintained with manicured lawns.

"We have some people who don't have a complete understanding of what it does to the environment when you throw down garbage and litter. I just happened to pick an area for us to meet where there seems to be a lot of trash.

"I say as a chief that I don't like where the conversation is going," Weistche told me, backing away from me and my notepad and tape recorder. "You talk about Henry Hudson and you are trying to make the connection with the Cree, and 'boom' you throw in this thing about how the aboriginal people are supposed to be so respectful of the environment and yet you see garbage everywhere.

"Maybe the garbage is the garbage in people's lives."

I told Weistche that I had just flown in from Chisasibi at the top of James Bay after visiting the gigantic Hydro Quebec facilities there and inland at Radisson. I told him I had spent the day with a young public relations representative who spoke earnestly of how the company sought to work in cooperation with the Cree and other native peoples as stewards of the lands.

Weistche laughed, as many Cree seem to do in the face of bad news.

"Hydro lies," he said. "When the white man looks at [the river], they see millions of kilowatts going out to waste, and that's money. That's what Robert Bourassa said.

"I guess most of the time money is a good thing, but it does pose some consequences. Are you happy? Money doesn't always buy everything.

"The way we look at money," Weistche said, "is we figure the land will always be there. If you were to take money and see a crash of the stock market it would be gone, or maybe the money will just happen to go on fire."

The Fight Against Hydro Quebec

At the time of my visit, Weistche was one of three chiefs of Cree bands who were openly opposed to the 2002 agreement signed with Hydro Quebec. He was in company with Abraham Rupert of Chisasibi and Josie Jimiken of the Nemaska band. The next day was to be election day for the grand chief of the Grand Council of the Crees.

Weistche made no secret of his disapproval of some of the actions of the incumbent, Ted Moses. In particular, he felt that the individual bands and their chiefs had not been fully advised of the negotiations that led up to the agreement between the Crees and Inuit and Hydro Quebec and the resulting Paix des Braves treaty in 2002, an update to the original James Bay Treaty of 1975.

"At the time the agreement in principle was being negotiated secretly, without the full knowledge of the chiefs, the river was frozen over. You couldn't see it," Weistche said.

"But I can feel the river. It gives me life and strength. I do a lot of kayaking myself on the river. There is a lot of interaction with the river and people; it brings a lot of enjoyment and there is a spiritual connection we have with the river that is very important. It makes us well and balanced," Weistche said.

Work has already begun on the dams and canals that will divert a large portion of the Rupert River away from its natural channel into the bottom of James Bay. Hydro Quebec says it will maintain enough of a flow to allow traditional fishing and other activities, a promise Weistche does not accept. In the face of the huge utility, the provincial government, the Canadian federal government, and the treaty, he said he would do what he could to block the project.

"If you don't fight, you have no chance," Weistche said. "You have to understand Hydro Quebec; they are good salesmen. Nonaboriginal people agree that because money is generated that's what runs the economy.

"There are people who say, 'Give me the money.' There are people who want the jobs and the benefits.

"On the other hand, there is a part of an agreement that Indians should never have agreed to: the river. That fight should have been for another day."

Weistche said that the original James Bay agreement has never been fully delivered on, and the subsequent revisions were clouded in misunderstandings.

"I think a lot of people originally supported the deal because it brought a lot of benefits to the Cree," he said. "And it did. But I am saying we are not getting any real money from the government right now. Basically, what we are is an administrative arm of the government, and we are administering the programs that they should have done, and they failed to do.

"They are saying, 'Well, we didn't fulfill Section Twenty-eight of the James Bay [and] Northern Quebec Agreement, but here is the money. You do it. You decide how that money is going to be spent and in what areas.' "

When Grand Chief Moses worked out the agreement that led to the Paix des Braves that was voted on and accepted by the Cree Nation in 2002, Weistche said he was among a majority of the people who did not fully understand its scope.

"I went to agree to something that was already agreed to before," he said. "And on top of that they sold the river, knowing that the Crees were going to go for that money without even realizing that we were being deceived.

"I feel I was confused," Weistche said. "And now a lot of people are reflecting back on that decision and saying, 'Yeah, I voted yes to the agreement, now I regret it. I am sorry.'

"It was so very well orchestrated by scholars and lawyers and politicians and the government," Weistche continued. "The government knew how to divide the Cree people and that division is very evident in our community and in our politics."

Election Day, 2005

Before the signing of the original James Bay Agreement in 1975, there was no organized central government for the various Cree bands who lived in the bush and small communities along James Bay. For the Quebec government and the Hydro Quebec utility to have a political entity that could sign its agreement, the province included the setup of the Grand Council of the Crees in 1974; the natives called their homeland *Eeyou Istchee*, which means "land of the people."

Moses, who was only the third grand chief in history, reached a secret accord with the Quebec government in 2002 for the $3.6 billion Paix des Braves agreement. It is the most expensive land settlement ever reached with a Canadian First Nation. The Cree received a renegotiated agreement that promised fifty years of annual payments of $70 million; in exchange, the natives ended some $8 billion in lawsuits rising out of what the Cree said were unfulfilled promises in the 1975 original agreement.

In return, the Cree agreed—or more precisely, promised not to oppose—two additional hydroelectric projects that would flood nearly 400 square miles of traditional native hunting lands.

The term *La Paix des Braves* was adopted as a sort of government double entendre. It literally means "the peace of the braves," as in chiefs of the First Nations. It is also a nod toward the French premier Charles de Gaulle's 1958 peace proposal to end the Algerian conflict, in which the term meant "the peace of the brave."

By any measure, $3.6 billion is a lot of money, but spread out over fifty years it amounted to only about $7,000 per resident in 2006 and the amount will go down sharply over time as the population increases and as inflation reduces the value of the money.

Matthew Mukash, who served as the deputy grand chief under Moses in an earlier term, was formerly the chief of Whapmagoostui Nation, the northernmost Cree band that shares the mouth of the Great Whale River with the southernmost Inuit community, Kuujjuarapik. In the 1990s, Mukash paddled on the Hudson River as one of the leaders fighting against Hydro Quebec's Great Whale project; their success in halting diversion of that river for a hydroelectric plant is considered by many Cree to be the only political battle ever won by their people.

Mukash opposed the Paix des Braves in 2002. He said that it was being pushed too hard and too fast, without enough time for study and debate. And he called for certain issues to be excluded, including removing a clause that committed the Cree Nation not to oppose the diversion of the Rupert River.

In the election for grand chief that took place the day after my visit, Waskaganish overwhelmingly rejected the incumbent Moses, preferring Mukash by a 45 to 30 percent vote in the first round. In the runoff election between the top two candidates, Mukash won by 56 percent of the vote across the Cree Nation, ousting Moses. There were 5,787 votes cast.

Mukash was sworn into office on October 19, 2005, in Chisasibi, one of his strongholds. "Thirty years ago, the Cree leaders took a bold step and signed an agreement that affected the course of our history, our lives, our relationship to the land and has brought our Nation to its present path," Mukash said in his inaugural address. "We used the JBNQA [James Bay and Northern Quebec Agreement] to create entities to service our Nation in areas such as health and education.

"For a number of years, some of us have expressed our objection to the way in which the Paix des Braves Agreement was negotiated and presented to the Cree Nation for approval. We must ensure that in the future there is more time to consider such agreements and more dialog about the content before they are ratified.

"Our relationship to Creation is what has sustained us for thousands of years," Mukash continued. "This relationship came with numerous responsibilities and obligations. As we strive to work together to implement the Paix des Braves, we will honor this relationship while carefully assessing the impacts of our decisions and promoting cleaner alternative and renewable sources to energy, such as wind, solar, and biofuel.

"We must do our best to avoid decisions that may jeopardize our children and grandchildren's inheritance," Mukash said.

Then Mukash and his deputy were presented with traditional jackets that made note of their position. Embroidered symbols included moose and bear, representing strength. The goose—an important part of Cree spirituality—adorns the right sleeve, the side the men would use when they shook hands to make future deals.

An earlier grand chief, Billy Diamond, gave Mukash a carving of a wolf. The wolf, he said, has a dangerous bite.

Parting with a Handshake

Before Weistche and I parted ways at the riverside, I changed the subject to the weather. We spoke about the spectacular rainbow that had crossed over a corner of the settlement down to the river.

I told the chief that as an outsider I could see both the beauty and the contradictions in a place like Waskaganish.

"I think that's what life is about, contradictions," Weistche said.

My home, I told him, is not what he imagined: a place with man-icured lawns.

"That's what I saw when I went to America," Weistche said. "I was in Boston and they had white picket fences."

Nantucket, the island where I live, was once Wampanoag land, I told him. The Wampanoag are distant Algonquian linguistic cousins of the Cree.

"What happened to the native people?" he asked.

"They're all gone," I said.

CHAPTER 26

The Company Men

James Wilson Brown has chosen to spend his life in the remote northeast of Canada, including a stint as one of the last in the line of Hudson's Bay Company (HBC) traders and managers.

He began his career with the HBC in northern Ontario at Fort Severn—one of the most isolated places in Canada or anywhere else—working twenty-one straight months before he had a day off. He stayed with the company ten years.

Fort Severn is the most northerly community in Ontario, at the edge of the tree line about five miles from the mouth of the Severn River, where it flows north into Hudson Bay. Like most of the other settlements of the North, there are no year-round roads to the community; for two or three months of the cold winter, an ice road runs along the shore of the bay about 125 miles to Shamattawa, where snowmobile trails and rough winter roads connect to the outside world. In the summer of 2005, only one barge came up to the community from Moosonee. An airstrip is serviced several days a week by small plane.

Fort Severn was one of the first trading posts in the New World; the HBC set up shop there in 1680. Today, the population of registered Cree is about 578, and government sources report the unemployment rate is as high as 90 percent.

Married into the Community

As a factor, Brown traded cash and goods with trappers; the business was a tiny fraction of what it had been in HBC's heyday. He bought mostly beaver skins with a smaller market in lynx, fox, and otter. "And we had a retail operation with groceries and basically whatever the community needed to survive," he told me.

"The market would determine the price for beaver. Sometimes the people would complain that the price was too low, but that was the market value. It's like the price of oil today.

"Many times the company lost money. By the time the furs were shipped to the head office in London the price had already dropped.

"I thought the HBC was a good company," he said. "It depended on the manager. You had offices in London and Winnipeg or Montreal, and some guys were doing things that they shouldn't have."

Even in the 1980s, Brown said, the HBC was mostly managed from afar. "You still get a lot of that today," he said. "With many of the companies that are in business up north, the bosses might come to visit one day a year and that is it. They have no idea of what is really happening in those communities. They form an opinion on the basis of a one-day visit."

"The worst part of the year was when all of the people were out on the traplines in the bush," he said. "Then, the only ones left in town would be the older people and the younger people. There might have been one hundred seventy-six people in the community at most and sometimes only twenty-five were left."

During his first assignment, as a single man, Brown lived with the manager and his wife and two children. There was a shortwave radio, he said, and sometimes he might be lucky enough to get a call through to his parents in Newfoundland or somewhere else down south.

"I would read half a book a day by candlelight," he said. "We had a diesel plant for Bell Canada but the houses weren't wired up.

"We couldn't keep anything cold; we'd bring in our cold stuff in the winter time—as much as a thousand pounds of meat—and our fresh stuff in the summertime. And any chicken legs or pork chops that arrived in the summertime we had to sell right away," Brown said. The air temperature for much of the year was more than cold enough to keep food cold or frozen without the need for refrigeration.

"It was an exciting life," Brown said. "We were a part of history. The company promoted that a lot when they hired you. They didn't pay that much, though. I started in 1972 making thirty-nine hundred dollars a year. I was passing through Pickle Lake [in central Ontario] one time and sat down at the bar with this guy who was a geologist. And he said to me, 'You must be paid big money to go up to Fort Severn. You are totally isolated.'

"So I showed him my contract and he started to laugh at me," Brown said. "He showed me his pay stub, and he made forty-one hundred dollars that month and I made thirty-nine hundred dollars a year."

After Fort Severn, Brown went on for short assignments in Moosonee and Waskaganish before landing a position as the manager of the Eastmain HBC store. Along the way, he met and married a native woman from Waskaganish.

Eventually, the company moved him all the way up to Iqaluit in Frobisher Bay in what is now Nunavut for a three-year assignment. Iqaluit, which is on the other side of the Meta Incognita Peninsula from Hudson Strait, was the northernmost posting he was given by the HBC, but Brown said it was his first job that was the most isolated.

When Brown first came to Waskaganish in the winter of 1974, there were just a few houses on the river bank and a few more behind that, and a school. The community has grown drastically in the past few years, he said, with the money that came in because of the James Bay Agreement.

"This is the first place in the North that I saw sidewalks and fire hydrants," he said. Other communities are working on that sort of infrastructure now.

When I met him, at age fifty-four he was the manager of the Kanio-Kashee Lodge in Waskaganish, working for the tribe.

An Outsider's View of the Politics of Water

"I don't want to get into politics," Brown said. "But people want power. They want TV. They want electric stoves. The power has got to come from somewhere. Nuclear, hydro dams, coal-fired generators that damage the environment. Where do you draw the line? I don't know. The Cree and everybody else say, 'not in my back yard.'"

I told him about my encounter with Chief Robert Weistche down along the banks of the Rupert River.

"I can understand Robert's point of view," Brown said. "Very much so. I'm from a small island off the coast of Newfoundland. You can't fish in Newfoundland. Can you imagine that?

"I spoke to a guy from Yamaha a few years ago. He couldn't understand the situation in Newfoundland. 'There you are with the largest fishing grounds in the world and you can't employ 100,000 people in fishing,' he said. 'In Japan we employ 2.2 million people in fishery.'

"My grandfather fished all his life. So did my great-great-grandfather going back as far as Newfoundland was there. But now stocks are low and there is a moratorium. It's all government screwups and bureaucracy. It's a sad thing to see.

"I can see the same situation through Robert's eyes. Change is something that happens, and sometimes we can't stop change. Is it good? Is it bad? Only time will tell."

A Political and Business Dynasty

At age fifty-four, Albert Diamond is an elder of the Cree First Nation, a member of a respected political dynasty, and a major economic player in the Canadian North. We met in the tiny airport at Waskaganish; he was waiting to catch an Air Creebec flight to Mattagami while I watched the skies for the plane that would take me some 500 miles southeast to Montreal.

Diamond, the president of the Cree-owned airline, seemed to know every passenger in the terminal except me; I introduced myself and arranged an interview.

The family dynasty goes back at least to the 1940s, when Albert's father, Malcolm, was elected as the chief of the Waskaganish band, a post he held for more than twenty years. Brother Billy was chosen as the chief when he was just twenty-one, and when the Grand Council of the Crees was established in 1974, he was elected as the first grand chief, a post he held for ten years.

Billy Diamond was the lead negotiator with the province of Quebec for the James Bay and Northern Quebec Agreement, the treaty that laid out the framework for the insertion of Hydro Quebec in the region and the first coordinated political organization for the First Nations.

The oldest sibling, Annie Whiskeychan, is honored in much of the region as the first Cree to earn a certificate to teach the native language. One of the outcomes of the James Bay Agreement was the establishment of a local school board in each community, and a priority was to save the traditional language. A new wing of the elementary school in Waskaganish was named in Annie's honor after her death.

The oldest brother in the family, Charlie, was taken out of school when he was only fourteen or fifteen years old. "The trapline system is handed down from father to son," Albert said. The Diamond traplines are south of Waskaganish and just northwest of Mattagami, in Quebec.

"When my father retired from trapping, he handed over the stewardship of the trapline to Charlie; he looks after it. And of course Charlie is teaching one of his sons to take it over when he gets ready to stop trapping."

Brother George works with the Cree health board; the youngest son, Stanley, runs a family-owned ferry and delivery service. Sister Gertie is an educational administrator in Waskaganish. And Agnes lives with her husband in Manitoba.

"In my own family, most of us were encouraged to go and get educated," Diamond told me. "But my father said, 'Then I want you to come back and work for our people.'

"During my time, the residential school system was in place. The residential schools were initially run by the church organizations and funded by the federal government through the Department of Indian Affairs. There was a Catholic mission and an Anglican church.

"When I first started school, there was a one-classroom school and then many of the kids were sent to Moose Factory in Ontario," Diamond said. "After high school, only then were we given a choice of where we wanted to go for university.

"It was difficult. We would leave at the end of August and we wouldn't come home until the end of June. At that time, most of our parents were trappers, so they would leave the communities in September or the first part of October and they would come back to the community in February or March and then they would go out again for the spring goose hunt and be back at the end of May."

An Airline to Connect a Nation

Through the 1970s and into the 1980s, there was very little in the way of medical services in James Bay, Diamond said. If someone became seriously ill, an emergency airlift would sometimes be arranged. "Usually, when people were flown out, a body came back," he said.

With the establishment of the Grand Council of the Crees and promises—some kept, some not—by the provincial government, one of the priorities was to establish air service to connect the road-less communities of the North. Grand Chief Billy Diamond recruited his son Albert, who was chairman of the board of compensation that managed the disbursement and investment of the funds coming in from Hydro Quebec and the provincial government.

Although the Cree generally opposed the James Bay hydroelectric project, once it was approved and underway the chiefs were determined to get a piece of the pie for their own workers.

Once again, it was the Hydro Quebec project that both harried the Cree and helped them; the construction work required installation of an access road and airports. Among the first businesses was the Cree Construction and Development Company. Another piece of the puzzle was the construction of airports for the various scattered Cree communities; before the agreement, nearly all of them were inaccessible by road or by air.

When the airline first started, one of its principal assignments was to ferry equipment and workers up to Radisson for the Hydro Quebec projects.

The Cree sought out an airline company to help set up operations as a partner; Air Creebec took to the air in the summer of 1982, and its operations were run for the tribe for the first six years by a Canadian company. In 1992, Albert Diamond, who had been running the construction business for the tribe, was asked to move over to run the airline.

Today, Air Creebec has eleven airplanes and concentrates on scheduled passenger service. Its newer planes are Canadian-built De Havilland Dash-8s; other craft include smaller twin-engine equipment.

Besides scheduled passenger service, one plane is primarily dedicated to the use of the health board in Ontario to transport passengers and medical personnel to and from communities and to the hospital in Moose Factory. The fleet is also available for charter for passengers and freight. At the time I spoke with Diamond, he was negotiating with a gold mining operation in a remote part of Ontario to provide service for employees.

And Air Creebec holds the contract to transport Hydro Quebec workers on the controversial Eastmain Hydroelectric project.

Air Creebec is owned by the Cree Nation of Quebec, essentially making the 14,600 registered members of the tribe shareholders. Just under half of the 204 employees are natives; about 20 of the 36 pilots are French- or English-speaking Canadians. Diamond said the company has been slowly building a staff of native pilots, with fourteen Cree flying planes in Ontario and two in Quebec.

Diamond said the principal reason for the smaller number of native pilots is the cost of training—about $60,000. At the time we spoke, the newest pilot for the airline was breaking a new barrier: a young Cree woman had just received certification to fly for Air Creebec.

Earnings go to Creeco, the tribal holding company, and to the Board of Compensation, which distributes income to communities. In 2004, Creeco's revenues were approximately $160 million, about $140 million in U.S. funds.

The various Cree communities make their own decisions on economic development. In Waskaganish, the band spent some of its money on a tourist lodge and a small strip mall, and is the majority shareholder in Moosonee Transport Limited, which is based in Moosonee on the Ontario side of the border.

"I would say the majority of the Crees understand that if there is going to be development in Quebec up north where their territory is, they will oppose it if it impacts the land and the environment," Diamond said, "but they also understand that if the projects go forth there could be some benefit for the Cree people if they get involved or participate in that development."

CHAPTER 27

An Archaeologist
in the Bush

Jim Chism came from Kansas in 1972 and has spent most of the succeeding three decades working as an archaeologist in the bush, isolated islands, and native communities of James Bay. He more or less settled in Waskaganish in 1986.

His office is within a narrow wooden and corrugated tin building that at first glance appears abandoned. There was no sign out front and I walked past it twice, jangling the heavy padlocks on the two front doors before finding a third entrance around back that was slightly ajar. An interior door, with a handwritten sign reading KEEP CLOSED—BLACK FLIES was wide open. Inside was a jumble of charts, maps, photos, and artifacts. A corner of the room held hundreds of books, monographs, and other documents.

I had spoken with Chism by phone before my visit and he had set aside some materials for me to examine. His assistant apologized several times for the disorder on the shelves: "We don't have a librarian. You have to kind of remember where things came from and where they go back."

The assistant left to attend to other business including checking on some work being done to maintain the old cemetery fence at the crumbling Anglican church along the river; he asked me to reinstall the heavy padlock on the back door when I was done.

"We have formed a nonprofit cultural corporation called the Waskaganish Cultural Institute," Chism told me when we spoke. "It's politically independent, but we are supported by the band and other organizations around the region. We help train people from other communities, and we do research for regional Cree organizations."

As Hudson Saw Waskaganish

I asked Chism to describe the territory around Waskaganish as it exists now, and as it may have appeared four centuries earlier when Henry Hudson and the crew of the *Discovery* wintered over somewhere in the area in 1610 and 1611.

"We have highlands and good habitable land that comes pretty much to the edge of the water," Chism said. "When you move away from this area to the west on the Ontario side, you have a lot of foreshore flats; sometimes you have to go for a mile or so inland before you are anywhere except in high grasses."

To scientists, a foreshore is the strip of land that exists between low-water and high-water marks—land that is not appropriate for habitation.

"We have four major rivers flowing into Rupert's Bay: the Nottaway, the Broadback, the Rupert, and the Pontax. And so there is a fair bit of freshness to the water in Rupert's Bay. It is not until you are out a ways that the salt is more present," Chism told me.

As a result, the soil around Waskaganish is relatively rich, allowing many crops and animals to grow and flourish. "It's much known for its migratory water fowl. We have seals and beluga whales, the occasional foot-wide stingray, and we even have reports of people seeing killer whales," Chism continued.

"We get really nice migrations of whitefish coming up the Rupert River every late summer; it draws people to the area, particularly to the second rapids, which has always been a very well known traditional fishing site especially at that time of the year."

According to Chism, the area has been occupied from early times. "If you go a few miles inland, they have dated archaeological sites that would be around four thousand years old. Right here on the coast [the uplift of the land] would give you the possibility that there could have been people here two or three thousand years ago.

"At Smoky Hill, near the second rapids, there is a fishing spot that looks like it probably dates anywhere from one thousand to twenty-seven hundred years ago. There hasn't been that much actual digging along the coastal area. Almost all the archaeology that has taken place has been because of the hydroelectric projects, particularly inland and farther north from here.

"There is a really nice row of hills that lead from inland right out to the coast. There were two glaciers—one over on the Ontario side and one over here on the Quebec side—and there was a bit of a space between them. As those glaciers went away, it left a sandy area between.

"We are very interested in looking to see if that would have formed a kind of natural passageway, particularly in winter. When things were still wet and marshy down below because the sea hadn't retreated that much yet, this might have made a nice penetration route coming into the coast.

"These would have been archaic people, perhaps from interior areas of the Labrador, the Quebec peninsula, and the Gulf of Saint Lawrence. Some people call them the Laurentian Archaic."

A Hudson River–Hudson Bay Connection

One of the many interesting theories I had come across in my own research was that the Cree of James Bay were distant relatives of the Native American tribes who met Henry Hudson when he traveled up the river from New York.

"That's pretty speculative, but probably yes. They were probably Algonquians if you can push that back that far. There were movements coming out of the mountains, south of the Great Lakes, perhaps five or six thousand years ago. For some reason, people started moving and they dispersed, some heading this way and some heading toward New York."

We spoke about how the shores of the James Bay near Waskaganish might have changed since the time of Hudson.

"About four hundred years ago the water level here at the coast would have been between three and four feet higher than now," he said. "We can see former beach lines going back like stair steps as we move inland. A friend of mine who was doing a survey around the bay found a couple of sites with pottery and chip stone tools back behind today's shore.

"There is a peninsula between Waskaganish and Ontario that forms the other side of Rupert's Bay," Chism said, "and there are still local stories that people used to go through with their boats behind the highland to get across to the other side. You can see a fairly low place, a break in that string of hills, where that could have happened.

"So the tip of that peninsula might have been an island, perhaps at the time when Hudson was here."

Some historians and supposed experts are flat-out certain that Hudson camped along the banks of the Rupert River near Waskaganish.

"We haven't found anything to support that," Chism said. "It is a bit like searching for a needle in a haystack.

"Some of the people who were doing maps for the Dominion of Canada say that Hudson's camp was the present site of Rupert's House, which is now Waskaganish. They say that Charles Fort was built right on the site, but we have seen nothing to suggest that. We have done testing along the edge of the water and here in town.

"The oldest stuff we have found is from about 1668, from the period of the first colonial effort by what became the Hudson's Bay Company."

We discussed the journal of Zachariah Gillam, the captain of the *Nonsuch*, who sailed into Rupert Bay in 1668. He reported as a fact that he found a house he estimated to be about sixty years old, and the supposition is that this was the house that Hudson's carpenter built in 1610. Onboard the *Nonsuch* was the French explorer Médard Chouart des Groseilliers.

Gillam and Chouart des Groseilliers did winter over at the mouth of the river, which they named the Rupert and built a house they called Charles Fort; this later became the Rupert House trading post.

According to Chism, the report of the house at Charles Fort may not have come from Gillam but instead may have been inserted over the years by the British Admiralty, which stitched together all sorts of logbooks, journals, and unsubstantiated stories from various explorers and captains.

"The stuff we have seen speaks about the fact that they were sailing along and desperately trying to find someone they could trade with and they saw this smoke on the shore," Chism said. "And Gillam's journal says they came over to the mouth of a river. The people they traded with told them they would tell all their friends to come.

"And there is a comment about going out walking on the winter ice and there being an island in the mouth of the river where birch trees were growing," Chism said. "Today, there is no island with birch trees on it, but the way the ice scours the ground, they could have been rubbed off. We don't have anything in those notes that talk about his seeing a hut."

And so I asked a scientist to step back from the facts and speculate.

"I don't think there is anything against Henry Hudson being here," Chism said. "This is a nice spot. Rupert's Bay would be an appealing place to come in.

"Out in James Bay there are lots of rocks and very shallow spots and especially in the fall when the waves are pretty bad it can be a pretty horrible, nightmarish place to be trying to sail through.

"You get a very clear impression of that from looking at Thomas James's log, which was published as a popular best seller in England," Chism said. (The book carried the very marketable title *The Strange and Dangerous Voyage of Captain Thomas James for the Discovery of a Northwest Passage to the South Sea.*)

Chism said that James might have dramatized his experience a bit, but you nevertheless get the clear idea that any place is going to look good to you if it is out of all those reefs and shallows and into Rupert's Bay.

Hudson may have been coming into the area from the west, from near Moosonee. Chism said that though the waters at the mouth of the Moose River were a bit easier than those near Waskaganish, there were plenty of reefs in between and around Charlton Island.

I asked him about Charlton Island and its smaller neighbor, Danby Island. Once the Hudson's Bay Company (HBC) was up and running, Charlton Island was used as a depot for transferring cargo to and from larger ships that came into the bay. Some Hudson followers have speculated that the captain and those abandoned with him could have made landfall there after they were forced off the ship in the spring of 1611.

"Charlton and Danby are kind of the same," Chism said. "There is a beautiful little protected harbor between them, a natural harbor out of the winds and storms. It is deep and there is very fast water going through there.

"It would be a good place if you could get in there, and of course that is what James did. I don't know if it was by luck or by looking at the 'Hudson' map [brought back by the survivors] whether he was able to plan on going there. He does not claim to be doing that in his journal. He just says, 'Here is this big island' and that's where he drew his dotted lines.

"On Danby, we haven't seen any sites, but we have only looked—we have not done any digging," Chism told me. "James claimed that he saw a camp on Danby. He was quite excited about that because all the time he was on Charlton Island he never saw anybody else; he never saw any hunters or trappers and he never even saw any smoke from someone's fire."

Some historians and fablists extrapolate from James's report of seeing some stakes in the ground that these had to have been made by technologically advanced Europeans.

"There is nothing to suggest from what he said that it was anything other than a Cree camp," Chism said. "He was excited because he thought this could only be done with metal tools.

"Of course, you can get a nice point with something besides a metal tool," Chism said. "In any case, we haven't been fortunate enough to stumble across what he was looking at.

"No one really knows where Hudson ended up," Chism said.

"When you talk about Hudson with folks around here, they kind of chuckle and say, 'If those guys wanted to get rid of him and really didn't want him to get back to England on his own and talk about what they did to him, maybe they put him adrift or maybe they just did him in: tossed him into the water and claimed to have put him adrift.'

"One way or another, they apparently didn't make it too far, although there are all these rumors of people descended from Hudson. People come looking around for those folks once in a while," Chism said.

"No one in Waskaganish makes that claim. There was a former school teacher from Wemindji who said there were people who claimed they were descendants from Hudson," Chism said.

Wemindji is also called Paint Hills because that is a word for a red paint stone. Locals speak of a place near Paint Hills that is called *Waamistikushish*, a Cree word said to mean "young Englishman." Thus far, this particular thread has gone no further than a place name.

"I don't know of anyone who has come up with anything concrete there," Chism said. "There was a fellow who went up there and supposedly was taken to a kind of stone cairn or something like that. He did a bit of poking around, for which he had his wrists slapped by the authorities, but nothing was found."

Rushing Ahead of Rising Waters

Although geologists and archaeologists tend to think in time periods of millennia and longer, there was also a bit of urgency in some of Chism's work. Much of his field work has to be accomplished during the relatively brief late spring and summer periods in the subarctic, and then there is the problem of Hydro Quebec.

The utility has already submerged huge swaths of northern Quebec beneath water and changed the paths of dozens of rivers and lesser streams. The prospect of further alteration to the land is on the minds of the natives and scientists.

Chism planned to spend a precious portion of the short summer working with a digging team near the Eastmain River north of Waskaganish, assisting a university research team. "There is a hydroelectric project going on the Eastmain River and so they are trying desperately to salvage what they can before the waters come up sometime during the fall or winter," Chism said.

The Hydro Quebec project is supposed to divert much of the flow of the Rupert River into the Eastmain. As Chism and others pointed out to me on numerous occasions, Hydro Quebec seems to have the habit of beginning work on projects before they have all the necessary governmental and environmental agency approvals.

I asked Chism what the effect of the diversion would be to the Crees he lives with in Waskaganish. "It's really hard to say," he said. "If you can believe the engineers, they say they are going to put some kind of retaining stations along the river below the diversion that are supposed to hold back some water at places where people might want a little deeper water. I don't think they really know if those things will work.

"I read that a footbridge collapsed on a truck out in British Columbia yesterday. Some engineer probably told them that that footbridge would never collapse, but it killed that driver."

Adopting the Modern

In Chism's writing, he often notes how the natives have "adopted" modern, outside technologies and methods. As an archaeologist, he echoed the words of the Reverend Tom Martin.

"You don't survive unless you are pragmatic in the boreal forest," Chism said. "If something is useful or exotic or interesting or beautiful, or otherwise appeals to your sense of aesthetics, those are the kinds of things you would adopt. Where things go from there is a matter of what the next generation considers pragmatic.

"Sometimes the function is the same but the form is different. Efficiency has a big impact on where people choose to live or how big an area you can exploit in one winter from one base camp.

"If you have metal tools, you can put a camp in the side of a very tough clay or rock hill, using what a modern engineer would call 'cut and fill' to make yourself a nice level place to have a tent."

If something works, if it does not offend their sensibilities, and if it is not dangerous, the Cree will integrate it into their lives, he said. The Cree had been trading with Europeans before the HBC arrived, and even before Hudson sailed into James Bay.

"I think you could push it even further than that," Chism said. "There were trading systems already existing before the arrival of the Europeans. We know that in prehistoric sites you find seashells from the Gulf Coast and exotic stones that would be valued for their beauty and for use in making tools.

"All kinds of things were moving back and forth, including food. Corn might have been coming up here from other areas, although we haven't found evidence of corn being burned in anyone's fireplace.

"When the Hudson Bay Company came here, it was a matter of plugging into an already existing trading pattern, a symbiotic relationship," Chism said. "People up here were at the tail end of the trading system that would have been bringing exotic goods from farther south."

It's an interesting observation: four centuries ago, just as now, the people living in the far north of Canada were at the very end of the distribution system and the very beginning of the production chain.

As the consumers, they had to pay the highest prices for goods that were brought in; the buyer, the middleman, and the trader each added a profit along the way.

And at the same time, the native traders were being paid wholesale price for their pelts and other objects of worth; several layers of profit would be added before those items were resold in Europe or elsewhere.

"When the English came sailing in," Chism said, "the natives made it obvious that they wanted to trade. These guys knew about that trading system and they knew about goods that were interesting because they were exotic.

"We do it today, too, don't we? We all want to be the first one to have a new computer, the first one to have new software, the first one to have a new game. The natives had the same kind of curiosity."

The history of colonization is a mixed one, Chism said. Some of the visitors to the New World were looking for a place to conquer and plunder. Some were looking for a place to farm. And some were looking for a place to trade. In the Far North, colonization was almost entirely a matter of setting up trading posts.

"If I am a Cree hunter and I have this trading post sitting there, I am going to make sure that they are taken care of and that they survive," Chism said. "I am going to be a good caretaker of this resource just as I am a caretaker of other resources."

In a commercial relationship like a trading post, there is likely to be less stress than in other situations such as those farther south in the United States, where the first settlers were taking over the land for farming, he said. In James Bay and Hudson Bay, it was more of a symbiotic relationship than parasitic.

Chism said that for the first century-and-a-half of operation of the HBC and the competing Northwest Company there was no attempt to take over the land for farming colonies. They came to trade, and they let the locals manage the resources.

Thomas Douglas, who was elevated to the title of Lord Selkirk in 1799, came to the North in 1807 with hopes of establishing a huge farming community in and around HBC territory in Red River, Manitoba, and extending south deep into present-day Minnesota and North Dakota.

The fertile land—about 116,000 square miles, or an area four times larger than Scotland and just slightly smaller than all the British Isles including Ireland—would be used to ship food back to starving Scotland and Ireland and help support representatives of the United Kingdom and the HBC already in Canada. The cost to Selkirk for the land grant: ten shillings.

There was great resistance from within the HBC, the Northwest Company, and natives. Selkirk's plan never came to fruition.

In the 1840s, missionaries began to traveling to the North to places like Waskaganish and with them came the idea of setting up residential schools to "civilize" the natives. This was also not something that the HBC had sought; it was only interested in the trade.

One of the first schools, with a specialty in agriculture, was set up on Moose Factory Island after 1870, Chism said. "Moose Factory is actually one of the few places where you have really great soil for gardening and growing crops," he said. "We have photographs from the Anglican Church collection showing flowers and vegetables growing above people's heads. Of course, the minute you get away from Moose Factory Island the soil is not so great."

But the biggest impediment to establishing farms in the area was the fact that the Cree were not farmers, Chism said. They were, and are, hunter-gatherers.

CHAPTER 28

A Young Man Keeps
the Old Traditions

I took the land route to Moosonee: a two-day train trip on one of the last single-track wilderness railroads. Passengers for Ontario Northland's *Northlander* were directed to gather at Gate 12 at Toronto's Union Station; the "gate" turned out to be a U-shaped spot in the middle of the departure hall demarked by ropes on stanchions. There was a door for Track 11 and another at Track 10, with real trains awaiting passengers for VIA Rail's long-distance cross-Canada service.

But like Harry Potter's assignment to Track 9¾ at King's Cross Station, the twenty-five or so customers waiting for Ontario Northland's daily one-train one-track service due north were held apart, in a world of our own. Finally, five minutes before the scheduled 8:55 morning departure, a conductor emerged from an unmarked door to escort us through to the train.

The *Northlander* meandered all day on a ten-hour trip to the frontier town of Cochrane, where I overnighted in a hotel above the train station. The next day, the *Little Bear* headed past the end of the road at Fraserdale; beyond here, only the railroad track continues north to Moosonee, a five-hour trip.

Moosonee, on the west bank of the broad Moose River, is a nondescript secular town with the feel of a frontier: there are no roads leading in or out except for the railroad, which comes to an end there. On the other side of the river is Moose Factory Island, home of the Moose Cree First Nation.

The Moose River flows north between the two communities to the bottom of James Bay. Henry Hudson sailed across the mouth of the river in 1610 as he methodically explored the bay, and may have passed by again after wintering on the eastern shore near Waskaganish.

Moose Factory was the site of the first English settlement in what is now the province of Ontario. The Hudson's Bay Company (HBC) post was set up in 1673, and Moose Factory was the administrative center for the company's James Bay or southern department. The presence of the factor drew nomadic Cree from the bush with pelts, meat, and other objects to trade. Smaller trading ships would sail north, down the river, to make deposits and withdrawals at the company's depot on Charlton Island.

Ontario is the most populous of Canada's provinces; like most of the country, almost all of its 12.5 million residents live in a 100-mile band just above the border with upstate New York and Michigan. Nearly 90 percent of its 415,598 square miles of land lies in the mostly empty regions above North Bay, Sudbury, Sault Ste. Marie, and Thunder Bay near Lake Superior and the states of Michigan and Wisconsin.

Upper Ontario begins as vast forest land; the trees support a huge industry in logging, mostly as softwood for paper and newsprint. Above Cochrane, the trees give way to clay, then tundra, and finally water; the great Missinaibi, Mattagami, and Abitibi rivers flow north and come together into the Moose River, which empties into the bottom of James Bay at the settlement of Moosonee on the west bank and Moose Factory Island on the east.

Captain Thomas James visited in 1631; his name was attached to the bay soon thereafter. The freelance explorers and fur traders Pierre Esprit Radisson and Médard Chouart des Groseilliers (known to millions of English-speaking Canadian schoolchildren by their easier-to-pronounce nicknames of Radishes and Gooseberries) set up trading posts for the HBC in 1672. Radisson and Chouart des Groseilliers had started out aligned with the French but changed allegiances to the British—or at least to British money.

For the next two centuries, nearly all trade was conducted from above: ships came through Hudson Strait and down Hudson Bay into James Bay. The trading season was open only when the waters were free of ice, generally from about May through early September. A small number of expeditions made the long, hard slog north from the lower portion of Canada. Among the travelers by land were French canoemen and explorers—the *coureurs des bois* (runners of the woods)—who came from the St. Lawrence River settlements.

Trading between the local Cree and factors from the HBC was a major economic force in Canada; in 1884, records show that about $100,000 in customs duties was collected on Moose Factory Island. In 1903, the HBC was joined by French enterprises including Révillon Frères, the predecessor to the Revlon cosmetics company and a global financial and luxury furs company.

About that time, the provincial government in Toronto began to hear from business interests in Ontario with dreams of a counter to the developing economic power of Quebec. They proposed building a railway from Toronto to James Bay to open up Moosonee as the province's own seaport, independent of Montreal and Quebec. (The fact that James Bay was frozen over for much of the year and that the Moose River was too shallow to allow large freighters to enter seemed not to receive much consideration.)

The provincial government had made the decision to send a pair of rails north in 1902, meeting up with the expected east-west tracks of the transcontinental railway in Cochrane in 1908. Among the lures for the railroad were the discovery of silver at Cobalt and even larger lodes of gold at Porcupine in 1909 and Kirkland Lake in 1912. And even a century ago, it was apparent to government and private sectors that there was a huge potential for hydroelectric plants on the rivers of the North.

The tracks went no farther than Cochrane until 1923, when the final push to Moosonee began. That stretch of track presented some very daunting challenges: much of the land was unyielding frozen ground for most of the year and soggy muskeg in the brief summer. And the railroad had to cross over the Moose River at the place where the Missinaibi and Mattagami join the main channel; the flamboyant Canadian builder Harry McLean built a half-mile-long bridge over an island in the stream.

And then finally on July 15, 1932, Moosonee's isolation from lower Canada came to an end with the completion of the Temiskaming and Northern Ontario Railway. Today, the single-track line is called the Ontario Northland Railway. The *Northlander* runs once a day from Toronto to Cochrane, and on alternate days the *Little Bear* chugs its way 186 miles from Cochrane north to Moosonee carrying residents, fishermen, hunters, and freight. During the summer, the *Polar Bear Express* takes tourists to the end of the line in the morning, returning to Cochrane each afternoon.

Near the end of the tracks is a cairn erected by McLean; inscribed on the monument are lines from Rudyard Kipling's poem "The Sons of Martha," which celebrates the workers of the world who "say to mountains, 'be ye removed.' "

In 1920, the first airplane touched down at Moosonee. And on August 1, 1931, Charles Lindbergh landed his float plane *Sirius* at the remote settlement on an airborne Northwest Passage to Asia. To this day, a popular name for babies is Lindy.

In the early cold war, Moosonee was home to an isolated military radar station that was an element of the Pinetree Line, the chain of early warning stations to alert Canada and the United States. The installation is long gone, but many of the former military buildings have been converted to other uses, and a section of town is still referred to as "the base."

Ice Floes, Sandbars, and Mosquitoes

I hauled my bags a few blocks east from the train station to the banks of the Moose River. There, I met Clarence Trapper, my driver on the river and on Moose Factory Island. Trapper was also my deeply spiritual guide to the rich mix of old traditions and new ways that exist among the people on the island and in the bush.

Clarence Trapper on the Moose River.
Photo by the author

The final leg of the journey took place in Trapper's freighter canoe, a broad-beamed canoe with a powerful outboard motor; these
boats are the taxis between Moosonee and Moose Factory Island for
about half the year, wending their way around shifting sandbars and
tricky currents that make a two-mile trip into a windy and sometimes
wet fifteen-minute expedition.

In the winter, the river freezes over thick enough to allow snowmobiles and trucks to drive across. The difficult time comes in late
fall, when the river is crusted over with thin ice and again in the late
spring when the breakup leaves large patches of water between
floes of ice; in recent years, a helicopter company has come north
to fill the gap at these times.

A cold north wind blew down the river; it was 46 degrees on June
25, and some pellets of ice were mixed into a light drizzle. At din-

ner, we were treated to a spectacular lightning storm that crossed the river south of us. And then the lights went out.

As the *Little Bear* chugged along the single track of the Ontario Northland Railroad, I had watched the poles of the power line march from a large hydroelectric plant across the sparse trees of the subarctic. Moosonee's connection to the outside world, even in 2006, was so obviously fragile.

I could picture a lightning strike on one of the towers and imagined the process of sending a crew of linemen out in the pounding rain to find the wire. After dinner, I took a candle back to my room.

Outside, the sun was still evident until nearly 10:30 at night, and as it finally set, lights flickered back to life.

The next morning Trapper took me out onto the river and we bounced through cold six-foot waves as we headed north toward James Bay about seven miles down the river. The twenty-two-foot-long Norwest freighter canoe had no name. "I've never heard of any Cree giving a boat a name," Trapper said. "It's not alive."

The land is very flat along the shore of the river, an extension of the delta. There are four miles of mud flats inland and out into the bay. Near James Bay is Shipsands Island, a bird sanctuary that each spring is covered with geese, ducks, and shorebirds.

Flying overhead were red-throated arctic loons, and thousands of common loons—better known as loonies and featured on Canada's one-dollar coin; in typical understated northern humor, the two-dollar coin (decorated with a polar bear) is called a Twonie or Toonie. (There's little mention of Queen Elizabeth II, who appears on the face of both coins, although a wag dubbed the two-dollar coin as "The Queen with the Bear Behind," which led, of course, to the "Moonie.")

Temperatures warmed in the afternoon as we drove around Moose Factory Island; Trapper had the windows up and the air conditioner running. I started to lower a window, and he firmly said, "No."

Before I had the chance to ask him why, we turned the corner to approach the river and the van was suddenly assaulted by huge horseflies. It was like a scene out of *Jurassic Park* or maybe *Day of the Dead*.

The Legacy of Treaty Number Nine

The local band of Cree have been coming to the island for longer than any records can tell, many centuries before anyone thought to build and name a town.

"The Moose Cree First Nation are the ones who were originally here," Trapper said. "These are the people who were recognized by Treaty Number Nine that was signed in this community in 1905.

"But there were still nomadic families back then. They would come to Moose Factory and live here just for the spring or summer season and then they would head back out into the bush."

To many natives, the 1905 treaty was just one in a string of "agreements" between unequal partners. When the Hudson's Bay Company and provincial authorities arrived at Moose Factory Island and other campsites, one of the first things they had to do was create a leadership to have someone to sign the paper.

"We have always been nomadic people," Trapper said. "Then when the treaty was signed, they tried to set up communities as a reservation where there would be a chief and a governing body.

"We didn't have a chief. We weren't set up that way. There was a head man of each family's last name.

"When our treaty was signed in 1905, the translator was white," he continued. "When the commissioners who were here to sign the treaty came into the community, they said 'Okay, you are going to be chief.'

"So when the treaty was signed in this area, it was interpreted in two different ways: the nonnative way and the native way. The nonnative way was the signing of the right to the land.

"We signed over the rights to the land to the Canadian government for certain perks. We got free education and free medical services. And then there was a promise that each Indian recognized in that treaty would receive four dollars on an annual basis. Four dollars on each anniversary of that treaty. In 1905 that was a lot of money. Now, four dollars can't even buy a pop and chips.

"And then they tried to set us up as farmers up the river," he continued. "And what happened was when harvest season came there

386

Moose Factory Island in the brief subarctic summer.
Photo by the author

was nobody around to harvest because everybody was still practicing the traditional ways: we went to the bay to harvest geese. We are gatherers instead of farmers."

Government documents from 1905 record the following:

The Indians were informed that by signing the treaty they pledged themselves not to interfere with white men who might come into the country surveying, prospecting, hunting, or in other occupations; that they must respect the laws of the land in every particular, and that their reserves were set apart for them in order that they might have a tract in which they could not be molested, and where no white man would have any claims without the consent of their tribe and of the government.

And His Majesty the King hereby agrees with the said Indians that they shall have the right to pursue their usual vocations of hunting, trapping and fishing throughout the tract surrendered as heretofore described, subject to such regulations as may from time to time be made by the government of the country, acting under the authority of His Majesty, and saving and excepting such tracts as may be required or taken up from time to time for settlement, mining, lumbering, trading or other purposes.

And with a view to show the satisfaction of His Majesty with the behaviour and good conduct of His Indians, and in extinguishment of all their past claims, He hereby, through His commissioners, agrees to make each Indian a present of eight dollars in cash.

His Majesty also agrees that next year, and annually afterwards for ever, He will cause to be paid to the said Indians in cash, at suitable places and dates, of which the said Indians shall be duly notified, four dollars, the same, unless there be some exceptional reason, to be paid only to the heads of families for those belonging thereto.

The modern Cree looks back at the signing of Treaty Number Nine and sees two cultures that did not understand each other and that had very different views of the world. "The natives looked at it as the sharing of the responsibility of the land," Trapper said. "They thought they would help watch the land along with the nonnative people."

Even today, Trapper said, there is a divide between some of the members of the band over the meaning and impact of the treaty, and the band's relationship to the provincial and federal government in Canada.

"Some of the elders say we should celebrate the treaty because of all the stuff we received from the government like free education, free health care, and all that," Trapper said. "But slowly the benefits we were offered are being taken away."

According to Trapper, among the sore points are new criteria on higher education that make it more difficult for natives to pursue postsecondary and university schooling; such education almost always requires travel and residence in one of Ontario's major cities located hundreds of miles to the south.

In 1949, the Moose Factory Indian Hospital was built on the island, primarily as a 200-bed tuberculosis sanitarium; the facility was laid out in a version of the shape of the Cross of Lorraine, the almost-forgotten symbol of the Canadian Tuberculosis Association, now the Lung Association.

"There was a big tuberculosis epidemic throughout all of James Bay and Hudson Bay and patients came from Cree and even Inuit communities," Trapper said. "Many people came to this place and some of them never left."

Today, the hospital, renamed as Weeneebayko General Hospital (the Cree word means "of the two bays") serves as the primary care facility for much of Ontario's northeast frontier.

The second group on the island are the MoCreebec, native people who came across the provincial border from Quebec and settled; they are recognized by the Canadian government as a First Nation tribe and participate in Grand Council of the Cree elections on the Quebec side. They are, though, a band without a reserve. "Mostly, they do their own thing and we do ours," Trapper said.

"The Moose Cree First Nation claims the surrounding territory: this whole area—the islands and the land—as their traditional territory. Each of the families on our reserve has a traditional hunting territory.

"Someone from the MoCreebec First Nation has to ask permission to go out onto the land and do some harvesting because their traditional hunting territories are in Quebec with their families."

The Moose Cree First Nation lands extend west along the bottom of James Bay toward Fort Albany and east toward Rupert House or Waskaganish, which is across the border in Quebec. I asked Trapper if the fact that their traditional lands spanned two provinces presented a problem.

"There was no border when our people first came here," he said. "But for instance in my family, our traditional hunting land is actually cut in half because in my grandfather's territory the Quebec and Ontario border went right through it. So they asked my grandfather where he was going to reside. He decided to follow my grandmother; my grandmother wanted to move here to Moose Factory in Ontario. So they resided in Ontario instead of Quebec."

In more modern times, one of the major efforts of the Moose Cree

First Nation has been to collect data to draw paper and then computer maps of the territory in their land claim. Some of the data traces family traplines going back decades.

The fact that the band is recognized by the government and can produce a map of traditional family territories does not mean that the Moose Cree own the land, though; all they have is preferential treatment for hunting and gathering and a wobbly leg to stand on in any attempt to fight hydroelectric or mining development.

Before There Was a History

The white man's history of Moose Factory Island goes back to the 1670s or so, when the first trading post was established there.

"Well, that's what they say," Trapper responded. As far as nonnatives are concerned, he continued, history only dates as far back as when the first book was written.

"We didn't have a written language," he continued. "It was all basically legend. And that's how we told our stories."

How far back do the legends go?

"It is hard to say because there were no years in the stories," he said.

What about Cree creation legends?

"If you go to other native societies besides Cree tribes, they all have a similar story of creation where they call this earth an island. We call North America 'Turtle Island.' We think of ourselves as living on the back of a turtle."

There is a parallel to Noah's Ark and the Great Flood in the native legend, Trapper said. After a flood, "all the land washed away and the only way we were able to survive was on the back of the turtle. There was a man and a woman, and muskrat, mink, beaver, and otter.

"Back then, men and women were more spiritual, I guess, and they were able to speak to the animals and the animals were able to speak back," Trapper continued. "And so they asked the beaver go down to the bottom and bring up some mud—bring up some land—and we will make it grow.

"The beaver went down a long time. And finally the beaver came up, and he said he couldn't do it. He couldn't get to the bottom.

"And so they said to the otter, 'Okay, it's your turn.' The otter went down and the same thing happened. He couldn't do it.

"They said to the muskrat: 'Your turn. Go dive down there.' And the muskrat went in and he came up on the other side right away, and he said, 'No, I am too scared.'

"So they said, 'Mink, it's your turn.' The mink dove in the water and he was gone and he never came up. It became dark and then daylight came. Early in the morning the mink pops up, almost half-dead. But in his paw he had a piece of mud.

"The man, Gistabesh, had the power in him to make things grow," Trapper said. "So he blew on that piece of dirt, and all over the turtle that is where the land grew. And that's how we live on the turtle."

I asked Trapper if he thought the creation legend had any basis in fact; was the Great Flood related to the melting of the glaciers of the North at the end of the ice age?

"No. It is my belief that we were always here," Trapper said. "We didn't come across a land bridge from somewhere else.

"I asked my grandmother one time what does it mean when they say we were always here," he continued. "And she said the land was here, and we come from the land, and we go back to the land. After a while, I thought about it and said, 'We live off the land, and when we die we go back into the land.' "

A Family from the Bush

"I grew up with my parents in the bush," Trapper said. "For the first two years of school, I was in residential school at the Ministik Public School here in Moose Factory Island. But once I got old enough, the school let me take up a big pile of schoolwork—all kinds of math, English, and science—and have my mom teach me from grades three through seven.

"I spent that time in the bush with my parents," Trapper said. "Today, my parents are seventy-five years old and still live in the bush."

Trapper said his mother and father have been living on the land for more than sixty years as nomads. "What I mean by nomadic is that they are here [in Moose Factory] in the summer, go out to the bay in the fall, and back into the bush into the winter."

I asked him why they would spend the winter in the bush, which would seem to be much more difficult than the comforts of town.

"No, it is not difficult. It is more abundant than here, with hunting and trapping."

Although Trapper now lives in a home in Moose Factory Island, with a job working for the tribal council, he told me that's as close to the outside world as he wants to get. "If I was in the city—New York or Boston or wherever—I don't think I would survive. I would be like a fish out of water.

"When I am in the bush I am in my element," Trapper said. "I know which plants are edible and which plants aren't. Which plants get you really itchy, and which plants can help you get rid of the itchiness.

"And in the winter, I know which plants can actually feed you. There are trees that have a bark you can scrape and mix up and eat, and it gives you energy. When we are in the bush it is our supermarket.

"If I feel I want to eat fish today, I will go to the lake and set a net or go ice fishing. If I feel like eating a rabbit or partridge, I go hunting."

Although today many bush camps have gas-powered electric generators, when Trapper grew up with his family in the bush they had no electricity. The tent frame was made of logs split in half with the cracks filled with moss. "That was me and my mom's job: filling in the moss," he said.

Trapper's parents are among the last from the Moose Cree community who still follow a version of the nomadic lifestyle. "My parents do have a house here, and they call it the summer home, but it is not really their home; their camp in the bush is where they live most of the time."

Memories of Henry Hudson and the Missionaries

In Moose Factory, there is no oral history of Henry Hudson, the *Discovery*, or the crew. Trapper did not find this at all unusual.

"If there was any contact," he said, "I'd say the first reaction was probably to run away.

"My grandmother told us what happened when my great-grandmother first saw an airplane," Trapper said. "A bush plane came in and when it landed it came to shore and people got out. Everybody ran away from the camp. They ran in the bush to hide. My grandmother remembers hiding in the bush.

"In some of the stories I have heard, they thought those were not real people who got out of the plane," Trapper said. "They were told, 'Don't laugh at them.' They just looked at them as something very strange."

About seeing Hudson and the *Discovery*, then: "I can imagine back in those days native people of this area seeing a big boat going by, and then seeing people coming ashore in rowboats. Curiosity would probably overwhelm them, but at the same time they would be afraid of them."

Hudson arrived at the bottom of James Bay in 1610 near the end of the summer and spent a lonely winter somewhere east of the mouth of the Moose River near Waskaganish. "I would say there's at least a fifty-fifty chance that he would have bumped into somebody," Trapper said. "There were always people traveling, and in the spring the people would be coming out of the tributaries of all the main rivers and coming to these summer meeting places."

The Cree began to come out of the bush within a few decades once the fur traders arrived in the area: the HBC on Moose Factory Island and Révillon Frères in Moosonee. Trapper took me to the former headquarters of the HBC on the island; it houses a small museum of artifacts from the former factors and managers.

On the main wall of the small building I came face to face with Henry Hudson once again: an antique painting of the explorer that had been distributed to many HBC posts in Canada. It shows the same forlorn, scraggly bearded Hudson portrayed in John Collier's 1881 romanticized image, "The Last Voyage of Henry Hudson."

The original painting, owned by the Tate Gallery in London, shows Hudson at the tiller of the shallop that is surrounded by floating mountains of ice; his young son is pitifully curled at his knees. The small version in the HBC post shows only the sad face and upper body of Hudson, his eyes focused directly on those who stand before him.

Along with the goods that the traders brought to exchange for furs came Christian missionaries. In most communities, the English traders brought Anglican ministers, while French traders brought Roman Catholic priests. Trapper told me the history of how Christianity had influenced two small Cree communities west of Moose Factory Island along the bottom of James Bay: Fort Albany and Kashechewan.

"There used to be one community on an island right in the middle of the Albany River. But when the fur trade came into that area, there were two missionaries who landed at the same time; one was Roman Catholic and the other was Anglican.

"They started baptizing the community, and what happened is it separated the community. Today, Fort Albany is all Roman Catholic and Kashechewan on the other side of the river is Anglican. They are still related like family, but separated."

At the time the missionaries came to James Bay, most of the Cree bands were still gathering for shaking tents, traditional ceremonies involving shamans or mediums. "When Christianity came in, they saw that and they said 'That is the Devil's practice and that is not God's way. God's way is the church.' "

The summer meeting places were not just about hunting and fishing, Trapper said. They also served other important social functions, including marriages that were mostly arranged between the parents as recently as seventy years ago.

Family names and hierarchies are passed down through the father's side. Trapper said he can trace his own name back to his great-great-grandfather Wan-hikan, whose Cree name was translated as Thomas Trapper when he was baptized by an Anglican minister.

A portrait of Henry Hudson inside the old
Hudson's Bay Company trading post at Moose Factory Island.
Photo by the author

Most of the Cree on Moose Factory Island are Anglican; there are five churches on the reserve. There is a small Roman Catholic congregation and two Pentecostal churches.

Look Me in the Eyes, If You Dare

The differences between native and outside culture include a great deal more than just religion and lifestyle. I had already noticed how most of the Cree I had met seemed very shy, almost childlike; even with an articulate and driven man like Trapper, it seemed hard to make a connection. I asked Trapper about it.

"Nonnative people such as yourself have to have direct eye contact," he said. "If someone doesn't look you in the eyes, you think that person is either being deceitful or is afraid of you. With us it is totally different.

"If you are staring into my eyes, you are either in love with me or you are being hostile or threatening," Trapper said. "That's because in the Cree culture we believe that the eyes are a very personal space."

Trapper had been with me when I had checked into my room at the lodge. "When my friend brought the keys here, I didn't even look at him, and he didn't even look at me. He just says, 'Here are the keys.' And that's the way it is with all the people in our community. They say, 'Hello, how are you?' They are very friendly. But eye contact is something they hold very dear to themselves.

"I only look into my wife's eyes," Trapper said.

There is another disconnect when it comes to the concept of time. To an outsider, the idea of doing something in a "while" means soon, perhaps within an hour or so; Trapper said to his people "in a while" might mean as much as twelve hours later. "Time is more expanded for us," he said. "Some things will be done when they are done. But there are also some times when we look at our environment and we know something has to be done soon because of something like the tide."

The ebb and flow of the tide is one of the most important clocks in Moose Factory Island. It affects travel downriver toward Shipsand Island, where many locals go to hunt geese; it changes the shape and contours of the sandbars that make it impossible to head straight across the river in a freighter canoe from Moose Factory Island to Moosonee on the mainland.

"Every twelve-and-a-half hours the tide comes in," Trapper said. "If we were to travel out in the bay today, we would have to do it at high tide. At low tide you are not going anywhere because it is too dry.

"Another thing we know, for instance, is that there is a certain plant that has huge leaves and a long stalk and on top of the stalk there is a white flower. And when that white flower blooms—pretty soon now, actually—and starts to fall off and blow away, we know that's the time we go out and set nets along the river here. That's when the whitefish start coming into the river from out in the bay.

I don't know how we know that, but it was something we were always told by our elders."

As we spoke, we heard the rumble of thunder down the river toward James Bay.

"In my family, we say thunder and lightning [are] a cleansing of the land," Trapper said. "We have different names; I don't know if you call them gods, but we call them spirits.

"There is a spirit that watches over all the animals and the land," Trapper told me. "This spirit is the one that shows you the way when you are hunting. It is hard to explain in English, but in Cree it is easy because I understand the concept."

If Trapper was to kill a moose in the bush, he would put aside a piece of the cooked meat and throw it into the fire, along with a piece of tobacco; he would do the same with a fish caught in the river or lake. "That is an offering back to the spirit; we hope the spirit will then feed us again another day. That's how we do it with all the food that we harvest.

"We pray to these spirits to help us before we go out," he said. "Guide me in the right way, help me in the harvest of the food."

Some of the creatures of the forest have special status. "For instance, the black bear is considered in Cree society as one of the most respected animals. We believe it is actually our brother.

"If we were hunting and shot a bear, before I even would touch the bear I would prepare an offering," Trapper continued. "Then I would crack all the knuckles of the bear. Our belief is that releases the spirit from the body. Then we would gut and clean the bear.

"And then we take it back to the camp," he said. "The eldest ladies in the camp skin the bear. And there are only certain parts of the bear that we deal with.

"The paws are only eaten by females," he said. "The head is only eaten by males. We believe that the bear spirit came along and said 'I don't want any men eating paws, only women.'

"In our family, the Trapper family, when we kill a beaver, we hang the carcass in the trees to show respect to the animal. And we show respect to a bear by putting its bones up on a platform."

What Do the Elders Say?

Even though Moose Factory Island is 200 miles away from Chisasibi and the mouth of the La Grande River—the largest of the Hydro Quebec projects—Trapper says that the community has seen changes in the Moose River and surrounding territory in recent years because of diversion of water. And other effects have come from industrial plants hundreds of miles south in Ontario, he said.

"The hydroelectric dams in Quebec have affected the population of geese and waterfowl in our area," Trapper said. "We used to get millions and millions of birds out there on the bay, and they would nest along the coast of James Bay. All the rivers started drying up out up there and it changed the ecosystem."

Many of the birds now come no farther south than Cape Henrietta at the bottom of Hudson Bay on the Ontario side, according to Trapper; after nesting, they fly west to Manitoba, a change in the historic pattern.

"It has to have something to do with the hydroelectric reservoirs." According to Trapper, the water levels in the Moose River have dropped since the dams were installed farther north. Twenty years ago there was only a small sandbar between Moosonee and Charles Island, which is the barrier island to Moose Factory Island, and today it is an island that the freighter canoes have to navigate around.

"There is also more silt in the water," Trapper said, "and it settles at the delta of the river. We're starting to see more and more shoals popping up in our area."

Trapper said that he remembers when the canoes used to be able to travel very close to the shore. Now, though, the river bottom is very flat, from the shore out into the flow.

The James Bay Agreement compensated the First Nation tribes on the Quebec side of the bay for the use of their land and the diversion of many of the major rivers for use in the hydroelectric plants. The Crees of Quebec excluded the Crees of Ontario from the payments.

"We didn't really mind," Trapper told me. "How we looked at it was that they were selling their land and we didn't. We still have our land. We still have a good fighting chance to claim our land."

The Moose Cree have other concerns besides changing water levels from the Hydro Quebec plants. There are also large dams and hydroelectric plants on the Abitibi River in the vicinity of Cochrane; there are five plants at Abitibi Canyon, and four more at Otter Rapids. The Abitibi merges with the Moose River about twenty miles south of Moosonee.

These dams regulate the flow of the river, making it slower at times when it used to be fast and fast at times when the water level used to drop; they also affect the content of the water, from silt to fish.

Added into the mix are the effluent of pulp and paper mills and tailings and pollution that finds its way into the river from gold, silver, and other mines in Timmins, Cobalt, and other areas that lie north of the big population centers of Toronto but south (and up-river) of Moosonee.

Another major industry that uses the resources of the region is the Abitibi-Consolidated newsprint mill in Iroquois Falls, near Timmins. The plant, though reduced in size in recent years, produces about 280,000 tons of newsprint and 47,000 tons of other stock, including colored paper each year, and harvests mostly black spruce from a 6,000-square-mile area of government-owned land plus its own property.

Trapper told me that years ago he had met a former biochemist for the paper company, a man once responsible for environmental assessment at the plant. He said, "You didn't hear this from me, but in the Abitibi River system thirty-two miles down that river there was no life in that section, it was just biologically dead."

According to Trapper, the former worker had a photograph of the paper mill that showed the river on a day when the plant had set up to produce red paper but then shifted to an order for blue. "So they drained all the red dye into the river, and he had the photo; for sixteen miles down the river it ran completely red. And that all comes down to Moose Factory.

"I tell that to the government," Trapper said, "and they tell me, 'they are just under their regulations and policies' for pollution and the dumping of their process solutions and waste."

After spending a few days with Trapper, I came to realize that he was a young man who in some ways was holding on tighter to tradition than many of the older members of the tribe. I asked him what the elders thought of the pace of change on Moose Factory Island.

"When it comes to some of the newer technologies, they praise it," he said. "They say, 'We used to do this the hard way all the time. We used to have to paddle all the way across the bay, and now you guys have motorized boats and skidoos. Some of the things are so easy for you.'

"But then there are some of the bad things that come along with it, like pollution. We live in a world where everything comes in a package.

"One of the biggest peeves some people have is the amount of garbage we produce," Trapper said. "When you go out into the bush, bring your garbage back. Don't leave it out there.

"Our culture is very important to us, and we are surrounded by our bush life here. My father took me out in the bush. He showed me how to hunt, he showed me how to hunt for myself and for my family. It was always a learning process.

"So now that I've become a man, I've got my own family," he continued. "I've got my son and we've been hunting for geese together for two years now. He's starting to get the hang of it."

Protecting the Homeland

On the last day of my visit to Moose Factory Island, Trapper opened up a bit more, at least when it came to the political slogan on his t-shirt. It read: "Homeland Security: Fighting Terrorism since 1492."

We spoke about the Canadian and provincial government's history of attempting to assimilate the native population into what they considered to be a superior and more modern society. At the heart of this was the establishment of residential schools throughout

Canada; young children were pulled from the bush or native communities and taken to schools, where they were given an English or French education and culture. One of the schools happened to be located on Moose Factory Island, and the government would send out a ship each fall to collect children from settlements on the Ontario side of James Bay as far away as Attiwapiskat above Fort Albany.

"They gathered all the children and brought them back here for ten months of the year, out of the traditional family structure," Trapper said. "What that did was cause a breakdown in tradition and culture.

"Some people were very influenced by the residential school," he continued. "It made them think: 'You're an Indian and being an Indian is not as good as being a white, a nonnative.

"When I was in residential school, and when my mom was in school, we were forbidden from speaking our native tongue. We were punished anytime we spoke it at school." When no one was watching, the students would speak Cree among themselves, but they would have to watch over their shoulders, he said.

"We need to retain our language in order to retain our culture," he continued. Otherwise, we just become English-speaking Indians.

I asked him if he remained hopeful about the future of his family and his culture.

"Oh yes," he said. "I say to my children that we are growing up in a new society, a new age of technology, and can communicate with anybody across the world. I see that we could use technology to help us keep our language strong. I see communities farther up the coast that are very strong in keeping their language," he continued.

"We've got to keep our identity," Trapper said. "Or someday someone is going to come up and ask, 'What is an Indian?'

"An Indian is a person who comes from a long line of people who learned from the bush. We still believe in the bush, and also use those same values that are taught in the bush.

"I just started to play hockey here six years ago," Trapper said. "I didn't know how to skate. But when I [was on the ice], I played until the game was over. I didn't stop. Never give up. That mentality, my father taught me that.

"I remember when I was fourteen years old and I was moose hunting with my father," Trapper said. "We were running after a moose, and he said, 'Here.' He gave me a rifle, and he said 'Go,' and I had to chase the moose.

"And I ran and ran. After about forty minutes of running I stopped. And I waited for my father to come.

"The first thing he did was, smack! 'What are you doing?' he asked. 'There isn't a moose here. The moose is still over there.' Then he told me, 'Don't ever give up on a moose. Because if you give up on him, he's always going to beat you. He'll always beat you.'

"And that's what I'd like to see my son do. I'd like to pass that on."

I ended my visit sitting with Trapper along the shore of the Moose River; we had crossed over to Moosonee in his freighter canoe and I was getting ready to head into town to catch the southbound *Polar Bear Express* train back to Cochrane. I said to him, "You are a Canadian, a Christian, a proud member of the Cree First Nation. In what order would you put those descriptions?"

He thought for a moment.

"I'd say being a Cree person, that's first because that's who I am. We identify ourselves by the way we live here on the earth," Trapper said.

"Then I'd be a Christian," he said. "That depends on personal preference. My mother is very strong in the church, probably because of the influence of the residential schools. I chose to follow the traditional ways.

"Then I'd be a Canadian. Anybody can be a Canadian now. Anybody can come from a different world and they can be classified as a Canadian."

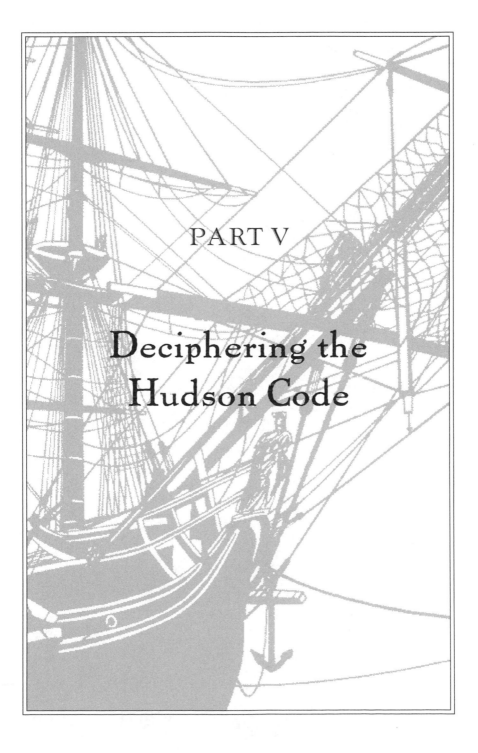

PART V

Deciphering the
Hudson Code

CHAPTER 29

Hudson's Bones,
Undiscovered

I traveled in the wake of Henry Hudson for more than a year to the northern corners of the globe, laid hands on an ancient altar rail touched by the captain, inhaled centuries-old dust from original copies of collections of English and Dutch ships' logs and journals, and otherwise devoted a large portion of my thinking to trying to decode 400 years of mystery.

By the end of my journeys, I had visited or passed by most of the places Hudson had explored, and spent time in the dead end of James Bay, where he most likely met his death.

Some of the places had changed remarkably, most notably the great city of New York that now stands at the entrance to the Hudson River. But most of the distant and difficult places where he ventured in his four voyages from 1607 to 1610 would have been immediately recognizable to the crews of the *Hopewell, Half Moon,* and *Discovery.*

Magdalenefjord in Svalbard is still scarcely touched by human hands and visited only by an adventuresome few each year. The sprawling islands of Novaya Zemlya above Russia remain among the most remote places on Earth, not easy to get to, and offering little reason to try.

Many of the Inuit of the Canadian Arctic and Hudson Bay and the Cree of James Bay have moved out of the bush and settled—a bit uneasily—into scattered communities. But when I sailed a few miles offshore on an icebreaker, it was easy to miss some of the tiny villages tucked into river bays.

And the markers of the sea—Bear Island in the frozen Arctic Ocean, the eastern coast of Greenland, Hudson Strait between Ungava Bay and Baffin Island, and treacherous Cape Wolstenholme at the top of Hudson Bay—are as immediately recognizable and foreboding as they were 400 years ago when Captain Hudson noted them in his log books.

When I first set out, I did not have serious hopes of finding Hudson's bones; many others have tried since 1611.

If we are to believe the testimony of the mutineers who returned to England without the captain, then we might expect that someday, someone may find remains along the east coast of James Bay or on one of the islands there. If instead Hudson's end was even more brutal than portrayed, then it may be that the captain and the others were killed in the bay and dumped overboard. And if we want to place any credit in the stories of the fablers and the bloviators, then Hudson may have made it to shore and even survived a few years: red-headed Cree, you know.

But it is also true that in the past four centuries there has been very little in the way of systematic exploration of most of the hundreds of big and little islands and uninhabited coastline of James Bay.

For me, though, the most stunning revelation of my journey was to learn the stories of the people and the places he visited.

The more I followed Henry Hudson, the more it seemed to me that in some ways he really was a Forrest Gump of the early 1600s; he seemed to stumble into accidental history at every turn, almost in spite of himself. And Gumpdom has continued in the four centuries since.

How else to explain threads like the connection between coal mining in Svalbard and Christian Scientists in Boston; between the plague, John Smith, Pocahontas, William Shakespeare, and Hudson; between Theodore Roosevelt, Fiorello H. La Guardia, Robert Moses, and the only significant statue of Henry Hudson anywhere in the world.

The Economics of Exploration

"The investors who backed Hudson's trips were looking for the big payoff," according to Chip Reynolds, the captain of the replica of the *Half Moon* that sails the Hudson today. "They wanted to hit three lemons off that roulette machine. But they were going to be happy if they got a pair, because at least they would get some return on their investment."

As I've noted, Hudson was an economic explorer; he wasn't making voyages merely for the honor of discovering unknown lands, and he wasn't sailing to claim colonies for a greedy superpower. He was the manager of a business unit of an investment company.

The seventeenth century was a time of great technological innovation and economic expansion. Most of the resources of northern Europe had been pretty well exploited, and there were political limits on other areas of exploration.

"When Hudson goes to these unexplored places and finds natural resources and fertile soil and fur-bearing animals that are going to be available for trade, he makes note of it all," Reynolds told me.

"The whaling industry in Spitsbergen exploded after his reports, but it would have happened irrespective of him. He was there at a timely moment, and he also demonstrated that the ability to sail there wasn't a fluke. He was thorough enough in his explorations around Spitsbergen to give a level of comfort to other investors to get back up there and continue this exploration," Reynolds said.

"Less than ten years after Hudson was in Spitsbergen, you have ships carrying twenty thousand men a year to that area. You don't have wood and fuel and food there. These guys have to carry everything. They have to build all their structures. They have to carry in their food."

A settlement of 20,000 people was a significant city at the time: there were only about 200,000 living in London and 100,000 in Moscow.

The whale fishery near Svalbard was all but killed off by about 1645. The same thing happened on the Hudson River with the beaver trade: within fifty years of the start of commerce there, the animal was almost gone from the region. But fortunes were made.

The Model of a Methodical Explorer

Comparing Henry Hudson to Forrest Gump does not set well with Reynolds. Hudson was not a guy who was just blundering around and having these things happen accidentally around him. "That's just not the case. He was systematically and thoroughly looking for these things and documenting them," Reynolds insists.

And I had only to hint at some of the conspiracy theories to get Reynolds launched on a defensive tack.

"One of the problems that Hudson suffered is the lack of documentation about aspects of his life and what happened on his voyages," he said. "But the other part of it is that because of the way he died you have people speculating; it all sounds very dramatic and compelling even when it is way off base.

"There are people who claim Hudson was actually a spy," Reynolds said. That's the conspiratorial view of his 1609 voyage on behalf of the VOC, which was preceded by two voyages for his native England.

And then there was Hudson's fourth and final voyage—back in the employ of an English company—and here the *X-Files* crowd sometimes chimes in with a theory that he wasn't really looking for the Northwest Passage when he sailed into upper Canada but instead was searching for mineral deposits in James Bay.

Reynolds buys none of it. "There is a straightforward and plausible explanation for everything Hudson did."

Hudson and his financial backers knew everything there was to know about the four supposed routes to Asia that would not bring ships into conflict with the other political and economic powers of the time. There were two [routes] to the Northeast: over the North Pole, or across the top of Russia. And there were two to the Northwest: a passage through northern Virginia (which mapmakers of the time defined as stretching from the Jamestown colony north to Cape Cod) or a route that would wend its way through the ice of upper Canada.

There were reports coming back from French explorers who had gone into the St. Lawrence River that although it was a great waterway for trade, like the Hudson River it eventually came to shallows and rapids that blocked the passage of large ships.

(In the mid-1600s, the French gave the rapids west of Montreal the mocking name of Lachine, a pun based on the efforts of early explorers including René Cavelier de La Salle, who thought the riverway was the passage to La Chine, or China.)

"If there is one thing that typifies Henry Hudson," Reynolds said, it is that he was "methodical, thorough, and precise in everything he did."

On his first voyage, from London to Spitsbergen, "he sails to the North and goes straight up and attempts to go down the other side; it is just as straightforward an approach as you can have. And he hits pack ice at a time of year when there ought not to be any if the theory of the open Arctic [Ocean] is true.

"So he comes back out, with a little side trip to the west. He has ruled out the northern route.

"On the second trip he goes to the Northeast and gets all the way up to Novaya Zemlya, once again in the time of year when if that route is going to be viable he should have been able to find a way through, and again it is just solid pack ice. So he comes back."

After the second voyage, the Muscovy Company in London cuts off his funding and Hudson tries the Dutch, flirts with the French, and finally signs a deal with the VOC. His new backers are very conservative, and they give him a contract that is explicitly restrictive: he is to sail to the Northeast and nowhere else. It's a stipulation that Reynolds says he can't explain, but in the end doesn't matter.

There are two incomplete fragments of journals for the 1609 voyage: one by the mate Robert Juet, and the other by Hudson himself. "We don't have a listing of the crew members, but there is not a chance in the world that the Dutch East India Company would have let this ship go without their company representative aboard," Reynolds said. "This was the common practice with all their sailings.

"The position in English commerce is the 'supercargo,' and he is the person who is actually in control of the strategic management of the ship. He does not sail the ship and he doesn't know about navigation. The supercargo makes decisions like, 'Do we go to Batavia, or do we go to Australia? What do we trade for, and what do we document?' "

According to Reynolds, even with their own captains—not to mention an Englishman on his first, and highly speculative voyage for the Dutch—the investment was too great for the company to send off a ship without a representative aboard. And so, when Hudson arrives at Novaya Zemlya and runs into the pack ice that he had to fully expect to be there once again, Reynolds believes that the supercargo made an executive decision.

It was still early in the season; the *Half Moon* turned away from Novaya Zemlya in the third week of May. "It is entirely plausible," according to Reynolds, "that the supercargo said, 'All right. We are already out here. We are not exposing the company to any greater loss of money. It is too late in the season to go to Batavia. Let's go look for the Northwest Passage.' "

Hudson Makes His Choice

Although we know very little about Hudson, it is apparent that he was a professional explorer. He studied the charts and logs of his contemporaries, met with scholars such as Richard Hakluyt, and was politically savvy enough to convince three sets of investors to back his four known commands.

Hudson didn't come back from his 1607 voyage to Spitsbergen and ask around to see if there were any other interesting theories out there. Less than a year later, he was off to Novaya Zemlya, and when that voyage quickly proved unsuccessful, he wrote in his journal that he considered turning around and crossing the Atlantic to explore Canada, but his crew seems to have objected.

On his third voyage, the Dutch sent him back to Novaya Zemlya, but when that did not work out, he made a U to the west. The common practice at the time was latitudinal sailing, and Hudson followed a near straight line in the water, which brought him to the coast of Maine.

Juet's journal notes that they lost the foremast halfway across, so when they reach land the first priority has to be repairing the ship before they think about exploring. Heading for landfall in upper Maine, the *Half Moon* sailed through the northern reaches of the Grand Bank, at the time one of the richest fishing areas in the world.

Basque fishermen from northern Spain had been visiting the area—just 150 miles offshore the coast of Newfoundland all the way down to Massachusetts—for several hundred years before Christopher Columbus "discovered" the Americas. They kept the source of the cod a closely held secret, but in 1497 the English explorer John Cabot, while searching for a northern route to Asia, stumbled across nearly a thousand Basque fishing vessels; he called the area New Found Land and claimed it for England.

Hudson and Juet headed right for the place Cabot had marked on the charts. Surviving charts from the fifteenth and sixteenth centuries show detailed drawings of islands, coastlines, and place names from Labrador to Cape Cod.

That knowledge was available to explorers such as Hudson as well as to geographers of his time such as Peter Plancius. And there is the possibility that Hudson might have visited the area on an earlier trip as a young sailor. After all, what little we know about him starts with his appointment as master of the *Hopewell* in 1607; it is a reasonable assumption that he had been out to sea somewhere before, in some role.

Once Hudson obtained a replacement for the broken foremast, he could have sailed to the north above Labrador—in search of the Northwest Passage—or to the south toward Cape Cod and down to Chesapeake Bay. He chose to go south, past the place where Boston would be founded by the Massachusetts Bay Company in 1629, around the outer hook of Cape Cod, out to sea offshore of Nantucket Island, and down the U.S. East Coast toward the Virginia colony.

"Some people have said they wanted to sail to the south because the Dutch were not cold-water sailors," Reynolds said. "That's absolutely preposterous. The Dutch had already been sailing extensively in the North Sea fishery, so they had sailors used to cold, hard conditions. They already had extensive trade in the Baltic countries and are trading extensively with Sweden, Norway, and Finland and over to Latvia and Russia. William Barents has already made his voyage up to Spitsbergen and Nova Zembla in the 1590s."

Instead, Reynolds said, there are some very straightforward reasons why Hudson and the *Half Moon* headed south down the coast. They head first for Cape Cod, which is a known point on the charts and then they sail offshore out of sight of land all the way down to Virginia.

"What you see is the systematic and methodical nature of Hudson," Reynolds said. "He goes off shore, not randomly but very specifically to the extent of known exploration [at Jamestown]. He makes the first documented entry into the mouth of the Delaware Bay. I say documented because perhaps the Basques had already been down there one hundred years before."

Then, Reynolds said, Hudson makes his way all the way back up the coast sailing very close to shore and taking the ship into some risky situations. But that is the only way to be thorough and make sure that they don't miss some possible entry.

When the *Half Moon* arrives at the outer harbor of New York, at Sandy Hook, Hudson uses the same cautious approach. They anchor and send the small sloop out to explore around what appears to be three rivers, and then they find the opening that leads through the Narrows and up the Hudson River.

The harbor at New York is immediately of interest to the men on the *Half Moon*. Even though a great deal was already known about the coastline of the New World, very little was known about the width of the North American continent. "Hudson didn't know whether this was going to be five hundred miles or three thousand miles," said Reynolds.

"But looking at the volume of water coming down through there, it is entirely within the realm of the possible that you could think that you go through the bay and river and come out into the Pacific Ocean."

Hudson's Final Voyage: Fool's Gold?

The last great mystery of Hudson's life, on his fourth voyage as captain, is this: Once he passed through the Hudson Strait and reached the top of Hudson's Bay in northern Canada, why did he not continue to proceed westward in the general direction of the expected Northwest Passage? Instead, he hung a left turn and headed south down into the dead end of James Bay.

Among the many theories put forth by some historians and storytellers is that Hudson was on a secret mission to find minerals, including gold; one earlier explorer, Martin Frobisher, had brought back tons of black rock from the area. Frobisher's haul turned out to be a form of worthless fool's gold.

"It is hard for me to imagine that anybody operating at Hudson's level would have been unfamiliar with the conclusion about that being fool's gold," Reynolds said.

"Again, it is a supposition, but it certainly falls well within the norm of sailing experience to expect that someone who is systematic and thorough is going to come into that area and follow the coastline around, just as he has done on previous voyages. He would sail in such a way that he couldn't inadvertently overlook a possible alternate route."

Winter comes and the crew of the *Half Moon* realizes they are in trouble. "They are scared about the cold. They know they are stuck and are going to spend the winter there," Reynolds said. "But that's where Hudson started showing signs of faulty judgment. Now here I think you have room for speculation. Maybe Hudson and the crew are already suffering the effects of vitamin A or vitamin C deficiency, or other things like that. That could have been affecting his thinking and his rationality, because they really did wait too long before they established their camp.

"Had they established their winter camp earlier, they would not have suffered as badly as they did. They were not adequately prepared. And that's giving the benefit of the doubt on every level about the accounts that exist after the fact, because who knows how much credence to give those who made it back to England. Were their accounts sanitized? Were the authors already trying to put the best face on it to avoid being charged with mutiny?"

The True Mystery of Henry Hudson

The Inuit and Cree of Arctic and subarctic Canada barely know of Henry Hudson. They call the waters around them by other names. They are more familiar with the Hudson's Bay Company, the private empire that brought trade and colonial power to their region; that company was named after the bay and not the explorer and the link is not obvious to all.

And though the Hudson's Bay Company still exists—it is Canada's oldest corporation—it is no longer in the fur trading business; the last pelt was bought in 1987. Today, as the country's largest department store retailer, it has dropped reference to the captain in its name. Its flagship stores, no longer in remote outposts but instead in big cities and shopping malls, are called the Bay.

There are people living in Manhattan who know the Hudson River that defines that city but know almost nothing of the man for whom the waters are named; the only major monument to Henry Hudson in New York stands in one of the city's most obscure parks. Tourists and residents of Maine, Nantucket, Delaware Bay, and Jamestown are not likely to know anything about Hudson's visits. So, too, are residents of lonely Svalbard and Greenland.

And so, back to the questions I asked at the beginning of this book.

Was Henry Hudson one of the greatest explorers of all time?
Was he merely an accidental tourist who stumbled into history?
Or was he the world's worst ship's captain, master of four failed expeditions, enabler of at least three mutinies, and creator of an atmosphere that led to his own ignominious death?

The answer to each question seems to be a qualified "yes."

On the one hand, Hudson was without doubt a brave, knowledgeable, and determined explorer. He took small and ill-equipped ships into dangerous and mostly uncharted waters and contributed a great deal of knowledge to British and Dutch trading companies. His reports of whales and other sea mammals in the waters near Svalbard launched a lucrative industry . . . for others.

On the other hands, he never accomplished any of the goals of his contracts: the Northeast Passage over the North Pole or across the top of Russia or the Northwest Passage through the Canadian Arctic.

As to the last question, we enter into ambiguous shades of gray: the true story of several mutinies is not known to us.

The writer Thomas Allibone Janvier, who collected some of the surviving Admiralty Court records of the trial of a few of the survivors, notes that on his last adventure, all of Hudson's "malign stars seem to have been in the ascendant." He is blunt in his assessment of both the captain and the men he brought with him.

"Sailor-men of Hudson's time—and until long after Hudson's time—were little better than dangerous brutes," Janvier writes. "And the savage ferocity that was in them was kept in check only by meeting it with a more savage ferocity on the part of their superiors."

To this I would add my own sense that Hudson may not have been the best manager of people. At various times, he seems to have been too willing to give his crew a vote instead of an order. On other occasions, he may have been too quick to explode with anger at loose lips or overt acts of disobedience.

He was willing to toss Master Coleburne off the ship even before he left England, apparently because he felt compromised in his ability to command the *Discovery*. And yet he was willing to take the malignant Robert Juet aboard for a third time and trusted Henry Greene, another bad choice.

And we will never know for certain whether, during that last desperate winter at the bottom of James Bay, Hudson lost his marbles. Did he press on when all logic argued for an escape? Did he hoard bread and cheese from the men?

All we have are the self-serving words of the survivors; they were seeking to save their own necks at the same time as their employers were hoping to capitalize on their experience in the New World for future expeditions.

His English and Dutch sponsors could not lionize him without beating the drums for the execution of the mutineers, and these men were literally worth more alive than dead. The search for fortune was more important than the search for justice.

Therein may lie the answer to why Henry Hudson is one of history's least-known most-important explorers. He disappeared without benefit of a knightship, a fortune, or even a proper oil portrait.

Index

Index

Index

Index